SERIES
IN
HUMAN
RESOURCE
DEVELOPMENT

THE 1983 ANNUAL FOR FACILITATORS, TRAINERS, AND CONSULTANTS

(The Twelfth Annual)

Editors

LEONARD D. GOODSTEIN, Ph.D.

and

J. WILLIAM PFEIFFER, Ph.D.

Associate Editor

BEVERLY BYRUM-GAW

UNIVERSITY ASSOCIATES, INC.
8517 Production Avenue
San Diego, California 92121

Printed in the United States of America

Published by
University Associates, Inc.
8517 Production Avenue
San Diego, California 92121
619-578-5900

University Associates of Canada
4190 Fairview Street
Burlington, Ontario L7L 4Y8
Canada

University Associates International
Challenge House
45/47 Victoria Street
Mansfield, Notts NG18 5SU
England

University Associates

PREFACE

This is the twelfth *Annual* in the University Associates series. The series has evolved to become the basic resource for trainers, facilitators, and consultants; *Annuals* can be found in numerous organizations in countries around the world.

From our original emphasis on human relations training, the *Annuals* have grown to encompass organization development and, now, the strongly emerging area of human resource development. Indeed, HRD has become the generic label for all types of training, consulting, and facilitation. This is appropriate, because the success of any endeavor depends largely on the *people* who are involved. The view of "human resources" as a basis for development reinforces our own theoretical bias—one that we have tried to present in all our publications over the years.

Another of our biases is that professional materials should be *user* oriented. The users are you, the readers—group facilitators, trainers, and consultants in education, business and industry, government, and nonprofit organizations—people whose work is to help others to learn about human behavior, about their own behavior, and how they can develop new behavioral skills. To further this end, we continue to allow users to duplicate and modify materials from the *Annuals for educational and training purposes,* so long as the credit statement found on the copyright page of this volume is used. However, *if University Associates materials are to be reproduced in publications for sale or are intended for large-scale distribution, prior written permission is required.* Also, if a footnote indicates that material is copyrighted by some source other than UA, *no reproduction is authorized without the permission of the actual copyright holder.*

The *Annual* is intended to serve as a clearing house for professional resource materials. The success of this concept is evidenced by the continued flow of new materials—structured experiences, instruments, lecturettes, theory and practice papers, and resource pieces—that we receive from our readers. We want to encourage the users of the *Annual* to continue to submit pieces that they feel would be of use to other practitioners. Continued sharing of tried-and-true methods as well as innovative approaches developed by our readers will assure that the *Annuals* continue to fulfill their purpose.

We want to express our appreciation to those who have worked with us to make this *Annual* possible: Beverly Byrum-Gaw, associate editor; Rebecca Taff, managing editor; Arlette C. Ballew, senior editor; Carol Nolde, staff editor; and Merilyn Britt, artist. As always, we also want to thank the authors—our colleagues and peers—for sharing with all of us their ideas, techniques, and materials.

Leonard D. Goodstein
J. William Pfeiffer

San Diego, California
December, 1982

About University Associates

University Associates is engaged in publishing, training, and consulting in the broad field of human resource development. UA has earned an international reputation as the source of practical publications that are immediately useful to today's facilitators, trainers, and consultants. A distinct advantage of these publications is that they are designed by practicing professionals who are continually experimenting with new techniques. Thus, UA readers benefit from the fresh but thoughtful approach that underlies UA's experientially based materials, resources, books, workbooks, instruments, and tape-assisted learning programs. These materials are designed for the HRD practitioner who wants access to a broad range of training and intervention technologies, as well as background in the field.

UA's practical, applied, theory-based approach is evident in its training and consulting activities as well. Its experienced trainers and consultants conduct training programs in both the public and private sectors, train trainers, and consult with organizations and communities to solve human and organizational problems. Activities include workshops on fundamental and current topics in human resource development and organization development, as well as workshops that are customized to meet specific client needs. In addition, professional certification is offered by the UA Graduate School through its intern program in laboratory education and its master's degree in human resource development.

The wide audience that UA serves includes training and development professionals, internal and external consultants, managers and supervisors, and those in the helping professions. For its clients and customers, University Associates offers a practical approach aimed at increasing people's effectiveness, on an individual, group, and organizational basis.

TABLE OF CONTENTS

---

*See Structured Experience Categories, p. 8, for an explanation of numbering.

     University Associates

GENERAL INTRODUCTION TO THE 1983 ANNUAL

This *Annual for Facilitators, Trainers, and Consultants,* a collection of practical and useful materials for practitioners in human resource development, is the twelfth in the series. Its format follows the previous volumes' division into five sections: Structured Experiences, Instrumentation, Lecturettes, Theory and Practice, and Resources. Although the organization of all *Annuals* is the same, each year's content is unique. Materials are chosen for their quality of thought, applicability to real-world concerns, relevance to current issues, clarity of style, and ability to offer the user an aid to more effective performance.

This year, among the twelve structured experiences, the reader will find several that speak to values clarification at different levels: individual, group, organizational, and cultural. Additionally, a number of the structured experiences in this *Annual* are helpful in developing specific skills, such as the PERT method, lateral problem solving, clear problem identification, and prioritizing and delegating. One theme centers on open-minded attitudes and behaviors targeted appropriately to the circumstances. While many of these experiences are relevant to contemporary issues in training, their ultimate value is critically dependent on the facilitator's understanding of the experiential learning cycle and the use of this knowledge in the appropriate preparation, processing, and closing of an experience. Some useful suggestions for conducting structured experiences are found in the introduction to that section.

Four new paper-and-pencil instruments have been selected for the second section, Instrumentation. Current issues are reflected in these instruments: career management within an organizational culture, the superior/subordinate communication relationship, values and skills in teamwork, occupational role stressors, and management of time, energy, and information. These instruments are intended primarily for training, consulting, and practical use rather than for research. Guidelines for choosing an instrument appropriate to the training design are discussed in the introduction to that section.

The nine pieces in the Lecturettes section are brief, focused, conceptual presentations of practical and theoretical issues in human relations training. Short enough to be used as handouts, they can highlight a structured experience. A proactive and realistic approach to the management of stress and conflict is a theme found in this year's lecturettes. Topics range from using encouragement and humor; to effective problem solving for individuals, groups, and organizations; to the current "hot" topic, quality circles. Because lecturettes can be a powerful means of clarifying participants' experiences, the introduction to this section provides ideas for making them both experiential and impactful.

Papers in the Theory and Practice section, intended for professional development of the practitioner, are often more complex than lecturettes. Some review ongoing theoretical issues and their application; for example, a number of pieces in this year's *Annual* speak to different aspects of learning theory. Others address current issues facing today's practitioners, such as the transition to new management and participatory organizational problem solving. One piece introduces a new topic to the *Annual,* and another applies related therapeutic techniques to human relations training. Because the majority of Theory and Practice papers apply a current model to practice or develop a new one, the introduction to this section reviews the method of model building.

The Resources section consists of materials for professional support and development, a source for keeping up to date on the latest "tools" of the trade. This year's section includes an updated list of consulting organizations, a team-building bibliography, a directory of biofeedback materials, and a directory of executive recruiters.

Although these sections are distinct from one another, they are not intended to be used in isolation. Instruments can enrich structured experiences, lecturettes are helpful in generalizing learning from experiential activities, and theory and practice papers and resources give the practitioner a more in-depth understanding of issues posed in structured experiences or instruments. By using the different sections to complement one another, the facilitator can render the total learning experience more powerful.

An alphabetical list of the contributors to the *Annual* can be found at the end of the volume. Users will find this list useful if they wish to locate the authors of specific pieces for feedback, comments, or questions. Further information about contributors is presented in brief biographical sketches at the conclusion of articles.

The editors are pleased with the continued high quality of materials submitted to us for publication. As is to be expected with such a wide variety of materials, however, not all users will find everything in this *Annual* of equal value. We invite comments, ideas, materials, or suggestions that will help us to make the next *Annual* as useful as possible.

INTRODUCTION TO THE
STRUCTURED EXPERIENCES SECTION

A structured experience is a process by which the participants in the experience learn inductively. Inductive learning, which proceeds from observation rather than from a priori "truth" (deductive), occurs within the framework of the experiential learning cycle. In this cycle, pictured in Figure 1, a person engages in some activity, looks back at the experience critically, abstracts some useful insight from the analysis, and puts the results to work through a change in behavior. (For complete examples of methods used in each phase, see the Introduction to the Structured Experiences Section in the *1980 Annual*.)

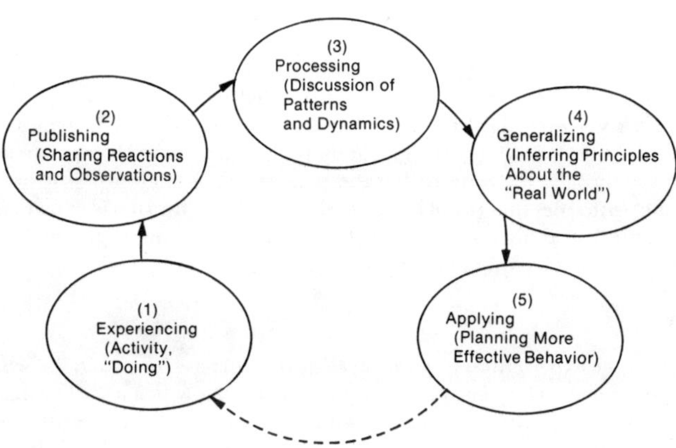

Figure 1. The Experiential Learning Cycle

Experiencing

The initial stage is the data-generating part of the structured experience. It is the step that is often associated with "games" or fun. Almost any activity that involves either self-assessment or interpersonal interaction can be used as the "doing" part of experiential learning. Activities can be carried out by individuals, dyads, triads, small groups, group-on-group arrangements, or large groups, as learning objectives dictate.

Objectives of structured experiences are necessarily general because inductive learning means learning through discovery, and the exact things to be learned cannot be specified beforehand. This stage of the learning cycle is used to develop a common data base for the discussion that follows. This means that whatever happens in the activity, whether expected or not, becomes the basis for critical analysis; participants may learn serendipitously.

Publishing

In the second stage of the cycle, the data generated are "published" or made available to the group. People have experienced an activity and now they can share what they saw and/or how they felt during the event. This step involves finding out what happened within individuals, at cognitive, affective, and behavioral levels, while the activity was progressing. Publishing can be carried out through free discussion as well as through structured methods.

Processing

This stage is the pivotal step in experiential learning. It is the systematic examination of commonly shared experience by those persons involved. This is the "group dynamics" phase of the cycle, in which participants essentially reconstruct the patterns and interactions of the activity from the published individual reports. Participants look at what happened in terms of interaction. A consciousness of the dynamics of the activity is critical for learning about human relations outside the laboratory setting.

Generalizing

An inferential leap is made at this point in the structured experience, from the reality inside the activity to the reality of everyday life outside the training session. The key question here is "So what?" Participants are led to focus their awareness on situations in their personal or work lives that are similar to those in the activity that they experienced. Their task is to abstract from the processing some principles that could be applied "outside." This step is what makes structured experiences practical. It is also possible for the facilitator to bring in theoretical and research findings in the form of a lecturette to augment the learning.

Applying

The final stage of the experiential learning cycle is the purpose for which the whole structured experience is designed. The central question here is "Now what?" The facilitator helps participants to apply generalizations to actual situations in which they are involved. Volunteers can be asked to report what they intend to do with what they learned, and this can encourage others to experiment with their behavior also.

It is important to note that on the diagram of the experiential learning cycle there is a dotted arrow from "applying" to "experiencing." This is meant to indicate that the actual application of the learning is a new experience for the participant, to be examined inductively in turn. What structured experiences "teach" is a way of using and owning one's everyday experiences as data for learning about human relations.

A structured experience, then, is a procedure used by the trainer to help the participants to initiate, process, complete, and integrate not only specified learnings but also the entire process of learning how to learn by moving from an experience to applicable results.

Structured experiences can incorporate instrumentation in the publishing phase, lecturettes in the generalizing phase, and the trainer's knowledge of theory and practice in the applying phase.

USING STRUCTURED EXPERIENCES

A structured experience is written with the purpose of giving the trainer adequate information to prepare and process that experience. *Goals* are established to focus the trainer on the general objectives of the experience—what it is expected that participants will learn. *Group size, time required, materials,* and *physical setting* set the limitations so that the trainer can choose a structured experience to fit within the constraints of his or her own training design. The *process* steps walk the trainer through the entire learning cycle, indicating what must be said or done in each step for the experience to work effectively. *Variations* give options for other ways of working with a particular structured experience.

The specific steps for each individual structured experience are based on general guidelines for conducting any structured experience. (For a more complete development of these "do's" and "don'ts," see the Introduction to the Structured Experiences Section in the *1979 Annual.*)

THINGS TO DO:

Prepare

- Have a design flow chart, at least in rough outline form.
- Check the timing of the various steps.
- Have more than enough back-up materials planned.
- If *you* have questions, get the answers *before* the session.

Plan for Contingencies

- Have alternative activities ready in case the group is more (or less) advanced than you expect.
- Have ready lecturettes, handouts, or instruments that you might possibly use.
- Examine your design plan to determine those points at which changes are most likely to be required.

Set up the Situation

- Give a broad overview of what will happen first.
- Provide further instruction in small segments.
- Always keep the learning objectives in mind.

Facilitate the Process

- Maintain a supportive atmosphere.
- Give everyone something to do at all times.
- Participate whenever possible.
- Let the group help you.
- Reinforce the concept of options.

Facilitate Learning

- Turn whatever happens into a learning experience.
- Manage the impact of the experience in accordance with participant readiness.
- In the learning cycle, make the stages clear and complete and prepare the way for the next step.
- *Experiencing:* keep the generation of data within bounds.
- *Publishing:* help the participants to separate themselves from the experience.
- *Processing:* work the discussion of dynamics thoroughly, focusing on interaction versus meaning.

THINGS TO DO (Continued):

- *Generalizing:* remain nonevaluative about generalizations and draw out all perspectives.
- *Applying:* encourage the participants to share their plans for action and change.

THINGS TO AVOID DOING:

Overinstructing

- Giving too much detail
- Excessive telling (versus listening or sharing)
- Pressuring people to participate

Negotiating the Design

- Arguing over interpretation of what did happen
- Defending your own views of what should happen
- Changing what will happen to meet the needs of one or a few of the group members

Playing Psychological Games

- Ridiculing individuals
- Deceiving people
- Interpreting an individual's behavior

Overloading

- Generating more data than can be discussed thoroughly
- Repeating an activity until it works
- Overanalyzing data

Ending Without Closure

- Leaving people to resolve their own exposed problems
- Leaving applications to chance

STRUCTURED EXPERIENCES IN THE 1983 ANNUAL

In this *Annual's* set of structured experiences, values are a strong theme—ranging from personal values that affect how we deal with people to organizational values that reflect the purpose of the organization. Additionally, specific skills such as problem identification, convergent and divergent thinking, planning a critical path to action, and deciding and delegating according to job priorities are presented through activities whose theme is the capability of focusing on exactly what is required in a given situation.

In this *Annual,* five of the six structured experience categories presented in the Introduction to the Structured Experiences Section of the *1981 Annual* are represented, providing the ongoing balance that we strive to present.

In the Personal category, "Feelings" increases the *feelings awareness* of participants through the verbal and nonverbal expression of emotions; "Manager's Dilemma" helps participants to identify their *assumptions* about human nature within the Theory-X/Theory-Y framework; and "Career Renewal" uses an inventory of the participant's present job as a means of evaluating *life/career planning* direction and involvement. The Communication category is represented by "Assistant Wanted," which gives participants the opportunity to practice *interviewing* skills in a role-play situation.

"Four Cultures," in the Group Characteristics category, aids in *values clarification/ stereotyping* by creating different cultural behaviors that participants role play in an interaction. Two *problem-solving/awareness* activities—"Pebbles," which increases awareness of vertical and lateral approaches to a dilemma, and "The Lawn," which discriminates between causes and symptoms of problems—constitute the Group Task Behavior category.

"Robbery" is the first of four experiences in the Organizations category. Use of the PERT technique teaches *decision making/action planning* skills. Further development of *decision making/action planning* skills is found in "Vice President's In-Basket," a management activity that teaches how to prioritize and delegate under pressure. "Organizational Blasphemies" and "Conflict Role Play" speak to *conflict resolution/values* in organizations. The first helps participants to identify values by creating their contradictions; the second heightens awareness of double standards based on stereotypes by surfacing them in an organizational role play.

In the category of Facilitating Learning, "Just the Facts" is a *getting-acquainted* activity through the process of interviewing participants.

STRUCTURED EXPERIENCE CATEGORIES

Numbers of Structured Experiences		Numbers of Structured Experiences	
1-24	Volume I, *Handbook*	185-196	1977 *Annual*
25-48	Volume II, *Handbook*	197-220	Volume VI, *Handbook*
49-74	Volume III, *Handbook*	221-232	1978 *Annual*
75-86	1972 *Annual*	233-244	1979 *Annual*
87-100	1973 *Annual*	245-268	Volume VII, *Handbook*
101-124	Volume IV, *Handbook*	269-280	1980 *Annual*
125-136	1974 *Annual*	281-292	1981 *Annual*
137-148	1975 *Annual*	293-316	Volume VIII, *Handbook*
149-172	Volume V, *Handbook*	317-328	1982 *Annual*
173-184	1976 *Annual*	329-340	1983 *Annual*

329. JUST THE FACTS: GETTING ACQUAINTED

Goals

    I. To provide an opportunity for members of a group to become acquainted with one another in a nonthreatening manner.

  II. To create an atmosphere conducive to group interaction and sharing.

Group Size

    Five to ten participants.

Time Required

    One to one and one-half hours.

Materials

    A sheet of blank paper and a pencil for each participant.

Physical Setting

    A room that is large enough for all participants to move around and interact.

Process

    I. The facilitator introduces the activity as an opportunity for members of the group who do not know one another to become acquainted.

  II. The facilitator distributes blank paper and a pencil to each member, then instructs each member to list the names (or identifying characteristics if a name is not known) of the three persons in the room whom they would like to know better. (Three minutes.)

 III. After the names have been recorded, the group members are directed to interview each person on their lists and to record three facts about each person. The facilitator specifies the following rules:

    1. Only one person may be interviewed at a time.

    2. Each interview should take approximately two minutes.

    3. The interviewee may not tell the same facts to more than one interviewer.

    4. The facts may be obtained through the interviewer's questions or may be offered spontaneously by the interviewee.

    5. Twenty minutes will be allowed for the activity.

    (Two minutes.)

 IV. During the interviewing phase, the facilitator may need to remind the participants of the rule of one-on-one interactions only. The facilitator also should announce the time in five-minute intervals. (Twenty minutes.)

V. The facilitator calls time and directs the participants to form a circle.

VI. The facilitator solicits a volunteer to share the three facts about the first person on his or her list. (The person being described is to remain silent.) Other members are then asked to share any information they learned about that particular person. (Five minutes.)

VII. The participants continue (around the circle) to share information. If the first person on someone's list already has been described, the second person on the list is introduced. This process continues until all participants have shared all their facts about other members of the group. (Five minutes for each group member.)

VIII. After the sharing process is completed, the facilitator raises the following issues:

1. Do any participants need to correct information given about them?

2. Were any people not on a list? Would they like to share any thing about themselves or any feelings?

3. Were any people on a majority of the lists? What are their feelings about being introduced to the other members of the group?

IX. The facilitator initiates a brief discussion of the experience. The participants may review surprises they experienced in learning about one another, reactions to the experience, and any changes in their feelings about themselves or the group. The following questions may be considered:

1. How did participants feel during and about the interviewing process?

2. How did participants feel during and about the reporting process (both reporters and those being described)?

3. What were the surprises or disappointments?

4. How have people's feelings changed since the beginning of the experience?

Variations

I. The facilitator can provide a list of sample questions. These questions can vary according to the level of readiness of the group members, i.e., factual questions for low readiness, emotional or symbolic questions for high readiness. Examples are:

1. What do you want for your birthday?

2. What is your favorite song (color, food, book, dessert)?

3. Where were you born?

4. What do you like to read?

5. Do you have any pets? If so, what kind?

6. What would you change if you could change anything in the world?

7. What do you like best about yourself?

8. Who is your favorite actor or actress (writer, historical figure)?

9. What do you dislike most?

10. What color (sound, animal, title) typifies you?

Similar Structured Experiences: *Volume I:* Structured Experiences 1, 5; *Vol. III:* **49**; *'73 Annual:* **88**; *'80 Annual:* **263**; *Vol. VIII:* **293**.

Suggested Instrument: *'74 Annual:* "Self-Disclosure Questionnaire."

Robert N. Glenn, Ph.D., *is the coordinator of clinical supervision and training for the Henrico Area Mental Health and Retardation Services, Glenn Allen, Virginia. He is responsible for the professional development of staff members and for maintaining a clinical quality-assurance system. His primary activities include psychotherapy, supervision of psychotherapy, and consultation. Dr. Glenn is a licensed (by the State of Virginia) clinical psychologist and has published several articles.*

330. FEELINGS: VERBAL AND NONVERBAL CONGRUENCE

Goals

I. To provide an opportunity to compare verbal and nonverbal components of feelings.

II. To develop awareness of the congruence or lack of congruence between verbal and nonverbal components of feelings.

III. To increase sensitivity to the feelings of others.

Group Size

Three to five groups of three to six members each.

Time Required

One to one and one-half hours.

Materials

I. A copy of the Feelings Work Sheet for each participant.

II. A pencil for each participant.

Physical Setting

A room with space for the groups to meet or one room for the general sessions and a separate room for each small group.

Process

I. The facilitator gives a lecturette on verbal and nonverbal communication, emphasizing the need for both aspects of communication to be congruent. The facilitator points out that confusion and mixed messages often result when people say one thing (verbally) and do another thing (nonverbally). (Ten minutes.)

II. The facilitator separates the large group into smaller groups of three to six participants each and assigns space within the room to each group. (Three minutes.)

III. The facilitator gives each participant a copy of the Feelings Work Sheet and a pencil. The facilitator goes over the instructions and tells the participants that they have approximately twenty minutes in which to complete the Feelings Work Sheet. (Two minutes.)

IV. The participants begin to work on the Feelings Work Sheet. After fifteen minutes, the facilitator reminds the participants that they have five more minutes in which to work. (Twenty minutes.)

V. At the end of twenty minutes, the facilitator calls time and directs the participants to share their responses within their small groups. (Fifteen to thirty minutes.)

VI. The facilitator calls the entire group together to process the experience. Possible processing questions include:

1. In what types of situations is congruence most likely to occur?
2. In what situations is incongruence most likely to occur?
3. What causes these differences?
4. What types of emotions seem to lead to mixed messages?
5. In what situations might a mixed message be appropriate?
6. How can we give more congruent messages when we want to?
7. How can we deal with others who are giving mixed messages?

(Fifteen minutes.)

Variations

I. The Feelings Work Sheet can contain specific situations that are appropriate to the participant group.

II. Group members can give one another feedback on their experiences of one another in terms of verbal and nonverbal congruence.

III. The participants can develop role plays to practice verbal and nonverbal congruence in difficult situations.

Similar Structured Experiences: *Volume VII:* Structured Experience **251**; *'81 Annual:* **286**.

Lecturette Source: *'74 Annual:* "Making Requests Through Metacommunication."

Submitted by Stella Lybrand Norman.

Stella Lybrand Norman is the supervisor of the South Clinic, Crossroads Drug Abuse Program, Alexandria, Virginia. She facilitates two special groups: "re-entry/aftercare," for clients who are leaving the therapeutic community and re-entering the mainstream of society, and "dual diagnosed," for clients who abuse illegal drugs and are being medicated with major tranquilizers. She is also responsible for case supervision, counselor schedules, and crisis intervention. Her specialties are groups for families, parents, and women, and nonverbal communication.

FEELINGS WORK SHEET

Instructions: Listed below are situations that you probably have experienced. For each situation, write out the verbal and nonverbal components of your feelings.

1. When I am bored with what is going on in a group, I usually express my feelings

    a. verbally by saying

    to whom?

    b. nonverbally by doing

    when?

2. When I am annoyed with someone with whom I want to build a better relationship, I usually express my feelings

    a. verbally by saying

    when?

    b. nonverbally by doing

    when?

3. When someone says or does something that hurts me deeply, I usually express my feelings

    a. verbally by saying

when?

b. nonverbally by doing

when?

4. When my boss asks me to do something that I am afraid I cannot do well, and I want to hide that fact, I usually express my feelings

a. verbally by saying

b. nonverbally by doing

5. When a close friend is moving away and I am feeling lonely, I usually express my feelings

a. verbally by saying

b. nonverbally by doing

6. When I feel affection and fondness for someone but am not sure that the other person feels the same way, I usually express my feelings

a. verbally by saying

b. nonverbally by doing

7. When someone destroys my personal property, I usually express my feelings

   a. verbally by saying

      when?

   b. nonverbally by doing

      when?

331. MANAGER'S DILEMMA: THEORY X AND THEORY Y

Goals

I. To help participants to become aware of their own philosophies of human resource management.

II. To introduce the concepts in McGregor's Theory X and Theory Y.

III. To allow participants to compare and discuss alternative courses of action in a management situation.

Group Size

Five to twenty participants in groups of four or five members each.

Time Required

Approximately two and one-half hours.

Materials

I. One copy of the Manager's Dilemma Work Sheet for each participant.

II. One copy of the Manager's Dilemma Interpretation Sheet for each participant.

III. A pencil for each participant.

IV. Newsprint and a felt-tipped marker.

Physical Setting

A room that is large enough to allow each group to work without disturbing the other groups.

Process

I. The facilitator introduces the activity by saying that the participants will complete an instrument that will help them to explore some of their philosophies of management. The facilitator stresses that the instrument is not a test of management know-how, but is designed to provide feedback about differences in approaches to managing people. (Three minutes.)

II. The participants are divided into groups of four or five members each, and the groups are directed to establish themselves in different areas of the room. (Three minutes.)

III. Each participant receives a copy of the Manager's Dilemma Work Sheet and a pencil. The participants are directed to read the instructions on the work sheet, and then the facilitator answers any questions. (Five minutes.)

IV. The facilitator announces that fifteen minutes will be allotted for the participants to complete their work sheets and tells them to begin. (Fifteen minutes.)

V. The facilitator gives a time warning after ten minutes and calls time after fifteen minutes. The participants are directed to share their ratings within their groups and then to vote among themselves on a group rating for each item. These ratings are to be entered in Column II on the Manager's Dilemma Work Sheets. (Fifteen minutes.)

VI. The facilitator calls time and asks for a spokesperson from each group to report on the group's ratings. A summary of the spread of ratings can be posted on newsprint or made verbally at the end of the reporting phase. (Ten minutes.)

VII. The facilitator distributes a copy of the Manager's Dilemma Interpretation Sheet to each participant and allows time for the participants to read the background information. The facilitator then briefly expounds the implications of Theory X and Theory Y. (Fifteen minutes.)

VIII. The participants are directed to predict where they are on the X-Y continuum and then to score and interpret their instruments. (Ten minutes.)

IX. The participants are directed to discuss their reactions to the experience within their groups. They are directed specifically to consider how their predictions matched their scores and what insights they gained about their approaches to working with people. (Fifteen minutes.)

X. The groups then are directed to discuss their results from the instrument in respect to the three types of approaches (Theory X, Theory Y, and Avoidance) and the possible effects of these managerial approaches in situations such as the one described on the Manager's Dilemma Work Sheet. (Fifteen to thirty minutes.)

XI. The entire group is reassembled, and the facilitator solicits observations and questions from the group and from individuals regarding the application of Theory X and Theory Y to management situations. The facilitator may solicit responses to the following questions.

1. What were individuals' reactions to their actual scores compared to what they would have predicted for themselves?

2. What was the tendency of the group as a whole? How does this differ from the individual tendencies? What might account for any differences?

3. Which approach would seem to yield the best short-term results? Which would yield the best long-term results?

4. What influences might the supervisor or the organization have on a manager's tendency to favor Theory X or Theory Y?

5. How might a better understanding of Theory X and Theory Y be useful in the participants' back-home management situations?

(Twenty minutes.)

Variations

I. If time is limited, participants can receive and complete the Manager's Dilemma Work Sheets before attending the group session.

II. The film "The Self-Fulfilling Prophecy" (CRM-McGraw-Hill Films) can be shown during step VII to further demonstrate the effects of managerial attitudes on subordinates.

III. If group ratings differ from individual ones, during Step X, the participants can discuss the possible consequences of the actions chosen by the group as opposed to those chosen by individuals.

Similar Structured Experiences: *Volume I:* Structured Experience 3; *Vol. VI:* **207**; *Vol. VIII:* **296**.

Suggested Instruments: *Volume I:* "T-P Leadership Questionnaire"; *'72 Annual:* "Supervisory Attitudes: The X-Y Scale"; *'73 Annual:* "LEAD (Leadership: Employee-Orientation and Differentiation) Questionnaire"; *'81 Annual:* "Patterns of Effective Supervisory Behavior"; *Vol. VIII:* "People on the Job Work Sheet."

Lecturette Sources: *'72 Annual:* "McGregor's Theory X-Theory Y Model"; *'81 Annual:* "An Overview of Ten Management and Organizational Theorists."

Submitted by Rollin Glaser and Christine Glaser. Copyright © 1980, Organization Design & Development, Inc.

Rollin Glaser is the president of Organization Design and Development, Inc., Bryn Mawr, Pennsylvania. His background includes both academic and business experience. He holds an M.Ed. from Northeastern University and has done doctoral work in adult education at Boston University. Mr. Glaser's specialties include organization development and team-building activities with management groups. He has authored or co-authored three books on management and training as well as numerous professional articles.

Christine Glaser is the vice president of Organization Design and Development, Inc., a company that specializes in human resource development. She also serves as a group facilitator and management-skills trainer. Her previous experience includes work in public schools and business training. Ms. Glaser holds an M.Ed. in guidance and counseling from Northeastern University. She is a co-author (with Rollin Glaser) of Managing by Design.

MANAGER'S DILEMMA WORK SHEET

Background: Paul is group manager for the housewares department of McClurkens, a national discount-store chain that is located in a regional shopping complex just outside of Wheeling, West Virginia.

Paul, who graduated from a two-year college, has held this position for the past year. An hour ago, the store operations manager stopped by to tell Paul that his spring shortage was higher than that of the previous fall. The operations manager was upset because other departments also fared poorly and the total store was soon going to be under considerable pressure from the home office. Paul was surprised at his department's shortage. The fall figure had been acceptable, and things seemed to have gone well with the inventory.

During a fifteen-minute session, the operations manager stated that Paul's future with the company might be in jeopardy and that his shortage percentage had better be in line by the summer inventory. Paul is worried because he recently received an invitation from the director of executive development to join the executive training class at the home office in September. Paul has aspired to a buyer's job for the last two years and he does not want to destroy his chances now.

Nine employees, full and part-time, report to Paul. They all have appeared to be reliable. Their backgrounds are varied—a few are attending college part-time. Most, however, are older workers with longer service and modest levels of aspiration.

For the past hour, as he has tried to complete some paperwork, Paul's mind has been rambling over his possible courses of action. He finally decides to write them down and creates a list of twenty actions that he could take in response to the problem.

Instructions: Using the following scale of 1-5, in column I write the number that corresponds to the level of importance you would give to each of the twenty alternatives.

Rating Scale:

1 = Very important. You would do it immediately.

2 = Important. You would do it when time permits.

3 = Of some importance. You may or may not do it, depending on a number of variables.

4 = Not really important. You probably would not do it.

5 = You would try to *avoid* doing it.

I Your Ratings	II The Group's Ratings	
——	——	A. Insist that the training representative retrain all the sales and stock people in the proper cash-register and sales check procedures.
——	——	B. Call a meeting of your employees and explain the shortage problem firmly, making the point that "heads will roll" if the next inventory is not substantially better.
——	——	C. Ask the security department for closer surveillance of your employees.
——	——	D. Call a meeting of your employees and ask everyone for ideas and suggestions.
——	——	E. Meet with a select few of the sales and stock people to explain the problem.

I Your Ratings	II The Group's Ratings	
_____	_____	F. Put up a variety of shortage-improvement slogans and signs in the stock rooms and office areas.
_____	_____	G. With your employees, develop a specific action plan aimed at reducing the shortage in the department.
_____	_____	H. Remove or physically secure all the higher priced items in your area. Keep the keys on your person at all times.
_____	_____	I. Without further discussion, tighten all the paperwork controls in your department.
_____	_____	J. Although the store does not have such a policy, insist that all employees bring their personal purchases to you for checking and sealing.
_____	_____	K. Ask the store manager if you can establish an incentive program for your employees, to encourage a reduced shortage percentage.
_____	_____	L. You are suspicious of one of your employees, although you have no facts. Just to be on the safe side, find a way to fire that person.
_____	_____	M. Ask each employee to give serious thought to the possible causes of the shortage in your department and to give those thoughts to you in writing. Review the best ideas with the entire group.
_____	_____	N. Ask the store manager to give your employees an emotional, fire-and-brimstone speech about shortage, profits, and job security.
_____	_____	O. After your initial meeting with your employees, continue to meet weekly to share information and to check progress.
_____	_____	P. Make unscheduled visits to your department when your employees are likely to think that you have gone for the day.
_____	_____	Q. After sufficient input from your employees, establish a shortage objective and review it with the store manager.
_____	_____	R. Ask the personnel manager to raise standards and to get you better qualified, younger employees.
_____	_____	S. Personally develop a comprehensive check list of possible causes of the shortage in your department and review it in detail with the members of your department to get their input.
_____	_____	T. Closely monitor each person's work and let it be known that everyone is under suspicion.

Background: The problem that Paul faces is much like ones faced by all supervisors, from time to time. Paul is under considerable pressure to take effective action to solve his department's problem. As with any business problem, time is limited and a wide range of alternative actions is available. How Paul chooses to deal with the shortage probably reflects, to a great extent, the assumptions that he makes about people and how they are capable of acting at work.

In this activity, you take Paul's role. The actions that you consider important or unimportant may reflect your own attitudes about your employees and whether or not you feel that they should be involved in helping you to manage your department.

Douglas McGregor, an industrial psychologist, provided a convenient way of understanding the kinds of assumptions that managers make concerning their subordinates. He identified two sets of common attitudes, which he labeled Theory X and Theory Y.[1]

Theory X	**Theory Y**
People, by nature, generally:	*People, by nature, generally:*
1. Do not like to exert themselves and try to work as little as possible.	1. Work hard toward objectives to which they are committed.
2. Avoid responsibility.	2. Assume responsibility within these commitments.
3. Are not interested in achievement.	3. Have a strong desire to achieve.
4. Are incapable of directing their own behavior.	4. Are capable of directing their own behavior.
5. Are indifferent to organizational needs.	5. Want their organization to succeed.
6. Prefer to be directed by others.	6. Are not passive and submissive and prefer to make decisions about their own work.
7. Avoid making decisions whenever possible.	7. Will make decisions within their commitments.
8. Cannot be trusted or depended on.	8. If trusted and depended on, do not disappoint.
9. Need to be closely supervised and controlled.	9. Need general support and help at work.
10. Are motivated at work by money and other gains.	10. Are motivated at work by interesting and challenging tasks.
11. When they mature, do not change.	11. Are able to change and develop.

Theory X and Theory Y represent extremes in thinking. They are polarities. Although individual managers may hold "pure" Theory X or Y attitudes, it probably is more likely that their attitudes "tend" toward X or Y or are a blend of the two.

Before scoring your responses to the case, you may want to take a moment to mark the continuum below to indicate your own perception of your X/Y philosophy. Later, you can check your actual rating against what you predicted; this will give you some insight into the

---

[1]From *The Human Side of Enterprise* by Douglas McGregor. Copyright © 1960, McGraw-Hill Book Company. Used with permission of McGraw-Hill Book Company.

accuracy of your self-perception. Also, you can solicit feedback from others about how they perceive your attitudes. People's self-perceptions often do not coincide with the perceptions that others have of them.

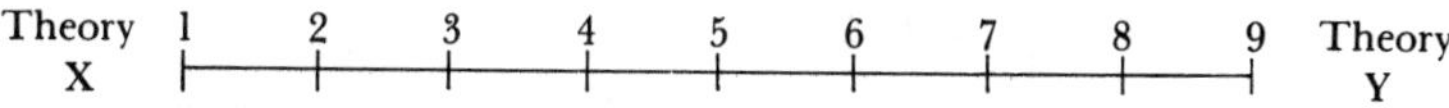

Effects of X and Y Assumptions

A manager's assumptions have a direct effect on his or her managerial behavior. Attitudes about how employees view their work will cause people to manage in various ways. A strong Theory-X manager, for example, will try to compensate for people's unwillingness to direct their own activities by doing most of the planning, organizing, and controlling of the work to be done. This person will monitor employee behavior closely.

A Theory-Y manager, on the other hand, thinks of people as having a great deal of unused potential and will manage in ways to exploit that potential, both for the organization and for the individual. This person's behavior will be geared toward getting employees involved in the planning process, in problem solving, and in the control of the work. This role is one of coach and facilitator.

Scoring and Interpretation

Manager's Dilemma is not a test. It is a learning instrument designed to assist you in discovering the assumptions that you may be making about your employees.

- The following items, if rated 1 or 2, suggest a Theory-X orientation: A, B, C, E, F, H, I, J, K, L, N, P, R, T.
- The same items, if rated 4 or 5, suggest a Theory-Y orientation.
- The following items, if rated 1 or 2, suggest a Theory-Y orientation: D, G, M, O, Q, S.
- The same items, if rated 4 or 5, suggest a Theory-X orientation.
- Any item rated 3, although possibly appropriate, should be considered an "avoidance-of-the-issue" response. A high percentage of such responses indicates an unwillingness to take a stand, for whatever reason.

Theory-X Orientation

Count the number of the following items that you rated 1 or 2 on the Manager's Dilemma Work Sheet and enter the total number of items on the line to the right.

A, B, C, E, F, H, I, J, K, L, N, P, R, T   ________

Count the number of the following items that you rated 4 or 5 and enter the total number of items.

D, G, M, O, Q, S   ________

Total of both lines: (1) ________

Theory-Y Orientation

Count the number of the following items that you rated 4 or 5 on the Manager's Dilemma Work Sheet and enter the total number of items on the line to the right.

A, B, C, E, F, H, I, J, K, L, N, P, R, T   ________

Count the number of the following items that you rated 1 or 2 and enter the total number of items.

D, G, M, O, Q, S   ________

Total of both lines: (2) ________

Avoidance

Count the number of items you rated 3 and enter the total
number of items.   Total: (3) ________

% of X responses: total for (1) ________=
                              divided by 20

% of Y responses: total for (2) ________=
                              divided by 20

% of Avoidance
     responses: total for (3) ________=
                              divided by 20

332. CAREER RENEWAL: A SELF-INVENTORY

Goals

I. To introduce the concept of job renewal.

II. To enable participants to examine their present jobs and to plan improvements.

III. To enable participants to evaluate their present jobs in light of their stated career goals.

Group Size

Five to fifteen participants.

Time Required

Approximately one hour.

Materials

I. A copy of the Career Renewal Work Sheet for each participant.

II. A pencil for each participant.

III. Newsprint and a felt-tipped marker.

Physical Setting

A writing surface for each participant.

Process

I. The facilitator introduces the concept of job renewal as viewing one's present job from the long-term perspective of one's career goals and using strategic planning to effect improvements. The facilitator says that because the object is to make purposeful changes within the existing framework, the concept can be said to be analogous to the concept of "urban renewal." Drawing parallels between a job or a career and an old house that needs to be repaired, the facilitator lists on newsprint the areas to be inspected. For example:

House	*Job*
Energy consumption	Time management
Landscaping	Physical surroundings

(Five minutes.)

II. The facilitator asks the participants for other parallels between the two areas and lists these on the newsprint. (Five minutes.)

III. Each participant receives a copy of the Career Renewal Work Sheet and a pencil. The facilitator briefly summarizes how the work sheet is to be filled out and tells the participants to begin. (Three minutes.)

IV. After eight minutes, the facilitator checks the participants' progress and gives a time warning. After ten to fifteen minutes, the facilitator directs everyone to stop writing.

V. The participants are divided into groups of four or five members each and are directed to share their overall reactions to the experience thus far, as well as similarities and differences in their job analyses. (Ten minutes.)

VI. The facilitator then reassembles the entire group and leads a discussion of the experience. The following questions may be included:

1. What seem to be the common problem areas in people's jobs?

2. What areas of job renewal are within the job holder's control? What areas are outside the control of the individual?

3. What types of improvements or changes seem to be required in the jobs of the group members? How easy or difficult will it be to effect these changes?

(Fifteen minutes.)

Variations

I. Participants can form dyads and make contracts with their partners about steps they intend to take to implement "back-home" changes in their jobs.

II. If time is limited, only one of the three sheets may be used.

III. Participants can write new job descriptions for themselves, based on what they have learned about job renewal.

Similar Structured Experiences: *Volume II:* Structured Experience 11; *'75 Annual:* 137; *'79 Annual:* 244.

Suggested Instrument: *Volume II:* "Life Planning Program."

Lecturette Sources: *'72 Annual:* "Job Enrichment"; *'74 Annual:* "Life/Work Planning"; *'80 Annual:* "Job-Related Adaptive Skills."

Submitted by Karen J. Troy.

__Karen J. Troy__ is a career development specialist for the Minnesota Gas Company, Minneapolis. Her major responsibilities are to identify and to respond to career needs and to design and implement programs, systems, workshops, and procedures to meet those needs. Her specialties are the facilitation of workshops in career planning, career coaching, team building, and organizational communication. Ms. Troy presently serves as Minnesota contact person for the National Career and Adult Development Network.

CAREER RENEWAL WORK SHEET

A. Analyze the good and not-so-good aspects of your current job. List your *most* important responsibilities below. Then place a check mark in one of the boxes for each category to the right to indicate the degrees of challenge, accomplishment, and enjoyment that each responsibility gives you (L = Low; H = High).

Most Important Responsibilities	Amount of Challenge					Feeling of Accomplishment					Level of Enjoyment				
	L 1	2	3	4	H 5	L 1	2	3	4	H 5	L 1	2	3	4	H 5
1.															
2.															
3.															
4.															

B. Briefly describe the aspects of your work listed below and check the degree of satisfaction that each one affords you.

	Level of Satisfaction				
	Low 1	2	3	High 4	5
Working Conditions:					
Relationships with Co-Workers:					
Supervision Received:					
Having Clear Responsibilities:					
Job Security:					
The Kind of Work I Do (The Work Itself):					
Feeling of Personal Accomplishment:					

	Level of Satisfaction				
	Low				High
	1	2	3	4	5
Opportunity for Growth:					
Compensation:					
Operating Style of Department:					
Recognition for Doing the Job Well:					
Other:					

C. Below are some items that will help you to examine your job duties and how you experience them. Check the questions that you would like to address as part of your career-renewal project.

_____ I am not aware of all of the job duties required of me.

_____ I need to better understand my job requirements and how to accomplish them.

_____ I need to identify my key strengths and problem areas on the job.

_____ How can I keep up with new developments in my field?

_____ In my present job, are there skills required of me that I can improve?

_____ In my present job, what new things can I do that will enhance my skills?

_____ Are there new activities that I can do or skills that I can acquire that will further my approach toward achieving my overall career goal?

D. Review your responses to parts A, B, and C. Decide what aspect of your current job you *most* want to focus on as an object for renewal. Describe it in your own words.

333. ASSISTANT WANTED: AN EMPLOYMENT INTERVIEW

Goals

    I. To provide participants with an experience in interviewing and in being interviewed.

    II. To explore the dynamics of the interviewer-interviewee relationship.

    III. To introduce the components of the employment interview.

Group Size

    An unlimited number of participants, divided into two groups of equal size.

Time Required

    Approximately two to two and one-half hours.

Materials

    I. A copy of the Assistant Wanted Interviewer Role-Description Sheet for each participant.

    II. A copy of the Assistant Wanted Interviewer Assessment Sheet for each participant.

    III. A copy of the Assistant Wanted Acceptance Sheet for each participant.

    IV. A copy of the Assistant Wanted Rejection Sheet for each participant

    V. A copy of the Assistant Wanted Interviewee Role-Description Sheet for each participant.

    VI. A copy of the Assistant Wanted Job-Application Sheet for each participant.

    VII. A copy of the Assistant Wanted Interviewee Assessment Sheet for each participant.

    VIII. A pencil for each participant.

    IX. Newsprint and a felt-tipped marker.

Physical Setting

    A room that is large enough for each interview to be conducted without disturbance from the others, in chairs arranged in pairs in separate portions of the room.

Process

    I. The facilitator introduces the activity as an experience in interviewing and being interviewed, then identifies half the participants as interviewers and the remaining half as interviewees. The interviewers and the interviewees are directed to assemble in separate portions of the room. (Five minutes.)

    II. Each interviewer is given a copy of the Assistant Wanted Interviewer Role-Description Sheet, a copy of the Assistant Wanted Interviewer Assessment Sheet, a copy of the Assistant Wanted Acceptance Sheet, a copy of the Assistant Wanted Rejection Sheet, and a pencil. Each interviewee receives a copy of the Assistant Wanted Interviewee Role-Description

Sheet, a copy of the Assistant Wanted Job-Application Sheet, a copy of the Assistant Wanted Interviewee Assessment Sheet, and a pencil. (Five minutes.)

III. The facilitator directs the interviewers to read their Assistant Wanted Interviewer Role-Description Sheets and to begin to construct questions to use during the interview. The interviewees are instructed to read their Assistant Wanted Interviewee Role-Description Sheets and to complete their Assistant Wanted Job-Application Sheets. (Ten minutes.)

IV. After ten minutes, the facilitator collects the completed Assistant Wanted Job-Application Sheets from the interviewees. The facilitator assigns an interviewee to each interviewer or directs the two groups to count off and pair off. Each interviewer is given the copy of the assigned interviewee's completed Assistant Wanted Job-Application Sheet. The interviewers are given five minutes to review these materials. (Ten minutes.)

V. The interviewers are seated at the interviewing stations and are directed to call their interviewees to their interviewing stations and to begin the interviews. The facilitator allows ten minutes for the interviews to be conducted. (Fifteen minutes.)

VI. After the interviews, both the interviewers and the interviewees are given five minutes to complete their respective Assistant Wanted Assessment Sheets. (Five minutes.)

VII. The interviewers and interviewees are directed to give one another feedback concerning the interview and to compare their responses to their Assistant Wanted Assessment Sheets. (Ten minutes.)

VIII. The interviewer and interviewee groups exchange roles, and steps II through VII are repeated. (The new interviewers do *not* interview the persons who interviewed them during the first round.) (Approximately one hour.)

IX. The facilitator instructs each participant to decide whether the person whom he or she interviewed is qualified for the job. Participants are given five minutes in which to make this decision and to complete an Assistant Wanted Applicant Acceptance Sheet if the interviewee is qualified for the job and an Assistant Wanted Applicant Rejection Sheet if the interviewee is not qualified for the job. (Five minutes.)

X. The persons who were interviewers during round 1 are directed to personally deliver their acceptance and rejection sheets to the individuals whom they interviewed during the first round and to explain (briefly) the reasons for their decisions. (Five minutes.)

XI. The persons who were interviewers during the second round of interviews are directed to personally deliver their acceptance and rejection sheets to the persons whom they interviewed during round 2 and to briefly explain the reasons for their decisions. (Five minutes.)

XII. All participants are assembled, and the facilitator leads a discussion of the experience, including:

1. What were the participants' feelings during the interviewing process: about being the interviewer? about being interviewed?

2. How were the feelings of the interviewer and interviewee similar or different?

3. How were participants' predictions of their own acceptance or rejection confirmed or disproved?

4. What types of questions and reactions helped to make people feel at ease during the interviews? Which helped them to show their personalities? Which helped them to demonstrate their skills?

5. What types of questions or reactions hindered people during the interviews? Did participants feel that these affected the decisions to accept or reject them?

6. What stages or processes did the interviewers go through? Did a common sequence emerge?

7. How did the experience fit with participants' own experiences in interviewing others or in being interviewed?

The facilitator lists the salient points of the discussion on newsprint. (Twenty minutes.)

Variations

I. At the end of the experience, the facilitator can deliver a lecturette or give a demonstration of an effective (model) interview and have the participants conduct another round based on the model.

II. The interviewers can write their own job situations and requirements prior to the interview.

III. The interviewees can assume any backgrounds they like during the interviews.

IV. If time is limited, only one round of interviews can be conducted. Participants would then be divided into two groups (interviewers and interviewees) to discuss the experience and report salient points.

Similar Structured Experience: *'75 Annual:* Structured Experience **142.**

Submitted by Laura M. Graves and Charles A. Lowe.

Laura M. Graves, Ph.D., *is an assistant professor of management and organization in the School of Business Administration at the University of Connecticut, Storrs, Connecticut. Her areas of expertise are social psychology and organizational behavior. Dr. Graves has done research on leadership and recruitment and has published articles in professional journals.*

Charles A. Lowe, Ph.D., *is a professor of psychology and head of the Division of Social Psychology at the University of Connecticut. He also serves as a marketing consultant on new product development, line extensions, and advertising, for several corporations. Dr. Lowe's research interests are in the areas of person perception, attribution, and nonverbal behavior. He is a consulting editor for the* Journal of Personality and Social Psychology *and has published articles in several professional journals.*

ASSISTANT WANTED INTERVIEWER ROLE-DESCRIPTION SHEET

Background: One of the Vitalab Company's most famous products is Vitamax brand vitamins. In the last few years, Vitamax has been losing its "fair share" of the vitamin market, and Vitalab is looking for new ways to advertise and market Vitamax. Vitalab's concern is to win back some or all of the consumers who have switched from Vitamax to other brands and to encourage consumers who did not previously take Vitamax to begin to do so. Vitalab has hired Dr. Pat Roberts, psychologist-consultant, to (a) conduct research on why people take vitamins, why they take Vitamax, and why they switch to other brands; (b) generate some new, creative, marketing strategies; and (c) devise pilot tests for the new marketing strategies.

The Current Situation: Dr. Roberts is looking for a bright, energetic, and ambitious research assistant to work on the Vitamax project. The pay is extremely good, and the exposure to marketing and consulting could be invaluable. The research assistant would be responsible for trying to find out why consumers take vitamins and why they prefer one brand over another. The project would involve talking to vitamin users and nonusers about vitamins and obtaining in-depth information about how consumers think about vitamins. The applicant should be flexible, be able to become involved in new experiences, be able to adapt to immediate and specific circumstances, and be at ease with people.

Your Role: You will play the role of a research assistant who already is working with Dr. Roberts. You have been asked to interview applicants who have applied for the position of research assistant. In the interview, you should attempt to:

1. Discover any relevant skills of the applicant,
2. Ascertain the applicant's personality,
3. Keep the interview spontaneous,
4. Make the applicant feel relaxed,
5. Make the applicant want the job.

Write down some questions that you will ask each applicant to assess his or her skills and personality.

ASSISTANT WANTED INTERVIEWER ASSESSMENT SHEET

1. Judging from the content of the interview, I believe that I know the skills, abilities, and qualities of the applicant, relevant to the job.

   Disagree   1   2   3   4   5   6   7   Agree

2. Judging from the content of the interview, I believe that I know the applicant as a person.

   Disagree   1   2   3   4   5   6   7   Agree

3. I feel that the interview was very spontaneous.

   Disagree   1   2   3   4   5   6   7   Agree

4. I feel that the applicant was very relaxed during the interview.

   Disagree   1   2   3   4   5   6   7   Agree

5. I tried hard to recruit the applicant for the position.

   Disagree   1   2   3   4   5   6   7   Agree

6. Overall, I feel that the interview went extremely well.

   Disagree   1   2   3   4   5   6   7   Agree

ASSISTANT WANTED ACCEPTANCE SHEET

———————————————
Marketing Research Assistant
Vitalab, Inc.

Dear ————————————:

It is with great pleasure that I inform you of my decision to hire you to work as a marketing research assistant on the Vitamax project. I look forward to working with you in the near future.

Sincerely,

———————————————

ASSISTANT WANTED REJECTION SHEET

———————————————
Marketing Research Assistant
Vitalab, Inc.

Dear ————————————:

I regret to inform you that I am unable to offer you a position as marketing research assistant on the Vitamax project. I will keep your application on file in the event that any other positions should be available in the near future.

Sincerely,

———————————————

ASSISTANT WANTED INTERVIEWEE ROLE-DESCRIPTION SHEET

Background: One of the Vitalab company's most famous products is Vitamax brand vitamins. In the last few years, Vitamax has been losing its "fair share" of the vitamin market, and Vitalab is looking for new ways to advertise and market Vitamax. Vitalab's concern is to win back some or all of the consumers who have switched from Vitamax to other brands and to encourage consumers who did not previously take Vitamax to begin to do so. Vitalab has hired Dr. Pat Roberts, psychologist-consultant, to (a) conduct research on why people take vitamins, why they take Vitamax, and why they switch to other vitamin brands; (b) generate some new, creative, marketing strategies; and (c) devise pilot tests for the new marketing strategies.

The Current Situation: Dr. Roberts is looking for a bright, energetic, and ambitious research assistant to work on the Vitamax project. The pay is extremely good, and the exposure to marketing and consulting could be invaluable. The research assistant would be responsible for trying to find out why consumers take vitamins and why they prefer one brand over another. The project would involve talking to vitamin users and nonusers about vitamins and obtaining in-depth information about how consumers think about vitamins. The applicant should be flexible, be able to become involved in new experiences, be able to adapt to immediate and specific circumstances, and be at ease with people.

Your Role: You will play the role of a job applicant who wants a position on Dr. Roberts' staff. Try to put yourself in the frame of mind of someone who really wants this job. Try to put your "best foot forward" during the interview. You will be interviewed by an individual who currently is employed by Dr. Roberts.

ASSISTANT WANTED JOB-APPLICATION SHEET

Name ____ Telephone _________

Address ____

____

Employment (Give two most recent positions):

    Current or Last Position: Dates held: _______________________________

                               Employer's name and address: _______________________

____

____

                               Describe position: _______________________________

____

    Previous Position: Dates held: _______________________________

                               Employer's name and address: _______________________

____

____

                               Describe position: _______________________________

____

Education:

    Education beyond high school:

1. School: _______________________________ Dates of attendance: _________

    Major: _____________________ Degree: _________ Date of degree: _________

    G.P.A.: _________

2. School: _______________________________ Dates of attendance: _________

    Major: _____________________ Degree: _________ Date of degree: _________

    G.P.A.: _________

ASSISTANT WANTED INTERVIEWEE ASSESSMENT SHEET

1. During the interview, I demonstrated that I was flexible.

   Disagree   1   2   3   4   5   6   7   Agree

2. During the interview, I demonstrated that I possess the necessary skills for the job.

   Disagree   1   2   3   4   5   6   7   Agree

3. I demonstrated that I enjoy working with people.

   Disagree   1   2   3   4   5   6   7   Agree

4. I demonstrated that I could elicit information from people.

   Disagree   1   2   3   4   5   6   7   Agree

5. I was enthusiastic during the interview.

   Disagree   1   2   3   4   5   6   7   Agree

6. I think the interviewer believes I want the job.

   Disagree   1   2   3   4   5   6   7   Agree

334. ROBBERY: PLANNING WITH PERT

Goals

    I. To illustrate the use of the Program Evaluation and Review Technique (PERT) and Critical Path Method (CPM) in planning.

    II. To allow participants to experience the scheduling and timing of both simultaneous and sequential activities.

    III. To demonstrate the creation of a basic PERT chart.

Group Size

Any number of groups of approximately five participants each.

Time Required

One and one-half to two hours.

Materials

    I. A copy of the Robbery Instruction Sheet for each participant.

    II. A copy of the Robbery Answer Sheet for each participant.

    III. Newsprint for each group.

    IV. Felt-tipped markers for each group.

    V. Masking tape.

Physical Setting

A room that is large enough for the groups to work without disturbing one another, and wall space for posting newsprint.

Process

    I. The facilitator delivers a lecturette on PERT and CPM. The lecturette must show how both simultaneous and sequential activities are dealt with by PERT and how the critical path is constructed. The facilitator draws a PERT chart on newsprint as part of the lecturette. (Fifteen to thirty minutes.)

    II. The facilitator divides the participants into groups of five members each, if possible (four or six members each if necessary), and directs the groups to assemble in different areas of the room. (Three minutes.)

    III. The facilitator distributes one copy of the Robbery Instruction Sheet to each participant, allows time for the participants to read their sheets, and answers any questions. (Fifteen minutes.)

    IV. The facilitator distributes newsprint and felt-tipped markers to the groups, reminds them that they are to draw their PERT charts on the newsprint, and tells them that they have twenty minutes in which to complete the task.

   V. The facilitator gives a time warning after fifteen minutes and calls time after twenty minutes. Each group's chart is posted, and one member of each group, in turn, explains the group's chart. (Thirty to forty minutes.)

  VI. The facilitator distributes the Robbery Answer Sheets and describes the procedure, timing, and critical path step-by-step. (Ten minutes.)

 VII. The participants are directed to take ten minutes to discuss within their groups:
   1. Their reactions to the experience,
   2. Problems they encountered in developing their charts,
   3. Questions about PERT or CPM that they wish to ask.

VIII. The entire group is assembled, and a spokesperson from each group reports on the group's discussion. The facilitator lists the salient points and any questions on newsprint. (Fifteen minutes.)

  IX. The facilitator solicits answers and comments from all the participants regarding the questions and points listed. (Five minutes.)

   X. The entire group discusses the uses of the PERT and CPM processes and suggests situations in which these processes would be helpful. (Ten minutes.)

Variations

   I. The task can be made more difficult by the addition of more activities.
  II. Work groups can "act out" their charts for the total group.
 III. The facilitator can draw a PERT chart of the entire structured experience to illustrate the concept more vividly.

Similar Structured Experience: *'74 Annual:* Structured Experience **132.**

Lecturette Source: *'72 Annual:* "An Introduction to PERT... or...."

Submitted by Mark P. Sharfman and Timothy R. Walters.

Mark P. Sharfman *is the president of Programetrics Consultants, Tucson, Arizona. He also is an instructor at both the University of Arizona and the University of Phoenix and is completing his Ph.D. in organizational behavior at the University of Arizona. Mr. Sharfman's interests are in management training, the impact of computers on organizations, and the management of change.*

Timothy R. Walters *is a partner in Avant Video, an educational videotape production company in Phoenix, Arizona. He specializes in management training programs and educational/commercial video production. Mr. Walters also is a management consultant specializing in organization development for Programetrics Consultants. He currently is completing a Ph.D. in education at Arizona State University.*

ROBBERY INSTRUCTION SHEET

Background: You are members of a notorious bank-robbing gang. The secret of your success is that your robberies always are well planned. For your next caper, you have selected a rural branch of the Second National Bank. From your surveillance, you have discovered that it will take the police seven minutes and thirty seconds to reach the bank once the alarm has sounded. You now want to determine if the robbery can be completed successfully in that time.

To complete the robbery, two members of your gang (one gunperson and a safecracker) will be dropped off behind the bank and will be responsible for picking the lock on the rear door. The rest of the gang will be driven to the front of the bank to wait. Once the alarm has sounded, the entire gang will enter the bank. The gun people will point their weapons at the guards and the customers, the counter leaper will leap over the counter and empty the teller drawers, and the safe cracker will crack or blow open the safe and empty it. Once these things have been accomplished, the gang will leave.

Your task is to determine whether the robbery can be accomplished in the allotted time and, if so, what the critical path is.

Your Task: To create a PERT chart for the bank robbery scenario.

Questions to be answered:

1. Can the robbery be accomplished in the seven minutes, thirty seconds before the police arrive?

2. How quickly can it be accomplished? (What is the critical path?)

Participants:

2 gunpeople	1 counter leaper
1 safe cracker	1 mastermind (optional with six participants)
1 driver	

Activities:

1. Drop off one gun person and the safe cracker in the alley behind the bank.
2. Drop off the other gang members in front of the bank.
3. Everyone enters the bank at the same time.
4. The gun people take up their positions and point their weapons at everyone in the bank.
5. The counter leaper leaps over the counter and empties the tellers' drawers.
6. The safe cracker cracks open the safe and empties it.
7. All members of the gang leave the bank at the same time.
8. The driver meets the rest of the gang in front of the bank when the robbery is completed.

Timing:

1. Two minutes to pick the lock on the rear door.
2. The alarm goes off when the back door is picked; the police arrive in seven minutes, thirty seconds.
3. Forty-five seconds to drive from the alley to the front of the bank.
4. Thirty seconds for the gun people to enter the bank and take up their positions.

5. Sixty seconds for the safe cracker to reach the safe from the back door.
6. Thirty seconds for the counter leaper to leap over the counter and start to empty the drawers.
7. Three minutes to empty the tellers' drawers.
8. Two minutes to open the safe.
9. Two minutes to empty the safe.
10. Forty-five seconds to exit from the bank and reach the car at the front curb.

ROBBERY ANSWER SHEET

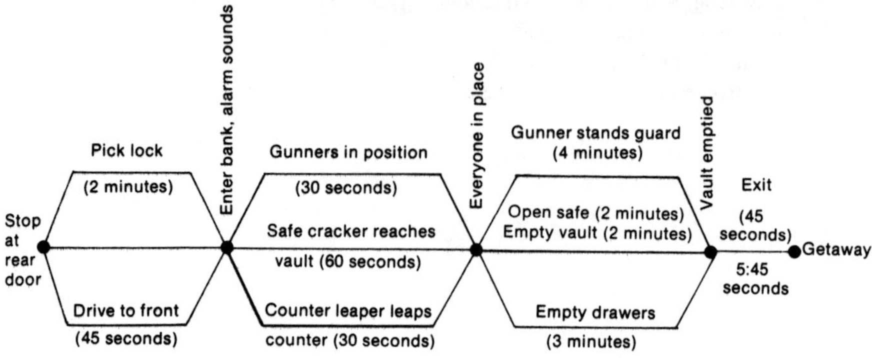

335. PEBBLES: VERTICAL AND LATERAL PROBLEM SOLVING

Goals

I. To provide an opportunity to compare vertical and lateral problem-solving approaches.

II. To increase participants' awareness of their preferences for and capabilities in these two approaches to problem solving.

Group Size

Several groups of three to five members each.

Time Required

Approximately one and one-half hours.

Materials

I. A copy of the Pebbles Problem Sheet for each participant.

II A copy of the Pebbles Solution Sheet for each participant.

III. A pencil for each participant.

IV. Newsprint and a felt-tipped marker.

V. Masking tape.

Physical Setting

A room in which all groups can work without disrupting one another.

Process

I. The facilitator briefly explains the goals and process of the activity. (Three minutes.)

II. The facilitator distributes a copy of the Pebbles Problem Sheet and a pencil to each participant and tells the participants that they have fifteen minutes in which to list their solutions to the problem. (Fifteen minutes.)

III. The facilitator calls time and divides the participants into groups of three to five members each. The facilitator tells the groups that they have thirty minutes in which to list and prioritize their solutions to the problem. (Thirty minutes.)

IV. After all groups have identified their solutions or when time has expired, each group is directed to explain the solutions or approaches that it selected to solve the problem. The groups alternate in reporting their solutions, starting with their first priorities. The facilitator lists the solutions on newsprint, putting the vertical solutions in one column and the lateral solutions in another column. (Fifteen minutes.)

V. The facilitator reviews the characteristics of the vertical and lateral problem-solving processes and refers to the solutions generated as examples of each. The facilitator then gives each participant a copy of the Pebbles Solution Sheet and reviews the information on the sheet. (Ten minutes.)

VI. The facilitator leads the participants in a discussion of which type of problem-solving approach they typically use and which type is most applicable to various kinds of problems. The facilitator may ask the following questions:

1. Which type of problem solving do you typically use? How effective is it?
2. Which type of problem solving typically is used at work? at home? Why might there be a difference?
3. What types of problems are best solved by vertical thinking?
4. What types of problems are best solved by lateral thinking?
5. When would a combination of the two approaches be appropriate?
6. Which approach is most effective for solving a problem for which there is no "right" answer?
7. If any participants are currently unable to solve a back-home problem, how might a change in the problem-solving approach help?

VII. Generalizations are drawn from the participants' learnings, and the group discusses applications. (Fifteen minutes.)

Variations

I. The facilitator can explain the differences between vertical and lateral thinking at the beginning of the experience and direct the groups to generate both types of solutions.

II. The facilitator can direct the groups to reassemble after step V and give them another problem to solve strictly by lateral thinking.

Similar Structured Experiences: *Volume IV:* Structured Experience **103**; *'77 Annual:* **185**; *Vol. VI:* **200**; *'79 Annual:* **240**; *'81 Annual:* **285**; *'83 Annual:* **337**.

Suggested Instrument: *'78 Annual:* "Phases of Integrated Problem Solving (PIPS)."

Lecturette Source: *'81 Annual:* "Creativity and Creative Problem Solving."

Submitted by Dan Muller.

Dan Muller *is the curriculum and training coordinator with the Value Management Resource Office of the City of Phoenix, Arizona. His areas of specialization are interpersonal communication, supervisory and management development, organization development, and team building. Mr. Muller is a member of ASTD and does external consulting in supervisory training. He also is an adjunct professor in the School of Communication at Arizona State University and teaches management courses at the University of Phoenix.*

PEBBLES PROBLEM SHEET

Background: The Pebble Story[1]

Many years ago, when a person who owed money could be thrown into jail, a merchant in London had the misfortune to owe a huge sum to a money lender. The money lender, who was old and ugly, fancied the merchant's beautiful, teen-aged daughter. He proposed a bargain. He said that he would cancel the merchant's debt if he could have the girl.

Both the merchant and his daughter were horrified at the proposal. So the cunning money lender proposed that they let providence decide the matter. He told them that he would put a black pebble and a white pebble into an empty money bag, then the girl would pick out one of the pebbles. If she chose the black pebble, she would become his wife and her father's debt would be cancelled. If she chose the white pebble, she would stay with her father but the debt still would be cancelled. But if she refused to pick out the pebble, her father would be thrown into jail and she would starve.

Reluctantly, the merchant agreed. They were standing on a pebble-strewn path in the merchant's garden as they talked, and the money lender stooped down to pick up the two pebbles. As he picked up the pebbles, the girl, sharp-eyed with fright, noticed that he picked up two black pebbles and put them into the money bag. He then told the girl to pick out the pebble that was to decide her fate and that of her father.

Instructions: Imagine that you are standing on that path in the merchant's garden.

1. What would you have done if you had been the unfortunate girl?

2. If you had to advise her, what would you advise her to do?

3. How did you reach your solution (briefly explain your thinking)?

PEBBLES SOLUTION SHEET

There are two general approaches to problem solving. The one most often used in business is "vertical thinking"—a logical analysis with one step or premise following another and building to a conclusion or solution. This may be described as "straight-line" thinking. The second is "lateral thinking," in which all the things that relate to the problem are considered. Lateral thinking is typified by the process of brainstorming, in which all solutions are considered, no matter how far-fetched they may seem at first glance. It may be described as "sideways" thinking.

In some cases, vertical thinking may be best and lateral thinking may indicate dishonesty. In other cases such as "The Pebble Story," vertical thinking may fail to produce a solution and lateral thinking may be the best approach.

Vertical thinkers are not usually of much help in the type of situation with which you have been dealing. The way they would analyze it, there might be three possibilities:

1. The girl should refuse to take a pebble.
2. The girl should show that there are two black pebbles in the bag and expose the money lender as a cheat.
3. The girl should take a black pebble and sacrifice herself in order to save her father from prison.

None of these suggestions is very helpful. If the girl does not take a pebble, her father will go to prison; if she does take a pebble, she will be forced to marry the money lender.

Vertical thinkers are concerned with the fact that the girl has to take a pebble. Lateral thinkers become concerned with the pebble that is left behind. Vertical thinkers take the most reasonable view of a situation and then proceed logically and carefully to work it out. Lateral thinkers tend to explore all the different ways of looking at something, rather than accepting the most promising and proceeding from that.

Solution: The girl in "The Pebble Story" put her hand into the money bag and drew out a pebble. Without looking at it, she fumbled and let it fall to the path, where it immediately was lost among all the other pebbles. "Oh, how clumsy of me," she said, "but never mind; if you look into the bag, you will be able to tell which pebble I took by the color of the one that is left."

Because the remaining pebble was, of course, black, it must be assumed that she had taken out the white pebble--the money lender dare not admit his dishonesty. In this way, by using lateral thinking, the girl changed what seemed to be an impossible situation into an extremely advantageous one. The girl actually was better off in this way than she would have been if the money lender had been honest and had put one black and one white pebble into the bag, for then she would have had only an even chance of being saved. As it happened, she was sure of remaining with her father and, at the same time, having his debt cancelled.

336. VICE PRESIDENT'S IN-BASKET: A MANAGEMENT ACTIVITY

Goals

    I. To focus attention on the issues involved in setting priorities for communications in organizations.

    II. To increase awareness of the role of delegation in organizations.

Group Size

Four to twenty-five participants.

Time Required

Approximately three and one-half hours.

Materials

    I. A copy of the Vice President's In-Basket Background Sheet for each participant.

    II. A copy of the Vice President's In-Basket Organizational Chart Sheet for each participant.

    III. A copy of the Vice President's In-Basket Situation Sheet for each participant.

    IV. A copy of the Vice President's In-Basket Calendar Sheet for each participant.

    V. One set of the fourteen Vice President's In-Basket Item Sheets for each participant.

    VI. A copy of the Vice President's In-Basket Solution Sheet for each participant (optional).

    VII. A pad of blank or ruled paper and a pencil for each participant.

    VIII. Fifteen paper clips for each participant.

    IX. Newsprint and a felt-tipped marker.

Physical Setting

Tables on which the participants can spread out their materials, a chair for each participant, and space to conduct small-group discussions.

Process

    I. The facilitator introduces the activity and states its goals. (Five minutes.)

    II. The facilitator distributes all materials *except* the Vice President's In-Basket Solution Sheet to the participants and directs them to read the Vice President's In-Basket Background Sheet, Organizational Chart Sheet, and Situation Sheet before beginning to work. The facilitator tells the participants that they will have two hours to complete the activity and that they probably will not have time to finish everything in their in-baskets in that amount of time; therefore, they will need to make some choices about priorities and delegation. The facilitator announces the time at which the participants will be asked to stop working and to turn in their responses to the original materials. The facilitator then tells the participants to begin working, suggesting that it will save time if they clip responses to items as they go. (Five minutes.)

III. The participants work on their in-basket items for two hours. At the end of this time, the facilitator directs them to turn in their fourteen in-basket items with the response to each item paper clipped to it, whether they have finished all the items or not. (Two hours.)

IV. The facilitator directs the participants to form groups of four or five members each and to discuss:

1. Their thoughts and feelings as they worked through the activity.
2. *How* they prioritized the items.
3. *How* they decided which items they should attend to themselves and which should be delegated.

(Fifteen minutes.)

V. While the groups are conducting their discussions, the facilitator prepares the following chart on newsprint:

Item	Topic	Priority	Action	Reason
1	Internal Reporting Format			
2	Guidelines for Clarifying Material			
3	Rejection Letter Memo			
4	Rejection Letter Form			
5	Request from Eric Short			
6	Speech Outline			
7	Writing Check List			
8	Clarifying Employee Benefits			
9	Note from Lorraine			
10	Newspaper Article			
11	Memo on Ad Meetings			
12	Annual Report Format			
13	Letters of Condolence			
14	Exhibit on Gross Revenues			

VI. At the end of the discussion period, the facilitator reassembles the entire group and examines the disposition of each item, summarizing the group's discussions and writing in the priority, action step, and reasons offered by the participants on the newsprint chart. The Vice President's In-Basket Solution Sheet may be distributed at this time. If the following points are not made by the participants, the facilitator may advance them:

1. The first working day after the trip will be Tuesday, May 26.
2. Some requests have been on Rick's desk since the first week in May.
3. Lorraine Short will not be able to type anything before Tracy leaves.

4. Some requests (e.g., art work) require lead time.
(Twenty minutes.)

VII. The facilitator concludes the activity with a discussion of the following questions:

1. How did your personal style of working help or hinder you during this experience? Did you handle work that was easiest for you or most essential for the company?

2. What other options are available besides "Do, Delegate, or Dump" (e.g., working on the airplane, mailing in work from New York, calling the office between meetings)?

3. What is the difference between delegating to a peer and delegating to a subordinate?

4. How can the most important factors affecting priorities in this activity be summarized? What were the highest priority items? (The facilitator may give participants the Vice President's In-Basket Solution Sheet at this point.)

5. How can this activity help the participants in their back-home work roles?

(Fifteen to thirty minutes.)

Variations

I. In-basket items can be added or deleted to lengthen or shorten the activity.

II. The background situation and in-basket items can be modified or written to reflect the work situation of the participants.

III. The participants can pair off after step VII to reassess priorities.

IV. The groups can be given the task of reaching consensus on priorities for the items.

V. Responses can be collected during step III in order to assess the participant's skills in business communication.

Similar Structured Experience: *Volume II:* Structured Experience 41.

Suggested Instruments: *'75 Annual:* "Decision-Style Inventory"; *Vol. VIII:* "When To Delegate Inventory Sheet."

Submitted by Annette N. Shelby.

Annette N. Shelby, Ph.D., is an associate professor of managerial communication in the School of Business Administration at Georgetown University, Washington, D.C. In addition, she consults in the areas of communication (both written and oral) and performance counseling and appraisal. Dr. Shelby's education is in the field of speech communication. Her areas of expertise include organizational communication and rhetorical theory. She previously taught speech communication and business courses at the University of Alabama.

VICE PRESIDENT'S IN-BASKET BACKGROUND SHEET

The Acme Company is rapidly becoming an energy conglomerate. Begun as a partnership between Paul and Harold Anderson (brothers), the company incorporated in 1975. Although the Andersons retain only 25 percent of the company's stock, company policy and procedure remain under their tight control.

Originally an oil-exploration company, Acme has pumped resources into shale oil and coal development, setting up separate corporate divisions for each.

A major thrust now is in strip mining—of both coal and shale. Acme's projected plans to "strip" five hundred miles in Colorado and three hundred miles in Alabama have environmentalists "up in arms," and they have filed law suits in both states.

"Sixty Minutes" ran a special last Sunday on what it called Acme's "excessive profits" and "rape of the environment."

Yesterday, an explosion at a test site near Steamboat Springs, Colorado, claimed forty-two lives.

Coal miners in Alabama's underground mines are threatening to go on strike next month.

VICE PRESIDENT'S IN-BASKET ORGANIZATIONAL CHART SHEET

Acme Company

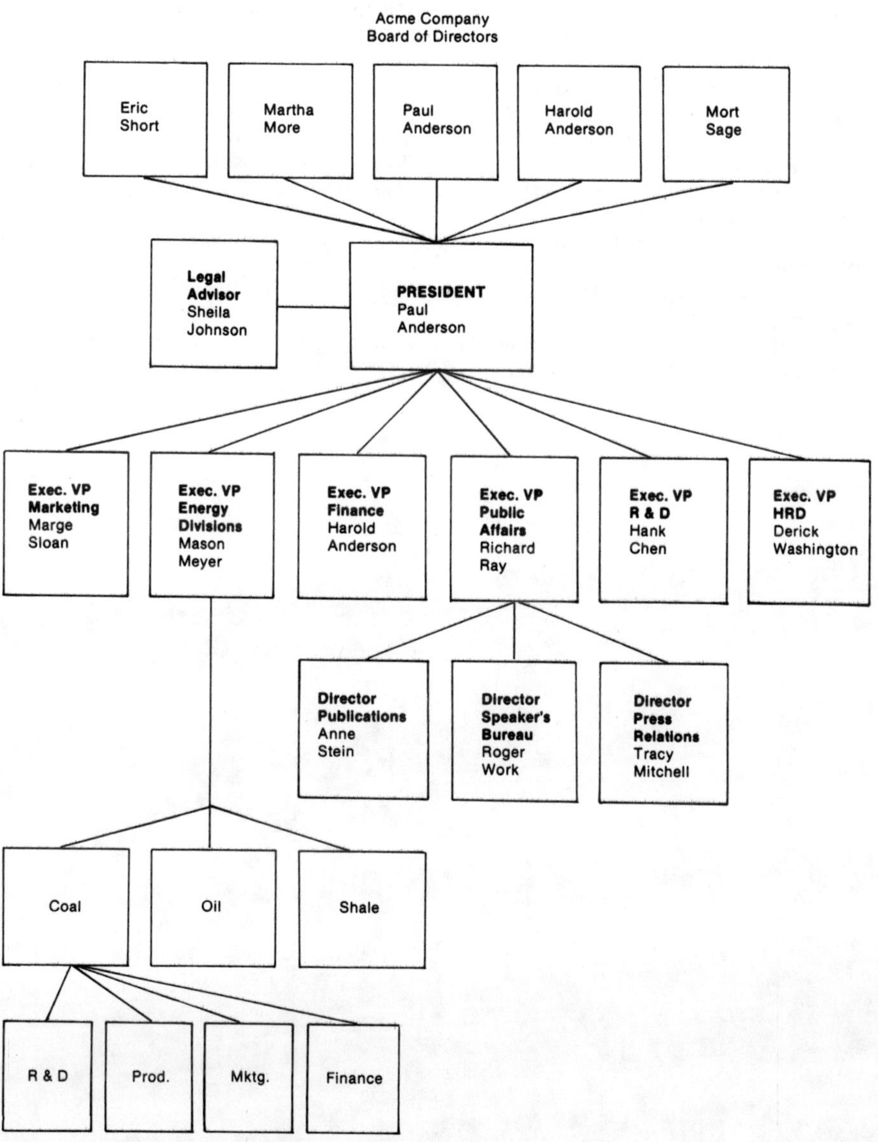

VICE PRESIDENT'S IN-BASKET SITUATION SHEET

Assignment

You are Tracy Mitchell. At 7 a.m. this morning (May 19), Paul Anderson phoned with the news that Richard Ray is in critical condition at Memorial Hospital following a massive coronary. You (Tracy) are to take over immediately as Acting Vice President for Public Affairs.

You are to continue your liaison responsibility with the press and, Mr. Anderson reminded you, you are to sit in on the meetings in New York City this week to discuss plans for a new corporate advertising campaign. Although the campaign is primarily the responsibility of the marketing division, Mr. Anderson wants you to be involved because of your sensitivity to the public relations implications. This is most important because of recent negative news coverage and the impending strike.

You are scheduled to fly to New York at 10:30 this morning. You cannot count on leaving New York before noon on Friday.

You have just arrived at the office (8 a.m.). By pushing it, you will have about two hours in the office.

Note: All typing and other secretarial work is channeled through Lorraine Jones. Neither Mr. Ray nor you has a personal secretary.

May

Sunday	Monday	Tuesday	Wednesday	Thursday	Friday	Saturday
					1	2
3	4	5	6	7	8	9
10	11	12	13	14	15	16
17	18	19	20	21	22	23
24 31	25 MEMORIAL DAY HOLIDAY	26	27	28	29	30

Office Memorandum

TO: Richard Ray   DATE: May 1, 19____

FROM: Mason Meyer *mm*

SUBJECT: *Internal Reporting Format*

With the expansion of our energy divisions, we need to standardize formats for our internal reporting. Paul suggested that I ask for your suggestions.

Office Memorandum

TO: Richard Ray   DATE: May 6, 19____

FROM: Paul Anderson *PA*

SUBJECT: *Guidelines for Clarifying Material*

Rick, I'm calling on your communication expertise again!

OSHA has ordered that we rewrite mining procedures so the miners will be able to understand the safety instructions more easily. Currently, they are written in engineering terminology.

You'll be glad to know that I'm not asking you to do the rewriting; I feel that's best done at the job site. However, I do want you to draft some guidelines for simplifying material, which I'll ask Mason Meyer to distribute under my signature to all managers and line supervisors. They will do the actual rewriting.

**VICE PRESIDENT'S IN-BASKET
ITEM SHEET 3**

Office Memorandum

TO: Richard Ray   DATE: May 12, 19____

FROM: Derick Washington *DW*

SUBJECT: *Rejection Letter*

I need your help. The (attached) letter that we send to applicants we don't intend to hire sounds pretty harsh.

Since PR is your "bag," would you give the letter a once over? Thanks.

**VICE PRESIDENT'S IN-BASKET
ITEM SHEET 4**

Date:

Dear Applicant:

We have received your application for a position here at Acme. Unfortunately, we cannot hire you at this time. We know how tough the job market is these days and we do wish you the best of luck in finding employment.

Yours truly,

Derick Washington

Derick Washington
Vice President,
Human Resource Development

486 High Forest
Mulga, OH 33221
May 11, 19____

Richard Ray
Executive Vice President
Public Affairs
Acme Company
1312 Macon Square
Cambridge, IL 24613

Dear Rick:

I received a copy of the last annual report and want to compliment you on its production. The only thing that bothered me was that I felt it was a little too worker-oriented. It seems to me that we are interested in getting more investors. You had pictures of miners. But that's just my own reaction.

The reason that I am writing is to ask a personal favor of you. As you know, I recently have been re-elected as president of the Rotary Club here in Mulga, and we are celebrating National Industry Week, May 25-29. Could you send someone to speak at our Rotary-Friend Luncheon on May 26th?

Thank you for your attention to this matter. I hope that you can send someone.

Yours truly,

Eric Short

ES: an

Office Memorandum

TO: Richard Ray

DATE: May 18, 19____

FROM: Paul Anderson *PA*

SUBJECT: *Speech Outline*

I received an invitation today to speak at the Chicago Press Club on May 29. (Somebody must have died.)

Could you get a bare bones outline to me by noon on the 21st so I can send it to research? Time is short!

I've listed a few ideas below, but feel free to add your own.

> Address environmental concerns
> We need to justify profits
> Take free-enterprise stance
> The work progress is key
> Should we talk about balance of payments?
> What about governmental regulation?

Office Memorandum

TO: Richard Ray

DATE: March 12, 19___

FROM: Paul Anderson *PA*

SUBJECT: *Writing Check List*

I continue to be appalled at the poor quality of writing at Acme. Because you're our "in-house communications expert," please draw up a check list that managers can use to give feedback to subordinates on writing problems.

Make the list short, simple, and easy to use, but make it comprehensive enough to be worthwhile.

Office Memorandum

TO: Richard Ray

DATE: May 4, 19___

FROM: Derick Washington *DW*

SUBJECT: *Clarifying Employee Benefits*

A recent survey shows that 58 percent of Acme's employees do not understand the company's benefit package. What are your ideas on how to correct this?

cc: Sheila Johnson

5/18

Mr. Ray —
I have a dentist's appt. Tuesday, the 19th, and will not be in the office before noon.

Lorraine Jones

From the Desk of
Paul Anderson

Tracy—
you'll have to handle this—

Let me see a draft before you leave town—
Paul A.

STEAMBOAT SPRINGS, COLORADO—Yesterday about 5:00 p.m., an explosion claimed the lives of forty-two miners in nearby Brat's gulch. Survivors blamed lack of safety precautions for the explosion. According to one miner, who does not wish to be identified, the company stored flammable chemicals near the construction site. A spark from the drilling rig ignited the chemicals. Spokespeople for Acme Company, owner of the drilling operation, could not be reached for comment.

Rick— The press is pushing for a response. Let me see a draft a.s.a.p. Express regret, tell them we're investigating, and generally smooth the waters.

Paul A.

From the Desk of
Paul Anderson

Rick —
I've asked Tracy to
sit in on the ad meetings
in NYC this week.
Tracy will be out of
the office Tuesday through
Friday.   Paul
5/18

Office Memorandum

May 18, 19____

TO: Richard Ray

FROM: Paul Anderson *PA*

SUBJECT: *Annual Report Format*

    Rick, thumb through several annual reports from other companies and give me some feedback about formats we may wish to consider using this year.

    I think our research library should have copies of several reports.

VICE PRESIDENT'S IN-BASKET
ITEM SHEET 13

From the Desk of
Paul Anderson

Tracy—
While you're working on that press release on the mine explosion, you may as well draft some letters of condolence to the families.
Thanks!
Paul

VICE PRESIDENT'S IN-BASKET
ITEM SHEET 14

From the Desk of
Paul Anderson

Rick—

Prepare a preliminary sketch for an exhibit on the following data on gross revenues. This is to be used in Congressional testimony on the 27th (May). How about giving me two alternatives?

Data: Over the past five years, gross revenues increased from $1.5 million in 19____ to 2.3 million in 19____, 4.5 million in 19____, 5.9 million in 19____, and 7.1 million in 19____

VICE PRESIDENT'S IN-BASKET SOLUTION SHEET

Using the Calendar:

1. Note carefully the dates and times that you will be out of town.
2. What are the implications of Lorraine Jones being out of the office until noon?
3. Note the dates of requests and the lead time needed to complete the materials (for example, the art work).

Setting Priorities:

1. *Speech Outline* (#6). The president has asked for this material. Time does not allow you to put it off. You are not safe delegating it to Roger Work because his position is likely to be administrative.
2. *Letter to Eric Short* (#5). You may delegate the task of finding a speaker to Roger Work, but you need to write to Eric Short to tell him you have done so. A carbon copy to Paul Anderson would be advisable in case Roger fails to follow through. Because Eric is on the Board of Directors, he is too important not to give special attention to his request.
3. *Sketches* (#14). The president has asked for the sketches, and you have a time constraint. To delegate might be very dangerous, although the actual art work will be produced by someone else from your sketches, so you need to provide lead time.
4. *Press Release* (#10). The president wants a copy on his desk *before* you leave town.
5. *Letters of Condolence* (#13). Time is a critical factor here, and you may not be able to trust anyone else with the "tone" of the letter.

Delegating Responsibilities:

1. Numbers 1, 2, 3/4, 7, 8, and 12 probably can be delegated to others. However, you must ultimately take responsibility for their work. You must decide whether you want to see the work before it goes out and whether this will be possible. You need to build in some check points.
2. Delegating work for which the president of the company is holding you personally responsible may not be a good idea.
3. You must be careful about delegating too much to any one individual. That person also has other work to do, and yours may not receive top priority.
4. Some items can be taken to New York.
5. You must leave very clear instructions for Lorraine Jones.

Throwing Away:

Items 9 and 11 should be thrown away.

337. THE LAWN: PROBLEM OR SYMPTOM?

Goals

   I. To provide an experience in clearly defining a problem.

   II. To increase awareness of the difference between the causes of a problem and the symptoms of a problem.

   III. To demonstrate how using only oral communication can affect the problem-solving process.

Group Size

Several groups of five members each.

Time Required

Approximately one and one-half hours.

Materials

   I. One set of twenty-five statements for each group, to be prepared from The Lawn Statement Sheet, on individual 3"x 5" index cards or slips of paper.

   II. A sheet of blank paper and a pencil for each group.

   III. Newsprint and a felt-tipped marker.

   IV. Masking tape.

Physical Setting

A room with space for the small groups to interact separately as well as for total-group discussion.

Process

   I. The facilitator briefly explains the activity. The participants are told that they will be given data and are to define the problem from the data given.

   II. The facilitator divides the participants into groups of five members each.

   III. The facilitator informs the groups that each group will receive twenty-five statements of data concerning a situation. The facilitator then gives each member of a group *five* of that group's statements. (Five minutes.)

   IV. The facilitator announces the rules for the activity:

     1. The members are not permitted to exchange cards or to show their cards to other members of their group.

     2. All data must be communicated orally to the other members of the group; these statements may be repeated as often as the group feels is necessary.

     3. If all members of the group feel that a statement (data) is not relevant to arriving at the definition of the problem, the statement is to be placed face down and not repeated.

4. Group members may *not* take notes during the process.

5. Only one problem definition may be presented from each group.

(Five minutes.)

V. The facilitator tells the groups that they will have thirty minutes in which to define the problem and that at the end of the allotted time, each group must submit a definition of the problem. The facilitator directs the groups to begin working.

VI. While the groups are working, the facilitator prepares a list on newsprint of the twenty-five statements.

VII. At the end of thirty minutes, the facilitator calls time, distributes a sheet of blank paper and a pencil to each group, and directs the groups to write their definitions of the problem on their sheets of paper. (Five minutes.)

VIII. The facilitator collects the groups' problem definitions and posts them. The entire group is reassembled, and a spokesperson from each group reports on how the group arrived at the problem definition. (Ten minutes.)

IX. The facilitator posts the appropriate definition of the problem: How to rid the lawn of grubs. With the participants' input, the facilitator checks the relevant statements on the newsprint poster, indicates why other data are irrelevant, and explains how the answer was reached. The facilitator answers any questions that may arise. (Fifteen minutes.)

X. The facilitator solicits comments from the participants regarding:

1. Their reactions to the experience.

2. Whether they had difficulty in separating irrelevant from relevant data.

3. How the groups decided which data were relevant.

4. Whether any groups reached total agreement on the definition of the problem.

5. How the use of only verbal communication affected the difficulty of the task.

(Fifteen minutes.)

Variations

I. The facilitator can give a lecturette on the "Phases of Integrated Problem Solving (PIPS)" instrument, the total problem-solving process, or some other appropriate aspect of problem solving.

II. Group members can be directed to discuss and to list behaviors that either contributed to successful task completion or hindered the group.

III. The rule about oral communication only can be eliminated.

IV. Other problems with lists of relevant and irrelevant data can be developed.

V. The participants can be encouraged to focus on problems of their own and to determine what aspects are symptoms and what are causes, with the help of the group.

Similar Structured Experiences: *Volume II:* Structured Experience 31; *'74 Annual:* 133; *Vol. V:* 155, 156; *'79 Annual:* 240; *'81 Annual:* 284; *'83 Annual:* 335.

Suggested Instrument: *'78 Annual:* "Phases of Integrated Problem Solving (PIPS)."

Submitted by William W. Kibler and William T. Milburn.

William W. Kibler is the director of organization and management development for the R.J. Reynolds Tobacco Company, Winston-Salem, North Carolina, where he directs the organization development and managerial training activities. Mr. Kibler has twenty-one years of line and staff experience and has developed and facilitated many training programs for the company. His structured experience "Dynasell"appears in the 1981 Annual. His special interests include conducting organizational analysis activities and workshops on oral presentations.

William T. Milburn is the training and development manager for the R.J. Reynolds Tobacco Company, Winston-Salem, North Carolina. His present activities include the development, implementation, and facilitation of management development programs for the company. Mr. Milburn was educated at the University of North Carolina. He has held line and staff positions with R.J. Reynolds for the past twenty-four years. His special interests include creative problem solving, values clarification, time management, goal setting, and financial planning.

THE LAWN STATEMENT SHEET

Instructions: These twenty-five statements are to be distributed individually to the members of each group (five separate statements to each of the five group members).

In the past, I always have had a beautiful lawn.

The lawn is dying in spots and it looks awful.

The dead spots have ridges.

Moles make ridges.

The lawn has never had ridges before.

I take great pride in my lawn.

My neighbor's lawn does not have dead spots.

My neighbor is making fun of my lawn.

I don't like my neighbor.

My lawn does not need water.

My lawn does not need fertilizer.

My riding mower is broken.

I want to get rid of the dead spots in my lawn.

Moles have tiny eyes.

Moles have concealed ears.

Moles work in the dark.

Moles have soft fur and eat grubs.

My neighbor has a mole on his neck.

My main concern is my lawn.

My push mower is working fine.

Moles are eager eaters.

My lawn has good drainage.

My lawn is frustrating me.

Moles tunnel in search of food.

I do not like moles.

338. FOUR CULTURES: EXPLORING BEHAVIORAL EXPECTATIONS

Goals

    I. To explore the effects of cultural behaviors or traits on others.

    II. To experience cross-cultural encounters.

    III. To increase awareness of how cultural mannerisms and rituals are derived from cultural attitudes.

Group Size

    Four groups of four to eight members each.

Time Required

    Two and one-half hours.

Materials

    I. A copy of the Four Cultures Instruction Sheet for each participant.

    II. A pencil for each participant.

    III. A copy of the Four Cultures Traits Sheet, cut into four strips so that each strip contains a different Trait Description.

    IV. A paper cup for each group.

    V. A box or bag of raisins, peanuts, or small candy for each group.

    VI. A newsprint poster on which is printed the schedule of visits for the groups, as follows:

Round 1: Group 2 visits Group 1 and
           Group 4 visits Group 3.
Round 2: Group 3 visits Group 2 and
           Group 1 visits Group 4.
Round 3: Group 3 visits Group 1 and
           Group 4 visits Group 2.

    VII. Masking tape.

Physical Setting

    A room large enough to provide each group with privacy and with an area in which to entertain, and eight movable chairs for each group. Separate rooms are ideal for the development and rehearsal stages.

Process

I. The facilitator introduces the activity as an opportunity to explore the effects of cultural behaviors or traits. The participants are divided into four groups, and the groups are assigned to different areas in the room or separate rooms, if available. (Five minutes.)

II. The facilitator distributes a copy of the Four Cultures Instruction Sheet and a pencil to each participant and one of the four Trait Descriptions from the Four Cultures Traits Sheet to each group (a different description for each group). The groups are directed to read their sheets quietly and to keep their information within their groups. (Five minutes.)

III. The facilitator tells the groups that they will have fifteen minutes in which to develop and rehearse their six cultural activities and then instructs them to begin. (Fifteen minutes.)

IV. When all groups have developed their six activities or at the end of fifteen minutes, the facilitator calls time and gives each group a paper cup full of raisins, peanuts, or small candy. The facilitator says that this food will be the refreshments that each group will have available to offer to visitors. The facilitator then posts the schedule of visits and directs the groups to take two minutes to prepare themselves for the first visit. (Five minutes.)

V. The facilitator announces the beginning of round 1, and the groups conduct their first visits according to the posted schedule. (Fifteen minutes.)

VI. At the end of ten minutes, the facilitator suggests that the visitors begin their farewells. At the end of fifteen minutes, the facilitator calls time and directs the members of each group to return to their area and to discuss their reactions to the activity among themselves. During this time, the facilitator refills the groups' paper cups. (Five minutes.)

VII. The facilitator conducts rounds 2 and 3 in the same manner as round 1, allowing a few minutes for group discussion and refilling of the cups at the completion of each round. (Forty minutes.)

VIII. When the groups' discussions of round 3 have been completed, the facilitator announces that the visiting groups are to "go native"—that is, adopt the mannerisms and customs of the groups they are visiting—during round 4. The facilitator then announces the schedule for round 4:

> *Select one of the following:*
>
> Group 2 visits Group 3 and Group 4 visits Group 1 OR
> Group 1 visits Group 2 and Group 3 visits Group 4 OR
> Group 1 visits Group 3 and Group 2 visits Group 4.

Round 4 and the groups' discussions of it are then conducted. (Twenty minutes.)

IX. The entire group is assembled, and the facilitator leads a discussion of reactions to and perceptions resulting from the experience. The following items may be included:

1. What were common themes in the groups' discussions following each round?
2. How did it feel to play the role of a member of another culture?
3. What were some of the most difficult or negative aspects of dealing with members of another culture?

4. What were some of the most enjoyable or positive aspects of dealing with members of another culture?

5. How did it feel to attempt to "go native"? Which was more comfortable: the role your group had been assigned or "going native"?

6. What were the reactions of the host groups when the visitors attempted to "go native"?

7. Which of the four cultures are most like our own? Which are like other cultures that the participants have experienced?

8. What implications do the reactions described have for real life?

9. What other things did the participants learn about cross-cultural interactions?

10. What generalizations can be drawn from these insights and learnings?

11. How can these be applied in real-life situations?

(Twenty minutes.)

Variations

I. The visits can be conducted nonverbally.

II. Following step IX, participants can be asked to volunteer ways in which they, as individuals, will change their behavior as a result of their learnings from the experience.

III. The issue of leadership can be examined as part of the groups' behaviors.

IV. Different cultures can be developed to accommodate more groups, and additional rituals (e.g., buying and selling or trading) can be added.

Similar Structured Experiences: *'73 Annual:* Structured Experience **94**; *'79 Annual:* **239**; *Vol. VIII:* **298**.

Lecturette Source: *'75 Annual:* "Nonverbal Communication and the Intercultural Encounter."

Submitted by Dwight L. Gradin.

__Dwight L. Gradin__ is the language coordinator at Missionary Internship, a missionary cross-cultural training center in Farmington, Michigan, He directs the program in language acquisition techniques and his specialty is the development and teaching of techniques for self-directed learning of language. Mr. Gradin previously served with the Summer Institute of Linguistics (Viet Nam); as chairman of the Language Department Asia Training Center, University of Hawaii/USAID; and as an instructor at the Toronto Institute of Linguistics.

FOUR CULTURES INSTRUCTION SHEET

I. The following is a fairly natural sequence of welcoming visitors. Your group is to create specific ways of expressing each activity below in accordance with the traits and characteristics that are distinctive of your group. Be as verbal as you want to be and create as many gestures as you wish, but be careful that the *way* in which you express yourself reflects your cultural traits. (This is a group activity.)

1. The equivalent of waving "Hello" as guests approach from a distance.
2. The equivalent of a close greeting, such as the custom of shaking hands.
3. The equivalent of inviting your guests to come in or to come with you.
4. The equivalent of inviting your guests to sit down (on a chair, the floor, etc.).
5. The equivalent of inviting your guests to partake of refreshments.
6. The equivalent of seeing your guests to the door and bidding them farewell.

Time will be allotted for you to develop and rehearse this sequence within your group.

II. The second part of this activity will be to act out your roles by conducting visits with other groups.

If you are the Host group: Demonstrate your traits and act out your host activities as you have designed and rehearsed them.

If you are the Visitor group: Maintain the traits and attitudes that are characteristic of your group, but allow your hosts to treat you according to the dictates of their own culture.

FOUR CULTURES TRAITS SHEET

Trait Description

You are Group 1.

You are a lordly, martial, highly regimented people with a sense of superiority that shows in your gestures and speech. You like organization and you like things to be in their proper places.

When guests arrive, you take charge and, although you treat them well, you insist that they do things *your* way.

Trait Description

You are Group 2.

You are a gentle, meek, submissive people with much grace and movement in your gestures.

When guests arrive, you put them in a superior position and are apologetic in the way you treat them.

Trait Description

You are Group 3.

You are a very warm, friendly, expressive people with gestures that demonstrate your warmth and friendliness.

When guests arrive, you are open and free in the way you treat them, and you try hard to please.

Trait Description

You are Group 4.

You have a very calm, relaxed outlook on life—one that borders on being lackadaisical. You are unhurried in what you do.

When guests arrive, you acknowledge their presence and do get around to serving them, but hurry is abhorrent to you.

---

339. ORGANIZATIONAL BLASPHEMIES: CLARIFYING VALUES

Goals

I. To provide an opportunity for the participants to be creatively open about aspects of their organizations.

II. To identify and compare the organizational values of the group members.

III. To provide an opportunity to explore the match between the goals or values of the participants and those of the organization.

Group Size

Three or more participants who work in the same organization, department, or temporary system.

Time Required

One to one and one-half hours.

Materials

I. Three sheets of blank paper and a pencil for each participant.

II. Newsprint and a felt-tipped marker.

III. Masking tape.

Physical Setting

A writing surface or floor space for each participant.

Process

I. The facilitator introduces the activity by stating that it is useful for the members of an organization to think from time to time about the organization's objectives and whether they, as individuals, are working toward those objectives.

II. The facilitator distributes three sheets of blank paper and a pencil to each participant and explains that each participant is to write an organizational blasphemy[1]—a phrase or slogan so alien to what the group represents that the members will squirm in their seats when they hear it. The facilitator then gives examples of blasphemies for other organizations:

University Associates: "You can't teach an old dog new tricks."

Four-Star Restaurant: "If we run out of veal, use lean pork; no one will notice."

(Five minutes.)

---

[1]The idea of an organizational blasphemy was suggested in *The Corporation Man* by Anthony Jay, Penguin Books, Ltd., 1975.

III. The participants are told that they will have five minutes in which to invent their own blasphemies and are instructed to write them on one of their sheets of blank paper. (Five minutes.)

IV. The facilitator calls time, collects the blasphemies, and reads them aloud while a member of the group posts them on newsprint. (Ten minutes.)

 V. The group discusses the activity so far. The following topics may be included in this discussion:

1. How did it feel to consider and write down ideas of this nature?

2. Why did members select these particular blasphemies?

3. Is there a common theme running through the blasphemies? What might this mean in terms of the way the members perceive the organization?

4. What blind spots or biases in the organization might these blasphemies indicate?

5. What taboos are there within the group that appear clearly in the list of blasphemies?

6. What does this imply about the goals of the organization? The way in which the organization works?

7. Does any group member's blasphemy differ significantly from the rest? What might be the reason?

8. What implications do the results of this activity have for the organization? The group? The individual members? The fit among these three?

(Fifteen to thirty minutes.)

VI. The facilitator states that blasphemies often highlight beliefs or aspects of behavior that have been "socialized out" of the group members by the organization's processes. The participants then are invited to contribute their own examples of how this process of socialization has operated, if at all, within the group. (Ten minutes.)

VII. The facilitator states that groups are often cultures within other cultures and that the values of these cultures can differ to a great extent. The facilitator then posts the following diagram:

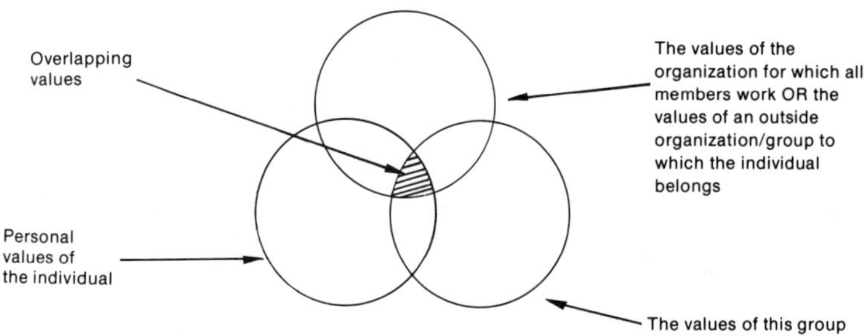

The facilitator explains that the larger the shaded area, the more "comfortable" individuals are likely to feel in the organization or group. If the shaded area is large, the individual is confronted by less value conflict. The facilitator says that tension can be present whenever the individual perceives a clash between the values of one culture and the values of another culture to which it is connected (e.g., personal and work or department and organization) and that these values may conflict more than one often realizes. (Five minutes.)

VIII. The facilitator asks the participants to think of two departments or groups to which they belong. Ideally, these would be groups that form part of a larger organization. The participants then are directed to think about themselves in relation to these groups and, using the diagram of the three circles as a model, to draw circles (of approximately the same size) to represent their own values in relation to their two chosen groups, departments, or organizations, and to list the values in each circle. (Ten minutes.)

IX. The facilitator divides the group into dyads and directs the members of each pair to discuss their respective drawings. Each individual is to explain to his or her partner the rationale behind his or her drawing. (Ten minutes.)

X. The facilitator reassembles the entire group and leads a discussion of the experience, focusing in particular on:
1. The shaded areas on the drawings and what these indicate about the match between the individual and the work area.
2. What values are seen as common (shaded area)? What values outside the common areas are shaded by individuals in the group?
3. Is there a common theme running through the blasphemies? What might this mean in terms of the way the members perceive the organization?
4. How can the blasphemies be turned around and stated in terms of agreed-on goals? (Ten to fifteen minutes.)

Variations

I. The facilitator can ask for the group members' perceptions of what their individual bosses would give as blasphemies. These blasphemies can be compared with the participants' own blasphemies. The group can discuss whether issues highlighted by the bosses' blasphemies differ significantly from those of the subordinates.

II. The activity can be made less sophisticated by ending after step V.

Suggested Instruments: *'75 Annual:* "Diagnosing Organization Ideology"; *'78 Annual:* "Organizational Norms Opinionnaire"; *'80 Annual:* "Organizational Diagnosis Questionaire."

Lecturette Sources: *'75 Annual:* "Understanding Your Organization's Character"; *'77 Annual:* "Organizational Norms."

Submitted by Tony McNulty.

Tony McNulty is a senior training adviser with Lucas CAV Limited, London, England, where he is responsible for developing and conducting management training courses. Mr. McNulty's background includes a bachelor's degree in modern languages and a two-year period as faculty assistant in organizational behavior at INSEAD, Fontainebleau, France. His current interests are in career management, creativity, and trying to relate concepts of behavioral science to organizational life.

340. CONFLICT ROLE PLAY: RESOLVING DIFFERENCES

Goals

    I. To examine individuals' reactions to situations in which a "double standard" of behavior operates.

    II. To allow participants to explore their emotional responses to conflict.

    III. To examine the problem-solving behavior of participants in conflict situations in which a power difference exists.

Group Size

Two or more groups of three members each.

Time Required

Approximately two hours.

Materials

    I. Two copies of one of the three sets of Conflict Role Play Sheets for each group (the sheets are cut to separate the manager and subordinate roles).

    II. A sheet of blank paper and a pencil for the observer in each group.

    III. Newsprint and a felt-tipped marker.

    IV. Masking tape.

Physical Setting

A room that is large enough for each group to meet without disturbing the other groups.

Process

    I. The facilitator introduces the activity as one that will examine problem-solving behavior in situations that involve conflict. No mention is made of the "double standard" aspect of the role play.

    II. The facilitator separates the participants into groups of three members each and instructs the members of each group to assume the roles of manager, subordinate, and observer. The manager and subordinate in each group receive only their own role descriptions from the Conflict Role Play Sheet; the observer in each group receives the complete Conflict Role Play Sheet (both role descriptions), a sheet of blank paper, and a pencil. If there are only two or three groups, each group receives a different Conflict Role Play Sheet. (Five minutes.)

    III. The facilitator directs the members of each group to study their role descriptions in preparation for a meeting between the manager and the subordinate. (Five minutes.)

IV. The facilitator directs each group to a separate area and tells the managers and subordinates that they will have fifteen minutes in which to conduct their meetings while the observers watch. The observers are told that they may take notes during the role plays if they wish. The role plays begin. (Fifteen minutes.)

V. The facilitator calls time and reassembles the complete group.

VI. The facilitator solicits the participants' reactions to the experience, including:

1. Reactions of the subordinates to the situations involving double standards.
2. How the managers felt about presenting situations involving double standards.
3. Comments from the observers regarding whether the issue of double standards was raised in each of their role plays and how that issue was dealt with.

(Five minutes.)

VII. The discussion then is focused on the problem-solving behaviors (or lack of them) that emerged during each role play. The participants' various attempts to solve their problems are discussed, and the observers offer their comments. (Fifteen minutes.)

VIII. The facilitator divides the participants into three groups: one of managers, one of subordinates, and one of observers. The group members are directed to discuss their responses (both feeling and behavioral) to the role-play conflicts in which there was unequal power and to compare these with their typical responses to conflict. (Fifteen minutes.)

IX. The total group is reassembled, and the facilitator asks for reports from the discussion groups on the members' typical modes of response to situations involving conflict. These may be listed on newsprint. (Ten minutes.)

X. The facilitator then introduces a discussion of the problem-solving behaviors that worked and why these were effective. The facilitator then summarizes the most effective modes of response to conflict and solicits additional ideas and comments from the participants. Key points are noted on newsprint and posted. (Fifteen minutes.)

XI. The participants are directed to form discussion groups of four or five members each and to discuss ways in which they can apply their learnings from the experience to real-life situations. (Fifteen minutes.)

Variations

I. The role plays can be used to focus primarily on double standards across sexes.

II. The same role play can be conducted with two groups in which the sexes of the manager and subordinate are reversed across groups for comparison.

III. The facilitator can provide each participant in a group the opportunity to be the manager, subordinate, and observer by conducting all three role plays with each group and rotating the roles.

IV. The facilitator can provide each participant the opportunity to be the manager and the subordinate by eliminating the role of observer and conducting two of the role plays with each group.

V. If there are only four to six participants, role plays can be conducted consecutively by two persons, with the non-role players serving as observers.

Similar Structured Experiences: *Volume III:* Structured Experience **62;** *'75 Annual:* **144;** *'77 Annual:* **186;** *Vol. VI:* **215;** *Vol. VII:* **268.**

Suggested Instrument: *Volume III:* "Polarization: Opinionnaire on Womanhood."

Lecturette Sources: *'73 Annual:* "Confrontation: Types, Conditions, and Outcomes"; *'74 Annual:* "Conflict-Resolution Strategies"; *'77 Annual:* "Constructive Conflict in Discussions: Learning To Manage Disagreements Effectively," "Handling Group and Organizational Conflict."

Submitted by Robert P. Belforti, Lauren A. Hagan, Ben Markens, Cheryl A. Monyak, Gary N. Powell, and Karen Sykas Sighinolfi.

Robert P. Belforti is the distribution services manager for IBM Corporation in Hartford, Connecticut. He is a member of the Hartford Area Private Industry Council and has been working with handicapped and disadvantaged youth in the area of job placement. A former teacher, coach, and athletic administrator, Mr. Belforti currently is attending the M.B.A. program at the University of Connecticut.

Lauren A. Hagan is a life insurance agent (college market representative) for the Fidelity Union Life Insurance Company in Milford, Connecticut. She is currently taking a C.L.U. course in taxation and investments. Ms. Hagan has an M.B.A. in marketing.

Ben Markens is the operations manager at Laurino Packaging Corporation, West Springfield, Massachusetts, where he has established a new policy and personnel changes to revise the customer-service department, as well as a standard operating procedure and new machine hour rates and cost systems. Mr. Markens currently is working toward an M.B.A. at Fairleigh Dickinson University.

Cheryl A. Monyak is an assistant underwriter in the Special Accounts Marketing division of the Travelers Insurance Company, Hartford, Connecticut. She has an M.B.A. from the University of Connecticut, where her graduate work focused around the field of human resource management.

Gary N. Powell, Ph.D., is an associate professor of management and organization at the University of Connecticut, Storrs, Connecticut. Dr. Powell has published several articles on management in such journals as Group & Organization Studies, *the* Academy of Management Journal, *and* Personnel. *He also is active in the field of experiential learning and presently is chairperson of the Eastern Experiential Learning Association, which is affiliated with the Eastern Academy of Management.*

Karen Sykas Sighinolfi is a sales representative for Thomas J. Lipton, Inc., Englewood Cliffs, New Jersey, where she is involved in selling and merchandising at wholesale and retail levels. She has an M.B.A. from the University of Connecticut.

CONFLICT ROLE PLAY SHEET

Role Play 1: *Manager's Role*

You are Kenneth Potter, northeastern regional sales manager for the APEX Corporation, a manufacturer of heavy industrial equipment. You have worked as a sales representative and instructor in the company for twenty-three years and have been in your present position for five years. You have sixteen sales representatives working for you; of these, only Janet Wilson and two males qualified for the prestigious "100% Club" this year. You recognize that Janet is the brightest salesperson you have seen in years. The hard work exhibited by Janet and the two men has resulted in their being invited to the annual 100% Club awards convention, to be held in a city that is known for its exotic entertainment. The convention consists of meetings and expositions during the day, and the various award winners go their separate ways at night. Ninety percent of the convention attendees are male. In addition to the daytime activities, many informal parties have been planned for the evenings. However, Perry Smith, the general sales manager, has reminded you that these are not the types of parties that "nice women" attend and he has suggested that you discourage Janet from attending. You realize that Janet's attendance at these parties could have detrimental effects on her future with the company as well as on your own career. You have decided to approach Janet on the subject.

CONFLICT ROLE PLAY SHEET

Role Play 1: *Subordinate's Role*

You are Janet Wilson, a twenty-four-year-old sales representative for the APEX Corporation, a manufacturer of heavy industrial equipment. You have been with the company for eighteen months and have made your full quota in your first year. As a result, you have been invited to the annual "100% Club" awards convention, to be held in a popular resort city. The convention consists of meetings and expositions during the day, and it seems to you that the various award winners go their own ways at night. About ninety percent of the convention goers are male. You are looking forward to attending the awards ceremony on the last night of the convention and to the informal parties that follow. You have been told that it is a "super time" and that many valuable business contacts are established at these events. You have just seen your boss, Kenneth Potter, approaching, and you have decided to tell him how glad you are to be attending the convention.

CONFLICT ROLE PLAY SHEET

Role Play 2: *Manager's Role*

You are Pat Miller, the manager of an accounting unit within the Great Northwest Insurance Company, where you have worked for the past ten years. At a recent company cocktail party, you became engaged in a stimulating conversation with Lee, the *very* attractive spouse of one of your subordinates, Chris Rogers. As the conversation progressed, you had the distinct impression that Lee, the spouse, had more than a casual interest in you. Deciding that there was no harm in taking advantage of the situation, you felt compelled to "make a move."

Now you have the feeling that Lee has told Chris about your behavior, and the relationship between you and Chris has become strained. You are willing to let bygones be bygones, but Chris seems to be holding a grudge.

There is a meeting scheduled for today between you and Chris to discuss Chris's possible promotion, which would depend in large part on a good recommendation from you. You are wondering just what tone the meeting will take.

CONFLICT ROLE PLAY SHEET

Role Play 2: *Subordinate's Role*

You are Chris Rogers, a young accountant with the Great Northwest Insurance Company. You have been in a stagnant position with GNI since you started working there seven years ago. There is a position open in a higher level of management, and you are a candidate for the job.

You were very pleased recently to be invited to a cocktail party that was also attended by the corporate vice presidents and all of your supervisors. You realized the importance of your attendance at such a function and the possible implications for your career. Because it was a "couples" gathering, you brought your spouse, Lee, who is *very* attractive. As you hobnobbed with the VIPs at the bar, Lee came up to you and asked to speak with you privately for a moment. Obviously disturbed, Lee then told you that your boss, Pat Miller, had made obvious advances. You know that Lee is not one to blow a situation out of proportion and you wonder if you should confront Pat or ignore the issue.

You are upset about what has happened. The relationship between you and Pat has become strained, and the open-door policy between the two of you has ceased to exist. Communication now usually is through written correspondence.

You realize that you need your supervisor's recommendation if you are to have a good shot at the promotion. A meeting has been scheduled for today between you and Pat to discuss the promotion.

CONFLICT ROLE PLAY SHEET

Role Play 3: *Manager's Role (if the subordinate is male)*

You are Lynn Baxter, the head architect and building designer for Pyramid Ltd., a large and growing firm in the Sun Belt. Several months ago, you hired Seth Malloy, a promising young architect. When you interviewed Seth, you had some misgivings about his effeminate manner, but you had to admit that he was the top candidate for the job.

Your entire staff was invited to Ace Construction's open-house cocktail party, to celebrate the opening of its latest facility. Because you wanted to maintain a good relationship with such a potentially good client, you urged each of your staff members to come and to bring a guest. Because you never had heard Seth mention a female friend, you expected to see him alone at the party.

However, Seth has just arrived at the party with a "friend," whose name is Virgil. It is obvious that they are more than just friends. Mr. Chambers, the vice president of Ace Construction, has just pulled you aside and stated that this is a largely conservative gathering and that he does not approve of such a couple being present. He strongly suggested that you take steps to remedy the situation immediately.

CONFLICT ROLE PLAY SHEET

Role Play 3: *Manager's Role (if the subordinate is female)*

You are Lynn Baxter, the head architect and building designer for Pyramid Ltd., a large and growing firm in the Sun Belt. Several months ago, you hired Karen Malloy, a promising young architect. When you interviewed Karen, you had some misgivings about her masculine manner, but you had to admit that she was the top candidate for the job.

Your entire staff was invited to Ace Construction's open-house cocktail party, to celebrate the opening of its latest facility. Because you wanted to maintain a good relationship with such a potentially good client, you urged each of your staff members to come and to bring a guest. Because you never had heard Karen mention a male friend, you expected to see her alone at the party.

However, Karen has just arrived at the party with a "friend" whose name is Jill. It is obvious that they are more than just friends. Mr. Chambers, the vice president of Ace Construction, has just pulled you aside and stated that this is a largely conservative gathering and that he does not approve of such a couple being present. He strongly suggested that you take steps to remedy the situation immediately.

CONFLICT ROLE PLAY SHEET

Role Play 3: *Subordinate's Role (for Seth or Karen Malloy)*

You are a promising young architect and you are determined to become a star in your field. You graduated from an established school and now hold a good position with Pyramid Ltd., a large and growing firm in the Sun Belt.

At a recent staff meeting, it was announced that Ace Construction, a potentially lucrative client, would be holding a cocktail party at which staff members and their guests would be welcome. You decide to attend with a date, who is of the same sex as yourself. You feel justified in bringing your companion, because everyone else has his or her own choice of guest.

You and your guest always enjoy each other's company, and you like the looks of this party. Your guest is very affectionate, which is one of the qualities that you admire, but you recognize the inappropriateness of such a display at a public gathering.

You notice that people seem to be avoiding the two of you. Just now, you have spotted your immediate supervisor, Lynn Baxter, approaching the two of you. Lynn has a great deal of influence over any promotion that you might receive, and you are anxious to engage Lynn in conversation to see if you can learn anything about your prospective future with the firm.

INTRODUCTION TO THE INSTRUMENTATION SECTION

An instrument is a survey, questionnaire, or inventory that, unlike a test, has no predetermined "correct" answers. Instruments generate data that can be used for personal growth, training, measurement, or research.[1]

Instrumentation can be intended primarily for either the end user, the participant, or for the professional trainer or consultant. In the first instance, as a part of the experience phase of the experiential learning cycle, an instrument can be used to promote self-awareness and analysis for participants' *personal growth,* generally in the area of attitudes, values, and personality characteristics.

When specific behavioral change is the focus, instruments can also be helpful in participant *training.* While the data generated for personal growth and training purposes can be used by the trainer to develop generalizations about a group, the focus is primarily on the instrument as feedback to the participant; to a large extent, the participant develops his or her own plan for applying the results, rather than one suggested by the trainer.

When instruments are used for *measurement* they become a professional tool for the trainer or consultant. Used to assess personal, interpersonal, group, or organizational phenomena, an instrument is helpful for purposes of analysis and diagnosis. Instruments used for measurement purposes provide base-line data that can be fed back to the population and also used to help determine consultant interventions.

Finally, instruments used for *research* generate, validate, or test a theory. When used for theoretical rather than practical purposes, they are academic tools for the trainer or consultant who wishes to gain insight into and knowledge about human behavior.

ADVANTAGES AND DISADVANTAGES

In using an instrument, the trainer should be aware of its advantages and disadvantages, the major questions that must be asked about it, and the careful process of administering it. With this knowledge, the trainer can employ instrumentation in the most productive way for participants.[2]

Advantages	Disadvantages
1. Involves participants with data, feedback process, and theory.	1. Triggers anxiety from "test" connotation and personal experience.
2. Develops understanding of terms, constructs, and theory.	2. Encourages "labeling" and nitpicking.
3. Supplies feedback in a low-threat condition.	3. Can result in feedback overload.
	4. Allows feedback distortion through manipulation of scores.

---

[1] See Introduction to the Instrumentation Section in the 1982 *Annual* for a complete model on the uses of instrumentation.

[2] For a complete explanation of both advantages and disadvantages, see *Instrumentation in Human Relations Training* (2nd ed.).

<table>
<tr><td align="center">Advantages</td><td align="center">Disadvantages</td></tr>
</table>

4. Provides comparison of individuals within the group and with norm groups.

5. Surfaces latent issues.

6. Allows the trainer to focus and control the group appropriately.

7. Facilitates contracting for behavioral change and assessment of change over time.

5. Makes it possible to avoid confronting key issues.

6. Fosters dependency on the trainer as "expert."

7. Relieves tension that potentially could lead to personal growth.

AREAS OF CONCERN

The trainer or consultant can avoid many of the disadvantages of instrumentation by finding accurate answers to the questions in the following areas of concern:

1. *Reliability.* Does the instrument yield the same results for the same people at a different time, given the same conditions? Do different parts of the instrument yield the same results?

2. *Validity.* Does the instrument measure what it purports to measure? Is this measurement useful? Are instrument scores related to measurable characteristics of the person tested as predicted by the logic of the instrument?

3. *Transparency.* How obvious is what the instrument is to measure? How likely is it that desirable results can be faked?

Having answered these questions satisfactorily, the trainer can proceed to other areas of concern.

Usage Concerns

1. How much special training is required to administer the instrument?
2. Is there a standard key for scoring? Can the instrument be self-scored?
3. Are other options available?
4. Does the instrument require special materials?
5. How much time is needed for the administration process?
6. Are the materials readily available?
7. Can the instrument be adapted to a particular situation?
8. What is the cost of the instrument and the interpretive materials?

Content Concerns

1. Would any of the items offend respondents?
2. Is it likely that the respondents have taken this instrument before?
3. Is the instrument's terminology readily understandable?
4. Can the scores be related to and validated by observable behavior? Are the scores derived from respondents' reports of behavior? Will the instrument yield additional knowledge for the respondents?

5. Can the scores be summarized for ease in interpretation?

6. Are distributable materials available to aid in interpretation?

7. Is relevant normative data available?

8. Is the instrument based on a realistic theoretical model?

THE ADMINISTRATION PROCESS

Once the areas of concern have been resolved, the trainer will consider how to administer the instrument effectively. The following procedure is based on the discussion in Pfeiffer, Heslin, and Jones (1976). The trainer should plan to take the instrument before using it with participants in order to obtain an indication of how or whether to alter the following steps.

1. Administration
   - Create a nonthreatening atmosphere by using the word "instrument" rather than "test"; diffuse anxiety by indicating that there are no "right" answers.
   - Legitimize the use of instrumentation by showing how it fits into the goals of training and by discussing the margin of error.
   - Give clear, objective instructions:
     - Explain without giving clues as to the nature of the instrument.
     - Give directions sequentially before the participants begin the instrument.
     - Encourage the participants to answer honestly to promote greater self-learning.
   - Establish the expectation that those who finish first will wait quietly for the rest.

2. Theory Input
   - Clarify the theoretical basis of the instrument and explain through analogy and visual aids.
   - Allow participants to explore the design of the instrument and the derivation of scores.

3. Prediction
   - Ask the participants to predict how they will score on the instrument's dimensions.

4. Scoring
   - Make sure that the scoring process does not detract from the data being generated:
     - Use simple explanations or handouts if scoring is fairly understandable.
     - Use clerical help over a break if scoring is difficult and return the scores to the participants immediately after the break.

5. Interpretation
   - Use your own scores as a basis for the interpretation process:
     - Compare actual scores to predictions.
     - Compare actual scores to available norms.
     - Examine category scores for significance.
     - Summarize and make meaning out of the whole.
   - Set up dyads for the interpretive process.
   - Avoid diagnosing or labeling participants.

6. Posting
   - Put scores on newsprint or chalkboard to generate data about group and subgroup profiles:
     - Emphasize that scores will not be reported to superiors.
     - Allow participants freedom not to post their scores.

7. Processing
   - Allow sufficient time for this critical step in the integration process.

- Form groups to allow participants to compare their scores and develop an understanding of how their scores "fit" with their self-images and others' images of them.
- Legitimize differing behaviors, orientations, and perspectives.
- Solicit feedback on the administration process.

8. Optional Next Steps
   - Validate the instrument through use (Jones & Pfeiffer, 1979, pp. 77-78):
     - Form homogeneous groups based on scores.
     - Administer a task.
     - Process the differences in results.
     - Integrate the experience with the instrument's theory.

INSTRUMENTS IN THIS *ANNUAL*

The four instruments in the 1983 *Annual* are useful to participants in developing both internal and external awareness and to trainers for diagnostic and planning purposes. Some themes touched on are also developed in the Lecturette and Theory and Practice sections: stress created by role changes and climate within the organization, differences in approaches to teamwork, and individual management of time. These instruments can be useful in identifying existing or potential stress and thereby leading to its management and/or prevention.

"Styles of Career Management" helps participants identify and assess their personal styles of career management and how those styles fit with their organizational cultures. Using the most basic dimensions of group behavior, task and maintenance, "The Team Orientation and Behavior Inventory" aids participants in learning more about both their values and their skills in handling team performance. Pareek's "Organizational Role Stress Scale" examines participants' understanding of ten different types of role stress they may be experiencing in their organizations. Finally, "The TEM Survey" helps people discover whether they are wasters, users, or achievers by assessing their attitudes toward and knowledge of the management of time, energy, and information retention (memory).

REFERENCES

Gibb, J.R. Defensive and supportive communication. *Journal of Communications*, 1961, *11*, 141-148.

Jones, J.E., & Pfeiffer, J.W. Introduction to the instrumentation section. In J.E. Jones & J.W. Pfeiffer (Eds.), *The 1975 annual handbook for group facilitators*. San Diego, CA: University Associates, 1975.

Jones, J.E., & Pfeiffer, J.W. Introduction to the instrumentation section. In J.E. Jones & J.W. Pfeiffer (Eds.), *The 1979 annual handbook for group facilitators*. San Diego, CA: University Associates, 1979.

Pfeiffer, J.W., & Goodstein, L.D. Introduction to the instrumentation section. In J.W. Pfeiffer & L.D. Goodstein (Eds.), *The 1982 annual for facilitators, trainers, and consultants*. San Diego, CA: University Associates, 1982.

Pfeiffer, J.W., Heslin, R., & Jones, J.E. *Instrumentation in human relations training* (2nd ed.). San Diego, CA: University Associates, 1976.

ASSESSING STYLES OF CAREER MANAGEMENT

Tom Carney

Different ways of pursuing a career are discussed daily in the work place and in various publications. We all tend to have views on how to pursue a career. Although the style of career management that a person favors may not be the one that is appropriate to his or her work situation, this style will largely determine the person's loyalty to the organization and the people in it. The more conscious a person is of various career styles—and of the biases that accompany these styles—the better for all concerned.

The consciousness-raising instrument that follows makes it possible to assess various styles of career management and at least some of their consequences.

ELEMENTS OF THE INSTRUMENT

Four organizational character types appear throughout the literature on organizations:

1. *The Careerist:* These people build networks and find mentors. They are shrewd at all aspects of office politics and very careful to be associated with the right people. Rapid advancement is their primary objective.

2. *The Organizational Entrepreneur or Task-Force Manager:* These people reorganize systems and put together task forces to solve difficult problems. Their constant reshuffling is done with great innovation. Problem solving is their main focus.

3. *The Organization Person:* These people identify with the organization itself. They work at being accepted and think they can advance through loyal, steady service. They primarily "go by the book."

4. *The Specialist/Expert:* These people see the organization as providing resources for them to develop their specialites. They believe that technical expertise is more important than managerial ability. The attainment of technical proficiency is their primary goal.

Perhaps the most strikingly visible of these character types is the *careerist*, whose view of organizational communications could be summed up by the common expression: "It's *who* you know that counts." Careerists tend to think that "organizations are people." They are convinced of the importance of the "grapevine," of knowing the "right" people, of building a network, and of finding a sponsor. Careerists view an organization as individuals in interaction, with certain individuals interacting more than others. They may see the organizational chart as a network of cliques. Careerists are apt to be shrewd about finding quick paths to advancement.

To the *organizational entrepreneur*, organizations drive industrial society but they are subject to malfunctions and breakdowns and sometimes need extensive redesign. Organizational entrepreneurs are able to restructure the organization in radical new ways with drastic changes in staff and procedure. They can put project teams together rapidly, ignoring rank and status, and can manage these teams to bring projects to production quickly.

The *organization person* thinks that the effectiveness of organizations comes precisely from "going by the book"—filling role prescriptions and norms—and having a well-structured, clearly differentiated, chain of command. They identify with "their" organizations and see the organization as an entity in which one progressively becomes more and more of an "insider."

For them, a career involves three types of movement: upward through promotion; laterally to a more prestigious function or department; and inward to an inner circle of power and prestige.

The *specialist/expert* sees the organization as providing the resources—facilities, finance, administrative backup—necessary to his or her specialty. As the specialist sees it, organizations exist to "do things," and the technical experts "get things done." Specialists see managers as mere paper shufflers.

In their approaches to their jobs, most people exhibit aspects of each of the styles described. The question is: In what proportions and with what level of awareness?

This instrument is composed of issues in career management. For each issue, four options, each with a different cost-benefit ratio, are presented. The four options for each issue represent the four career-management styles. Thus, the instrument provides a series of rank orderings for which cumulative choices indicate preferences among the styles.

This is a new type of instrument, not obviously tied to any specific theory or viewpoint. Its contents relate directly to everyday dilemmas of the work place. It is often difficult for respondents to make a choice among the various options, which are scrambled and posed in different ways. The respondents are given only about forty minutes to complete the inventory so that there is little time for second guessing. The cumulative implications of the inventory are not apparent. Usually, the inventory is perceived as an intriguing exercise in consciousness raising, but its findings can be used in a variety of other ways as well.

USES OF THE INSTRUMENT

The most obvious use of the instrument is to assess which style is most prominent, which appears least, and so on. The next most obvious use is to determine what mix of styles is favored by the organization for which the respondent works. Step three follows naturally: to determine how well the first two match.

The next round of investigations probably will be to find out how accurate the respondent's perceptions are. So someone (or, better, *several* people) who know(s) the respondent will rate the respondent's most likely choices on the inventory. Then several other persons from the organization in which the respondent works rate the *organization's* probable choices on the inventory. Again, there is a check to see how well the respondent's perceptions match those of the other people. Some biases of style(s) will become evident by this time. Differences in perceptions will not be random.

Another type of investigation is to pick out the type of person with whom the respondent would most (or least) like to work and to have that person complete the inventory. The comparison of the respondent's and the other person's preferences will show what mix of styles complements (or jars) those of the respondent. If an individual who is an extreme type of one of the four styles completes an inventory, the results can show how differently the organizational world is perceived by someone with a more extreme style. Discussions between different types of respondents can increase their sensitivity about communicating and working with people whose styles differ from their own.

By comparing one's own mix of styles with those of the people who are highly successful in the organization, one can see whether the style mix that he or she has—perhaps unconsciously—chosen is realistically matched to the requirements of the organizational situation.

This inventory also can be used to obtain *group* data. Aggregate data from the inventory also can indicate what strategies people in an organization perceive as rational for survival or advancement. These perceptions are likely to be linked closely with loyalty—or the lack of it.

Obviously, this instrument can be used in conjunction with other instruments or approaches. For instance, it complements a communications audit or JoHari Window activity.

If another instrument reveals marked differences in the respondents' perceptions of an organization, this inventory can be used to investigate the likely sources of perceptual bias.

WORKING WITH SCORES

The respondents may wish to compare their responses with those of "the organization" or they may wish to compare their self-perceptions with someone else's perceptions of them. Individuals also may wish to contrast their own mixes of styles with the average mixes for their work groups. The instrument also may be used to contrast an individual's early (on entry) mix of styles with the styles that the person has adopted after a certain period of time within the organization.

The format for comparing scores in Figure 1 presents the data and their implications more clearly than a string of numbers can.

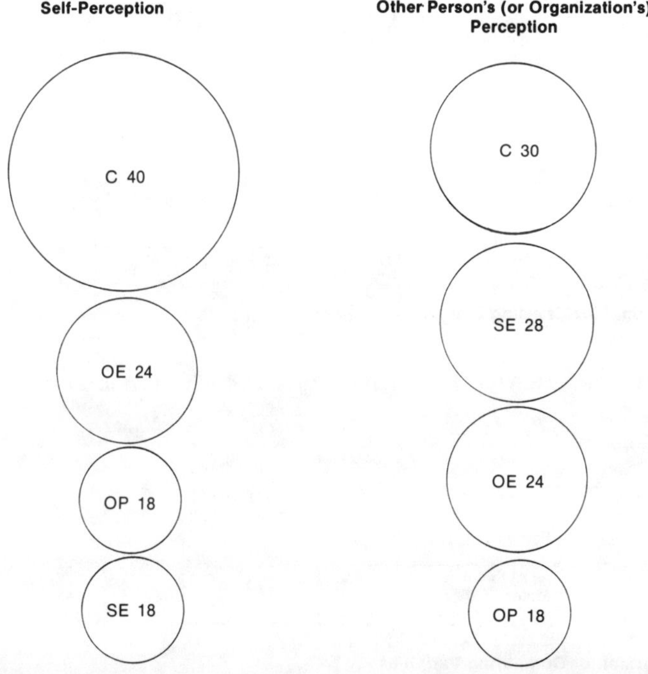

Notes:

1. Make the size of the circles proportional to the number of points that each style recieves.
2. Put the style with most points first and the rest in descending order.
3. Put styles with equal points side by side.

Figure 1. Format for Comparing Scores

A three-by-four table with aggregate data such as the one in Figure 2 can be used to review the primary tendency plus the extreme scores in each category (across, top) for various groups of organizational personnel (down, side). A chart could be used to determine, for instance, which groups "play it safe" in regard to their style mixes and which groups gamble on one particular style or strategy. The possibilities for charting are numerous.

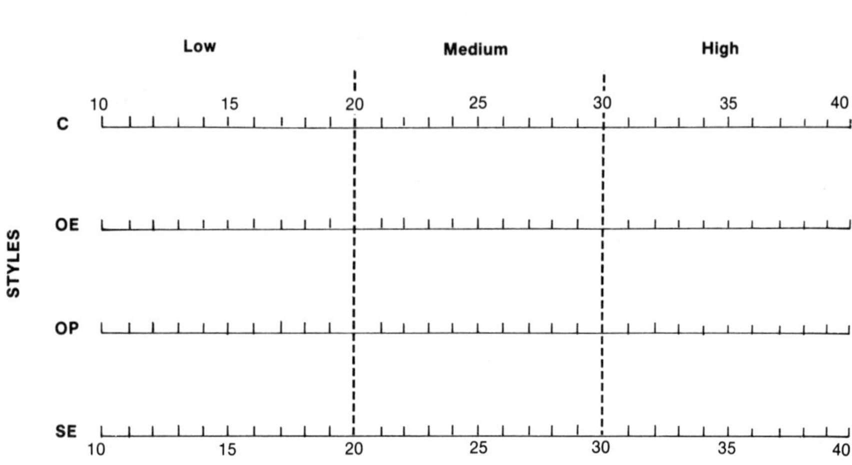

Figure 2. Format for Charting Scores

A simple table such as the one in Figure 3 can be used to compare data across variables. For example:

	Below Age 35	Above Age 35
Females		
Males		

Figure 3. Format for Comparing Variables

The following points should be considered in working with the instrument or in interpreting scores derived from it.

1. The stereotypes in the organizational and career literature do not fit actual practice very well. Organizational personnel tend to adjust their style mixes quite rapidly to fit the objective reality of their work situations. Thus, young women may gamble quite aggressively on a single style when an affirmative action program goes into operation. Young men may, equally realistically, operate cautiously with a balanced mix of styles in such a situation.

2. There is a tendency for people to verbally espouse different styles from those that they actually employ. This disparity can lead to discrepancies between the self-perception of the person involved (often influenced by the talk, despite the actions, of the person involved) and the perceptions of others who are very close to the respondent. Typically, highest and lowest scores are perceived identically by both parties, but styles with the two middle scores are perceived differently.

3. There may be more adherence to a "company person" style than one might expect in light of the findings commonly published about the decline in loyalty to organizations.

People differ remarkably in regard to the clarity and detachment with which they interpret their scores. Merely listening to another person discussing his or her scores can be a source of insight. It is wise to allow plenty of time for a follow-up discussion after the administration and scoring of the instrument. It may be advisable to structure the discussion somewhat, because a discussion of personal styles of any type can engender defensiveness and other dynamics. In particular, the style to which most objection seems to be taken is that of the careerist. Follow-up discussions of the merits and drawbacks of this style tend to become quite heated.

REFERENCES

Downs, A. *Inside bureaucracy*. Boston, MA: Little, Brown, 1966.

Handy, C. *Gods of management: Who they are, how they work, and why they will fail*. Pan Books, 1979.

Maccoby, M. *The gamesman: The new corporate leaders*. New York: Simon & Schuster, 1976.

Plutzik, R. What price loyalty? *Training/HRD, 17* (10), 1980, 22-30.

Schein, E.H. *Career dynamics: Matching individual and organizational needs*. Reading, MA: Addison-Wesley, 1978.

Tom Carney, Ph.D., is a professor of organizational communications at the University of Windsor, Ontario, Canada. He specializes in communication in career management and workshop and facilitation skills. He has received several awards for research (Fullbright, Killam) and teaching (Canadian Association of University Continuing Education: Award of Program Distinction; Ontario Confederation of Faculty Associations: Award for Excellence in Teaching). He is a consultant to business and government and has authored several books and numerous journal articles.

STYLES OF CAREER MANAGEMENT
Tom Carney

Instructions: There are no right or wrong answers to this instrument, and you cannot "beat" someone else by scoring higher. The instrument investigates the way you perceive and have adapted to your organization's culture. It does this by requiring you to consider and respond to a variety of organizational issues. You will see the strategies that are implicit in your dealings with the organization and the strategies that are implicit in its dealings with you.

The instrument presents a series of statements on practices, dilemmas, and attitudes that are prevalent in organizations. A variety of responses is possible for each statement; you are to indicate which response is most like what you would do. For purposes of comparison, you also may indicate the response that you think would be favored by your organization.

In each case, after the initial statement or question, four possible responses are presented. Rank order these options, that is, put a "4" next to the one that comes closest to your views on the matter, put a "3" next to the response that fits next best, and so on. Put a "1" next to the option that fits *least* well with your views. Use only one *each* of the numbers (4, 3, 2, 1) for each set of choices. Do not give two equal choices.

Try not to answer in terms of what you would ideally like to do or in terms of what you morally ought to do. Your answer should reflect what you feel you would *have* to do—what would be expedient. If you are answering from the organization's point of view, think about actual cases. Organizational logic and ethics differ from one organization to another.

    I. *By and large you can expect an organization to treat you in the following way:*

_______ 1. Organizations make most of their decisions *impersonally* through committees, task forces, standard operating procedures, and so on. You cannot expect an organization to treat you as though one individual is relating to another individual. You will be treated well if you know how to work in the system, have a lot of connections, and are prepared to move about—to go where the company needs to send someone or to threaten to take another job at a critical moment. Essentially, you have to fight for your rights in the dog-eat-dog competitive world of organizational politics.

_______ 2. Organizations look at the bottom line. If you can come through in a crunch, you will be rewarded and advanced. Those who produce get the rewards; otherwise the business goes to the competition. You will be treated well as long as you can identify problems that can be solved successfully, have yourself assigned to solving them, and keep producing results. You cannot expect the organization to support someone who is not pulling more than his or her weight. You have to be alert, on your toes, and productive.

_______ 3. You will be treated well as long as your expertise is crucial to the success of the product(s) on which the company depends. This includes expertise in *servicing* the main product lines. Technical expertise is basic to the firm's functioning, so it has to be maintained. Your position will be assured, although you may not rise rapidly, as long as you have technical expertise as the basis for your position.

_______ 4. You are safe enough as long as you are in an organization that provides some security of tenure for its employees—or where there is a union to protect you and your job. Basically, the due process protects your rights and guarantees fair and impersonal treatment for employees. After all, *all* employees are in the same boat, so protecting employee interests is something that most of them can be relied on to do in their own interests.

II. *The influence that your supervisor is likely to have over your career opportunities and your satisfaction with your job is:*

_____ 5. Important, but transitory. Supervisors change, and you advance through different units. What really matters are your peer-group relations (committees make most of the important decisions) and knowing the ropes—how your institution's procedures really work.

_____ 6. Critical. A bad supervisor can derail your career. You cannot afford to have serious problems at *any* stage in your career, given the competition at your level. Besides, there usually is a mentor behind the early career years of anyone who has "made good" in an organization, and mentors are not apt to back people who have bad relationships with their supervisors.

_____ 7. Important, but overrated. Most opportunities come through working on task forces, and these get you out of your supervisor's control or enable you to switch to another one. Anyone with skills in problem solving is not likely to have supervisor troubles because the supervisor needs the person too much and the person moves from supervisor to supervisor too often.

_____ 8. Overestimated. Your work should speak for itself. If your work is needed, and if you are the best in your job, you will advance because the company needs you. Of course, your supervisor can hold you back, but it will cost something because the work will not be done as well and higher management will notice (or you will leave for a more compatible supervisor). The power of your supervisor is in inverse relationship to the importance of your professional skills. You are better off putting your time and energy into cultivating them, rather than into cultivating your supervisor.

III. *The best way to get ahead in any organization is to:*

_____ 9. Know who the people are who decide your future, be visible to them, and perform in ways that they will think highly of. Also realize that these people may not all be in the firm for which you now work. Having contacts so that you have opportunities outside your firm does no harm; if your supervisor knows that you are wanted elsewhere, he or she is likely to treat you better.

_____ 10. Build up special skills and know-how that will make you the best in your job. Special expertise is always in demand, no matter what the fortunes of your firm may be, so you increase your options and opportunities by developing it.

_____ 11. Find the really big or complicated job that most needs to be done, determine how to do it, and make it happen. The people who produce in a crunch are the ones whom the firm advances furthest and fastest.

_____ 12. Proceed by the regular route: Obtain the training and experience, then advance in conformity with the career norms. Short cuts and climbing over other people are apt to misfire. Working night and day to solve problems will cause you to burn out and probably will cause problems at home. It is a question of balance: How much are you willing to pay for quick promotions? You have to weigh the consequences. You owe it to yourself and to your family to have a life outside the job.

IV. *By and large, you can expect your peers at work to be:*

_____ 13. Generally supportive. After all, you are all in the same boat. If the peer group does not look after its own interests within the organization, who will?

_____ 14. Important, of course, but the *really* important colleagues are those who can pull their weight in a crisis—when you have to put a special assignment out or cope with a sudden emergency. Only some of these people are likely to be your peers; many are superiors or subordinates. This is your *real* work group.

_____ 15. Critical to your own growth and development in your specialty and vital to the contribution that this specialty makes to the firm. These people provide back up or complementary services and skills.

_____ 16. Your main source of competition in regard to career advancement. Your peers are able to do you serious harm; because they work so closely with you, they know your weaknesses and can sabotage you easily.

V. *Personality-related problems erupt in your department or section. You are not directly involved, but the trouble could spread if not handled well and quickly. What would be the best way to react?*

_____ 17. Deal with the problems humanely and carefully, at the unit level. Problems of this sort rarely go away. If ignored they usually become worse, and people take sides. Once a unit's esprit de corps goes, it is hard to recover. Get involved if asked to.

_____ 18. If you wanted to manage personal problems, you would have become a manager. You *produce* work; that is what everybody should concentrate on. Let management cope. People should not bring their personality problems to work anyway.

_____ 19. You do not have serious personality problems at work without underlying organizational problems. Try an organizational intervention with a third party to defuse things.

_____ 20. It depends on who is involved and what the issues are. There are some people in any unit with whom it would not be wise to become involved, and some issues can leave long-lasting ill feelings, even if you manage to solve them in the best possible way.

VI. *You are in mid-career, progressing moderately well, and have just been offered the chance to move into a new line of work in another firm. The work seems more likely to be in demand five or six years in the future than the work you are in now. You might be able to go further in your personal advancement in the new position, but it would mean a lot of retooling on your part. Assuming that the move would create no problems in your family life, what would be the best thing to do?*

_____ 21. Given the state of the current job market, it probably is best not to switch jobs or firms. You have too much to lose in terms of seniority and "insider" status in your present firm, and too many unknowns if you move.

_____ 22. Progress in your present firm has been only "moderate"; if you are going to make a breakthrough in your career, it will not be in your present firm. The new line is promising, and there may be more opportunities for promotion in the new firm, so moving seems to be a good idea. You are probably going to have to retool sometime. Also, the broader experience probably will make you more valuable.

_____ 23. The move will be worth the risk only if the new firm will make you the project leader. Make your acceptance of the job conditional on that.

_____ 24. You only are really trained *once*. Mid-career retooling may be fashionable, but it just produces half-trained, overaged workers. You would never be accepted by the younger people who are properly trained in the new line. Forget it.

VII. *The current concern with impression management (business dress codes, status symbols, effective resume writing, and so on) is:*

______ 25. A waste of time and effort that would be better spent on doing the job properly. If you develop expertise in the most in-demand specialty within your line of work, the "window dressing" should not be necessary.

______ 26. Critically important to one's career. Appearances *count* in the real world. You simply cannot afford to be less sophisticated in these matters than your competitors are.

______ 27. Something you should know about. It probably is of less importance than job-related knowhow, but it is useful for smoothing the way in the work environment. There is no point in creating poor impressions.

______ 28. Probably quite important, something you really *should* work on. But, for the moment, there are more urgent problems to which you simply must pay attention.

VIII. *All this emphasis on "hidden agendas" and on "the games people play" in organizational life is:*

______ 29. Blown up out of proportion by people who have an interest in "training" you how to cope with these things. Business is there to get the job done; if these games *do* take place, they should not. It is best to ignore the matter.

______ 30. Something you should pay close attention to or you could find yourself sabotaged when promotions or pay raises are due. Office politics are a fact of life; you have to be able to cope with them.

______ 31. Something you need to watch for if you are involved in any ad hoc committees or project teams. The various members each tend to lay claim to the highest status and, if these status squabbles get out of hand, the assignment never will be completed on schedule.

______ 32. Worth knowing about. Such things do tend to happen, although, fortunately, not very much in your work group. But they are not nearly as frequent or as serious as the books would have you believe. In the long run, unless you are honest and play by the rules, you are likely to end up in trouble. Playing games creates too many enemies.

IX. *A crisis has developed at work, and your skills are related—marginally, not centrally—to its solution. The organization needs everyone who can to pitch in and help, but there are no sure ways of coping, and some of the proposed measures could misfire badly. What would it be best to do?*

______ 33. Volunteer to help, especially if you can generate good ideas in a crisis and know where to find effective people to help, on an emergency basis, to make things happen.

______ 34. Avoid getting involved. If they had a technical problem calling for your kind of special expertise, you would help in a flash. But you really would not be very effective working on an emergency task force dealing with an "iffy" project.

______ 35. Be careful. If the difficulty looked like one with which you could be of help, in regard to some *specific* part, you would be among the first to volunteer, but you would have to be pretty sure that you could be effective. You would not want to be associated with a disastrous failure.

______ 36. Rally 'round. If the organization suffers, you *all* suffer. So you should offer your services and pitch in wherever needed.

X. *You have a good chance of being promoted at work, but it involves moving out of your special line of work (at which you are expert) and moving into general management. Your reaction is:*

_____ 37. The management track will take you upward furthest and fastest; no one but an idiot would turn down a chance like this. Besides, if you turn it down, you will soon become known as someone who cannot move outside your specialty or as someone who has "peaked" or cannot respond to a challenge.

_____ 38. The general practice is for people at your stage to make this kind of move. There are not many advantages in swimming against the tide, and making the move will keep you in step with the majority of those who were recruited at the same stage.

_____ 39. If you want to broaden your expertise and general problem-solving capabilities, you will need to have *both* managerial and specialist skills. In fact, you will have *more* chance to use your specialist skills, in the long run, if you have some managerial experience. This combination will make you eligible to work on *bigger* projects that involve your special skills.

_____ 40. Management is a jungle, nowadays. It is not worth the hassles. Besides, in your current job, you are building up real expertise at doing something practical. You would be better off working at becoming a leader in your specialty; that should open all kinds of opportunities without requiring you to go politicking around as a manager.

STYLES OF CAREER MANAGEMENT SCORING SHEET

The instrument is composed of ten theme statements, each of which is followed by four possible responses. For each statement, the responses are rank ordered, so the response of first choice is assigned four points, the second choice is assigned three points, and so on.

Instructions: Below are the numbers of the various response options from the instrument. Insert the point value that you gave to each option on the line next to the number of that option. Then read the interpretation on the next page.

Scoring Code

First choice   = 4
Second choice = 3
Third choice   = 2
Last choice   = 1

C	OE	OP	SE
1 _____	2 _____	4 _____	3 _____
6 _____	7 _____	5 _____	8 _____
9 _____	11 _____	12 _____	10 _____
16 _____	14 _____	13 _____	15 _____
20 _____	19 _____	17 _____	18 _____
22 _____	23 _____	21 _____	24 _____
26 _____	28 _____	27 _____	25 _____
30 _____	31 _____	32 _____	29 _____
35 _____	33 _____	36 _____	34 _____
37 _____	39 _____	38 _____	40 _____
Total C _____	**Total OE** _____	**Total OP** _____	**Total SE** _____

The total of the scores for each statement is ten points (4+3+2+1). Ten statements times ten points each equals one hundred possible points in all, so the maximum score for any one type of response is forty and the minimum score for any one type of response is ten. You can check your totals as a check on your accuracy of recording.

The four types of response are indicative of four ways of looking at how people should manage their personal careers. A low score (10-19) indicates that you do not generally agree with a particular style of career management. A mid-range score (20-29) indicates that you sometimes employ that style. A high score (30-40) for any one style indicates that you tend to prefer this mode in managing your career.

The four styles of career management are:

C: The Careerist: These people build networks and find mentors. They are shrewd at all aspects of office politics and very careful to be associated with the right people. Rapid advancement is their primary objective.

OE: The Organizational Entrepreneur or task-force manager: These people reorganize systems and put together task forces to solve difficult problems. Their constant reshuffling is done with great innovation. Problem solving is their main focus.

OP: The Organizational Person: These people identify with the organization itself. They work at being accepted and think they can advance through loyal, steady service. They primarily "go by the book."

SE: The Specialist/Expert: These people see the organization as providing resources for them to develop their specialties. They believe that technical expertise is more important than managerial ability. The attainment of technical proficiency is their primary goal.

THE TEAM ORIENTATION AND BEHAVIOR INVENTORY (TOBI)

Leonard D. Goodstein, Phyliss Cooke, and Jeanette Goodstein

One of the most important strategies of organization development (OD)—perhaps the *most* important—is team building. Effective and productive teams, at both the worker and managerial level, are the desired end product of most OD interventions. As organizations become more complex in their structures, team work, through task forces, committees, staffs, and so on, will become even more important—and thus the importance of team building.

Surprisingly, there is no theoretically based approach to team building with the exception of the Tavistock model of group functioning (Rioch, 1975). The Tavistock approach, based on psychoanalytic theory, places primary emphasis on issues of authority and power in small groups. Clarifying how the group copes with the leadership issue is the major developmental focus or purpose of the group.

More generally, team-building efforts tend to be atheoretical. Beckhard (1972) saw four major purposes of team building:

1. To set goals or priorities.
2. To analyze or allocate the way work is performed according to team members' roles and responsibilities.
3. To examine the way the team is working—norms, decision making, conflict management, etc.
4. To examine relationships among team members.

Similarly, Dyer (1977), in his classic book on team building, supplied three check lists to examine the need for team building in a work group. Reilly and Jones (1974, p. 227) defined team building as providing the opportunity for a work group "to assess its strengths, as well as those areas that need improvement and growth." Solomon (1979, p. 181) defines team building as "the introduction of a systematic, long-range plan for the improvement of interpersonal relationships among those workers who are functionally interdependent." All these definitions are fairly clear and can readily be used, but no theoretical basis for team building has been presented.

The purposes of this article are to generate a theoretically based definition of team building and then to present a rational-theoretical (Lanyon & Goodstein, 1982) instrument for assessing both the need for and an approach to team building in work groups.

A THEORETICALLY BASED DEFINITION OF TEAM BUILDING

The primary work group is the most important element or subsystem of any organization, and the team leader or manager is the linking pin between that primary group and the rest of the organization (Likert, 1967). As Burke (1982) noted, work groups provide both the setting and opportunity for: (1) meeting the primary social relationship and support needs for all members of the work group; (2) providing work group members a view of the organization, its structure and goals; and (3) allowing work group members to connect with other organizational segments as well as the organization as a whole. Given these important functions, the degree to which work groups operate effectively is a critical determinant of the overall effectiveness of the organization.

Based on work by Bales (1950), Benne and Sheets (1948) found that group members assume social roles in order to influence the behavior of other group members. They identified three major classes of roles: those necessary to accomplish a *task*, those necessary to increase the supportive *climate* and *cohesion* of the group, and those necessary to satisfy their *personal needs*. Benne and Sheets labeled these three general classes as *group task roles, group maintenance roles*, and *individual roles* and said that effective team functioning requires a balance of the first two roles and a minimization of the last.

Their analysis provides the background for the following definition of team development or team building: Team development is the analysis of the relative strength of group task and maintenance roles in functionally interdependent teams for the purpose of establishing, restoring, or maintaining an adequate balance between these two roles in order for the team to function at its maximum potential.

The distinction between task and maintenance is scarcely a new one. The Ohio State Leadership Studies (Stogdill, 1974) clearly supported the notion of initiation of structure (task) and consideration for people (maintenance) as the two principal, independent axes for understanding leadership behavior. The extension of these dimensions to team work is natural.

Following the work of Blake and Mouton (1964), the two dimensions can be plotted on a grid, with maintenance orientation on the horizontal axis and task orientation on the vertical axis. An additional element, the distinction between attitudes or values on the one hand and skill on the other, appears to be pertinent. One can hold a strong value toward task accomplishment but lack the specific skills for effective group work, such as agenda setting, summarizing, or integrating. Or a person may place a low value on group work, believing that groups and meetings are primarily a waste of time. Such a person might develop strong task skills, but these skills are typically acquired by people who set about to make groups and teams operate more effectively.

Similarly, a distinction can be made between values and skill in team members' maintenance orientation. Team members either value the support and cohesion that groups provide or they do not, and they either have the skills to enhance maintenance functions, like gatekeeping or checking on feelings, or they do not. It is more likely that a person will value maintenance but lack maintenance skills than that a person will not value maintenance but possess the skills. A fully functioning team can be characterized as having members with a high value commitment to *both* task and maintenance and with high skills in both areas. Such a team profile is illustrated in Figure 1. This profile of a fully functioning team should be the goal of team-development activities.

Trainers and consultants frequently fail because they approach the problem as a lack of skills and do not work with the lack of appropriate values on the part of team members. This Lone Ranger profile is illustrated in Figure 2. The task is first to clarify values related to the use of teams, the synergy that teams can produce, when it is appropriate to use teams, and so on, then to concentrate on skill development.

Skills training is accomplished readily with group members who have high values but low skills, the Educably Retarded profile shown in Figure 3. In this situation, the group member values both task and maintenance, but has only good task skills, or has low task and low maintenance skills. The trainer must concentrate on increasing both sets of skills.

There are also some group members who have adequate skills in both task and maintenance but who tend to prize the maintenance functions so highly that little attention is paid to the task

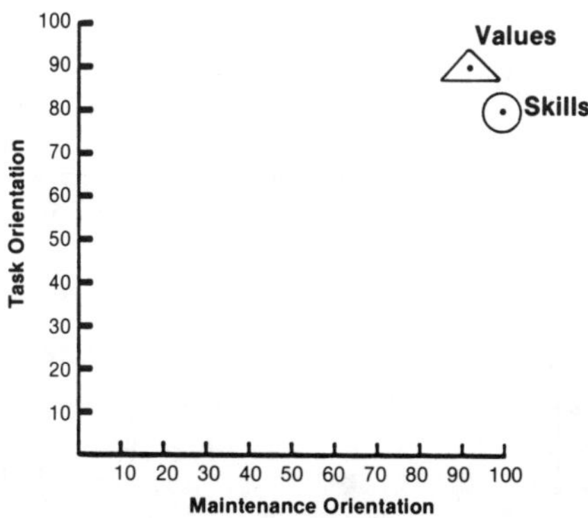

Figure 1. The Fully Functioning Team Member Profile: High Skills and High Values on Both Dimensions

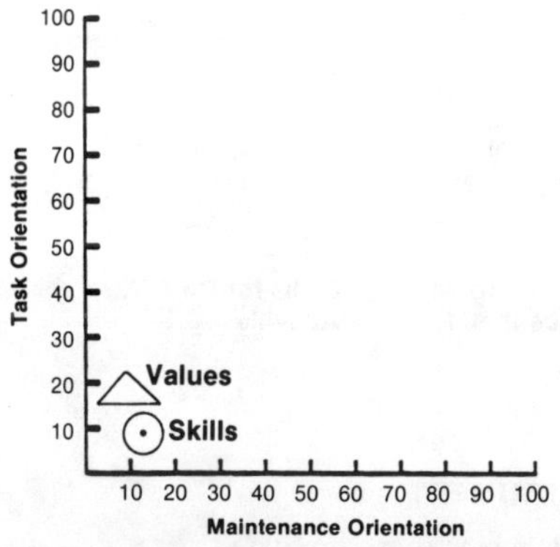

Figure 2. The Lone Ranger Profile: Low Skills and Low Values on Both Dimensions

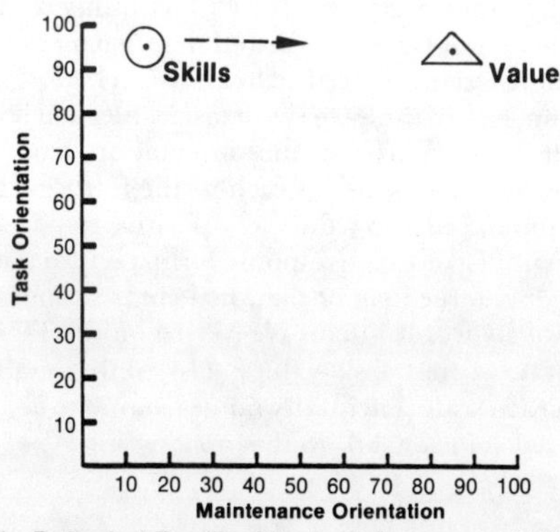

Figure 3. The Educably Retarded Profile: Weak Maintenance Skills with High(er) Maintenance Values

requirements. Such persons see groups as an opportunity to feel included, to practice their maintenance skills, and to feel good about themselves. This profile is often found among trainers and consultants and is shown in Figure 4 as the Trainer/Consultant profile. Such an orientation is appropriate for T-groups and personal-growth encounters, but not appropriate for work groups. Members with such an orientation are often a target of derision in work groups, and their lack of productivity is often the focus of management concern. Value clarification rather than skill development is necessary here.

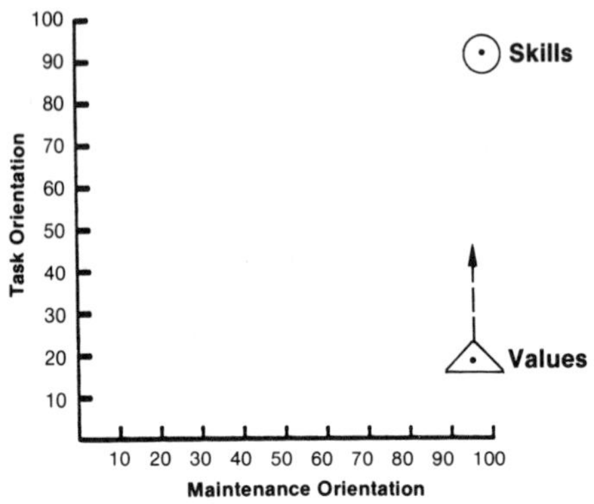

Figure 4. The Trainer/Consultant Profile: High Skills for Both Task and Maintenance but Higher Values for Maintenance than for Task Activities

DESCRIPTION OF THE INSTRUMENT

The Team Orientation and Behavior Inventory (TOBI) was developed to help the trainer distinguish issues of values from issues of skills. It provides a yardstick for assessing how much needs to be done on each dimension to achieve a fully functioning team. Fifty-six self-report items were developed from the descriptions of task and maintenance originally developed by Benne and Sheets (1948) and more recently described by Hanson (1981). Half of the items (28) are concerned with task orientation, half of these (14) with task values and half (14) with task skills. The other half (28) are concerned with maintenance orientation, half (14) with maintenance values and half (14) with maintenance skills. In each of the fourteen subsets, four items are worded in the negative direction in order to reduce any positive response set.

All items are on a seven-point Likert-type response format with a score of 7 indicating that the respondent strongly agreed with the item or that the item is strongly descriptive of him or her. The scoring on the negatively worded items is reversed on the TOBI Scoring Sheet. The instrument yields four separate scores: task values; task skills; maintenance values; and maintenance skills. Scores on each scale potentially range from 14 to 98, with the higher scores indicating a higher self-reported value or skill in that area.

Reliability

The reliability estimates, expressed in alpha coefficients, are presented in Table 1. The reported values indicate that the four scales are reliable, that is, the obtained scores can be regarded as reasonably stable or reproducible.

Table 1. Reliability of Scale Score (Alpha Coefficients)

Task Orientation		Maintenance Orientation	
Values	*Skills*	*Values*	*Skills*
.74	.79	.81	.83

Validity

Early validity data on the TOBI indicate that intact work teams that are given high ratings by independent observers for effectiveness tend to produce scores in the high 70s and low 80s on all four scales. These fully functioning teams show very little difference in the four scores, and the intercept for both task and maintenance orientations is in the upper right quadrant of the graph (see Figure 1). Teams rated as moderately effective yielded scores in the high 60s, again with little difference in their four scores, except for occasional scores of 50-55 on the maintenance-orientation scales.

USES OF THE INSTRUMENT

Administration

Although the instrument is self-administered, the trainer should read the instructions with the participants to make certain that they have no questions. The TOBI Scoring Sheet should not be distributed to the participants until after the instrument is completed. Rather than having participants score their own instruments, the trainer can collect the materials and score the items for the participants. Individual scores should be plotted on the TOBI Profile Sheet, and a group profile should be constructed by averaging the group scores on each of the four scales.

For best use of the TOBI, the trainer should follow the recommended procedure from Pfeiffer, Heslin, and Jones (1976). They recommend:

1. Administering the instrument;
2. Presenting the underlying theory to the group;
3. Helping participants to understand the instrument and to predict their scores;
4. Scoring the instrument;
5. Discussing the results;
6. Posting the results, openly or anonymously; and
7. Interpreting the results and discussing the implications of these results.

With Work Groups

Several potential uses for the TOBI can be found in team development with intact work groups: (1) the instrument can be used to assess the task and maintenance commitment and skills of a team and of the individuals on the team; (2) differences across teams can be assessed and compared; (3) posting of individual or team results provides a strong data base for assessing actual team development before and after team-building efforts; (4) the items also provide a starting point for team building by identifying desired attitudes and behavior; and (5) it provides a convenient research instrument for examining group profiles in various work settings.

REFERENCES

Bales, R. F. *Interaction process analysis*. Reading, MA: Addison-Wesley, 1950.

Beckhard, R. Optimizing team-building efforts. *Journal of Contemporary Business*, 1972, *1*(3), 23-32.

Benne, K. D., & Sheets, P. Functional roles of group members. *Journal of Social Issues*, 1948, *4*(2), 41-49.

Blake, R. R., & Mouton, J. S. The Managerial Grid. Houston, TX: Gulf, 1964.

Burke, W. W. *Organization development: Principles and practices*. Boston: Little, Brown, 1982.

Dyer, W. *Team building: Issues and alternatives*. Reading, MA: Addison-Wesley, 1977.

Hanson, P. G. *Learning through groups: A trainer's basic guide*. San Diego, CA: University Associates, 1981.

Lanyon, R. I., & Goodstein, L. D. *Personality assessment* (2nd ed.). New York: John Wiley, 1982.

Likert, R. *The human organization.* New York: McGraw Hill, 1967.

Pfeiffer, J. W., Heslin, R. E., & Jones, J. E. *Instrumentation in human relations training* (2nd ed.). San Diego, CA: University Associates, 1976.

Reilly, A. J., & Jones, J. E. Team building. In J. W. Pfeiffer & J. E. Jones (Eds.), *The 1974 annual handbook for group facilitators*. San Diego, CA: University Associates, 1974.

Rioch, M. J. Group relations: Rationale and technique. In A. D. Colman & W. H. Bexton (Eds.), *Group relations reader*. Washington, DC: A.K. Rice Institute, 1973.

Solomon, L. N. Team development: A training approach. In J. E. Jones & J.W. Pfeiffer (Eds.), *The 1977 annual handbook for group facilitators*. San Diego, CA: University Associates, 1977.

Stogdill, R. M. *Handbook of leadership: A survey of theory and research*. Riverside, NJ: The Free Press, 1974.

Leonard D. Goodstein, Ph.D., is the chairman of the board of University Associates, Inc., San Diego, California. He specializes in organizational behavior, consultation skills, and organization development and team building with executive groups. Dr. Goodstein is a diplomate in clinical psychology of the American Board of Professional Psychology, is the author or co-author of fifteen books, and was editor of the Journal of Applied Behavioral Science *from 1974 to 1979. He is co-editor of the* 1982 *and* 1983 Annuals.

Phyliss Cooke, Ph.D., is the director of professional services and dean of the Masters in Human Resource Development program and the Intern Program for University Associates, Inc., San Diego, California. She designs and conducts training events and consults with UA client systems. Dr. Cooke also schedules and plans the staffing of UA's professional development programs. She specializes in the design of training programs, leadership development, the training of trainers, and issues concerning women in management.

Jeanette Goodstein is a freelance consultant and trainer in San Diego, California. Her special interests are nonprofit and public agencies and cross-cultural issues. Ms. Goodstein previously taught public administration at the Center for Public Affairs, Arizona State University. She also has been a member of the Peace Corps staff in Washington, D.C., of Peace Corps training programs in India and Hawaii, and of the Neighborhood Health Center Program of the Office of Economic Opportunity.

THE TEAM ORIENTATION AND BEHAVIOR INVENTORY (TOBI)

Leonard D. Goodstein, Phyliss Cooke, and Jeanette Goodstein

Instructions: Taking this instrument will help you to learn more about your attitudes toward teams and work groups as well as your behaviors in such groups. There are no right or wrong answers. You will learn more about yourself if you respond to each item as candidly as possible. Do not spend too much time deciding on an answer; use your first reaction. Circle one of the numbers next to each statement to indicate the degree to which that statement is true for you (or the degree to which that statement is descriptive of you).

	Strongly disagree (very unlike me)	Disagree (unlike me)	Slightly disagree (somewhat unlike me)	Neither agree nor disagree (neither like nor unlike me)	Slightly agree (somewhat like me)	Agree (like me)	Strongly agree (very like me)
1. I am often at a loss when attempting to reach a compromise among members of my group.	1	2	3	4	5	6	7
2. I am effective in ensuring that relevant data are used to make decisions in my group.	1	2	3	4	5	6	7
3. I find it difficult to summarize ideas expressed by members of the team.	1	2	3	4	5	6	7
4. I believe that the existence of positive feelings among team members is critical to the team's efforts.	1	2	3	4	5	6	7
5. It often is important in my group to summarize the ideas and issues that are raised.	1	2	3	4	5	6	7
6. I think that, to be effective, the members of a team must be aware of what is occurring in the group.	1	2	3	4	5	6	7
7. I am able to convey my interest in and support for the other members of my team.	1	2	3	4	5	6	7
8. In my opinion, it is very important that team members be sources of support and encouragement for one another.	1	2	3	4	5	6	7
9. I am effective in establishing an agenda and in reminding the other members of it.	1	2	3	4	5	6	7
10. I am particularly adept in observing the behaviors of other members.	1	2	3	4	5	6	7

Persons using the TOBI are encouraged to share their data with the authors, whose addresses are in the Contributors List at the end of this *Annual.*

The scale header reads, from left to right:
Strongly disagree (very unlike me) · Disagree (unlike me) · Slightly disagree (somewhat unlike me) · Neither agree nor disagree (neither like nor unlike me) · Slightly agree (somewhat like me) · Agree (like me) · Strongly agree (very like me)

11. When the group becomes bogged down, it often is helpful if somone clarifies its goal or purpose.

    1   2   3   4   5   6   7

12. I frequently keep the group focused on the task at hand.

    1   2   3   4   5   6   7

13. I think that testing for members' commitment is one of the most important components of group decision making.

    1   2   3   4   5   6   7

14. In my opinion, summarizing what has occurred in the group usually is unnecessary.

    1   2   3   4   5   6   7

15. One of the things that I contribute to the team is my ability to support and encourage others.

    1   2   3   4   5   6   7

16. I think that examining the assumptions that underlie the group's decisions is not necessary in terms of the group's functioning.

    1   2   3   4   5   6   7

17. It is difficult for me to assess how well our team is doing.

    1   2   3   4   5   6   7

18. In my opinion, work groups are most productive if they restrict their discussions to task-related items.

    1   2   3   4   5   6   7

19. I believe that for the team to regularly evaluate and critique its work is a waste of time.

    1   2   3   4   5   6   7

20. In my opinion, it is very important that team members agree, before they begin to work, on the procedural rules to be followed.

    1   2   3   4   5   6   7

21. I think that, to be effective, a group member simultaneously must participate in the group and be aware of emerging group processes.

    1   2   3   4   5   6   7

22. It is really difficult for me to articulate where I think other members stand on issues.

    1   2   3   4   5   6   7

23. I am effective in helping to ensure that all members of the group have an opportunity to express their opinions before a final decision is made.

    1   2   3   4   5   6   7

24. I believe that one's feelings about how well the group is working are best kept to oneself.

    1   2   3   4   5   6   7

	Strongly disagree (very unlike me)	Disagree (unlike me)	Slightly disagree (somewhat unlike me)	Neither agree nor disagree (neither like nor unlike me)	Slightly agree (somewhat like me)	Agree (like me)	Strongly agree (very like me)
25. I am skillful in helping other group members to share their feelings about what is happening.	1	2	3	4	5	6	7
26. I usually am able to help the group to examine the feasibility of a proposal.	1	2	3	4	5	6	7
27. I believe that it is a waste of time to settle differences of opinion in the group.	1	2	3	4	5	6	7
28. I often am unaware of existing group dynamics.	1	2	3	4	5	6	7
29. I do not think that the participation of all members is important as long as final agreement is achieved.	1	2	3	4	5	6	7
30. I am skillful in organizing groups and teams to work effectively.	1	2	3	4	5	6	7
31. I feel that, to be effective, group members must openly share their feelings about how well the group is doing.	1	2	3	4	5	6	7
32. In my judgment, sharing feelings about how the group is doing is a waste of the members' time.	1	2	3	4	5	6	7
33. When the group gets off the subject, I usually remind the other members of the task.	1	2	3	4	5	6	7
34. One of the things that I do well is to solicit facts and opinions from the group members.	1	2	3	4	5	6	7
35. Ascertaining the other members' points of view is something that I do particularly well.	1	2	3	4	5	6	7
36. I think that it is important that my group stick to its agenda.	1	2	3	4	5	6	7
37. In my opinion, an inability to clear up confusion among members can cause a team to fail.	1	2	3	4	5	6	7
38. I feel that it is important to elicit the opinions of all members of the team.	1	2	3	4	5	6	7
39. It is not easy for me to summarize the opinions of the other members of the team.	1	2	3	4	5	6	7
40. A contribution that I make to the group is to help the other members to build on one another's ideas.	1	2	3	4	5	6	7

	Strongly disagree (very unlike me)	Disagree (unlike me)	Slightly disagree (somewhat unlike me)	Neither agree nor disagree (neither like nor unlike me)	Slightly agree (somewhat like me)	Agree (like me)	Strongly agree (very like me)

41. I believe that the group can waste time in an excessive attempt to organize itself. 1 2 3 4 5 6 7

42. I believe that it is very important to reach a compromise when differences cannot be resolved in the group. 1 2 3 4 5 6 7

43. I am effective in helping to reach constructive settlement of disagreements among group members. 1 2 3 4 5 6 7

44. I am effective in establishing orderly procedures by which the team can work. 1 2 3 4 5 6 7

45. I think that effective teamwork results only if the team remains focused on the task at hand. 1 2 3 4 5 6 7

46. I am particularly effective in helping my group to evaluate the quality of its work. 1 2 3 4 5 6 7

47. In my opinion, it is important that the team establish methods by which it can evaluate the quality of its work. 1 2 3 4 5 6 7

48. I find it easy to express ideas and information to the other members of my group. 1 2 3 4 5 6 7

49. In my judgment, searching for ideas and opinions is one of the criteria of an effective team. 1 2 3 4 5 6 7

50. I believe that it is critical to settle disagreements among group members constructively. 1 2 3 4 5 6 7

51. I believe that it is important that the members of the team understand one another's points of view. 1 2 3 4 5 6 7

52. I am adept in making sure that reticent members have an opportunity to speak during the team's meetings. 1 2 3 4 5 6 7

53. I think that the synergy that occurs among group members is one of the most important components of group problem solving. 1 2 3 4 5 6 7

54. I rarely volunteer to state how I feel about the group while it is meeting. 1 2 3 4 5 6 7

55. When my group wanders from the task at hand, it is difficult for me to interrupt the members and attempt to refocus them. 1 2 3 4 5 6 7

56. I am able to restate clearly the ideas that are expressed in my group. 1 2 3 4 5 6 7

TOBI SCORING SHEET

Name ________________________________ Date ________________________________

Directions: Transfer your scores from the response sheets directly onto this scoring sheet.

Task Orientation

Values		*Skills*	
Item Number	Your Score	Item Number	Your Score
5.	——	3.	——*
11.	——	9.	——
14.	——*	12.	——
18.	——	17.	——*
19.	——*	30.	——
20.	——	33.	——
32.	——*	34.	——
36.	——	39.	——*
38.	——	40.	——
41.	——*	44.	——
45.	——	46.	——
47.	——	48.	——
49.	——	55.	——*
53.	——	56.	——
TOTAL	——	**TOTAL**	——

Maintenance Orientation

Values		*Skills*	
Item Number	Your Score	Item Number	Your Score
4.	——	1.	——*
6.	——	2.	——
8.	——	7.	——
13.	——	10.	——
16.	——*	15.	——
21.	——	22.	——*
24.	——*	23.	——
27.	——*	25.	——
29.	——*	26.	——
31.	——	28.	——*
37.	——	35.	——
42.	——	43.	——
50.	——	52.	——
51.	——	54.	——*
TOTAL	——	**TOTAL**	——

* Reverse score item. Change your score as follows:

1 = 7	3 = 5	5 = 3	7 = 1
2 = 6	4 = 4	6 = 2	

TOBI PROFILE SHEET

Name _______________________   Date _______________________

Directions: Plot your values score by finding the place on the graph where your total scores on the task-values scale and on the maintenance-values scale intersect. For example, if your task-values score is 40 and your maintenance-values score is 35, find where 40 on the vertical axis and 35 on the horizontal axis intersect. Mark that spot with a small triangle.

Now plot your skills score by finding the place on the graph where your scores on the task-skills scale and on the maintenance-skills scale intersect. Mark that spot with a small circle.

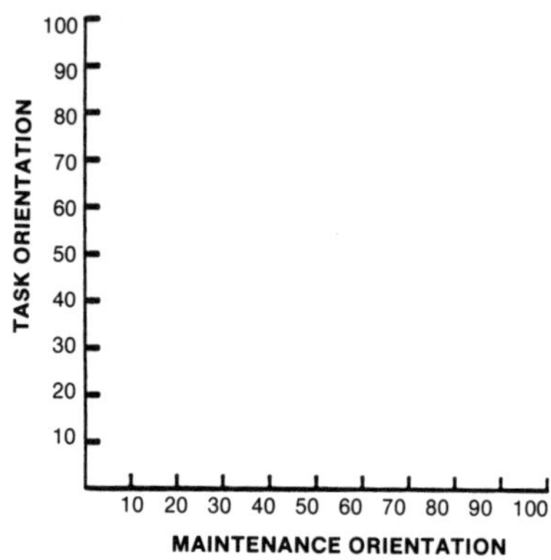

Interpretation Suggestions:

Individual: Compare your two points. Are they more or less at the same level? Which of the four profiles described earlier does your profile resemble? How strong is your personal commitment to your values? Do you need skills enhancement? What are your action steps?

Group: Compare your scores with the scores of the rest of your team. How do these scores help in understanding how your team conducts its business? Which team members are most committed to task? To maintenance? Who has the highest task-skill scores? The highest maintenance-skill scores? How do these compare with the group's perception? How can the team use its resources to improve its functioning?

ORGANIZATIONAL ROLE STRESS

Udai Pareek

Executive burnout is often the end result of stress experienced, but not properly coped with, by an executive. Burnout symptoms include exhaustion, irritation, ineffectiveness, inaction, discounting of self and others, and problems of bad health and drug use. On the other hand, stress properly coped with can lead to feelings of challenge, high job satisfaction, creativity, effectiveness, better adjustment to work and life, improved efficiency, career growth, and happiness. It is useful to look at the factors that contribute to the burnout of executives, and one of the most significant is role stress.

THE CONCEPT OF ROLE

The concept of "role" is key to understanding how any individual functions in any system. It is through his or her role that an individual interacts with and is integrated into a system (Pareek, 1976). Role has been defined in several ways. Here, it is defined as any position one holds in an organization as defined by the expectations various significant persons, including oneself, have for that position (Pareek, 1976). "Function" is defined as the set of interrelated expectations from a role. As here defined, sales manager is a role, while developing the sales force and customer contacts are functions.

Some conflict is always present because the very nature of role has built-in potential for conflict or stress. The main characteristic of role conflict is the incompatibility of some variables related to the role. Buck (1972) defines "job pressure" as the resultant psychological state of the individual who perceives that (1) conflicting forces and incompatible commitments exist in connection with work, (2) at least one of the forces is coming from outside, and (3) the forces recur or are stable over time.

Kahn, Wolfe, Quinn, Snoek, and Rosenthal (1964) were the first to draw attention to organizational stress in general, and role stress in particular. As suggested by Katz and Kahn (1966), an organization can be defined as a system of roles. Kahn and his associates used three categories (role ambiguity, role conflict, and role overload) to define role stress. This classification has been used by many other researchers. However, because each role is also a system of functions, from the point of view of individuals, two aspects of their roles are most important: *role set*, the role system within the organization of which roles are a part and by which individual roles are defined, and *role space*, the roles people occupy and perform.

Because the concept of role is inextricably linked with expectations, the organizational context is especially important. For example, authoritarian organizational structure and control systems are potent sources of stress because they breed dependency, afford little scope for initiative and creativity, and channel behaviors along narrowly defined paths. Many variables are involved, including oneself, the other roles in the organization, the expectations held by those in other roles, and one's own expectations.

USING THIS INSTRUMENT

Many classification systems have been used to describe role conflict and role stress. The Organizational Role Stress Scale was developed as one way to categorize role stress in terms of *role space* and *role set*. The instrument measures role-space conflict in terms of inter-role distance (IRD), role stagnation (RS), role expectations conflict (REC), personal inadequacy (PI) and self/role conflict (S/RC). Role-set conflict is measured in terms of role erosion (RE), role overload (RO), role isolation (RIs), role ambiguity (RA), and resource inadequacy (RIn). Definitions of these terms have been developed as follows:

Role-Space Conflicts

Inter-Role Distance. Conflicts may exist between two roles a person attempts to play. For example, executives often face conflicts between their organizational roles and their family roles. These may be incompatible and are quite frequently a source of conflict in a society in which people increasingly occupy multiple roles in various organizations and groups.

Role Stagnation. People "grow into" the roles they occupy in an organization. As they advance, their roles change and there is always a need to take on a new role for personal challenge. The problem is especially acute when a person has occupied a role for a long time and may feel secure and therefore hesitate to take on a new challenge. At middle age, and usually at middle-management levels, careers become more problematic and many executives find their progress slowed, if not actually stopped. Job opportunities are fewer, those jobs that are available take longer to master, and old knowledge and methods become obsolete. Levinson (1973) and Constandse (1972) depict these managers as suffering fear and disappointment in silent isolation.

Role Expectations Conflict. Because individuals develop expectations as a result of their socialization and identification with significant others, there is usually some incompatibility between a person's own expectations of a role and the expectations of others. For example, a professor may feel that the demands of teaching and of doing research are incompatible, whether they are or not. Others in the organization also are very likely have expectations of the person filling the role that conflict with the person's own.

Personal Inadequacy. If an individual has sacrificed his or her own interests, preferences, and values for the job, it may be because of fears of being inadequate otherwise to fill the role. The fear of demotion or obsolescence is especially strong for those who have reached a career ceiling, and most people will suffer some erosion of status before they retire. The company tends to sense an employee's feelings of inadequacy and often hesitates to promote because of it. McMurray (1973) describes what he calls "the executive neurosis": the overpromoted manager who is grossly overworked just in order to keep the job and at the same time hide a sense of insecurity and feelings of personal inadequacy.

Self/Role Conflict. Conflict often develops between people's self-concepts and their expectations of themselves in their job roles. For example, an introverted person may have trouble in the role of salesperson. It is also fairly common for people to experience conflict between the way they treat others in everyday life and the way they are required to treat others in their organizational roles, where maintaining distance from others may be necessary. Such conflicts are very common.

Role-Set Conflicts

Role Erosion. Employees often feel that some functions important to their roles are being performed by someone in another role. Role erosion is likely to be experienced in an organization that is redefining roles and creating new roles. As much stress is experienced by people with not enough to do or not enough responsibility for a task as by those with too much to do. People do not enjoy feeling underutilized.

Role Overload. On the other hand, when the role occupant feels that there are too many expectations, stress exists from "role overload" (Kahn et al., 1964). Kahn and Quinn (1970) suggested some conditions under which role overload is likely to occur: in the absence of role integration; in the absence of role power; when large variations exist in expected output; and when duties cannot be delegated. Marshall and Cooper (1979) categorized overload into "quantitative" and "qualitative." Quantitative refers to having too much to do, and qualitative refers to work that is too difficult. A number of studies have shown (Breslow & Buel, 1960; French & Caplan, 1970; Margolis, Kroes, & Quinn, 1974; Miller, 1969; and Russek & Zohman, 1958) that quantitative overload is significantly related to a number of symptoms of stress: alcohol abuse, absenteeism, low motivation, lowered self-esteem, and many physical ailments. Some evidence also shows that (for some occupations) qualitative overload is a significant source of stress and of lowered self-esteem (French, Tupper, & Mueller, 1965). French and Caplan (1973) summarize the research by suggesting that both qualitative and quantitative overload produce at least nine different symptoms of psychological and physical strain: job dissatisfaction, job tension, lowered self-esteem, paranoia, embarrassment, high cholesterol levels, rapid heart rate, and increased smoking.

Role Isolation. Role occupants tend to feel that those occupying other roles are either psychologically near or at a distance. The main criterion of perceived role-role distance is frequency and ease of interaction. When linkages are strong, the role-role distance is seen as low. In the absence of strong linkage, the role distance can be measured in terms of the gap between the desired and the existing linkages. Both Kahn et al. (1964) and French and Caplan (1970) came to the conclusion that mistrust of persons one worked with was positively related to high role ambiguity and to low job satisfaction.

Role Ambiguity. When people are not clear about the expectations others have of them in their roles, whether due to poor feedback or poor understanding, they experience role ambiguity. Kahn and Quinn (1970) suggested that role ambiguity may be in relation to activities, responsibilities, personal style, and norms. They suggest that it was created by the actual expectations held for the role occupant by others, the expectations of the role occupant, and the expectations the role occupant receives and interprets in the light of prior information and experience. According to Kahn and Quinn, four kinds of roles are most likely to experience ambiguity: roles new to the organization, roles in expanding or contracting organizations, roles in organizations exposed to frequent changes in demand, and roles concerned with process.

Kahn et al. (1964) found that people who suffered from role ambiguity experienced low job satisfaction, high job-related tension, a sense of futility, and low self-confidence. Kahn (1973) distinguished two components of role ambiguity: present ambiguity and future-prospect ambiguity.

Resource Inadequacy. Resource inadequacy refers to people's feeling that they do not have adequate resources to perform their roles effectively, whether through lack of supplies, personnel, information in the system, or historical data, or through lack of knowledge, education, or experience on their own.

The author's surveys using this instrument have shown that senior managers experience role stress in the following order: role isolation, self/role conflict, role erosion, and inter-role distance and that middle managers tend to experience more role stagnation (for more details, see Pareek, 1982).

RELIABILITY AND VALIDITY

Retest-reliability coefficients were calculated for a group of about five hundred managers after an interval of eight weeks. These ranged from .37 to .73 for the various role stresses. All were significant at the .001 level. Therefore, the Organizational Role Stress Scale would appear to be reliable for training purposes.

Some evidence of validity is provided by the measure of consistency of an instrument. Each item was correlated with the total score on the instrument for the approximately five-hundred respondents. All but two correlations were significant at the .001 level: one at .002 and another at .008. The results show high internal consistency for the scale. Mean and standard-deviation values of the items also were analyzed. The lowest mean value was 2.42 and the highest was 4.66. The two items that had low correlation with the total had high mean values.

The responses also were factor analyzed, which produced exactly ten factors, corresponding to the ten role stresses, explaining 99.9 percent variance.

SCORING THE INSTRUMENT

The instrument has an accompanying scoring sheet. The responses are ratings from a five-point Likert scale that indicates how descriptive a particular statement is for the respondent. The role-stress scale-score range is from a minimum of 5 to a maximum of 25. The total score ranges from 50 to 250. The columns are to be totalled to yield scale scores and the columns are summed to yield a total score.

REFERENCES

Breslow, L., & Buell, P. Mortality from coronary heart disease and physical activity of work in California. *Journal of Chronic Diseases*, 1960, *11*, 617-626.

Buck, V. E. *Working under pressure*. London: Staples Press, 1972.

Constandse, W. J. Mid-40s man: A neglected personnel problem. *Personnel Journal*, 1972, *51*(2), 129-133.

French, J. R. P., Jr., & Caplan, R. D. Psychosocial factors in coronary heart disease. *Industrial Medicine*, 1970, *39*, 383-397.

French, J. R. P., Jr., & Caplan, R. D. Organizational stress and individual strain. In A. J. Marrow (Ed.), *The failure of success*. New York: AMACOM, 1973.

French, J. R. P., Jr., Tupper, C. J., & Mueller, E. I. *Workload of university professors*. Unpublished research report, University of Michigan, 1965.

Kahn, R. L. Conflict, ambiguity and overload: Three elements in job stress. *Occupational Mental Health*, 1973, *3*, 1.

Kahn, R. L., & Quinn, R. P. Role stress: A framework for analysis. In A. McLean (Ed.), *Mental health and work organizations*. Chicago: Rand McNally, 1970.

Kahn, R. L., Wolfe, D. M., Quinn, R. P., Snoek, J. D., & Rosenthal, R. A. *Organizational stress: Studies in role conflict and ambiguity*. New York: John Wiley, 1964.

Katz, D., & Kahn, R. L. *The social psychology of organizations*. New York: John Wiley, 1966.

Levinson, H. Problems that worry our executives. In A. J. Marrow (Ed.), *The failure of success*. New York: AMACOM, 1973.

Margolis, B. L., Kroes, W. H., & Quinn, R. P. Job stress: An unlisted occupational hazard. *Journal of Occupational Medicine*, 1974, *16*(1), 654-661.

Marshall, J., & Cooper, C. L. *Executive under pressure: A psychological study*. London: MacMillan Press, 1979.

McMurray, R. N. The executive neurosis. In R. L. Noland (Ed.), *Industrial mental health and employee counselling*. New York: Behavioural Publications, 1973.

Miller, J. G. Information input overload and psychopathology. *American Journal of Psychiatry*, 1969, *8*, 116.

Pareek, U. Inter-role exploration. In J. W. Pfeiffer & J. E. Jones (Eds.), *The 1976 annual handbook for group facilitators*. San Diego, CA: University Associates, 1976.

Pareek, U. *Role stress scales manual*. Ahmedabad, India: Navin Publications, 1982.

Russek, H. I., & Zohman, B. L. Relative significance of heredity, diet, and occupational stress in coronary heart disease of young adults. *American Journal of Medical Sciences*, 1958, *235*, 266-275.

Udai Pareek, Ph.D., is the Larsen and Toubro professor of organizational behavior at the Indian Institute of Management, Ahmedabad, Gujarat, India. Dr. Pareek's background is in organization development, human resource development, organizational design, and change in persons and systems. He has consulted with industrial and nonindustrial systems in various countries and with many international organizations. He also is the author or co-author of five books on psychology and management.

ORGANIZATIONAL ROLE STRESS SCALE
Udai Pareek

Name _______________________________ Title_______________________ Date________

Organization____

Instructions: People have different perceptions of their work roles. Some statements describing such perceptions are listed below. Read each statement and decide how often you have the thought expressed in the statement in relation to your *role in your organization*. Circle the number on the scale that indicates your perception of your organizational role.

If you find that none of the categories given adequately indicates your opinion, use the one that is *closest* to your perception.

1 - Never or scarcely ever see things this way
2 - Occasionally (a few times) see things this way
3 - Sometimes see things this way
4 - Frequently see things this way
5 - Very frequently or always see things this way

	Never or scarcely ever	Occasionally	Sometimes	Frequently	Very frequently or always
1. My role tends to interfere with my family life.	1	2	3	4	5
2. I am afraid that I am not learning enough in my present role to prepare myself for higher responsibility.	1	2	3	4	5
3. I am not able to satisfy the conflicting demands of various people who are over me in the organization.	1	2	3	4	5
4. My role recently has been reduced in importance.	1	2	3	4	5
5. My work load is too heavy.	1	2	3	4	5
6. Other role occupants do not give enough attention and time to my role.	1	2	3	4	5
7. I do not have adequate knowledge to handle the responsibilities in my role.	1	2	3	4	5
8. I have to do things in my role that are against my better judgment.	1	2	3	4	5
9. I am not clear about the scope and responsibilities of my role (job).	1	2	3	4	5
10. I do not receive the information that is needed to carry out the responsibilities assigned to me.	1	2	3	4	5
11. My role does not allow me to spend enough time with my family.	1	2	3	4	5

12. I am too preoccupied with my present role responsibilities to be able to prepare for taking on greater
responsibilities.

13. I am not able to satisfy the conflicting demands of the
various people at my peer level and of my subordinates.

14. Many of the functions that should be part of my role
have been assigned to other roles.

15. The amount of work that I have to do interferes with
the quality I want to maintain.

16. There is not enough interaction between my role and
other roles.

17. I wish I had more skills to handle the responsibilities
of my role.

18. I am not able to use my training and expertise in
my role.

19. I do not know what the people with whom I work
expect of me.

20. I do not have access to enough resources to be effective
in my role.

21. I have various other interests (social, religious, etc,)
that are neglected because I do not have the time to
attend to them.

22. I do not have the time or opportunities to prepare
myself for the future challenges of my role.

23. I am not able to satisfy the demands of clients and
others because they conflict with one another.

24. I would like to take more responsibility than I
have at present.

25. I have been given too much responsibility.

26. I wish there were more consultation between my role
and other roles.

27. I have not had pertinent training for my role.

28. The responsibilities I have are not related to my
interests.

29. Several aspects of my role are vague and unclear.

30. I do not have enough people to work with me in my
role.

31. My organizational responsibilities interfere with my nonwork roles.

32. There is very little room for personal growth in my role.

33. The expectations of my seniors conflict with those of my subordinates.

34. I can do much more than what I have been assigned.

35. There is a need to reduce some parts of my role.

36. There is no evidence of involvement of several roles (including my role) in joint problem solving or collaboration in planning action.

37. I wish that I had prepared myself well for my role.

38. If I had full freedom to define my role, I would be doing some things differently from the ways I do them now.

39. My role has not been defined clearly and in detail.

40. I am worried that I lack the necessary resources needed in my role.

41. My family and friends complain that I do not spend time with them because of the heavy demands of my work role.

42. I feel stagnant in my role.

43. I am bothered with the contradictory expectations that different people have of my role.

44. I wish that I would be given more challenging tasks to do.

45. I feel overburdened in my role.

46. Even when I take initiative for discussions or help, there is not much response from other roles.

47. I feel inadequate for my present job role.

48. I experience conflict between my values and what I have to do in my job role.

49. I am not clear about what the priorities are in my role.

50. I wish that I had more financial resources for the work assigned to me.

ORGANIZATIONAL ROLE STRESS SCALE SCORING SHEET

Instructions: Enter your scores from the Organizational Role Stress Scale in the spaces provided below.

1._____ 2._____ 3._____ 4._____ 5._____

11._____ 12._____ 13._____ 14._____ 15._____

21._____ 22._____ 23._____ 24._____ 25._____

31._____ 32._____ 33._____ 34._____ 35._____

41._____ 42._____ 43._____ 44._____ 45._____

TOTALS

IRD: Inter-Role Distance	RS: Role Stagnation	REC: Role Expectations Conflict	RE: Role Erosion	RO: Role Overload

6._____ 7._____ 8._____ 9._____ 10._____

16._____ 17._____ 18._____ 19._____ 20._____

26._____ 27._____ 28._____ 29._____ 30._____

36._____ 37._____ 38._____ 39._____ 40._____

46._____ 47._____ 48._____ 49._____ 50._____

TOTALS

RIs: Role Isolation	PI: Personal Inadequacy	S/RC: Self/Role Conflict	RA: Role Ambiguity	RIn: Resource Inadequacy

GRAND TOTAL

Definitions:

IRD—*Inter-Role Distance:* conflict between one's organizational role and other roles, e.g., between travel on the job and spending time with one's family.

RS—*Role Stagnation:* a feeling of stagnation and lack of growth in the job because of few opportunities for learning and growth.

REC—*Role Expectations Conflict:* conflicting demands placed on one from others in the organization, e.g., producing excellent work, but finishing under severe time restraints.

RE—*Role Erosion:* a decrease in one's level of responsibility or a feeling of not being fully utilized.

RO—*Role Overload:* too much to do and too many responsibilities to do everything well.

RIs—*Role Isolation:* feelings of being isolated from channels of information and not being part of what is happening.

PI—*Personal Inadequacy:* lack of knowledge, skill, or preparation to be effective in a particular role.

S/RC—*Self/Role Conflict:* a conflict between one's personal values or interests and one's job requirements.

RA—*Role Ambiguity:* unclear feedback from others about one's responsibilities and performance.

RIn—*Resource Inadequacy:* lack of resources or information necessary to perform well in a role.

THE TEM SURVEY

George Petrello

The "knowledge worker," as defined by Peter Drucker (1969), is usually college educated, with expertise in some technical, professional, or administrative field. People who have freedom to control their time within their work environments are knowledge workers, in contrast to people who work on production lines, where their activities are controlled by the movement of the work along the line. Job success for knowledge workers depends largely on how effectively they use the time available to them.

BACKGROUND AND SUPPORTING THEORY

The literature on time management indicates that effective usage of time is greatly dependent on people's ability to pace themselves and their levels of recognizing and controlling human energy flows. Industrial psychologists have found that theories concerning "night people" and "morning people" are true for the vast majority of cases. In its simplest form, energy-level theory suggests that people realize, through self-observation, when they are at their best for physical activities such as dealing with people, presentations, and meetings and when they are at their best for mental activities such as writing, reviewing reports, and preparing budgets. If time is used for work that complements one's energy flows, one's use of time becomes more effective.

The literature indicates that effective time management also is greatly dependent on the individual's ability to process and retrieve information through a personal memory system. "Memory improvement" refers to the use of simple mechanical aids to help the person to store and retrieve information, rather than relying on the person's ability to remember in the traditional sense. Memory improvement involves careful record keeping through the use of diaries, project sheets, schedules, and so on. Thus, effective time management is linked to the individual's energy level and memory system. Research confirms that people can be taught to use their time more effectively. Sometimes the teaching does not involve communicating techniques but, rather, changing poor attitudes. Many people know or can learn what they should be doing to use their time more effectively, but they are not motivated to apply the techniques. Some people have attitudinal problems that are rooted in their environments or histories. Most people are able to change their attitudes and habits and to attain more effective use of their time.

The statements in The TEM Survey (time, energy, and memory) are derived from the author's experience in presenting time-management seminars and from the professional literature in the field. About 60 percent of these statements reflect knowledge and about 40 percent reflect attitudes. Reddin's Management Style Diagnosis Test (Reddin, 1977) was used as a model in the design of the instrument.

The author has used The TEM Survey with over three hundred knowledge workers. In post-test surveys, participants were asked if they thought that the instrument accurately described their attitudes and knowledge about time, energy, and memory. Eighty percent of the participants said that the survey was accurate; 12 percent of the participants said that they were not sure; and 8 percent of the participants said that the survey was not accurate. In almost all cases, the participants thought that the survey was an excellent way to introduce a seminar on time management.

Administration and scoring of the instrument take thirty to forty minutes. It can be used as the basis of a one- or two-hour session, or it can be used to introduce a longer seminar. It also can be used for personnel screening and as a prescriptive device.

INSTRUCTIONS FOR ADMINISTRATION

After distributing copies of The TEM Survey, the facilitator should instruct the participants to read the instructions carefully, but not to read the statements until they are instructed to do so. When all participants understand the instructions, the facilitator tells them to begin and allows twenty or thirty minutes for them to complete the instrument.

When all participants have completed the instrument, the following instructions for scoring it are given:

1. Add all the "A's" in Columns 1 and 3 of The TEM Survey Answer Sheet (Step I). Insert the totals on the proper lines of Step II. Add these totals and insert this sum on the blank line for Attitude Raw Score.

2. Add all the "B's" in Columns 2 and 4 of The TEM Survey Answer Sheet (Step I). Insert the totals on the proper lines of Step III. Add these totals and insert this sum on the blank line for Knowledge Raw Score.

3. Convert the Attitude Raw Score and Knowledge Raw Score to Graph Values (Step IV) and shade in the Attitude and Knowledge Graphs that appear in Step V to the appropriate levels.

4. To find your TEM Profile, total the Raw Scores from Steps II and III and find the Range into which this total Raw Score falls. The Range indicates your potential as a Waster, User, or Achiever.

REFERENCES

Bliss, E. C. *Getting things done: The ABC's of time management.* New York: Bantam, 1978.

Cooper, J. D. *How to get more done in less time.* New York: Doubleday, 1962.

Drucker, P. *The effective executive.* New York: Harper & Row, 1969.

Jay, A. *Management and Machiavelli.* London: Hodder & Stoughton, 1967.

Lakein, A. *How to get control of your time and your life.* New York: Signet, 1974.

Mackenzie, R. *The time trap.* New York: McGraw-Hill, 1975.

Raths, L. E., Harmin, M., & Simon, S. B. *Values and teaching: Working with values in the classroom.* Columbus, OH: C. E. Merrill, 1966.

Reddin, W. J. *The management style diagnosis test.* Fredericton, New Brunswick: Organizational Tests Ltd., 1977.

George J. Petrello, Ph.D., is the dean of the School of Business and Administration and a professor of management at St. Mary's University in San Antonio, Texas. He serves as a management consultant and trainer for the U.S. Air Force Social Actions Training Program and has presented seminars in the areas of time management and decision making for corporations, state and national governmental agencies, and nonprofit institutions. Dr. Petrello has co-authored two college-level textbooks and study guides.

THE TEM SURVEY

An Assessment of Your Effectiveness in Managing
Your Time, Energy, and Memory
George J. Petrello

Managers, administrators, professional practitioners, and educators are defined by Peter Drucker as "knowledge workers." These professionals are not expected to punch time clocks, nor are they expected to be clock watchers, but their use of time, energy, and memory (TEM) determines to a great extent how successful they will be in a work environment that is limited by hours, human energy, and the capacity to retain information. Many people have inefficient attitudes about time, energy, and memory management or they do not know how to become more effective users of these precious resources.

Most people can be defined as WASTERS, USERS, or ACHIEVERS in terms of their use of time, energy, or memory. The TEM Survey will help you to ascertain whether you need to improve your attitude or increase your skills in this area.

Directions: Following are fifty sets of statements concerning attitudes or knowledge about time, energy, and memory management. Each set contains *two* statements, one in Column A and one in Column B. Read each set carefully, select what you believe to be the *best* answer, and indicate your choice on The TEM Survey Answer Sheet by writing in an "A" or a "B" in the appropriate space. Note that the items go *across* the answer sheet, not down. Many of the statements in the sets are unrelated. Try not to let this frustrate you in your effort to select the *best* of the two statements. Although some alternatives may not apply to your work environment, select the *best* answer as if all statements did apply.

	A	**B**
1.	Your time is your responsibility.	We can always control our time.
2.	Committee meetings usually are a waste of time.	Most managers could not do their jobs well without meetings.
3.	In order to better manage our time, we need to learn to set priorities.	Training people to save time is really a waste of time.
4.	Time spent waiting is unproductive but a necessary evil.	On certain days at certain times, instruct your secretary to hold all non-emergency calls so that you have a quiet time for thinking and planning.
5.	Your time is your tool.	The individual controls time and energy; environment has little to do with it.
6.	Time analysis usually is an exercise in wasting time.	Your time is a company resource.
7.	Analyze and suggest ways to help your boss make better use of your time.	Chasing time (leg work) usually is a time saver in the long run.
8.	Prepare a weekly "to do" list in order to plan the work week ahead.	Ask others "What can I do to help you to make better use of your time?"

A	B
9. We have two choices: to control the amount of work for which we are responsible or to expand the amount of time that we spend doing the work.	Schedule recreation for weekends and evenings.
10. Have subordinates evaluate for you how wisely you use your time.	The skill of delegation is difficult to learn.
11. Prepare a job description of your work and relate it to your own use of time. Have your subordinates do the same.	Avoid taking notes while talking in person to others; it is threatening to them.
12. Do not expect a secretary to be more than a typist and file clerk.	Delegate work, not the job of figuring out what the work is.
13. We cannot always control our time because we often do work that involves other people.	Telephones usually are time wasters.
14. As a participant in a meeting, you are unable to save time.	Committee meetings are different from staff meetings.
15. Outline important telephone conversations in advance.	Luncheon meetings are often the most productive.
16. Handle business in person whenever possible.	Attempt to cut down on travel through the use of conference calls.
17. The telephone can be a great intruder on our time if we permit it to be.	Avoid meetings as often as possible.
18. Do not let courtesy stand in the way of good time management.	Control your work; do not allow your work to control you.
19. Proper training of subordinates usually is an important time saver.	Keep your appointment calendar in one central location, usually with your secretary.
20. Have a secretary take notes after each major appointment that you have.	Ending telephone conversations is difficult for most people.
21. Generally, "do it now" is the best philosophy in handling paperwork.	Generally, "do it now" is the best philosophy in making people or dollar decisions.
22. Train yourself in memory techniques to rely on instant recall.	Document telephone conversations while they are in progress.
23. Have your own special filing system.	Having subordinates present written proposals to you is unwise because it discourages creativity.
24. Handle minor decision-making problems while waiting for airplanes or such things as the dentist.	Use your watch as a time message for those who take up your time.

A

B

25. Most people are ill-equipped to manage their time.

Leave all files to your secretary or assistant to manage. Do not waste your time on them.

26. The larger the organization, the less actual time the chief executive will have.

Time spent truly relaxing is of no value to your career.

27. Take as long as time permits to make an important decision.

Require a secretary or assistant to schedule all your appointments.

28. Use discretionary on-the-job time to catch up on work-related reading.

Keep the ball in the other person's court as a way of keeping the paperwork moving meaningfully.

29. In trying to control time, there is a clear danger that one may cut back tasks and acttivities too drastically.

The best advice one can give a manager or executive is to plan one's work carefully and in advance, each and every day.

30. Think of work time as separate and distinct from personal time.

Interpersonnel problems may be a symptom of overstaffing.

31. Require completed work from your subordinates.

Carefully plan each day's schedule of activities as tightly as possible at the beginning of the day.

32. Visit with co-workers to get the job done right and quickly.

Use the telephone as a time-saving tool.

33. Try to increase your work pace from time to time.

Executives should avoid most time commitments that are nonproductive.

34. Be careful of setting deadlines for yourself and others; it can become too autocratic.

Concentrate only on one thing at a time.

35. Logging important meetings and conversations by date and title is a very effective means of memory control.

Plan routines for processing communication and be sure that those around you know them and follow them.

36. Keep meetings flexible; do not lock yourself into a specific agenda in advance.

Carry a pocket calendar and record all appointments.

37. Expect something useful to come out of every meeting.

Doing something yourself is often the best way to save time.

38. As a general rule, meetings should be 50 percent structured and 50 percent free to allow for creativity.

Inevitably, some portion of your time will be spent on activities outside your control.

39. Use a dictating machine as a memory log.

Answer or move on all correspondence within twenty-four hours.

40. Keep all short-term paperwork in neat piles on your desk.

After each important meeting, have the minutes printed and distributed.

A   **B**

41. Expect constant interruptions during your working hours.

"Know Thyself" and "Know Thy Time" are both difficult to impossible for mortal man.

42. Concentrate on details. Remember, the whole is made up of many parts.

Time analysis, like financial analysis, depends on carefully documented historical data.

43. Cut off nonproductive activities as quickly as possible.

When pushing paper, handle each piece of paper only once.

44. Wise use of small portions of time, as opposed to wise use of fairly large portions of time, is a key to managerial effectiveness.

Select the best time of day for the type of work required.

45. Do not allow immediate time demands to deter you from long-term goals.

Discretionary time available to executives is usually much greater than we think.

46. As a general rule, catch your supervisor in a casual, relaxed atmosphere to discuss important work issues.

There always is enough time for the important things.

47. On a large project, start with the easiest tasks.

Breakfast meetings and late afternoon meetings are nonproductive and should be avoided.

48. Take a memory course for the purpose of developing the skill of holding more data in your head.

On a large project, start with the most satisfactory tasks.

49. Few executives use delegation to a great extent as a time saver.

When tense, visit colleagues for a few minutes in their offices for a change of pace.

50. Committees should meet on a regular schedule.

Handle interruptions as rapidly and as thoughtfully as possible.

THE TEM SURVEY ANSWER SHEET

Instructions:

1. Add all the "A's" in Columns 1 and 3 of The TEM Survey Answer Sheet (Step I). Insert the totals on the proper lines of Step II. Add these totals and insert this sum on the blank line for Attitude Raw Score.

2. Add all the "B's" in Columns 2 and 4 of The TEM Survey Answer Sheet (Step I). Insert the totals on the proper lines of Step III. Add these totals and insert this sum on the blank line for Knowledge Raw Score.

3. Convert the Attitude Raw Score and Knowledge Raw Score to Graph Values (Step IV) and shade in the Attitude and Knowledge Graphs that appear in Step V to the appropriate levels.

4. To find your TEM Profile, total the Raw Scores from Steps II and III and find the Range into which this total Raw Score falls. The Range indicates your potential as a Waster, User, or Achiever.

STEP I

Column 1	Column 2	Column 3	Column 4
1 ______	2 ______	3 ______	4 ______
5 ______	6 ______	7 ______	8 ______
9 ______	10 ______	11 ______	12 ______
13 ______	14 ______	15 ______	16 ______
17 ______	18 ______	19 ______	20 ______
21 ______	22 ______	23 ______	24 ______
25 ______	26 ______	27 ______	28 ______
29 ______	30 ______	31 ______	32 ______
33 ______	34 ______	35 ______	36 ______
37 ______	38 ______	39 ______	40 ______
41 ______	42 ______	43 ______	44 ______
45 ______	46 ______	47 ______	48 ______
49 ______	50 ______		
A Total ______	**B Total** ______	**A Total** ______	**B Total** ______

STEP II

__________ + __________ = __________
A Total   A Total   Attitude
Column 1   Column 3   Raw Score

STEP III

__________ + __________ = __________
B Total   B Total   Knowledge
Column 2   Column 4   Raw Score

STEP IV

Raw Score:	0-5	6-10	11-15	16-20	21-25
Conversion Index:	20	40	60	80	100

STEP V

Attitude		Knowledge
100	Excellent	100
80	Good	80
60	Average	60
40	Below Average	40
20	Very Poor	20

TEM PROFILE

STEP VI

__________ + __________ = __________
Step II   Step III
Total   Total

Your potential level of effectiveness in the management of time, energy, and memory:

RANGE

0-30	31-41	42-50
Waster	User	Achiever

INTRODUCTION TO THE LECTURETTES SECTION

A lecturette is a short, conceptual presentation designed to establish a common language bond between the trainer and the participants. It provides a mutual frame of reference and promotes the cognitive understanding of individual experience and group dynamics. In the experiential learning cycle (see the Introduction to the Structured Experiences Section), a lecturette may be useful in solidifying the generalizing phase, during which abstract principles are drawn from specific observations. The lecturette caps the inductive process; consequently, it can then be used deductively to illustrate generalizations about human behavior.

Because the lecturette is a tool for increasing and clarifying participants' understanding of their experiences, the pieces in this section can be used as handouts for participants. Written in a simple style with a realistic focus, the material is immediately applicable to further practice of the basics that have been learned.

Because lecturettes, by their very nature, can set up a norm of "I talk, you listen" between trainer and participants, this important technique must be used carefully and creatively to keep participants actively involved in the learning process. The trainer can develop skills to prevent participant apathy and passivity. Two such skills important for the effective use of lecturettes are (a) making lecturettes experiential by involving the participants and (b) stimulating participant reaction by adding "punch" to the lecturette. These methods are summarized below; all must be used with discrimination to avoid overshadowing cognitive learning.[1]

MAKING LECTURETTES EXPERIENTIAL

Preparation

The purposes of the beginning phase of lecturettes are to (a) establish the climate of the group; (b) promote participants' readiness for learning; (c) reduce anxiety; and (d) provide a "sense of audience."

Helpful techniques are identified, with examples of their use.

- *Energizers*
  Applaud each participant.
- *Associations*
  Have participants verbally complete a sentence, e.g., "Conflict is . . . ."
- *Charts*
  Have participants list the good news/bad news about stress. Have participants express a positive statement (+), negative statement (–), and curiosity (?) about sexual stereotypes.
- *Fantasy*
  Have participants imagine that they are guiding a rocket through outer space.

---

[1]For a more complete explanation, see the Introduction to the Lecturettes Section of the 1979 and 1980 *Annuals*.

- *Assigned Listening*
  Divide participants into three groups. One listens for agreement; the second, disagreement; the third, clarification and amplification.
- *Impromptu Lectures*
  Ask participants to speak individually on different aspects of training: needs assessment, diagnosis, intervention, evaluation.
- *Self-Assessment*
  Have participants make personal statements about their experience with burnout.

Process

The purposes to be attended to during the lecturette include the following: (a) to provoke task-relevant thinking; (b) to keep participants active; (c) to correct and clarify misunderstandings; and (d) to keep a "sense of audience."

Techniques applicable to this phase of presenting lecturettes follow.

- *Soliciting Examples*
  Have participants think of personal or current-event examples that illustrate a statement such as "A manager may be required to use different styles with different employees."
- *Interviewing*
  Have participants form dyads or interview the people sitting next to them about their beliefs about quality circles.
- *Using Synonyms*
  Have participants devise other terms for jargon words such as "share," "growth," "awareness."
- *Asking Questions*
  Ask participants to tell what they have heard you say about negotiation as a strategy. Ask the question "How can communication reduce stress?" and then answer it. Ask additional questions, pause, and give the participants an opportunity to answer.
- *Answering Questions*
  Have the participants interview one another on the topic of time management.
- *Responding*
  Have participants complete the statement "Right now I'm feeling/thinking/wondering... ."

Closure

When closing the lecturette, the following purposes are pertinent: (a) to integrate cognitive input; (b) to clear up misconceptions; (c) to test learning; and (d) to plan for transfer.

Closing techniques useful to the facilitator include the following:

- *Q/A Period*
  Have participants rehearse questions with a partner and then ask you.
- *Quiz*
  Have participants take a test, share their answers with one another, and voice any disagreement they may have with your answers.
- *Statements*
  Have participants make opinion statements about the content of the lecturette.

- *Handouts*
  Give participants handouts summarizing the content of the lecturette.
- *Skill Practice*
  Have participants practice with a partner the skill of turning questions into statements. Role play a real or hypothetical situation developed for skill practice.
- *Goal Setting*
  Have participants contract by themselves or in pairs to apply assertiveness in a back-home situation.
- *Link with Other Methods*
  Use a lecturette on problem solving to lead into a problem-solving experience.

ADDING IMPACT TO LECTURETTES

Any of several methods will contribute to the effectiveness, power, and impact of lecturettes, thus making them a more useful tool for the trainer or facilitator.

- *Relevant Humor*
  Tell a joke or a "war story" based on your personal experience with performance appraisals.
- *Word Images*
  Draw a vivid word picture to illustrate the concept of communication climate.
- *Analogy*
  Make a comparison between assertiveness and target shooting.
- *Modeling*
  Demonstrate the skill of confrontation.
- *Visual Aids*
  Employ flip charts, posters, slides, or music to explain Situational Leadership™.
- *Problem Development*
  Give participants a problem from your own experience or a case study about dealing with a new boss.

LECTURETTES IN THIS *ANNUAL*

Although the majority of the selections in the 1983 *Annual* are philosophically grounded in humanistic and holistic values, they focus on the practical behaviors that follow from that foundation. The arrangement of the pieces proceeds from those focusing on the individual to those geared to use by an organization.

A general theme found in this year's lecturettes is the reduction of stress and the management of conflict to increase individual and organizational effectiveness. Further, the tone is proactive, emphasizing taking personal responsibility for the creation of productive contexts and the prevention of energy-draining contexts. The authors pay attention to the realistic constraints of larger systems, accounting for contingencies external to the individual, group, and organization. As a whole, they acknowledge the difficult times in which we find ourselves and provide ideas for intangible rewards.

"Using Humor in Workshops" offers eight guidelines for using humor to establish a positive atmosphere, increase teacher/learner collaboration, and develop listening and problem-solving skills. In a similar "up" approach, "Encouragement" offers ways to release energy often bound up in historical negative patterns and labels.

At a group level of interaction, "Toward More Effective Meetings" suggests simple steps for preparing, managing, and following up on meetings in order to eliminate the problem of ineffectiveness and to build collaboration into the problem-solving effort. Narrowing the focus specifically to the problem-solving process, "A Guide to Problem Solving" depicts a clear ten-step model to aid in the process of managing information both creatively and logically. Also including a problem-solving model is "Stress, Communication, and Assertiveness," which adds a fresh perspective to methods of stress reduction by viewing most stressors as symbolic threats. Eight potentially effective styles of managing conflict in organizations are diagramed in "Preventing and Resolving Conflict." Again at the organizational level, "A Look at Quality Circles" presents a thorough explanation of quality circles, including the history and implementation of a quality-circles program.

Finally, "Surviving Organizational Burnout" picks up the theme of stress at an organizational level. Suggesting that stress results from the pace of our time, this lecturette emphasizes the re-evaluation of values and reordering of priorities as a means of reducing disparity between resources and goals.

USING HUMOR IN WORKSHOPS

Joel Goodman

> There are three things which are real: God, human folly, and laughter. The first two are beyond our comprehension. So we must do what we can with the third.   (John F. Kennedy)

> Humor is essential to any smoothly functioning system of interaction, to any healthy person, and to any viable group. Humor is, in the last analysis, no joke.   (Dr. Gary Alan Fine, University of Minnesota)

Humor is serious business. It can serve as a powerful tool for leaders at all levels to prevent the build-up of stress, to improve communication, to enhance motivation and morale, to build relationships, to encourage creative problem solving, to smooth the way for organizational change, and to make workshops fun (Goodman, 1982).

WHY WE NEED HUMOR

In a workshop (or in consulting, teaching, or meetings), the participants are trying to learn new skills or to deal with important issues or to develop teamwork. If the workshop participants enjoy the experience, they will want to be there, they will be motivated to learn. Obviously, the leader or facilitator will enjoy the experience more, too, if humor is involved; and if the humor puts the participants into more receptive moods, the work of the leader will be made easier. Humor also conveys the message that the facilitator is a human being. If the facilitator can laugh with the participants and at herself or himself, it is much easier for the participants to relate to the facilitator. The use of humor decreases problems in discipline, increases listening and attention on the part of the participants, decreases the pressure on people to be perfect, increases retention (by freeing attention through laughter), and increases the comfort level in the workshop setting (by building interest and energy through laughter). The resulting positive attitude can greatly contribute to achievement and productivity.

Humor also is a powerful tool for enhancing self-confidence and for building empathy among people. In helping workshop participants to tap their own senses of humor, one helps them to develop an important skill for leadership and for dealing with challenges and problems. President Reagan's ability to use humor after the attempt on his life certainly is an illustration of this.

Humor also makes it easier to hear feedback and new information. Humor gives us perspective on problems; it helps us to get away from a problem situation in order to see the situation and possible solutions in perspective. This is a very important skill for leaders and problem solvers of any type to have.

EIGHT BASIC TECHNIQUES

Education and enjoyment are not mutually exclusive. In fact, the synergy between learning and laughing will produce more learning and more laughter—a great formula for a successful workshop! The eight basic techniques that follow will help to introduce humor successfully into a workshop.

Environment

The first step is to create a positive context by creating a humor-filled environment. This could be as simple as setting up a bulletin board that contains cartoons, funny photographs, or humorous quotations related to the topic of the workshop. The participants can check this bulletin board before the workshop begins as well as during any breaks as a way to socialize and to recharge their battteries. The use of the bulletin board allows the facilitator to avoid being a stand-up comedian. (In fact, there are hundreds of ways to build humor into an atmosphere without having to tell jokes.) For example, participants who are addressing very serious issues might enjoy reading some tongue-in-cheek words from Woody Allen (1979).

> More than any other time in history, mankind faces a crossroads. One path leads to despair and utter hopelessness. The other, to total extinction. Let us pray we have the wisdom to choose correctly.

Enter

It often is helpful to begin the workshop by sharing a humorous personal anecdote and/or a humorous example that illustrates the theme of the workshop. For instance, if the goal of the workshop is to help the participants to improve their communication and conflict-resolution skills, the following anecdote would be pertinent:

> Lieutenant Tomb was invited to be interviewed by an admiral for a particular job. "Sit down, Toom," said the admiral. "My name is pronounced 'Tom,' Sir," said Tomb. "I didn't ask you to speak," said the admiral. "Now, Toom, when did you first become interested in nuclear power?" The Lieutenant replied, "Well, Sir, I first became interested in nuclear power on the day that the United States dropped the first atomic boom."

When people have opened their mouths to laugh, they are more ready to open their minds to learn.

Ear Ye, Ear Ye!

Listening is the key to hearty laughter. After the facilitator has set up a positive environment and modeled the sharing of humor, it often is helpful for the participants to share their own humor. This could be in the form of a "whip," in which each person would have a chance, in turn, to share briefly a humorous quotation, joke, or perspective on the topic at hand. For example, at a recent workshop on leadership, these little gems were contributed by the participants:

> If all the politicians in the world were laid end to end, they wouldn't reach a conclusion.
> Congress is so strange. A man gets up to speak and says nothing, nobody listens, and then everybody disagrees.
> (Will Rogers)
> An optimist and a pessimist are right about the same number of times, but an optimist has more fun.
> A committee is a group that keeps minutes and wastes hours.
> Procrastination is the art of keeping up with yesterday.
> To do a superior job, a good leader needs a plan and not quite enough time.
> Everyone *talks* about the weather, but no one ever *does* anything about it. (Mark Twain)

Bringing a humorous item to share could be an enjoyable "ticket of admission" to a session of the workshop.

Exercise

Humor is an invitation to mental, emotional, and physical exercise. There are hundreds of activities that simultaneously evoke thinking, imagination, and hearty laughter. If used in a well-conceived sequence (fun with a purpose, not just "playing a game"), humorous exercises can be excellent ways in which to help workshop participants to develop the skills related to their goals. For instance, in workshops that focus on creative problem solving, brainstorming often is taught as a specific skill. In order to help the participants to internalize this skill, it can be extremely helpful to have them use it first on problems that are not "close to home"(so that they can focus on the *skill* without concerning themselves about the problems). The following problems can be explored in introductions to the technique of brainstorming:

What would happen if the human body were rearranged so that our mouths were located on the tops of our heads?

What would happen if our eyes were located on the tips of our thumbs?

What would happen if a popcorn popper didn't stop popping?

What would happen if orchestras played colors, not sounds?

What are all the ways you can think of to send love long distance?

What are all the different uses you can think of for a rubber band (an "Exit" sign, old tennis balls, unmatched socks)?

Such exercises are wonderful for building creativity and for making it easy to learn new skills. It also can be fun for the facilitator and participants to create the exercises.

Exaggerate

This is a most important technique. Exaggeration can help to maintain perspective in a challenging situation or to illustrate a point in a humorous way. Exaggeration can involve the use of metaphors—for example, describing the group's difficulty in making consensus decisions as similar to trying to nail Jell-O™ to a tree or comparing the consequences of a negative interpersonal conflict to what garlic has done for the good-night kiss.

One effective way to utilize exaggeration is in teaching workshop participants a new skill. Sometimes it is most helpful to see in an exaggerated way how *not* to do something. For instance, in a session on "motivation," the facilitator might begin by role playing in an obviously exaggerated fashion the most unmotivating, boring speaker imaginable. One well-known structured experience on listening requires one participant to attempt to communicate something while the other participant engages in exaggerated nonlistening behaviors, ranging from obvious boredom to outright rudeness. In such cases, the exaggeration brings both behaviors and feelings into perspective without threatening the participants.

Energize

Humor is contagious. It provides a "shot in the arm" and is effective for warming up a group. It also provides a refreshing break (remember, the head cannot take any more than the seat can). A good example of an energizing activity is found in Weinstein and Goodman (1980); it is called Four Up. The directions to the participants are as follows: *"This is a game with very simple rules. We'll start sitting down. Anyone can stand up whenever she or he wants to, but you cannot remain standing for more than five seconds at a time before you sit down again. Then you can get right up again if you want to. Our objective as a group is to have exactly four people standing at all times."*

Enhance

Humor is a powerful tool; it can be used for constructive purposes or it can be used destructively. A few guidelines can be employed to help to determine if humor is being used to enhance the workshop. If the humor (either spontaneous or planned) is related to the theme of the workshop—as opposed to jokes for the sake of telling jokes—it is most likely to serve a constructive purpose. If the humor is used to encourage the participants' readiness to learn, it probably will make a positive contribution to the program. If the humor is in the form of laughing with people, rather than laughing at people, it probably will enhance the experience. The check list that follows can help to distinguish between laughing *with* others and laughing *at* others.

Laughing with Others	*Laughing at Others*
1. Going for the jocular vein	1. Going for the jugular vein
2. Based on caring and empathy	2. Based on contempt and insensitivity
3. Building confidence	3. Destroying confidence through put-downs
4. Involving people in the fun	4. Excluding some people
5. Letting a person make the choice to be the "butt" of a joke (laughing at yourself)	5. Not letting a person make the choice to be the "butt" of a joke
6. Amusing and inviting people (to laugh)	6. Abusing and offending people
7. Supporting people	7. Putting people down
8. Bringing people closer together	8. Dividing people
9. Leading to positive repartee	9. Leading to a "onedownsmanship" cycle
10. Poking fun at universal human foibles	10. Reinforcing stereotypes by singling a particular group

The workshop atmosphere and the participants' self-esteem can be enhanced by laughing with people and can be destroyed by laughing at people. As a famous man did not say: You can make fools of some of the people all of the time, and all of the people some of the time, but you will pay for it. Negative humor is costly. It probably also is unethical.

Extend

The goal of most workshops is to help people to extend their workshop learnings to their roles in their private lives or organizations. The use of humor in the workshop setting can help participants to realize the benefits of incorporating more humor and more laughter into their personal and professional lives. This realization can be enhanced if the facilitator initiates some of the following.

1. *A Humor Chain Letter.* Make up a roster of workshop participants. After the workshop, send something humorous (a cartoon, joke, or quotation related to some topic or theme that was raised during the workshop) to the first person on the roster. That person would then add something humorous and send both items to the next person on the list, and so on.

2. *A Jargon Dictionary*. This is one way for professionals to take themselves with a grain of salt. Individuals could make lists of common words or phrases used in their organizations, along with humorous definitions. Here are some examples from one group:

"Negotiate" = argue.
"I'm comfortable with that" = "I'm tired" or "I trust you to do the work."
"Brainstorm" = No one knows the answer, but if we all talk at once... .
"Under consideration" = The issue is dead.
"I'll have to think about it" = I'll have to figure out how to get you to agree with me.

3. *Adding Some Magic—Literally*. Many magic tricks are excellent vehicles for illustrating ideas as well as for evoking laughter and a sense of wonder. Goodman and Furman (1981) suggest dozens of easy-to-do but impressive tricks along with hundreds of ways to use them in a workshop setting.

4. *The Court Jester*. On a rotating basis, have different people assume the role of court jester during the workshop sessions. The jester is responsible for providing an energizer or for injecting humor during a break (e.g., by doing a skit, by playing a funny excerpt from a comedy album, by sharing some of his or her definitions from the jargon dictionary). This helps to enable people to take themselves less seriously while continuing to take their jobs and responsibilities seriously.

5. *A Humor First-Aid Kit*. Laughter really is the best medicine! A humor first-aid kit should consist of sure-fire stimuli, e.g., favorite humorous sayings, a comedy record, cartoons, ridiculous photographs, or riddles. He (or she) who laughs, lasts!

CONCLUSION

The above guidelines (eight is enough) are some of the ingredients that can turn workshops into really enjoyable experiences, both for the participants and for the facilitator. Yes, it is possible to make sense of humor.

REFERENCES

Allen, W. My speech to the graduates. *The New York Times*, August 10, 1979.

Goodman, J. (Ed.). *Laughing matters*. Saratoga Springs, NY: Sagamore Institute, 1982.

Goodman, J., & Furman, I. *Magic and the educated rabbit*. Paoli, PA: Instructo/McGraw-Hill, 1981.

Weinstein, M., & Goodman, J. *Playfair: Everybody's guide to noncompetitive play*. San Luis Obispo, CA: Impact Publishers, 1980.

***Joel Goodman, Ed.D.**, is the director of The HUMOR Project and consultation services at Sagamore Institute, Saratoga Springs, New York. He is the author of seven books and over forty articles and is the editor of* Laughing Matters, *a quarterly that focuses on the use of humor. In recent years, Dr. Goodman has taught graduate courses, led workshops, consulted, and given speeches for over 30,000 facilitators, managers, teachers, business-people, and helping professionals on the constructive applications of humor.*

ENCOURAGEMENT: GIVING POSITIVE INVITATIONS

Daniel G. Eckstein

Parents, teachers, and managers (hereinafter called "helping persons") frequently ask how to motivate others more effectively. The philosophy and skill of encouragement are a means both of increasing motivation and of combating feelings of inadequacy.

Encouragement communicates trust, respect, and belief. Many psychologists contend that there are only two basic human emotions: love and fear. Encouragement communicates caring and movement toward others—love, whereas discouragement results in lowered self-esteem and alienation from others—fear. Yet, despite the intention to be encouraging, all too often, helping persons are, in fact, discouraging in their communications with others. An example is the manager or parent who "lets things go" as long as they are going well, and who comments only when things go wrong.

A crucial beginning to being a more encouraging person is to become more aware of and to eliminate discouraging messages. The five telltale signs that a message is discouraging are:

The "Red-Pencil" Effect, circling the mistakes of others. A frequent consequence of such "constructive criticism" is that the receiver of the message becomes preoccupied with his or her mistakes.

The Horizontal Versus the Vertical Plane of Interaction. The vertical plane is characterized by "oneupsmanship." The horizontal plane is characterized by equality and a mutual respect for all. Classification of people as superior or inferior and sexual, racial, and religious prejudice do not exist on this level.

Overperfectionism, an unrealistic notion that people should not make mistakes, leads people to become overly critical of themselves and to want to discover that others are worse. If people cannot make peace with themselves, they never will make peace with others.

Clinging to Old Patterns. A primary principle of child psychology is that children are good observers, but poor interpreters. When they observe someone dying, many children, being egocentric at the time, conclude that they killed the person. Many such irrational decisions and conclusions are habits, held over from the past. By means of a systematic life-style assessment, counselors often gently confront a client by noting: "Now that you are not a child anymore, perhaps you would like to look at some things differently." Reinforcing a static philosophy ("You've always been that way; you're not going to change") can actually inhibit change or growth.

Misused Psychological Tests. For people who doubt their own abilities, an "objective, scientific" test can be the ultimate discourager. Such tests often "label" people and the people then act in accordance with the labels. Although all tests obviously are not harmful, it is wise to remember that we build on strengths, not weaknesses. Thus, it is important to focus on people's assets whenever possible.

The goal is not to cease all discouragement completely; indeed, all helping persons at times need to confront others. The goal is to combine such confrontation with encouragement as a means of maximizing the ability to impact others positively. Dinkmeyer and Dreikurs (1963) note that the proper use of encouragement involves:

1. Valuing individuals as they are, not as their reputations indicate or as one hopes they will be. Believing in individuals as good and worthwhile will facilitate acting toward them in this manner.
2. Having faith in the abilities of others. This enables the helper to win confidence while building the self-respect of the other person.
3. Showing faith in others. This will help them to believe in themselves.
4. Giving recognition for effort as well as for a job well done.
5. Using a group to help the person develop. This makes practical use of the assumption that, for social beings, the need to belong is basic.
6. Integrating the group so that the individual can discover his or her place and begin working positively from that point.
7. Planning for success and assisting in the development of skills that are sequentially and psychologically paced.
8. Identifying and focusing on strengths and assets rather than on mistakes.
9. Using the interests of the individual in order to motivate learning and instruction.

Carl Reimer (1967) lists ten specific "words of encouragement."

1. "You do a good job of . . . ." People should be encouraged when they do not expect it, when they are not asking for it. It is possible to point out some useful act or contribution of everyone. Even a comment about something that may seem small and insignificant could have a significant positive impact.
2. "You have improved in . . . ." Growth and improvement are things we should expect from all. If any progress is noted, there is less chance of discouragement and individuals usually will continue to try.
3. "We like (enjoy) you, but we don't like what you do." People frequently feel disliked after having made mistakes or after misbehaving. A person, especially a child, should never think that he or she is not liked. Rather, it is important to distinguish between the individual and his or her behavior, between the act and the actor.
4. "You can help me (us, the others) by . . . ." To feel useful and helpful is important to everyone. Most people need only to be given the opportunity.
5. "Let us try it together." Individuals who think that they have to do things perfectly often are afraid to attempt something new for fear of making mistakes or failing.
6. "So you made a mistake; now, what can you learn from it?" There is nothing that can be done about what has happened, but a person always can do something about the future. Mistakes can teach a great deal, especially if people do not feel embarrassed for erring.
7. "You would like us to think that you can't do it, but we think that you can." This approach can be used when people say (or convey the impression) that something is too difficult for them and they hesitate even to try. An individual who tries and fails can be complimented for having the courage to try. One's expectations should be consistent with the person's ability and maturity.
8. "Keep trying; don't give up." When someone is trying, but not meeting with much success, a comment like this can be helpful.
9. "I am sure that you can straighten this out (solve this problem), but if you need any help, you know where you can find me." Express confidence that others are able and will resolve their own conflicts, if given a chance.

10. "I can understand how you feel, but I'm sure that you will be able to handle it." Sympathizing with the other person seldom helps because it suggests that life has been unfair. Empathizing (understanding the situation) and believing in the person's ability to adjust to it is of much greater help.

"Giving positive invitations" is another way to describe the process of encouragement. Such invitations help to increase people's self-confidence by at least four different methods:

1. Self-affirmation—a renewed appreciation of one's personal strengths, motivators, values, and peak experiences.
2. Self-determination—being able to take responsibility for one's life without blaming others.
3. Self-motivation—setting goals and taking the action necessary to reach those goals by integrating one's emotions and intellect with one's body.
4. Increased empathic regard for others.

Many people's feelings of inadequacy can be overcome by prolonged exposure to positive affirmation. Of course, the process of encouragement may take longer with some individuals than with others. One may be tempted to admit defeat and discouragement much too soon. An optimistic rather than a pessimistic attitude and a proactive rather than a reactive affirmation of the basic worth of all people can help anyone to be a more effective "helper." Encouragement can assist people to rediscover their values and joys, to identify their strengths instead of dwelling on their mistakes, to challenge and change old patterns, and to have the courage to be imperfect!

REFERENCES

Dinkmeyer, D., & Dreikurs, R. *Encouraging children to learn: The encouragement process.* Englewood Cliffs, NJ: Prentice-Hall, 1963.

Reimer, C. Ten words of encouragement. In V. Soltz, *Study group leader's manual.* Chicago: Alfred Adler Institute, 1967.

Daniel G. Eckstein, Ph.D., is a licensed psychologist and a senior consultant for University Associates, Inc., San Diego, California. He is the co-author of four books on life-style assessment and affective education. His current interests include personal and systems power; sports psychology; organization development; and encouragement laboratories. He also is a professor of psychology for the University of Humanistic Studies, San Diego/Maui.

TOWARD MORE EFFECTIVE MEETINGS

Mike M. Milstein

Meetings *potentially* can perform several integrative functions. First, they can provide an excellent forum in which members of a group can share information and clarify their preferences. Second, they can enable wide input into decisions that might affect the group's members. Third, when decisions for action are made, meetings can help to identify members who have the ability to perform tasks and increase the probability that these persons actually will carry them out. Finally, meetings can bring group members together to remind them that they share common values and purposes even though they may have different roles.

Unfortunately, most meetings do not live up to their potential. Organizational members frequently regard meetings as a waste of time and something to be avoided unless absolutely necessary. Common complaints are that meetings are:

1. Too long;
2. Boring;
3. Dominated by formal leaders or by a few influential or verbal people;
4. Poorly organized and/or poorly led;
5. Called too frequently or, just as bad, not frequently enough;
6. Diverted by members with hidden agendas;
7. Subverted by members whose behaviors are destructive; or
8. Not focused on important issues.

Most people who attend such meetings leave wondering how they are related to the group's purposes or ongoing activities and thinking that "there must be a better way!"

Meetings that come closer to fulfilling their potential functions are guided by basic rules regarding their planning, conduct, and follow-up. Such rules reduce members' frustrations while increasing the potential for productivity; thus, the meetings become meaningful encounters in which people work hard, produce important outcomes, and leave with a sense of accomplishment.

PREPARATION

What actually happens during a meeting is as dependent on careful planning as it is on meeting-management techniques. The following rules can help leaders to avoid some common traps.

1. *Define the Purposes of the Meeting.* A clear notion of what is to be accomplished is the foundation on which everything else rests. Not only should the leader have a good idea of what he or she wants to accomplish, but, equally important, the suggestions of the group members should be solicited. This feedback helps to assure that the meeting will focus on relevant issues. It also promotes anticipation, curiosity, and preparation.

2. *Develop an Agenda.* Once considerations are identified, they should be sequenced in a formal agenda so that those topics that are most urgent appear at the beginning of the meeting. This increases the likelihood that the most relevant issues actually will be considered.

3. *Distribute the Agenda Prior to the Meeting.* Keeping the group members informed about the pending meeting increases their senses of responsibility and helps them to be aware of the purposes of the meeting, prepared to attend it, and, one would hope, more enthusiastic about participating.

CONDUCTING MEETINGS: SEQUENCING ACTIVITIES

With the preparation completed, the next concern is to conduct the actual meeting. The following rules describe how to manage a meeting.

1. *Start on Time.* It is very frustrating for members to have to wait for other members before the meeting can begin. Starting on time, even if only a few people are present, sets a precedent and suggests that members should be more punctual. It also rewards those who arrive on time.

2. *Review the Agenda and Set Priorities.* Initially, agenda items may need to be removed, combined, reordered, or added (as new business at the end of the agenda). This review provides a check on the planning and gives the group members one more opportunity to take responsibility for the meeting.

3. *Stick to the Agenda.* A common problem occurs when the leader allows the members to explore new topics before completing the established agenda. Such a discussion is likely to be unsatisfactory because there has been no opportunity for systematic preparation of information. More important, it is likely that other agenda items will not be explored because discussion of the new topic will take up allotted time. Group members may not like being constrained to agendas, but they are even more dissatisfied when many agenda items remain unexplored. Leaders can minimize this problem by consistently requiring that any topic raised at a meeting be put under "new business" and considered after the listed agenda has been completed (or put on the agenda for the next meeting if no time remains).

4. *Assign Responsibilities and Establish Target Dates for Task Accomplishment.* Decisions that call for tasks to be performed require, either during the meeting or soon thereafter, that members be assigned to carry them out within established time periods. This not only promotes task accomplishment but also provides a clear sign to the group that decisions made at meetings will be pursued. Nothing motivates group members more than seeing that things are done!

5. *Summarize Agreements Reached.* Reviewing the outcomes of a meeting reminds group members about the major decisions that were reached. Assuming that feedback is permitted during the leader's summary, it also enables members to correct any misinterpretations the leader may have made. This activity also provides a sense of completion for the members and increases the potential that members will leave in agreement about what occurred.

6. *Close the Meeting at or Before the Agreed-On Time.* Leaders who ask group members to stay for "just a few minutes longer" to complete a "critical" agenda item may be perceived as being insensitive to others. It usually is better to end on time or even a few minutes early. Members will appreciate the leader's concern about their other commitments. If the agenda is organized appropriately, items that are scheduled for the end of the agenda, except in extraordinary circumstances, can be put off until the next meeting. It probably is an indication of insufficient planning if many agenda items are left over on a regular basis.

7. *Keep a Written Record.* Clear, complete, and accurate minutes are important because they provide the group and the leader with the ability to recall decisions that were made, actions that were called for, and responsibilities that were assigned. The minutes remind members to get on

with their tasks. Equally important, conflicting interpretations of meeting outcomes can be minimized if complete and accurate minutes are available.

CONDUCTING MEETINGS: DEALING WITH DIFFICULT MEMBERS

If some members of a group behave in ways that are disruptive, participation becomes difficult for others. The leader must learn to deal with the following behaviors:

1. Talking for the sake of being heard;
2. Conducting side conversations;
3. Challenging attempts to move the group toward decisions;
4. Joking about everything that happens;
5. Interpreting criticism of ideas as personal attacks;
6. Waving off or negating all suggestions or new ideas from others;
7. Urging the group to take action before a problem is clearly identified;
8. Insisting on a precise, clear definition of each idea to the point that the group becomes bogged down.

Such disruptive behaviors may occur because preparation for the meeting has been inadequate. Clarification of purposes and development of a tight agenda keep the group focused on tasks and can reduce disruptive behaviors.

However, even with careful preparation, some disruptive behaviors may be exhibited. It often may be possible to help difficult group members to channel their energies toward more positive effects. The following rules can help to improve the leader's ability to deal with difficult members (see also Jones, 1980).

1. *Listen, but Do Not Debate.* Troublesome members cannot simply be turned off or tuned out. Although it is difficult, it is best to work at bringing troublesome members into the mainstream of the discussion. When they feel that their views are respected, such members often begin to accept responsibility for controlling their own behaviors.

2. *Talk Privately with Members Who Continually Exhibit Disruptive Behaviors.* Publicly chastising difficult members can have detrimental effects: they may increase their negative behaviors or withdraw entirely from participation in the group. Public confrontations are best reserved as a last resort. Private conferences in which the leader's concerns are presented and the disruptive members' views are solicited provide confidential opportunities for members as well as leaders to explain their feelings and needs and promote the potential for agreements to be reached. This strategy preserves the members' sense of dignity, spares the rest of the group from witnessing embarrassing confrontations, and conserves precious meeting time. It is important to remember, during such conferences, that the focus is to be on the members' disruptive *behaviors*, not on the members' overall personalities or past histories.

3. *Turn Negative Behaviors into Positive Contributions.* It should not be assumed that all difficult members want to subvert meetings. Some may want to make positive contributions, but have not found the appropriate means to do so. Leaders can help disruptive members to find more productive ways of harnessing their energies to the group's needs. For example, leaders can encourage disruptive members to participate in planning sessions, ask for their suggestions during meetings, and give them the responsibility to perform tasks that result from decisions made in the meetings. Although some may not be responsive to such initiatives, many disruptive individuals, when so approached, become active and productive members.

4. *Encourage the Group to Share the Responsibility for Handling Difficult Members.* If the group members share maintenance activities with the leader, it is more likely that negative behaviors will decrease. Group censure puts pressure on disruptive members to modify their

behaviors. It is one thing to risk the wrath of the leader and quite another to risk censure by the entire group.

FOLLOW-UP

Following up is as important as conducting the meeting. It translates decisions made at meetings into tangible results, including, for example, the development of policy statements, the design of new procedures, and the collection of information. If the follow-up is adequate, subsequent meetings will be viewed positively. If the follow-up is not sufficient, subsequent meetings may be anticipated unenthusiastically. Following three specific rules can help to make this critical stage more effective.

1. *Edit and Distribute the Minutes Promptly.* Soon after a meeting, the leader, along with the recorder, should go over the minutes to check them for accuracy, completeness, and clarity. The minutes, once approved by the group at its next meeting, become a definitive record that can help to resolve differing interpretations and to remind the leader and others of commitments made to pursue certain activities. Therefore, it is a good idea to distribute the minutes to group members while the meeting is still fresh in their memories. The minutes also help to remind group members of the relationship of any given meeting to the purposes of the group or organization.

2. *Encourage the Completion of Tasks.* Nothing promotes belief that meetings are relevant as much as task completion. Leaders should not hesitate to remind members of their commitments and, periodically, to check on the progress being made. It also is a good strategy to publicize the progress of work that is being carried out. This gives recognition to those doing the work and encourages them to complete their tasks as expeditiously as possible.

3. *Put Unfinished Business on the Agenda for the Next Meeting.* Each agenda item is of interest to at least one group member or it would not have appeared in the first place. Those who requested discussion of a topic that is not treated at one meeting will watch closely to see whether it appears on the next meeting's agenda. Be sure to include such items on the agenda that is sent to group members for review before the next meeting.

SUMMARY

The full cycle of meeting-related activities includes preparation, conducting the meeting, and follow-up. Completion of the follow-up phase flows into the preparation phase for the next meeting.

REFERENCE

Jones, J. E. Dealing with disruptive individuals in meetings. In J. W. Pfeiffer & J. E. Jones (Eds.) *The 1980 annual handbook for group facilitators.* San Diego, CA: University Associates, 1980.

Mike M. Milstein, Ph.D., is a professor of educational administration for the State University of New York at Buffalo, where he teaches graduate courses in the areas of OD diagnosis and intervention in educational organizations. He also is doing long-term stress-management projects in schools. Dr. Milstein has published widely on the topics of changing organizations and the politics of education. He also is a founder of and partner in Creative Management Associates, a training and consulting firm.

A GUIDE TO PROBLEM SOLVING

Dean Elias and Paul David

Problem solving is a fundamental process that remains the same regardless of the problem. Of course, the complexity of the process changes with the nature of the problem.

CRITICAL VERSUS CREATIVE

Problem solving is, in many ways, simply a process of information management. Social scientists have discovered that one of the most significant barriers to effective problem solving is that people fail to make use of information that they already have. Like the computer, the brain consists of two components: a storage unit and a processing unit. Although the storage unit can hold a great amount of information, the capacity of the processing unit is quite limited. The average person can effectively manage no more than about seven independent variables of information at one time. When a problem begins to exceed this level of complexity, people overlook elements, perceive the wrong elements, or fail to make the right combinations of elements.

Another significant barrier to effective problem solving is that people often fail to use their creative faculties in searching for answers. The processing unit of the brain consists of both critical and imaginative functions. The critical function analyzes, compares, evaluates, and selects relevant information. The imaginative function generates, visualizes, abstracts, and foresees combinations of information. Both synthesize information, but the imaginative function creates ideas whereas the critical function delivers judgments. Both functions must operate mutually for successful problem solving.

For most individuals, judgment grows with age while creativity dwindles. The formation of adult habits and a critical self-image often limit creative abilities, while education and a career often promote the development of only judicial faculties. This overemphasis on judgment creates a tendency to see only the negative side of situations. In creative problem solving, one must turn off the critical function and use the imaginative function. Otherwise, premature judgment may limit creative possibilities or even eliminate any ideas that are generated.

Systematic Creativity

Creativity is mental activity characterized by both subjective and objective thinking. It is a process of alternating back and forth between what we sense and what we know. A key to productive creativity is to control the alternation of subjective and objective thinking so that the critical and imaginative functions complement each other.

A DEFINITION OF PROBLEM SOLVING

Problem solving is creating change to bring actual conditions closer to conditions that are desired. A problem is a discrepancy between current conditions and desired conditions. A goal is a result that will reduce the discrepancy. There are two basic aspects of problem solving:

decision making and *problem analysis*. Decision making consists of determining goals and choosing courses of action to reach those goals. Problem analysis consists of identifying factors that impede goal achievement and determining the forces that bear on those factors. The essential elements of *planning* depend on accurate problem analysis and shrewd decision making. These elements are determining if a particular problem is significant, setting realistic goals, describing the major forces that affect the problem, and showing how a specific set of interventions can ameliorate the problem.

Major Premises

The steps in the problem-solving process are based on the following premises:

1. The most powerful action in problem solving is becoming more aware of the problem. This is the so-called paradox of change: starting off by trying to change conditions seems to exacerbate the problem, while accepting the full measure of the problem begins to solve it.

2. Problems have many causes, not just one. Every situation can be described as a field of forces—various psychological, social, political, economic, and cultural factors—held in dynamic balance. To produce change, we first must see clearly what forces are at work and how they are balanced. Then we must search pragmatically for the most effective place(s) to intervene in the field of forces in order to change the balance, rather than search for the one "cause" that seems most logical.

3. Valid decisions depend on adequate information. Adequate means accurate, clear, and complete. To draw an analogy, the recipe (process) depends on the ingredients (information).

4. Working with others can improve the process. A group of informed people working on a problem can compress into a few hours the mental work that might take months for only one person. In addition, the members of a group tend to risk more novel approaches than do individuals working by themselves.

5. Getting good results from a valid decision requires that those who must carry out the decision understand and be committed to it. A decision might be technically sound, but politically unreliable, or those who are responsible for implementing it may not be committed to or capable of doing so.

6. The "change agent" must develop a supportive environment:

   a. The people who experience the problem should share authority for making any decisions for change.

   b. Those who participate in the problem-solving process should have a trusting relationship and should communicate openly about the problem.

STEPS IN PROBLEM SOLVING

The problem-solving process is a cyclical feedback system. It is essentially continuous, with no real beginning or end, and the completion of each step affects the definitions of the previous steps. These steps are depicted in Figure 1.

1. Assess the Situation

Before launching a strategy for change, it is important to assess the problem in terms of whether action really is needed and whether it actually will have some impact on the problem.

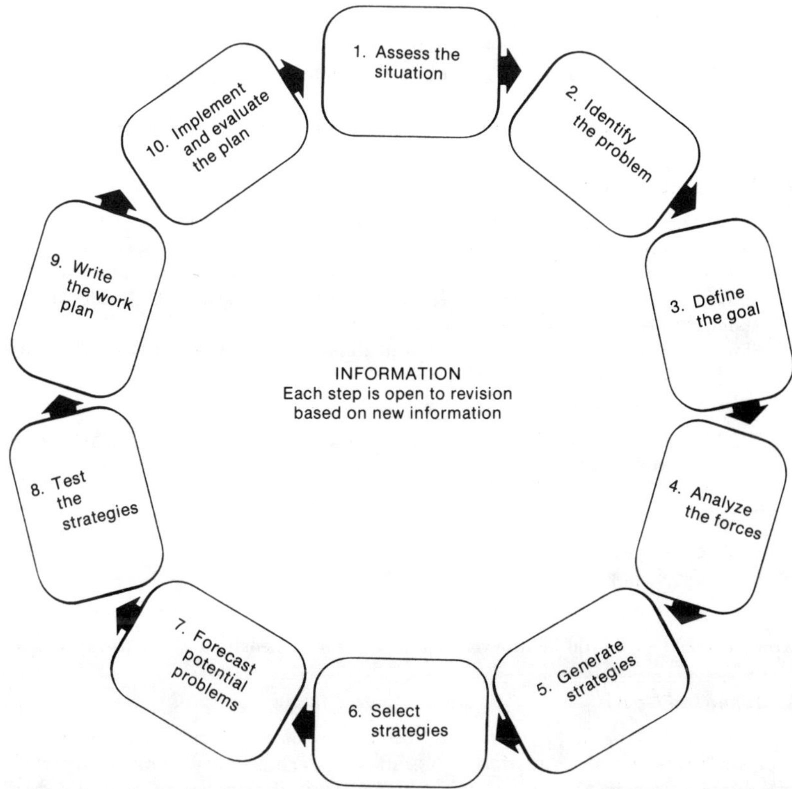

Figure 1. Cycle of Problem Solving

To assess the situation, answer the following questions:

1. What is occurring that requires change?
2. What will result if nothing changes?
3. Can any significant change actually be effected?
4. Can the relevant information be obtained?
5. Does the situation deserve the effort (right now) compared with other priorities and interests?
6. Are the persons involved in the situation committed to making a change?
7. At which step in the process should the effort begin?
    - To remove or reduce a deficient condition, begin with major step 2 and go through all the steps.

- To develop an improved strategy (rather than change a deficiency), begin with major step 5, although steps 3 and 4 can provide some useful tools.
- If there is a plan of action that has not been tested or put into practice, begin with major step 7.
- If a tested strategy simply has not been put into practice, begin with major step 10.

2. Identify the Problem

One of the most crucial and difficult steps in the process is identifying the actual problem. Problems usually are obscure, disguised, or locked inside some emotional distress, attitude conflict, or misleading outgrowth of another situation. Another major difficulty is in determining the standard by which a deficient condition is measured. Unless we are clear about our standards, we cannot be clear about our problems.

This step may take a long time and may include several revisions, but the effort is well spent. A problem that is well stated is half solved.

To identify the problem, answer the following questions:

1. What is specifically desired that is not happening? What are the standards or values that apply to the situation?
2. What is happening (described in objective and observable terms)?
   - Who is involved?
   - Where does it occur?
   - When does it occur?
   - What is the extent of the problem, that is, how many or how much?

Now the problem should be summarized in one comprehensive and concise statement.

3. Define the Goal

The definition of the goal is a statement of what is to be done about the problem. It should be expressed in measurable terms, that is, the results to be achieved in the form of observable and/or behavioral outcomes. Abstract or subjective statements of outcome are impossible to assess.

To define the goal (the desired conditions), define or answer the following:

1. Results—the outcomes expected:
   - What specifically is to result?
   - Who will be involved?
   - When will the result be achieved?
   - Where will the result occur?
2. Criteria—measures for acceptability:
   - What are the quantitative standards that indicate the minimum level of goal achievement?
   - What are the qualitative standards that indicate the minimum level of goal achievement?
3. Conditions—the perimeters of the effort:
   - What limitations or restrictions in terms of time and/or money are to be imposed?
   - What resources in terms of people and/or equipment are required?

Now the goal should be summarized in one comprehensive and concise statement, then checked to make sure that it describes an outcome rather than a strategy. It is important not to confuse *ends* with *means* at this point.

4. Analyze the Forces

This step is to collect, organize, and analyze all the relevant information regarding the current situation as a foundation for creating a creative and realistic plan for change. At this point, it is very helpful to involve people who are familiar with the situation.

This step has two aspects: past circumstances that have influenced the formation of the problem and present factors (forces) that affect the achievement of the goal.

1. Past Circumstances

    To have a clear picture of the circumstances from which the issue evolved, answer the following questions:

    - What are the past decisions, occurrences, and factors that created the present problem situation?

    - What was the context in which these circumstances occurred?

    - Were any payoffs or benefits derived from these past decisions or actions? If so, what were they and who benefited from them?

2. Present Factors (Force-Field Analysis)

    Force-field analysis, developed by Kurt Lewin (1951), is a tool for organizing and analyzing information as a basis for a change effort. Any situation can be considered as a dynamic balance of forces working in opposite directions. Forces moving toward change, helping forces, are opposed by an equal number of forces moving in the opposite direction, hindering forces. No change will take place in the situation unless an imbalance of these forces is created. The procedure involves identifying the problem, determining the goal that the group or individual wishes to achieve, listing the helping forces and the hindering forces, and assessing each force in terms of its strength and vulnerability to change.

    An important aspect of this procedure is brainstorming, a group process designed to produce a large number of ideas in a short period of time. While someone writes down what is said, the members of the group spontaneously and quickly express their ideas, more or less by free association. No comments or criticisms are permitted; anything and everything offered is noted. Each participant is encouraged to say whatever he or she wishes, no matter how unusual or unrealistic it may appear.

The Procedure

Summarize the problem in the middle of a sheet of paper. Summarize the goal at the right side of the sheet. Then use brainstorming to create a list of present helping forces and enter these on the left half of the sheet. Make a similar list of present hindering forces on the right half of the sheet. Be as specific as possible.

The next step is to eliminate repetition and clarify items. Then, for each of the two lists, rate each item in terms of its strength, with the strongest being rated 10 and the rest rated on a scale of 1 to 10, compared with the strongest.

Next, for each of the two lists, rate each item with a strength of 5 or above in terms of how vulnerable it is to change efforts. Start by rating the easiest to change as 10; then weigh the other items on a scale of 1 to 10, in contrast with the easiest. This will provide a picture of how easily each force can be controlled or influenced.

Finally, identify and list the items for additional information as needed and proceed to obtain that information.

Once the analysis is completed, alternative strategies for creating an imbalance—or creating change—can be developed. In general, this change can occur through any of the following alternatives:

- Changing the strength of any force,
- Changing the direction of any force,
- Withdrawing hindering forces, or
- Adding new helping forces.

It often is best to begin by working with hindering forces. Increasing helping forces often increases resistance (it is a law of physics that every action has an equal and opposite reaction). Strategies for change that are directed toward reducing hindering forces generally are more effective.

5. Generate Alternative Strategies

The first step is to review and revise the goal if the intervening steps have helped to clarify it. The next steps are quite unlike the systematic problem analysis. They require quite a different orientation—an openness to the absurd, spontaneous, and poetic resources of the preconscious. In these steps, creativity and invention are employed and logic and proportion are suspended.

1. Fantasizing

   Attention is focused on the specifications of the goal and the people involved. For about two minutes, everyone fantasizes freely about a solution to the problem. The fantasies are then shared and compared to see what patterns are present as well as what elements are different from others.

2. Brainstorming

   First considering those hindering forces that are strong and vulnerable, brainstorm actions to remove or minimize them. The process then is repeated with the helping forces that are strong and vulnerable. When ideas no longer flow freely, repetition is eliminated and statements are clarified.

3. Synthesizing

   The list of items is synthesized by identifying logical combinations. All items that have an organic or logical connection (e.g., credit checks or interest charges) are identified with the same letter. Each combination is then defined by a brief description of the strategy to be used, and, where appropriate, one or more are linked to provide more comprehensive possibilities.

6. Select the Best Strategy

This step uses a matrix to compare alternative strategies with decision-making criteria. This enables decision makers to be as precise as possible about the relative value of any one strategy or combination of strategies. There are two alternative procedures.

Fixed-Criteria Procedure

A "quick and dirty" distinction can be made by selecting the criteria of most benefit and least cost. Cost/benefit criteria are listed vertically and alternative strategies are listed horizontally. Using the rating system employed in the force-field analysis, assign a value of 10 to the alternative with the highest benefit and lowest cost and then rate the others on a scale of 1 to 10. Select the alternatives with the best combinations of benefit and cost.

Goal-Criteria Procedure

Review the goal and identify each element that can be described as a criterion or measure. Segregate into two categories (IN/OUT and WANTS) criteria by which to measure alternatives. IN/OUT criteria represent minimum conditions that an alternative must satisfy to be considered further, i.e., alternatives meet these criteria or are tossed out. Alternatives that do meet minimum conditions are then evaluated by WANTS criteria, i.e., which is preferable? The key measure is the comparison among the criteria. If the relative importance of the criteria listed under WANTS differs, assign each a weight of 10 and weigh each against that criterion using a scale of 1 to 10.

Screen out alternatives using the IN/OUT criteria; then compare the alternatives against each WANT criterion in turn and assign a rating. Use the rating mechanism described previously. Multiply the *weight* for each criterion by the *rating* for each alternative. Compare the resulting scores.

If the alternative with the highest score has face validity, a tentative decision can be made. If it does not, the next highest alternative should be reviewed.

7. Forecast Potential Problems

The next step is to test the feasibility of the selected course of action. Again, it will help if people who are involved, affected by, or have technical knowledge about the situation participate. Looking at the preferred course of action, carry out the following steps:

1. Brainstorm a list of things that could go wrong and list every idea.
2. Rate each potential problem in terms of *probability*. Using 10 as a rating for certainty, assign each item a score from 1 to 10.
3. For each item that received a rating of 5 or more (seems probable), rerate it in terms of *threat*. Using 10 as a rating for catastrophe, assign each item a score from 1 to 10.
4. For items with ratings of 4 or more on both scales, seek preventive actions; if you cannot prevent the problem, seek a contingency action to keep the problem from having a serious impact.
5. For an alternative with preventive or contingency actions, if no crippling potential problems seem likely, the preferred course of action should be sound.
6. If problems still seem likely, return to major step 6. Select another alternative and repeat the steps for forecasting and analyzing potential problems.

8. Test the Strategy

Before beginning to carry out any strategy for change, it is important to test the strategy. Testing may reveal more potential problems and also may clarify the extent to which the ability and commitment exist to carry out the strategy. The result in most instances is a refinement of the strategy that will increase its effectiveness.

The test to be used will be dictated by the nature of the strategy. If the strategy is interpersonal, role playing may suffice. If the strategy is technical (change in policy, procedures, or methods), a brief trial period with a small number of people may suffice. The test should give some indication of the plan's feasibility.

9. Write a Work Plan

The next step is to develop a work plan that delineates the activities necessary to carry out the strategy. This should account not only for the activities that directly relate to implementing the strategy but also for any contingency to prevent potential problems. To complete this step, complete the following:

1. List all the tasks required to carry out the selected course of action.
2. Order the tasks in chronological sequence.

3. Write a plan that (at minimum) accounts for the following:
   - Tasks—What needs to be done.
   - Primary responsibilities—who is going to carry out the tasks, and
   - Deadlines—when the tasks are going to be accomplished.

10. Implement and Evaluate the Plan

The process at this point may seem overwhelming. However, if the chosen strategy seems to be right, the following may help:

1. Act as if you can carry it out. Simply go ahead and do it.
2. Forgive and remember. If errors are made while the strategy is being carried out, forgive the lapse, remember the goal, and carry on.
3. Evaluate and revise. Be aware of the consequences of any action, and if the plan is not progressing, either revise it or return to major step 1.

REFERENCES

Kepner, C. H., & Tregoe, B. B. *The rational manager.* New York: McGraw-Hill, 1965.

Lewin, K. *Field theory in social science* (D. Cartwright, Ed.) New York: Harper & Row, 1951.

__Dean Elias__ is the regional director of Antioch University, Seattle, Washington, and teaches group process, consultation, adult learning, and organizational learning. He also is a private consultant, specializing in executive team development and planning of preferred futures. Mr. Elias has developed models for using higher education programs in community development with Indian reservations, learning models for preparing work groups to develop new institutions, and strategies for peer teaching in undergraduate and graduate education.

__Paul David__ is a psychotherapist in private practice and a consultant-trainer with Human Development Trust, Inc., Seattle, Washington. His clinical interests are in therapy for couples and groups, and his consultation specialties are in training trainers, interpersonal communication, and team building. Mr. David is an adjunct faculty member at Antioch University West and at Western Washington University. He teaches counseling and industrial psychology and is engaged in research on characteristics of mental health practitioners in private practice.

A LOOK AT QUALITY CIRCLES

H.B. Karp

In the past twenty years, the field of human resource development has evolved from the vast amount of theories and techniques produced in the behavioral sciences and aimed at increasing organizational productivity and/or individual effectiveness. The latest addition to the field of human resource development, and one that is enjoying a great deal of success, is the concept of quality circles (QCs). Although the QC certainly is not a panacea for all organizational problems, the data derived over the last three years indicates that, if installed properly and nurtured carefully, this approach has high potential for dealing with issues of productivity and worker involvement.

BACKGROUND AND DEFINITION

First implemented in Japan in 1962, quality circles are an outcome of American thinking, the result of quality-control technology introduced to Japan by Deming and Juran and behavioral science inputs from Herzberg, McGregor, and Maslow. In effect, quality circles are the latest refinement of organization development technology that has been developed and practiced in the United States since the early Sixties.

A quality circle is a group of three to ten people from the same work area that voluntarily meets on a regular basis—usually for one hour, once a week—to identify, analyze, and solve problems in that work area. Although frequently thought of only in terms of manufacturing plants, the quality circle is useful in any organization in which effectiveness can be measured and there is an authentic concern for increased productivity and human potential.

A quality-circle program has two major objectives: (a) to improve the quality of management within the organization, and (b) to tap the creative problem-solving skills of the workers. Although increased productivity and cost reductions usually are two of the results, these are the *measures* of a successful program and *not* its objectives. Some other benefits derived from an effective quality-circle program are improved communication, improved attendance, increases in performance and productivity, better teamwork, and enhanced technical knowledge.

STRUCTURE

Although the quality circle focuses on the worker, everyone in the organization is, to some degree, actively or passively affected. In a QC program, there are seven categories that encompass the entire working force of an organization.

Steering Committee

The steering committee is comprised of people who represent various functional areas in the organization, usually mid- and upper-level managers, and it may include the chief executive officer (CEO) and union leaders from within the organization. The responsibilities of the steering committee are to establish the quality-circle program; set policies, philosophy, procedures, and objectives; provide guidance and support; demonstrate management's commitment by setting high priorities on circle recommendations; meet and work closely with the facilitator; monitor effectiveness (usually quarterly); and provide needed resources.

The steering committee usually meets weekly during the organization phase of the program and may meet bimonthly once the program is established. Regardless of its scheduled meetings, the committee is always "on call" to respond to specific needs.

Facilitator

The facilitator is the key to the success of the program. When there are more than six circles operating, the facilitator usually holds a full-time position. The facilitator is responsible for training the circle leaders and members; meeting with each circle leader prior to the circle meeting to review the plans; forming the necessary links between the circle program and the rest of the organization; locating specialists to assist the circles with particular problems; maintaining records; coordinating circle activities; working with and being a member of the steering committee; assisting leaders and members with problems; and attending and monitoring circle meetings.

Circle Leader

Usually the circle leader is the first-line supervisor of the people who make up the circle. In some cases, however, the circle leader is selected by the steering committee or elected by the members. (This usually occurs when new circles are formed in one work area or department.) The responsibilities of the circle leader are to run the circle meetings; assist the facilitator in training the circle members in problem-solving techniques; meet with the facilitator prior to each meeting to review that meeting's agenda; act as liaison to other departments and support personnel; know and understand quality-circle tools and techniques; plan circle activities; and be an active member of the circle. The circle leader *must* use a participative approach during the circle meeting. The leader has only one vote and, generally, will use it only in order to break a tie.

Circle Member

The circle member is a worker who volunteers to participate in a quality circle. No one is required to participate and no one is barred. The responsibilities of the circle member include being trained in quality-circle techniques; attending and participating in all meetings; and identifying, analyzing, and implementing solutions to problems in the work area.

Top Management

Top management's support will either make or break the quality-circle program. Top management's responsibilities include making the final decisions concerning the quality-circle program and the recommendations of the individual circles; actively supporting the program; attending meetings at the invitation of the circles; and providing role models for participative management.

Middle Management

Although middle management plays no active role in the program, its support is vital to the success of the program. Middle management's responsibilities include not scheduling activities that conflict with circle meetings; openly supporting circle activities; implementing circle recommendations or explaining why they are not to be implemented; including circle activities in reports to higher management; and meeting periodically with circle leaders.

Noncircle Worker

Because participation in a quality circle is voluntary, there is always a segment of the work force that prefers not to be involved in the program. The noncircle worker continues on the job when the circle(s) for his or her department meet(s). The noncircle worker may, on occasion, be asked to provide consultative help on a circle project.

IMPLEMENTATION

If they are to be effective, quality circles must be planned thoroughly before being introduced into an organization. Typically, an organization will start with four to six circles and add one or two more circles at a time. A *minimum* of six months of planning and preparation is required from the time a decision is made to initiate a QC program until the first circles are operative. In most organizations, it is eight months to a year from the time of the decision before any results are expected. The process cannot be rushed! With minor variations, a typical start-up process will proceed through twelve steps.

Deciding to Proceed

The decision to begin a quality-circle program is made by the CEO of the organization, with whomever the CEO chooses to include in the process. This decision is made after the top management has been fully informed about the concept of quality circles.

Using a Consultant

Although it is not essential, using an external consultant has advantages. A qualified consulting firm can explain the program to top management, train the facilitator and the leaders, and help the organization to avoid pitfalls during the implementation of the program.

Introducing QCs to the Management Team

Once the decision is made to proceed, it is essential that all managers in the organization be informed and be given an opportunity to voice their support or resistance. It is also wise to include union leaders as soon as possible in the process. All managers and union leaders can be invited to a half-day training program in which a formal presentation of the nature and benefits of the QC program is made (by the external consultant or CEO). The participants then ask questions about how the program would affect their work areas.

Establishing a Data Base

Although not essential, it frequently is wise to obtain various measures of productivity in key areas of the organization before starting the program. Although increased productivity and decreased costs are not the objectives of the program, they are two of the usual benefits, and obtaining a data base in the beginnning is a good way to monitor the cost effectiveness of the program.

Selecting the Steering Committee

Because the steering committee is to provide the necessary support, especially during the early stages of the program, every functional area in the organization, including the union, should be represented. However, it is best not to *force* any manager to participate because it is necessary that the members of the steering committee be committed to the concept.

Selecting the Facilitator

The facilitator is the most important individual in terms of the success or failure of the program. The facilitator (usually chosen by the steering committee) can come from anywhere within the organization, but knowledge of the organization and its technical basis is a solid advantage. Some of the qualities essential in the facilitator are enthusiasm for the position; an ability to relate well to the workers; the respect of management and easy access to the CEO; a willingness to work hard (and at odd hours if circle meetings are to occur during second or third shifts); the capacity to teach others to teach; and good communication skills.

Informing All Employees of the Plan

Employees can be informed of the plan to start the program in a number of ways. The only requirement is that the approach be well thought out and well executed. One approach is to call a meeting of all employees and make a formal presentation. Another approach is to inform the employees in small groups. A third option is to inform the employees through letters sent to their homes. These letters would explain the program and would be signed by the CEO. Any approach can include subsequent meetings in which employees can ask questions and discuss their concerns about the program.

Selecting Circle Leaders

When all supervisors understand the nature of the program, the best approach is to ask for volunteers. Because a program usually begins with only four to six circles, there usually are more than enough volunteers. Circle leaders should have enthusiasm for the program, should work well with people, should not be involved in any serious union issues; and should be able to obtain measurable results from their units. Their units also should not have any unusual problems. If a supervisor refuses to participate, additional time is needed to explain the purpose and benefits of the approach and to understand the supervisor's resistance. If the supervisor still chooses not to participate, the steering committee can select a worker from the unit to be the circle leader, but this must be done with the supervisor's consent.

Forming Circles

Once the units and the circle leaders have been identified, workers from those units are asked to volunteer. In most cases, there will be more volunteers than the circle can absorb. The steering committee can provide a policy for selection, or the volunteers themselves can be asked to determine who should be included in the first circles. It is important that all volunteers be assured that they will be included as the program expands.

Training the Facilitator

Generally, a forty-hour program is required to train the facilitator. The first phase deals with the cognitive, problem-solving techniques that will be used in the circles: problem identification, data gathering, problem analysis, and presentation techniques. The second phase focuses on process (consultative) skills such as participative leadership, communication, team building, conflict management, and training people how to train.

Training the Circle Leaders

Generally, circle leaders undergo a twenty-hour training program. They are trained in the same problem-solving methods as is the facilitator and also in participative leadership skills.

Training the Circle Members

The first eight weeks of the circle's life are dedicated to the training of its members. After a thorough introduction to quality circles, the members receive eight hours of training in problem-solving techniques and presentation skills. Although the facilitator and the circle leaders may be trained by an outside consultant, the circle members are trained by the circle leader, with the facilitator's assistance.

THE CIRCLE MEETING

When all training has been completed, the circle picks a name for itself and then begins to meet for one hour, once a week, to deal with problems relating to the work area. The typical, one-hour, weekly meeting include opening remarks by the leader, a brief reading of minutes of the last meeting, the introduction of new topics, "next steps" on existing projects, work assignments (for circle projects) for the next week, and the closing.

Certain guidelines are always in effect and are agreed to by all members, for example: (a) criticize ideas, not people; (b) the only stupid question is the one not asked; (c) everyone in the group is responsible for the group's progress and process; and (d) be open to the ideas of others.

The types of issues that the circle will address are work quality, cost reduction, safety, work methods, tools and equipment, interorganizational communications, and process and procedures. A quality circle does *not* deal with issues such as wages and salaries, hours of work, personalities, new product design, hiring, firing, and disciplinary decisions. Ideas for discussion topics can come from many sources, e.g., circle members, managers, customers, or staff members; however, the selection is the circle's prerogative. Most circles can handle three to ten projects per year, depending on the complexity of the problems. If the circle requires outside information or assistance, the circle leader will contact the resource needed. Should the involvement of top management be needed to complete or approve a project, the circle will prepare a formal presentation. The circle also will make a presentation to top management periodically to review its progress.

PROGRAM COSTS

There obviously is a wide range in the cost of quality-circle programs. Much depends on whether or not an external consultant will be used, whether training packages will be developed or purchased, what the facilitator will be paid, and so on. If an organization were going to develop a complete program starting with six circles, but had no existing resources of its own, the total cost for the first year, including the cost for time off the job for the circle members, could be between $45,000 and $60,000. After the first year, the cost would be approximately $200 per week, per circle, including participants' time, the training room, materials, and so on. The most accurate perspective, of course, is to view the expense not in terms of "cost" but, rather, in terms of *investment*.

CAUSES OF PROGRAM FAILURE

Merely installing the technology correctly does not guarantee success in a quality-circle program. The following is a partial list of the factors that can cause a program to fail.

1. *Management Impatience:* demanding a rapid return on investment, expanding the program too quickly, cutting down on training time and/or start-up time, demanding that certain issues be considered by the circles, or unrealistic expectations.

2. *Lack of Management Support:* not making all needed information available to the circles; postponing circle meetings for *any* reason; not educating managers in the process; denying or forcing participation in the program; not publicizing the program internally; or establishing arbitrary criteria, deadlines, or cost-savings demands.

3. *Inadequate Implementation and Planning:* not using a facilitator or poor choice of facilitator; little support from the steering committee; little or no training; not following a formal pattern; not including union representatives; not planning for turnover of members or leaders; little management involvement; inadequate assessment of organizational readiness for the program; or poor coordination among the facilitator, the steering committee, and the CEO.

UNIQUE BENEFITS

The concept of quality circles is an *evolutionary* step in human resource development, but several aspects make it uniquely different from other techniques that have been and are being used.

It is the only approach that is initiated by management but run solely by the work force.

Although participative principles are underlying and essential elements of a quality-circle program, it actually has evolved into what could be called a "partnertive" approach. Management does *not* participate in a quality-circle program after it is installed and running; it merely provides support when needed. This is quite different from participative management, in which the goal is to include the worker in relevant management considerations.

It allows the installation of participative values in segments of the organization without abruptly changing the structure or value system of the organization.

The most important element in the survival and growth of a quality-circle program is management's philosophy concerning human resource development and quality of work life. There is no room for lip service. If there is an authentic commitment by top management to "humanize" an organization, but the commitment of middle and lower management is not strong, imposing "humanism" on these managers only increases their resistance. The quality-circle program provides a safe and functional structure in which those who are enthusiastic can participate and in which those who are not enthusiastic can observe and evaluate over time. In effect, it provides a mechanism whereby participative and humanistic work procedures can be absorbed slowly by the organization, rather than being forced on it.

The most beneficial payoffs occur externally to the program.

Although the circle meets under a strict set of participative rules, the circle leader is bound by them *only* during the circle meeting, one hour per week. The rest of the time, each leader is free to lead in his or her usual style. However, circle procedures gradually begin to permeate the day-to-day work life of the unit. Most successful programs report specific returns on investment in excess of 3 to 1, but the greatest payoff is in the increase in consciousness of quality and the better work relationships that result from the program.

It provides a constant, established base for ongoing training and development.

The circle provides a rich resource of training criteria. Workers learn to identify objectives, to analyze and solve problems, and to explore resources, along with numerous other work-related skills. The circle provides an established setting into which training can be introduced. Training can be more readily accepted and absorbed when the learner can see how the information can help in dealing with and overcoming work problems. Facilitators and leaders can apply additional process training not only to their circles but also to their day-to-day jobs.

H. B. Karp, Ph.D., serves as a consultant through his own organization, Personal Growth Systems, in Norfolk, Virginia. He conducts public and in-house workshops in the areas of leadership and supervisory effectiveness and consults to organizations in the areas of team building and conflict management. Dr. Karp's background is in organizational psychology, organization development, human motivation, and Gestalt applications to individual and organizational growth.

PREVENTING AND RESOLVING CONFLICT

Udai Pareek

Conflicts are not necessarily dysfunctional. Functional conflicts result in a desire for excellence and creativity and may take the form of healthy interpersonal or intergroup competition or Comp+ (Pareek, 1981). Functional conflicts also help a person to develop a sense of identity, a sense of responsibility, internal standards of performance, an urge to excel, individual creativity, and feelings of autonomy.

Conflicts are dysfunctional (Comp-) when they drain the energy of people or groups and reduce their effectiveness (Pareek, 1981). Unhealthy and dysfunctional competition often can be prevented by early diagnosis. The concept of "preventive medicine" applies to the management of conflict, as well as to the management of disease.

UNDERSTANDING THE SOURCES OF CONFLICT

Seven main sources of interpersonal and intergroup conflict are listed in the first column of Figure 1. Columns 2 and 4 show how group members perceive the various sources under each of two modes: conflict escalation or conflict prevention and resolution.

1 Sources of Potential Conflict	2 Perception Under Conflict-Escalation Mode	3 Resultant Orientation	4 Perception Under Conflict-Prevention-and-Resolution Mode	5 Resultant Orientation
Concern with Self	Narrow (Own)	Short-Term Perspective	Broader	Long-Term Perspective
Different Goals	Conflicting	Individualistic	Complementary	Superordination
Resource Issues	Limited	Fighting	Expandable	Sharing
Power Issues	Limited	Lack of Trust	Sharable	Trust
Different Ideologies	Conflicting	Stereotyping	Varied	Understanding
Varied Norms	Must Be Uniform	Intolerance	Diverse and Evolved	Tolerance
Relationship	Dependent	Dominance/ Submission	Interdependent	Empathy and Cooperation

Figure 1. Some Potential Sources of Conflict in a Group and The Perceptions of Group Members in Two Different Modes

Reading across the figure, conflict is likely if group members' *main concern is with themselves*. Their perspectives will be *narrow*, and their orientation will be *short term*. It is ironic that the interests of individuals are not served properly by their being narrowly concerned with themselves. The group is likely to remain in conflict unless members can *broaden* their perceptions—what Sherif and Sherif (1953) called "superordinate goals." Superordinate goals are those which are critical for all individuals in a group, but cannot be achieved by any one person alone. Only by all members working together can the needs of individuals be met.

Conflict is also likely if members in a group perceive their *goals* as *conflicting*. Instead of taking an *individualistic* orientation, members should try to meet several goals at once. This may not be difficult, as goals are often *complementary*. For example, one person may want to learn everything he can, and another may want to share her knowledge with the group. These are complementary goals that can both be met. Some people also must be willing to *subordinate* their goals for the group's good.

Often intra- or intergroup conflicts arise from difficulties on how to share available *resources*. Group members perceive the resources as *limited* and tend to *fight* over who will receive what. However, if people are able to perceive resources as *expandable*, the energy of the members may be spent on efforts to share them. Even if resources are not expandable, they can at least be perceived as *sharable*.

Power also is often perceived as *limited*. For example, in a group the "chair" position may be very important, and the person who holds it may exercise most of the power. This leads to *lack of trust* among members, and conflict results. If the chair position can be seen as *sharable*, this can lead to *trust* among members and an actual increase of power for everyone.

If *ideologies* are *conflicting* in a group, *stereotyping* may result, and people will act out their "parts" rather than cooperating for the good of the whole. If members of the group can accept that ideologies are *varied* and that people can work together in spite of differences, *understanding* may result.

Many groups work toward uniform *norms* or standards of behavior, but expectations of *uniformity* may lead to *intolerance* of differences. If group members realize that *diverse* norms always exist early in the life of a group and that in time some commonly shared norms will *evolve*, they can learn *tolerance* of the various norms and keep differences from causing conflict when they have no effect on achieving the main goals of the group.

One other basic problem, especially in intercultural groups, is what *relationships* people have to each other in a hierarchical structure. Some people are comfortable taking a dependent role, but others fight to attain positions of authority. The expectation that others should be *dependent* often results in conflicts and *dominance* or *submission* needing to be determined for every member before the group can begin to work. If relationships are perceived as *interdependent* (that A depends on B for some things, and B depends on A for some other things), people are more likely to have *empathy* for others and to *cooperate* on problem solutions.

To summarize the discussion thus far, if people in a group perceive their own concerns to be high priority; want their own goals met at all cost; fight over available resources; distrust those in power; stereotype those with conflicting ideologies; refuse to tolerate varied norms; and attempt to dominate the group, conflicts will surely escalate. If, however, group members attempt to see differences as opportunities to *prevent* or *resolve* conflicts, they will consider the broader group concerns; realize that goals can be complementary and subordinate their own; share resources; trust those in power and share the burdens of leadership; attempt to understand separate ideologies; tolerate varied group norms; and cooperate with and have empathy for others. Conflicts cannot be resolved unless people are willing to take these risks.

STYLES OF CONFLICT MANAGEMENT

People usually attempt to manage conflict, once it exists, in one of three ways: (1) by avoiding the issue; (2) by approaching the problem and attempting to reach a solution; or (3) by defusing the situation and sharing in problem solving. These attitudes can be put on a continuum from avoidance to approach.

Members of a group also tend to take an "us" versus "them" view of conflict. Sometimes, an "outer" group is perceived as opposed to the interests of the "inner" group. If the outer group is seen as belligerent, conflict will seem inevitable; but if the outer group is simply seen as disinterested or distracted, conflict will seem less likely. Once conflict exists, the outer group can still be perceived in two separate ways: as unreasonable (in which case, there is little hope for a solution) or as open to reason (in which case, a solution seems possible). A combination of these two types of perception of the outer group with the avoidance-approach continuum results in the eight modes of conflict management presented in Figure 2. Determining just where a group can be placed on the avoidance-approach dimension is significant in determining the effectiveness of its behavior. Avoidance is based on fear of conflict and is dysfunctional;

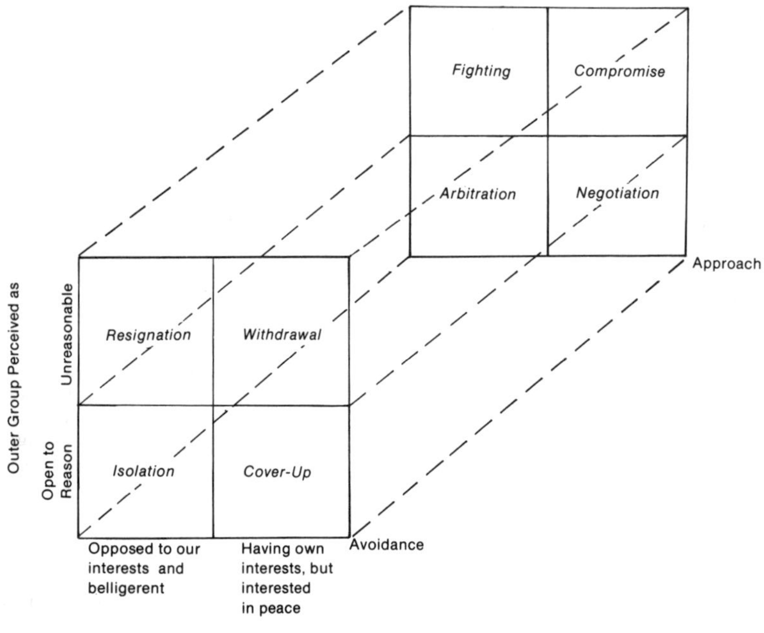

Figure 2. Eight Styles of Conflict Management

approach is based on optimism and is the more functional. Avoidance is characterized by a tendency to deny, rationalize, or avoid the problem; displaced anger or aggression; and emotional appeals. Approach is characterized by efforts to find a solution with the help of others.

Four Avoidance Styles for Handling Conflict

Extreme avoidance of conflict—when the outer group is seen as belligerent and unreasonable—results in a fatalistic *resignation* to fate and a sense of helplessness. However, if the outer group is perceived as interested in peace, avoidance takes the form of *isolation* from the other group to minimize the opportunities of interaction (and possible conflict).

When the outer group is seen as open to reason, avoidance takes a more positive form: *withdrawal* from the conflict. If both groups are interested in keeping the peace, they may *cover up* the conflict and prevent hurt feelings or disruption. No solution is attempted—or found—for any conflict by using the avoidance modes.

Four Approach Styles for Handling Conflict

Approaching a conflict can take aggressive forms or more positive forms. If the "inner" group perceives the "outer" group both as opposed to its interests and as unreasonable, group members may opt to *fight* for a solution in their own favor. Blake, Shepard, and Mouton (1964) called this the "win-lose trap." If the outer group is seen as interested in peace, but still unreasonable, an attempt may be made to seek a *compromise*. Both groups then share some gain, but there is no solution to the conflict. On the other hand, if the outer group is perceived as belligerent, but not unreasonable, *arbitration* by a third party may be sought to assess the situation objectively. The conflict remains unresolved but is postponed for some time. The most satisfactory solution may emerge only when both groups confront the problem through *negotiation*.

NEGOTIATION: TOWARD CONFLICT RESOLUTION

The negotiation mode of conflict resolution is the most mature of the approach-style modes. Negotiation is possible only when the outer group is perceived both as interested in peace and as reasonable. Negotiation involves continuous interaction and dialog between groups in order to find a solution with maximum advantages to both. Through negotiation, mutual interests are met and the most satisfactory solution is determined. The negotiation style for managing conflict can be described in a number of steps. These steps are presented below in a sequence, but this need not be followed strictly (Pareek, 1982).

Unfreezing. Two groups in conflict may be "frozen" into a stereotyped relationship. Unless the expectations and patterns of the relationship are unfrozen, any movement toward negotiation may be impossible. To thaw out the atmosphere, group members can generate images they have of each other and of members of the other group. The ensuing discussion may provide an opportunity for members of both groups to say many things that they otherwise would not. Or members of both groups can be mixed in order to discuss some issues. In this way, people may increase their understanding of each other's perspectives.

Being Open. Group members may be "closed" with each other and may need to develop norms of voicing different points of view or alternatives without fear of repercussions. Openness is usually most difficult when the conflict involves critical issues and the atmosphere is emotionally charged, but openness is even more vital at such times.

Learning Empathy. Group members may see only their own points of view, but can gain empathy for others by sharing their main concerns, apprehensions, or goals. Such sharing may help people to gain new insight about themselves and others.

Searching for Common Themes. Groups involved in conflict may be helped to search for common goals or other areas of overlap by listing their expectations, apprehensions, perceptions, goals, etc.

Generating Alternatives. Once the groups are aware of others' perspectives, they can generate alternatives for solving some of the issues. If both groups participate in generating alternatives, they are likely to feel mutually responsible for finding a solution.

Responding to Alternatives. After alternatives have been generated, members of both groups should study and respond to them. Every effort should be made to see issues in a positive, problem-solving way. Outright rejection of alternatives should be avoided, but all should be discussed by the whole group for clarification and for sharing concerns.

Searching for a Solution. A number of alternatives may be explored in depth by small groups made up from members of both large groups. The small groups can reach consensus on a solution and then report to the large group. Because many points of view are represented in the subgroupings, these groups are likely to come up with some innovative possibilities.

Breaking the Deadlock. Sometimes the conflicting groups may be so emotionally involved that they cannot move toward a solution by themselves. In such cases, a third party who is both objective and experienced with this type of problem may be brought in.

Committing to the Solution Within the Group. After solutions are generated by subgroups, the groups can debate and consider these solutions and make their commitments to some of these. Openness among group members will help for genuine commitment. All doubts must be resolved or must be put aside at this point.

Committing the Whole Group. The last phase of conflict resolution is for both groups jointly to accept a solution and to make public commitment to implement it. Group members may share the mechanisms they plan to use for following up on the commitments made. Arrangements can also be made at this point for a joint review of any remaining issues at a later time.

Resolving conflict through negotiation involves a continuous effort on everyone's part to build a climate of openness and nondefensiveness. The success of negotiation depends on the efforts made by members of both groups to develop their own group skills. The process of negotiation itself contributes to the development of the group. The process is difficult, but extremely worthwhile.

PARTICIPATION AND COLLABORATION: TOWARD CONFLICT PREVENTION

Preventing conflict is also an approach mode. Prevention means anticipating the potential causes of conflict and taking quick action to turn them into positive forces for better understanding and cooperation. Two main strategies for prevention of conflicts are described in the following paragraphs.

Everyone concerned in a common task must be involved in order to reduce the breeding ground for conflict. Whenever problems arise, everyone must be involved in finding alternative solutions. Such participation and the resultant sense of shared responsibility for a solution help to prevent many conflicts. The solution reached through participative decision making may be much more acceptable and pragmatic than one imposed from above. Representative groups from various levels of an organization can be formed for dealing with grievances, work norms and deviations from them, procedures for employee assessment, performance criteria, etc., before the issues arise in order to prevent unhealthy conflict.

An emphasis on collaboration and team building also helps to change the potential causes of conflicts into positive forces for cooperation. The main emphasis of collaboration is on identifying common goals, recognizing each other's strengths, and planning strategies for achieving goals by working together.

REFERENCES

Blake, R.R., Shepard, H.A., & Mouton, J.S. *Managing intergroup conflict in industry.* Houston, TX: Gulf, 1964.

Pareek, U. Developing collaboration in organizations. In J.E. Jones & J.W. Pfeiffer (Eds.), *The 1981 annual handbook for group facilitators.* San Diego, CA: University Associates, 1981.

Pareek, U. Managing conflict and collaboration. New Delhi: Oxford & IBH, 1982.

Sherif, M., & Sherif, C.W. *Groups in harmony and tension.* New York: Harper, 1953.

Udai Pareek, Ph.D., *is the Larsen and Toubro professor of organizational behavior at the Indian Institute of Management, Ahmedabad, Gujarat, India. Dr. Pareek's background is in organization development, human resource development, organizational design, and change in persons and systems. He has consulted with industrial and nonindustrial systems in various countries and with many international organizations. He also is the author or co-author of five books on psychology and management.*

STRESS, COMMUNICATION, AND ASSERTIVENESS: A FRAMEWORK FOR INTERPERSONAL PROBLEM SOLVING

Brent D. Ruben

In recent years countless books and articles have appeared on stress, assertiveness, and interpersonal communication. As interesting and popular as each concept is in its own right, the relationship among the three is even more intriguing, in terms of both theory and training.

STRESS

In very general terms, *stress* results when we are confronted by environmental threats or demands to which we cannot easily adjust. In such situations the body mobilizes itself to restore equilibrium. For most animals, stress is brought about by threats from the physical environment—an impending attack by a predator, a wound, or a loud noise. The response is a generalized physiological arousal. Neural, hormonal, and muscular reflexes are activated in preparation for the maximum physical output necessary for a fight or flight. Either action dissipates the physical and emotional energy (Pelletier, 1977; Seyle, 1976).

From a biological point of view, the stress-adjustment cycle of humans directly parallels that of other living systems. In terms of the origins of stress and the means available for dealing with it, however, humans are substantially unlike other animals, largely as a result of the role that symbols play in our lives. As humans, most of the stressors to which we strive to adapt are symbolic, rather than physical: the threat of rejection by a loved one, a heated argument with a colleague, the prospect of failure on an important exam, the tension of a long wait in line, or the pressure of an approaching project deadline. These symbolic threats are capable of triggering the same sorts of hormonal, muscular, and neural reactions that, for other animal species, are associated with physical threats.

Stress is, on the one hand, a very necessary and positive life force. It is the impetus for growth, change, and adaptation (Ruben, 1978). By adjusting to the demands of our physical and symbolic environments and to one another, we gain opportunities for personal and social growth, creativity, and discovery. On the other hand, chronic and accumulated stress can have devastating physical as well as emotional consequences. Research suggests that stress lowers our resistance to illness and can play a contributory role in diseases of the kidney, heart, and blood vessels; migraine and tension headaches; gastrointestinal problems; asthma and allergies; respiratory diseases; arthritis; and even cancer (Pelletier, 1977).

COMMUNICATION

Communication has two important functions in the stress-adjustment cycle (Ruben, 1982). First, many of the stressors we face daily have their origins in the symbols and meanings we have created through communication. As we rush to be on time, strive for promotions, or anguish over relationships, we are essentially troubled over problems of our own creation. The concern with promptness, for example, is socially created and varies greatly from culture to culture, as does a preoccupation with success and achievement. Those who are disturbed by relationship problems are upset because it has been communicated to them that relationships are important and to be valued.

Second, communication is the primary means through which we deal with the various stressors we encounter. We have learned that physical combat and running away are simply not "civilized" ways of dealing with problems. We hold our bodies in check, and usually react by "fight" or "flight" in a symbolic sense only. Ironically, our complex society leads to an increase in stress factors, while it decreases the opportunities for coping with that stress physically.

Interpersonal communication is our primary means for coping with the stressors we encounter daily. Over the course of time, largely through force of habit, we have evolved particular strategies that we characteristically use in threatening circumstances. Two typical styles familiar to most of us are the *marshmallow* and the *machine gun* (Ruben, 1972) shown in Figure 1.

Marshmallow Style	Machine-Gun Style
Cautious	Reckless
Passive	Aggressive
Inhibited	Uninhibited
Controlled	Controlling
Submissive	Pushy
Dominated	Dominant
Uncomfortable	Insensitive

Figure 1. Two Typical Styles of Dealing with Stress

The Marshmallow Approach

Those who utilize a marshmallow approach to dealing with stress in interpersonal relations take the path of least resistance, choosing simply to go along or comply with the demands of others, regardless of how unreasonable or uncomfortable these demands may be. This approach is the behavioral enactment of the philosophy that there is no value in "rocking the boat," when instead one can put up with the uncomfortable or annoying circumstance or individual.

Those who use this approach opt for passive resignation and acceptance, often internalizing frustration, hostility, and anger. The marshmallow approach dictates that one give all outward signs of being accepting, comfortable, and cordial, even if seething with hostility and resentment inwardly. The "marshmallow" may feel helpless, taken advantage of, and victimized. Yet at the same time he or she may well be uncomfortable reacting in any other way for fear of endangering the other's regard for him or her or jeopardizing what outwardly appears to be a stable, harmonious relationship.

The Machine-Gun Approach

Those who utilize a machine-gun approach to dealing with stress in interpersonal relations tend to say what is on their minds, regardless of the consequences. Unlike the marshmallow, the machine gun has no difficulty speaking up in public and in fact may be seen as highly verbal, outgoing, uninhibited, and—in extreme cases—insensitive, "pushy," aggressive, threatening dominant, or overpowering. Because of the forceful, even intimidating, way in which the machine gun approaches people and circumstances, others seldom make unreasonable demands of them.

A Comparison

The marshmallow is essentially *submissive*. The approach has advantages: It preserves surface harmony, and others appreciate one's willingness to comply with requests or meet demands. Disadvantages include: (a) stress and discomfort from continually internalizing feelings of hostility, frustration, and resentment; (b) a perpetuation of the pattern of being taken advantage of; and (c) a lack of self-respect or respect for others as a result of vulnerability and continued abuse.

In contrast, the machine gun is *aggressive*. This style lets others know very clearly where one stands and what to expect. It also has disadvantages: Others with whom one might have meaningful relationships are often frightened away and may perceive the machine gun to be disinterested and self-centered. The consequences ultimately may be stressful for the machine gun.

Both the marshmallow and the machine-gun styles are dysfunctional in terms of stress. The marshmallow steams on the inside while meeting the needs of others. The machine gun meets his or her needs by ventilating feelings, and, particularly in the short run, denies the needs of others.

The Assertive Response

Assertion theory (Bower & Bower, 1976; Kelley, 1979) provides a way of thinking about and dealing productively with stressful people, situations, and topics, avoiding many of the pitfalls of the machine-gun and marshmallow approaches, while benefiting from the care, sensitivity, and concern often characteristic of the marshmallow.

To use a similar metaphor, an assertive response can be seen as *target shooting*. Overall, the strategy of the target shooter is to conceive and aim messages purposefully, taking care to make the intended point clearly, logically, and without falling short of or overpowering the target. The target shooter makes an effort to separate issues from people.

The Target-Shooter Technique

The target-shooter technique consists essentially of five steps: (1) introduction/transition; (2) statement of the problem; (3) explanation of feelings; (4) proposed solution; and (5) closure.

Introduction/Transition. The target shooter begins with an introductory or transitional comment that alerts the other person that there is something important to be discussed. An example might be: "Jim, do you have ten minutes? There's something important I'd like to discuss with you."

Statement of Problem. The target shooter then states the problem in simple, specific, nonemotional and nonjudgmental terms, presenting a newspaper-type account of the situation and explaining who, what, when, and where.

Explanation of Feelings. Following the statement of the problem, the target shooter indicates his or her own feelings about the situation, i.e., "troubled," "concerned," or "disturbed," and why. The person avoids guessing at other people's motives and states only personal feelings. Comments like "I am annoyed because you seem to be trying to take advantage of me" generally serve to make others defensive and have the net effect of moving the discussion farther from, rather than closer to, a positive resolution.

Proposed Solution. Next, a solution to the problem is proposed in specific and reasonable terms. Target shooters avoid asking for less than they can accept or more than others can reasonably give and then are specific enough so that everyone will easily be able to determine whether the proposed solution has been followed or not.

Closure. A statement of closure softens the climate and indicates satisfaction with the outcomes of the conversation. Depending on the circumstances and the relationship, the closing statement might be "Thank you for the time" or "I'm glad we had this talk; I've been bothered by these issues for some time." Target shooters avoid the temptation for one last recrimination and do not enlarge the discussion at this stage.

A NEW MODEL FOR INTERPERSONAL PROBLEM SOLVING

Unfortunately, no single interpersonal strategy is likely to serve the wide-ranging needs of the individual in dealing with the many stressful situations he or she encounters. The great appeal of the target-shooter approach and other assertive approaches is their simplicity and promise of success. Ironically, these are also the major liabilities of these strategies. There is no doubt that assertive approaches do work very well in many situations, but there are times when there is really no substitute for the humility, silence, and submissiveness of the marshmallow approach. There are even times when there is no useful alternative to the outward expression of extreme emotion so typical of the machine-gun approach.

To deal with a wide range of situations, what is needed (from a theoretical and training perspective) is an approach that: (a) assumes the potential validity and value of a wide variety of interpersonal styles or strategies; (b) assumes there is merit in learning the skills and meta-skills necessary to use any of a number of different approaches; and (c) provides a framework for enabling the individual to select the approach that is most appropriate for the particular circumstances. One possible model for interpersonal problem solving for stress management (Ruben & Siegel, 1980) is presented in Figure 2 and described in the following paragraphs.

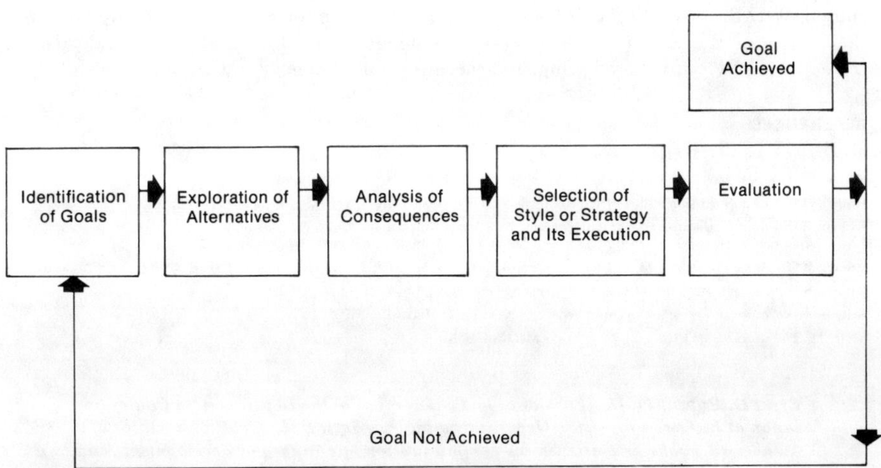

Figure 2. An Interpersonal Problem-Solving Model for Stress Management

Identification of Goals. One of the most difficult, yet most important, tasks to perform in stressful interpersonal situations is to identify goals. It is crucial to be clear as to one's goal or goals before trying to solve any interpersonal problem. The key question is *"What do I want to accomplish?"* It is critical to determine whether the primary goal is to (a) preserve the relationship; (b) express one's feelings; (c) put an end to the other person's requests or particular annoying habit; or (d) work toward some combination of these. The best way to handle any situation depends greatly on one's goal. If the goal is merely to preserve the relationship, the easiest approach is simply to comply with whatever requests are made. This is the marshmallow approach. If the goal is merely to rid oneself of frustration, the machine-gun approach is to mow down the opposition. If, however, one desires the relationship to develop into a healthier and more harmonious one, the goals might be to acknowledge the differences, the need for the various parties to be true to themselves, and the need to approach the situation in a problem-solving way. Alternatives then can be explored in a less stressful and more productive way.

Exploration of Alternatives. After identifying one's goals—but before selecting an approach and embarking on a specific communication strategy—it is important to explore alternatives. Several possible options usually exist, such as: (a) accepting things as they are; (b) letting a situation go a while longer in hopes that it will work itself out; (c) using devious, indirect tactics; (d) using subtlety or sarcasm; or (e) confronting the issue directly. Each of these options may be viable and appropriate in certain circumstances, and it is useful to consider all possible options and their consequences rather than settling on one by default.

Analysis of Consequences. The alternatives can be compared by considering the possible consequences of each one. Ideally, an option with the maximum likelihood of producing positive gain and minimum likelihood of negative outcomes would then be chosen.

Selection of Style or Strategy and Its Execution. After the style for dealing with a situation has been selected, a specific plan of action must be developed and perhaps even scripted. What to say, when to say it, and how, are factors that need to be considered, as well as various possible responses from the other person. Then the strategy must be executed.

Evaluation. The last stage in the process is evaluating the effectiveness of the strategy chosen. Were the goals achieved? If so, the problem has been solved. If not, a recycling through the phases of the model is necessary—checking goals; exploring alternatives; analyzing consequences; selecting, developing, and executing a new strategy; and so on.

REFERENCES

Bower, S.A., & Bower, G.H. *Asserting yourself: A practical guide for positive change.* Reading, MA: Addison-Wesley, 1976.

Kelley, C. *Assertion training: A facilitator's guide.* San Diego, CA: University Associates, 1979.

Ruben, B.D. Communication and conflict: A system-theoretic perspective. *Quarterly Journal of Speech,* 1978, *64*(2), 202-210.

Ruben, B.D. *Communication and human behavior.* New York: Macmillan, 1982.
    paper presented at the Western Speech Communication Annual Conference, Honolulu, 1972.

Ruben, B.D. Communication and conflict: A system-theoretic perspective. *Quarterly Journal of Speech, 64*(2), 1978, 202-210.

Ruben, B.D., & Siegel, R. *Personal power.* New Brunswick, NJ: Johnson & Johnson, 1980.

Ruben, B.D. *Communication and human behavior.* New York: Macmillan, 1982.

Seyle, H. *The stress of life* (Rev. ed.). New York: McGraw-Hill, 1976.

Brent D. Ruben, Ph.D., *is professor and chairperson of the Department of Communication at Rutgers University, New Brunswick, New Jersey. He is author or editor of a number of books and articles on communication, training and development, and research and he has served extensively as a consultant. Dr. Ruben's areas of expertise include intercultural and interpersonal communication as well as communication training.*

SURVIVING ORGANIZATIONAL BURNOUT

John M. Shearer

The phenomenon of individual burnout has received considerable attention recently (Adams, 1978, 1980; Lauderdale, 1982). People in organizations wonder how they can keep up with the demands made on them. If enough people in an organization feel that they cannot keep up, general productivity goes down and the organization starts to decline. The result is organizational burnout.

Certain steps can be taken to reduce the pressures that push an organization into decline. Priorities can be altered to reduce the strain on individuals. The following steps can be applied to all organizations—public or private, large or small—but most organizations need outside assistance to begin. The aim is not to point out faulty management practices or to correct inefficiencies but to stop to take stock of what is causing the stress on employees.

1. *Identify Functions.* Why does the organization exist? What were the original goals and subgoals? Are they out of date? What values are implicit in each goal? Do the goals accurately reflect company values? Unfortunately, organizations tend to add to the work force or change structure before reviewing function or goals. This often means perpetuating a losing situation. If goals have changed, employees may have the impossible task of striving to achieve the unachievable.

2. *Identify Resources.* What staff, funding, physical space, equipment, and materials are available? Are these permanent resources? What other resources are available through the community, the state, or Federal government? Should priorities be adjusted according to resource availability? What costs are associated with adding resources?

3. *Compare Goals with Resources.* Are resources available to carry out the goals identified? What do others in the organization think? What do clients say? Is the probability of additional resources high enough to justify existing or expanded functions? Functions must be compared with resources before decisions are made about priorities. Limitations in resources must be identified so people are not attempting to meet impossible deadlines or to produce products that cannot be produced.

4. *Set Priorities.* After identifying any disparities between resources and goals, it is important to identify priorities. This may require obtaining outside legal interpretation, interviewing clients, or checking with supporting organizations or suppliers to find out how they assign priority to a group. If good public relations or interagency relations is an issue, a marketing approach may be needed to find out what others want.

It may be that there is no hope of success with a particular client group. To provide equal services is to reduce the impact on groups with whom success is even more likely, thereby increasing organizational decline and poor public relations. Consider who can be served adequately before assigning priorities. If enough resources are not available for recognized priorities, documentation can be provided to those who have the authority to make policies and allocate resources. They can choose among alternatives available or find more resources.

5. *Revise Organizational Form and Structure.* Determine what new forms and service

structures must be adopted to carry out all necessary functions. Look at all three phases of the work flow: *intake of orders, delivery of services,* and *long-term follow-up.*

One or all of these phases of doing business may require modification. For example, priorities may not be set at the intake point. High priority business should receive better service than low. Low priority business may need to be channeled elsewhere. Or delivery of services may be inefficient. For example, educational services could be delivered to groups rather than to individuals, leaving more staff time for other services. Or follow-up may be taking a disproportionate amount of time so that priority services suffer. This is akin to police officers spending so much time giving court testimony that high crime neighborhoods are not patrolled.

6. *Stick with Priorities.* It is difficult for most organizations to stick to their priorities because they are diverted by feelings of responsibility and helplessness. It is seductive for those running organizations to think that no one else can do something "right," or that something will not be done if the organization does not take it on as a project. Informal mandates from "higher authorities" are compelling and hard to resist. The answer is to learn to say "No" and to stick with preset priorities. Organizations need to practice assertion as much as individuals do.

7. *Take Time to Plan.* Planning time must be allowed as an organizational renewal mechanism to incorporate changes in need, mandate, or market. Although time consuming, planning at regular intervals can save time and effort in the long run and may increase productivity (Fordyce & Weil, 1971).

REFERENCES

Adams, J.D. Improving stress management. *Social Change,* 1978, *8*(4), 1-12.

Adams, J.D. On consuming human resources: Perspectives on the management of stress. In W.B. Eddy & W.W. Burke (Eds.), *Behavioral science and the manager's role* (2nd ed.). San Diego, CA: University Associates, 1980.

Fordyce, J.K., & Weil, R. *Managing with people: A manager's handbook of organization development methods.* Reading, MA: Addison-Wesley, 1971.

Lauderdale, M. *Burnout: Strategies for personal and organizational life; Speculations on evolving paradigms.* San Diego, CA: Learning Concepts, 1982.

John M. Shearer *is a program manager of the Montana Department of Social and Rehabilitation Services, Community Services Division. He functions as an internal consultant to county welfare departments and middle management teams, with an emphasis on planning, problem solving, and decision making. His major interests include interpersonal communication, leadership training, and conflict management. His background is in community organization, workshop design, and consultation to public service organizations.*

INTRODUCTION TO THE
THEORY AND PRACTICE SECTION

A theory and practice paper published in the *Annual* series is a view of or a way of working with human behavior that can be or has been used in practice. It can be developed in two ways: *inductively*, when theory emerges from or is linked to those techniques and methods already in practice because of utility or necessity, or *deductively*, when practice is developed from tested and validated theory. In the applied behavioral sciences, a unified and systematic theory provides a model that can be applied in practice to human beings and human systems.

Because theory and practice papers speak to the "state of the art" of human resource development, the pieces in this section are designed to be used by practitioners to increase the knowledge base from which they work and to inspire further theory building. More abstract, complex, and research-based than lecturettes, theory and practice papers can, nevertheless, be used productively in conjunction with lecturettes to provide a broader and deeper grounding of the material to be presented to participants. The lecturette is the tip of the iceberg—what the participants are told and shown—while the theory and practice is what is underneath, what the practitioner needs to know.

Just as models can be used to explain human behavior, they can also be developed to guide professional behavior. A method for model building that can be useful to the practitioner concerned with continuing growth and development is outlined in this introduction.[1]

MODEL-BUILDING PHASES AND STEPS

I. *Delimiting:* Examining, narrowing, and selecting the phenomena

   1. *Observe* the phenomena.

   2. *Identify* areas of interest.

   3. *Specify* which areas are to be covered.

II. *Defining:* Explaining the specific variables and their interrelations

   1. *Develop* salient dimensions by thinking about:

      a. factors/components/elements/variables

      b. systems/constructs

      c. perimeters/boundaries

      d. functions/roles

      e. forces

      f. resources

      g. routines

---

[1]For additional discussion of developing theoretical models, see the Introduction to the Theory and Practice Section in the 1980 *Annual.*

    h. contingencies

    i.   effects

  2. *Define* interactions among dimensions by thinking about:

    a. randomness

    b. cause and effect

    c. correlation

    d. dependence

    e. intervening processes

    f. complexity

III. *Describing:* Writing and visualizing the model

  1. *Describe* the model in writing.

  2. *Depict* the model visually through the use of:

    a. lists

    b. tables

    c. ranking

    d. continuum

    e. categorization/taxonomy

    f. morphology

    g. facet design

    h. whirlpool

    i.   concentric circles

    j.   grid

    k. cube/triangle

    l.   diagram

    m. graph

    n. flow chart

    o. "black box"

    p. cyclical representation

IV. *Demonstrating:* Showing that the model works

  1. *Test* the model in a new situation.

  2. *Refine* the model based on results from the situation.

  3. *Review* relationships and graphic presentation.

THEORY AND PRACTICE PAPERS IN THIS *ANNUAL*

The theory and practice articles in this *Annual* progress from emphasis on the individual to group, intergroup, organization, and organization development applications. For the most part, these papers offer step-by-step models, often visual, to guide the practitioner in the use of the theory. Additionally, the majority of the selections are based on philosophical as well as theoretical assumptions. Values such as openness, participation, collaboration, growth, and integration are evident.

A theme threading through this year's Theory and Practice Section is the maintenance and expansion of health at various individual, dyadic, group, intergroup, and organizational levels.

Some pieces focus on the need to maintain health in an environment of scarce resources while under pressure to increase productivity, and others look at increasing health through heightened awareness, learning, and the development of new, more flexible behaviors. A number of the papers emphasize the importance of the holistic integration of cognitive, affective, and behavioral dimensions and the incorporation of polarities or opposites. What can be perceived clearly throughout the section is the value placed on the individual human being as a starting point for change within the complexity of human systems.

Three of the papers draw models specifically from learning theory. Byrum-Gaw and Carlock present a method of spontaneous behavior modeling by the trainer that is linked to the participants' stages in learning. Fryrear and Schneider focus on another successfully used approach to modeling through the use of participant-developed scripts and videotape recording and replay of those scripts-in-use as a means of behavior change. Simpson's training design is also firmly grounded in the theory of adult education, with a carefully built sequential model that gives the trainer precise strategies for various types of learners, content, and situations.

Two other papers use learning theory as a base for organization development. Zugel develops a transition-meeting model for new managers to ensure the necessary exchange of information during this often ambiguous and stressful organizational change. Nadler's approach is based in systems theory as well as learning theory, presenting the concept of system "congruence": a structured, research-based participative approach to organizational problem solving.

The Karp article deals with the tension between self-interest and interdependence and highlights the existence of influential relationship dynamics within the larger organizational system.

Finally, there are two unusual pieces in the 1983 *Annual*. Bates applies the values, theory, and technique of organization development to the small business, suggesting that it may be better equipped than a larger organization to treat the whole employee through caring behaviors and actualizing relationships. Eckstein and Wallock's presentation on dance therapy suggests that dance movement therapy is a means of expanding both individual expression and group creativity and cohesion.

In summary, the papers in this section of the 1983 *Annual*, all prepared by active practitioners, are intended to link theory to practice and provide a basis for good practice by the users of this *Annual*.

ORGANIZATIONAL HEALTH IN SMALL ENTERPRISES

Ralph R. Bates

Most of the literature about organization development (OD) is based on the experience and research of practitioners who have applied the theory and technology of OD in medium- to large-sized organizations. It often appears that such knowledge is not transferable to small organizations. However, smaller organizations often have leaders and managers who are knowledgeable about and skilled in OD, although they may not be able to spend large amounts of their own time or money engaged directly in OD activities. Small companies usually cannot afford full-time internal consultants or long-term external consultants. Consequently, planned change must occur in different ways using various modes of facilitation. Several OD approaches that small enterprises can adopt are not often described in the popular literature.

The model presented here is based on organizations with certain common characteristics, although the variables listed here do not comprise an exhaustive list. Generally, to the extent to which these variables exist for a small organization, the more relevant this model. The intent of this paper is not to provide a check list permitting complete transferability of the model to other settings, but to outline a model that may make sense to and be some help for those connected with small organizations.

DEFINING A SMALL ORGANIZATION

Small enterprises, for the purposes of this model, are those organizations, or units of larger organizations, with twenty to seventy-five employees. The small enterprise is conducting business, making products, or providing services in a volatile environment, that is, external forces impact frequently and uncontrollably on the internal environment (Jones & Reilly, 1981). Such things as government regulations, competition, changing technology, and funding sources permeate the boundaries of the organization and alter decisions, plans, or projections. Ambiguity and uncertainty about the future are ever present. Organizational leaders are keenly aware of and responsive to external conditions, although not always able to adjust quickly or to avoid adverse impact on their organizations. Leaders and key managers are opportunists, pragmatists, and entrepreneurs driven by a need to survive. They require great flexibility to plan, and long-term planned change seems almost impossible.

The organization's mission and purpose often tend to be articulated vaguely, which causes employees to be confused at times about its direction. Goals are unclear and seem to shift depending on circumstances and opportunities. The clearest organizational focus is on surviving, while providing a broad range of services to stay in business. Financial resources are a constant source of concern and debate. Income fluctuates depending on short- or long-term contracts for goods or services. Volume tends to increase threefold over a three-year period. Staff frequently also triples, and human resources are a mixture of skills and academic qualifications, but probably not oriented toward "high technology." Managers and professional staff have the most influence on change, rather than nonprofessional staff or the unions. Most employees are in their early thirties and tend to be enthusiastic and motivated.

Quite apart from the products or services they sell, many small entities fit this description. Although the types of products or services it deals in do have an impact on the small organization's strategy for achieving and maintaining organizational health, these variables are not considered here, nor are technological aspects of the work place or the production process. The focus of this model does include OD and behavioral and management science technology that are often not thought of as the "technology" of the work place.

DEFINING ORGANIZATIONAL HEALTH

One element especially critical for the health of small organizations—because of the potential for community that is difficult to achieve in large groups—is *actualizing relationships*; that is, interactions between people that nurture the "whole" person, not just the person in a job role. The growth of individuals as skilled workers and more self-actualized individuals is important and is supported in a healthy work place. Training in a healthy atmosphere is not just performance and task oriented but extends to people's career goals and lives outside the organization. People are interested in others' nonwork concerns; relationships tend toward joint problem solving, coaching, and self-responsibility and away form commiserating and rescuing.

Another element common to healthy organizations is *job satisfaction*. People are challenged but not overwhelmed; they receive recognition from others; and they value their own efforts. Workers are satisfied that they are rewarded fairly. Elements such as task variety, role negotiability, upward mobility, responsibility, appropriate and fair supervision, and the ability to influence and participate in change are all present.

Profitability must also be good to maintain organizational health. Recurring losses create a climate of concern, tension, and fear. Scapegoats are sought, top management worries about job stability, those in lower-level jobs fear layoffs, and the atmosphere is filled with uncertainty. Recurring profits create optimism, a "can-do" attitude, and a more relaxed atmosphere. Typically, education and training are valued in profitable times. Promotions and generous raises are more frequent. People allow time to plan, to organize, and to dream of the future. Risks are taken, and there is more room for creativity and synergistic behavior.

Finally, people in a healthy system believe that they are providing *good quality products and services*. Enthusiasm for high quality is shared, and high standards are set and reinforced through the formal and informal appraisal system. People are held accountable for the quality of their work. Clients and customers give positive feedback on the quality of goods or services. Both internally and externally, products and services must be seen as meeting high standards in order to have an impact on decision making and planning. One without the other does not contribute to organizational health.

KEY VARIABLES PROMOTING HEALTH

For small organizations to be healthy, eight variables must be attended to over time: *leadership, values, staff selection, rewards, norms, roles, decision making,* and *communication*. These represent interdependent internal variables that are interrelated with the external environment, that is, affected by the market place, government regulations, boards of directors, etc. No one variable by itself can affect organizational health positively, although the absence of key elements will have a negative impact.

Leadership

For small organizations, leadership is the key dimension of organizational health. Because of the leader's visibility and potential for frequent interaction with a large percentage of the work force, the opportunity for positive or negative impact is great. Whether he or she intends to do so or not, the leader models behavior for the rest of the organization. What the behavior is, how it affects others, and how people cope with its impact are important dynamics of any small organization. It is important that the leader recognize the impact his or her behavior (either through direct interaction or through observation) has on others. This phenomenon must be legitimized so that it can be used positively. Either direct or indirect confrontation of the leader's behavior must be allowed. Either the leader must be willing to be confronted by the person the behavior affected or the employee must be coached on how to cope with or understand the leader's behavior. The leader must be accessible on both a personal and a task level. Being sensitive and responsive to both work and nonwork interactions is more crucial for organizational health in smaller settings.

Finally, the principal leader or a designated top manager must take the responsibility to be the facilitator of and advocate for organizational health. With top-level support, considerable promotion and maintenance of organizational health will occur. Although long-term, planned change may seem nearly impossible for organizations operating in a volatile environment, the commitment of top management is adequate when coupled with the elements described in the following paragraphs. If the role of advocate is designated to another manager, that person must be a part of both formal and informal decision-making processes within the organization.

Values

Values underlying the mission or purpose of a small organization and of the work itself are set mostly by the leadership. However, because the organization is small and its work is not likely to be as diverse, the value base of the leaders is likely to affect people throughout the system. Also, it will be more obvious whether or not individually held values agree with those of the organization. If these assumptions are true, then the task of making organizational behavior consistent with values becomes a high priority. Otherwise, managing the consequences will take energy, time, and money. For example, if a core value is the fair and humane treatment of people, the unfair administration of raise and promotion policies becomes an issue sooner than it would in large organizations. Or if cooperation is highly valued, the impact of conflict on the system will be greater in relative terms than when an organization is large and conflict can be covered up or go unnoticed.

Staff Selection

The selection of staff is of high priority for all organizations, but especially in smaller ones. Employees must be chosen who not only have the requisite skills to perform well but also have the potential for establishing good relationships with peers, subordinates, and supervisors. Values, norms, and personality, as well as job or technical skills, are important. The challenge is for management to account for differences and, at the same time, avoid hiring the perfect match or clone, which destroys the diversity and individuality that lead to a challenging, dynamic atmosphere. Because one person can have a very negative (or positive) impact on everyone else in the system, hiring must be done to suit both the job and the whole system.

Rewards

Rewards are difficult to define because they depend on the perceptions of the recipients and the perceptions differ according to the size of the organization. Large organizations tend to conceive of rewards in traditional terms: pay, fringe benefits, bonuses, promotions, etc. Small organizations need to pay attention to psychosocial rewards as well. Such things as flexi-time, affiliation with leaders, association with "good" people, recognition through timely feedback, work that has a higher purpose or meaning, fair treatment, being treated as responsible adults, etc., are considered to be psychosocial rewards.

Curiously, these rewards come to be expected in small organizations, yet hardly ever merit the formal attention of management. The impact on climate is great because everyone can compare notes and observe who has the largest share of psychosocial rewards. People inside the system will note every inequity, but people entering the system for the first time from a "traditional" system will feel liberated and ecstatic. Thus, managers and leaders of small entities must introduce various psychosocial rewards into the system and be wise and thoughtful about their use.

Norms

Leaders and managers of small organizations play a large role in setting and maintaining organizational norms. Because they are conducting business in a volatile and changing environment, it is vital that they foster positive rather than punitive norms. Creativity, innovation, and the ability to make quick responses suffer in a punitive system. Some positive norms include support for risk taking; tolerance for differences; willingness to confront; conflict resolution; promotion of interdependence, collaboration, trust, authenticity, and openness; expectations of flexibility and fairness; and accountability at all levels.

Roles

It is a well-established maxim that roles must be clearly delineated to ensure a well-run operation. However, there is an inherent danger in this principle for organizations confronted with rapid or unpredictable change brought on by outside forces—inflexibility. To manage volatile change a flexible approach to role definition is necessary. Workers must be hired who are not rigid in their expectations; they must expect their roles to fluctuate. Especially if an organization adopts a matrix structure, roles and jobs must be restructured to fit both the needs and demands of task accomplishment and the worker's abilities and interests. Temporary work groups might be necessary, or managers may be called on to become workers led by other managers. Titles, seniority, credentials, and hierarchy may need to be set aside temporarily to achieve the best results.

Decision Making

Theoretically, participative management should fit nicely in a small organization. Unfortunately, conditions are often unstable, and response time may be too short for decisions by a group. Managers in small organizations must understand and employ a variety of decision-making approaches, depending on the situation or problem they face (Hersey & Blanchard, 1977; Maier, 1970). They also must legitimize this variety and develop employee understanding and acceptance by dealing with challenges and by clarifying the method used.

Except for institution-wide issues or problems, it is best that decision making be decentralized. This helps to avoid the emergence of a bureaucracy and the resultant slow response time, rigidity, and caution. It also achieves more meaningful clusters of influence and participation. Responsibility and accountability can be readily assigned. Better conditions exist for personal and professional growth and motivation in a small system, because individuals do not have an obligation to pass the decision along to higher levels.

Communication

Small organizations are as susceptible to developing ineffective communication systems as large organizations. An added danger inherent to small entities is the illusion that communication takes place more easily. Consequently, many managers pay little attention to communication needs, assuming that information is spread around but not checking to see if it is accurate or if the right people have been informed and included.

Because so much information can be transmitted verbally, there is a tendency to let formal patterns slide. Unfortunately, this leads to the generation of *mis*information. Meetings, memos, reports, and newsletters are just as important for a small organization as for a large one. Because not all people need or want the same information, a variety of methods to achieve a variety of communication purposes must be used. Especially in small organizations, little can be kept secret. Salaries, raises, grievances, and conflicts will eventually filter through the informal communication system. Realizing this, managers need to share almost all information, which will reduce the gossip and misunderstanding associated with secretiveness. Job satisfaction and efficiency will increase, and costs to do business will go down.

SUMMARY

Small organizations operating in an unstable environment can achieve and maintain organizational health, but the approaches and strategies they must use are different from those in large organizations. The factors of size, time available for formal OD interventions, and money affect how they must be run. The variables of leadership, values, staff selection, rewards, norms, roles, decision making, and communication are the keys to analyzing a small entity and selecting the right methods to promote organizational health. These variables are presented in the following list.

LEADERSHIP
1. Develop leaders' awareness of their power as models.
2. Develop staff awareness of the impact of leader behavior.
3. Promote the confrontation of behavior.
4. Facilitate leader accessibility.
5. Have leaders facilitate/advocate/support organizational health.

VALUES
6. Monitor organizational behavior in terms of leader values.

STAFF SELECTION
7. Select staff for skills and ability to establish satisfactory relationships.
8. Have leaders consider the system-wide consequences of their staff choices.
9. Select compatible staff, but not "yes" people.

REWARDS
10. Build in psychosocial rewards.
11. Be aware of how and to whom these rewards are distributed.

NORMS
12. Promote positive norms to ensure creativity, innovation, and quick responses.

ROLES
13. Define roles, but allow for flexibility.
14. Build the expectation of flexibility, and select staff comfortable with role changes.

DECISION MAKING
15. Employ a variety of decision-making approaches.
16. Legitimize varied approaches among employees.
17. Decentralize most decision making.

COMMUNICATION
18. Avoid thinking that smallness means good communication.
19. Adopt a mix of formal communication methods.
20. Allow open access to most information.

The absence of elements within each category of variables tends to have a greater negative impact on small organizations. Control over the variables can be achieved so long as top management supports any OD effort. If the management does not possess skills in change and implementation, a part-time internal OD consultant should be given top-management authority to facilitate the process.

REFERENCES

Hersey, P., & Blanchard, K. H. *Managing organizational behavior: Utilizing human resources.* Englewood Cliffs, NJ: Prentice-Hall, 1977.

Jones, J. E., & Reilly, A. J. The organizational universe. In J. E. Jones & J. W. Pfeiffer (Eds.), *The 1981 annual handbook for group facilitators.* San Diego, CA: University Associates, 1981.

Maier, N. R.F. *Problem solving and creativity in individuals and groups.* Belmont, CA: Brooks/Cole, 1970.

Ralph R. Bates *is the vice president for organization development at Trans Century Corporation, an international management and organizational consulting firm headquartered in Washington, D.C. Much of Mr. Bates' work is with small organizations, focusing on team building, intergroup problem solving, conflict resolution, coaching managers, strategic planning, role clarification, and participative management. He specializes in organization development, team building, training of trainers, and design skills.*

MODELING: TEACHING BY LIVING THE THEORY

Beverly Byrum-Gaw and C. Jesse Carlock

Various sources have described modeling as one of the basic means by which new behaviors are taught or existing behaviors are modified. The concept of vicarious learning—learning through observation of models—has been widely researched within the framework of social-learning theory (Bandura, 1965; Bandura & Walters, 1963) and training methodology (Zemke, 1982). This application of modeling allows the learner to observe the behavior of appropriate models as well as the consequences of this behavior. Subsequently, the learner practices the observed activities until they are performed skillfully.

Most modeling is carried out through preplanned demonstrations during which the model sets up and highlights discrete behaviors to be observed (Robinson, 1982; Robinson & Gaines, 1980). According to Robinson and Gaines, modeling is particularly useful in teaching skills and specific ways to employ these skills, whereas other methods are useful in transmitting information.

The authors feel, however, that these descriptions and definitions are too limited in scope. The general purpose of modeling, as they see it, is to demonstrate an appropriate integration of theory and practice—to prove that theory is livable and viable by involving the learner cognitively, affectively, and behaviorally. This expanded viewpoint includes the notion that modeling benefits the model, the professional trainer, as well as the learner. For instance, competence is an issue of continual importance to the professional trainer. In discussing competence, Pfeiffer and Jones (1974) maintain that there are four facets of training with which the professional must be concerned: oneself, theory, technique, and skill. They suggest that theory, technique, and skill can be acquired through reading, education, and training; however, developing oneself (that is, maintaining awareness, clarity of purpose, and an orientation toward growth) is both the most important and the most difficult task that faces the professional.

Modeling offers the trainer a way to continue self-development as well as to demonstrate theory, technique, and skill in a clear and efficient manner. Through modeling, the trainer not only learns and relearns theory by living it, but also remains current and consistent with what he or she must be willing to speak to underlying issues of personal concern as well as those that appear to be affecting the learners' work. By modeling such openness, the trainer practices this value and demonstrates it for others, thereby increasing his or her consistency and credibility as well as encouraging others to take the same risk.

When presented with the idea that modeling can enhance professional competence, many trainers are skeptical. They fear that by revealing how they actually think and feel in a given situation, they will forfeit their professional distance. To acknowledge and express feelings of anger, for example, is to be involved in what is happening, and a number of trainers feel that such involvement might reduce credibility rather than increase it. The authors' observations, however, indicate that appropriate modeling in process, can and should move from the professional distance needed to establish credibility to the personal and spontaneous behavior that comes from living one's theory. The end result can be training that is more focused, relevant, and practical.

As a training or teaching approach, modeling offers the following benefits:

- *Provides Motivation.* The learner is motivated to become aware of beneficial alternatives to present behavior.
- *Fosters Self-Acceptance.* The learner is encouraged to accept his or her present identity and to continue personal development.
- *Promotes Change.* The learner makes a conscious decision to try behavioral alternatives.
- *Reduces the Tension of Learning.* The learner is allowed to practice the components of a skill one at a time; consequently, each learning task is simplified and is less stressful. In addition, the learner witnesses the model's comfort with practicing new behavior.
- *Allows for Reinforcement.* Skills are practiced over time until they become refined and ultimately integrated into the learner's own style.
- *Creates a Positive Learning Environment.* Throughout the process the trainer models the learner's development, thus equalizing power in the learning environment, reducing the distance between the role of the teacher and that of the learner, and creating an atmosphere in which each learner is permitted to progress at his or her own rate.

HOW MODELING WORKS

A prerequisite to the experiential training approach of modeling is to motivate the learners to become involved and to experiment, which is accomplished by explaining the benefits of the specific skill to be learned. Once this groundwork has been laid, the modeling process (Figure 1) can begin.

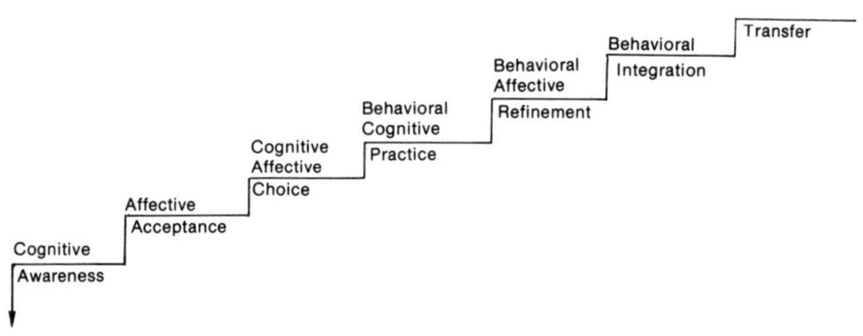

Figure 1. Steps Involved in the Process of Modeling

1. At the first step, *awareness,* the learners' pay attention to their present behavior; in addition, because modeling reveals untried or unthought-of alternatives, the learners realize the existence of options for behaving differently.

In this step, if the modeling involved is immediate and spontaneous, the appropriate climate must be established for it to be accepted in a nondefensive manner. For example, in establishing the climate for the skill of active listening, the trainer should discuss the purpose of and underlying attitudes essential to this skill, such as openness to others, nonevaluation, and receptivity. If the modeling is planned, the trainer as model may demonstrate or role play the skill, calling attention to it and consciously focusing on it.

2. The second step, *acceptance*, allows the learners to acknowledge that their present patterns of behavior no longer provide the benefits or payoffs that they once did.

3. *Choice*, the third step, consists of the learners' commitment to change and to adopting a new mode of behavior. To facilitate the accomplishment of this step, the trainer models the skill spontaneously as an appropriate response to what is occurring in the learning environment. For example, a learner expresses disagreement with something the trainer has said, and the trainer demonstrates the skill of active listening. Attention is not called to this skill, except perhaps in retrospect. This immediate and spontaneous modeling, which appears natural in the situation and fully integrated into the trainer's own behavior, motivates the learners to choose to invest time and effort in acquiring the new skill. If spontaneous modeling is not employed, the individual learner may see the skill simply as a technique that cannot possibly be incorporated into his or her behavioral repertoire.

4. The fourth step involves the *practice* of the new behavior, which usually takes place during a structured activity. For example, the learners may be given a formula for active listening to use in triads. During this phase the new behavior or skill is often formulary and rigid and involves strong feelings of self-consciousness.

5. The fifth step, *refinement*, is taken when each learner modifies the new skill to fit his or her personal style. At this point the skill is still undertaken consciously. Each learner receives feedback from the trainer regarding skill practice as well as reinforcement for continuing to work, which fosters refinement. Subsequently, the trainer structures the learning environment so that the learners have a chance to talk and listen to each other as they employ the new skill. In addition, each learner may be asked to list situations in which he or she can use the skill further as a means of refining and integrating it. Finally, in the trainer's own spontaneous and immediate modeling, he or she shows how the skill can progress from a formulary behavior to a characteristic behavior.

6. The sixth step, *integration*, occurs when the new skill is finally used unconsciously and effortlessly (Gaw, 1978).

7. *Transfer*, the final step, is accomplished when the individual learner uses the skill as part of his or her normal behavior pattern in situations other than the learning environment.

After refinement and integration, two problems commonly arise, making transfer difficult. When the learner leaves the learning environment, he or she may no longer receive accurate feedback on use of the skill or use of the skill may not be supported. The only way to handle these difficulties is to provide follow-up by contracting for post-tests or surveys, additional sessions involving those from the nonsupportive environments, and/or observations of these environments.

TYPES OF MODELING

Modeling can be explained further by viewing its dimensions: conscious/unconscious, verbal/nonverbal, and personal/impersonal (subjective/objective). These dimensions, which are described in the following paragraphs, are, in effect, types of modeling that can be used in various ways.

Conscious/Unconscious

Modeling may be employed consciously in any given situation. In other words, the trainer might assess a current situation; determine that modeling might be useful to show how a particular skill, such as asking open-ended questions, could be used; and then intentionally exhibit that skill. Similarly, the trainer might determine before a training session that a particular skill, such as reflecting feelings, might be modeled effectively with the group and then plan to model that skill. In both instances the trainer observes a condition in the environment and decides to model accordingly. This conscious employment of modeling implies that the trainer recognizes the steps involved in developing a particular skill and engages in these steps to heighten the trainees' awareness of the process. With conscious modeling the left brain predominates, and the trainer, using logical processes, determines what might be appropriate.

With unconscious modeling, the right brain is acting. In this case, modeling is spontaneous and is employed unintentionally; it is probable that the trainer is not even aware, at least initially, of modeling a given skill. For example, the trainer might spontaneously disclose at the start of a session that "This has been one of those days when nothing has gone smoothly, but now I'm going to block that out of my mind and start anew. Let's begin with a 'centering' activity; I could use one, and maybe you could, too." With this introduction to the training experience, the trainer begins with a self-disclosure and then provides an example of blocking out unrelated concerns as well as the technique of "centering."

Verbal/Nonverbal

The trainer may model verbal skills and/or nonverbal behaviors. With the modeling of verbal skills, the content of communication is emphasized, and the actual words that are useful in dealing with a particular situation are demonstrated. Verbal behavior is much more within conscious control than is nonverbal behavior; with nonverbal behavior, the process of communication is emphasized and its subtleties are demonstrated, although the behavior itself is often unintentional and unconscious. An example of employing conscious, verbal modeling as well as the unconscious, nonverbal variety is as follows: During an assertiveness-training workshop, six learners arrive for a session at intervals, ten to fifteen minutes late. The trainer becomes aware of feeling irritated and spontaneously begins the workshop by saying, "I'm annoyed that so many of you arrived late, making it impossible for us to begin on time without continual interruptions. In this situation we are all held back. I want us to begin on time." This verbal message contains all the elements of an effective, assertive statement. In addition, the trainer delivers the message in a strong voice; with a serious facial expression; with one hand on the hip; and from a stance in which the trainer's weight is equally distributed on both legs.

Personal/Impersonal (Subjective/Objective)

The trainer may use either personal or impersonal material. With the modeling of personal material, the trainer's experience of data in the environment is filtered through his or her feelings, self-concept, and life history. This type of modeling, consequently, involves some risk in that the trainer must be willing to deal publicly with personal issues. Another drawback is that subjective perceptions cannot be verified by other observers. Impersonal or objective material, on the other hand, is based essentially on unfiltered data gathered through the sensory apparatus. Thus, when it is used for modeling purposes, it offers the advantages of low risk for the trainer as well as easy confirmation by observers. For example, if the trainer states, "I've noticed that only the men have spoken up today," this assertion can be corroborated easily because it is based on observable data.

However, the use of personal data can also be advantageous. Bringing one's own feelings, thoughts, memories, and fantasies into the training process closes the gap of professional distance and allows for greater intimacy between the trainer and the trainees.

BEHAVIORS AND SKILLS THAT CAN BE MODELED

The specific behaviors or skills that can be modeled are numerous. Although it is possible to model technical skills, such as operating a machine, drawing a blueprint, or presenting a sales talk, the skills that the professional trainer is most interested in modeling are interpersonal ones. Figure 2 provides a list of interpersonal skills that can be modeled effectively as well as examples of ways in which the modeling of these skills can be accomplished in a training situation.

Skill	Example
Focus on Self	
Disclosure	The trainer discloses facts about self, here-and-now feelings, beliefs, values, desires, needs, and/or expectations.
Assertion	The learners resist, and the trainer uses the "broken record" technique: No matter what kinds of responses are received from the learners, the trainer simply keeps repeating exactly what he or she wants to have happen.
Focus on Other	
Acceptance	The trainer gives a nonevaluative response to a learner who is disagreeing with him or her.
Confrontation	The trainer informs a learner that a particular behavior manifested by that learner affects the trainer negatively; in addition, the trainer clarifies preferences and consequences.
Feedback	The trainer tells a learner how he or she perceives that learner.
Support	The trainer expresses appreciation for something that a learner has said or done.
Mutual Focus	
Conflict management	The trainer identifies an issue of conflict between a learner and himself or herself; the two parties generate alternatives and agree on appropriate action.
Immediacy	The trainer tells a learner how he or she is reacting to that learner at the moment.
Mutuality	The trainer cooperates with a learner for reciprocal achievement of goals.
Flexibility	The trainer abandons his or her original plan and accepts a new approach suggested by a learner.

Figure 2. Interpersonal Skills That Can Be Modeled Effectively

DETERMINING WHEN AND HOW TO USE MODELING

When determining whether to use modeling and what type of modeling might be appropriate in a given situation, the trainer should use his or her best judgment in assessing a group's readiness. The following factors should be considered carefully:

1. *The degree to which the group is attached to traditional sources of power.* For example, a trainer might use personal, subjective modeling earlier with a group of educators than with a group of learners from the armed forces. In general, if the trainer meets the group on its own familiar ground, trust and rapport can be developed; then the group can be led into unfamiliar territory.

2. *The extent of the trainer's credibility.* In some cases credibility is automatically established on the basis of a reputation that has preceded the trainer. For example, someone like Virginia Satir, a well-known leader of the human-potential movement, can have immediate credibility with a group, and, therefore, can successfully introduce radically different perspectives earlier than can an unknown trainer who must spend more time qualifying. However, credibility can be established not only through reputation and demonstrations of competence, but also through status-conferring elements such as gender, social power, ethnic status, credentials, and interpersonal attractiveness (Bandura, 1969). The higher the trainer's degree of credibility, the earlier he or she can use higher-risk modeling. All trainers, however, must observe certain unspoken boundaries of propriety in order to retain credibility.

3. *The degree to which the group is open to consideration of new ideas.* The learners' flexibility is an important issue, as is their motivation to discover alternative solutions, to acquire new skills, and to adopt different attitudes. When the learners are convinced that what they are presently doing is not working, they become committed to the training experience; under these circumstances, the trainer is justified in making a personal investment in the experience and taking risks with techniques such as modeling.

In addition, the trainer should examine the learner's patterns of reacting to change and providing support to each other. If they do not have experience in venturing into the unknown and supporting each other during the aftermath of such ventures, the trainer probably should not use modeling.

4. *The group's current stage of development.* In the early stages of a group's existence, developing trust and establishing valued norms are tasks of primary importance. Until these tasks have been accomplished to the group's satisfaction, the trainer should not involve the learners in the risks inherent in some types of modeling (Carlock & Byrum-Gaw, 1982). For example, highly personal disclosures that are delivered too early may alarm or alienate the learners (Weigel, Dinges, Dyer, & Straumfjord, 1972) and/or diminish the trainer's credibility.

5. *Technical considerations, such as number of learners and time frame.* In general, with groups of twenty or more participants, risks should be taken more slowly. Greater numbers of learners increase the anxiety of the trainer as well as that of the learners; consequently, interactions in such groups might best be kept to a level of safety not afforded by some types of modeling. With the high risks that are sometimes associated with modeling come intense reactions, which are more difficult to manage with greater numbers of learners.

The time frame within which the trainer must work also affects the level of risk that can be taken. It would be unethical to leave highly charged situations unfinished. Thus, before deciding to use modeling, the trainer must ensure that adequate time exists in which to deal with any repercussions.

6. *The learners' degree of psychological sophistication and psychological level of functioning.* The more psychologically sophisticated the group, the earlier that high risks can be taken. Familiarity provides the groundwork for moving more rapidly to deeper stages of

training. Also, the higher the learners' level of self-esteem, the less easily they will be threatened by new material.

7. *The degree of distance that the trainer wants to establish at the time.* For example, if the trainer is having difficulty blocking out some serious personal concern at the moment, he or she may want to maintain more distance than usual—particularly with a new group, with large numbers of people, or with an unsophisticated group. The trainer must respect his or her personal needs in this regard.

Even after a particular type of modeling has been selected and employed, the trainer must continue to be sensitive to cues from the learners; when any new data become available, the original assessment should be reviewed and revised as necessary. In addition to considering the factors previously discussed, the trainer might want to determine answers to the following questions:

- How much am I willing to risk?
- How can I legitimate my choice of a type or level of modeling?
- How might my choice of the type of modeling I employ coordinate with or expand my style?
- How competent do I feel in my understanding of an integration of the skill to be modeled?
- What is the nature of my contract with the learners (purpose, goals, time frame, and so forth)?

CONCLUSION

The modeling process offers the trainer an opportunity to grow professionally as well as to increase the effectiveness of training. In essence, the trainer as model is required to complete four functions. The effective model must structure the learning process by presenting objectives, purpose, rationale, and explanation, thereby serving as a knowledgeable *director*. He or she must also operate as an *encourager*, inviting the learners to participate in simulated activities and challenging them to experience fully. Similarly, the model functions as a *supporter* by maintaining a safe learning environment and by rewarding new behavior. Finally, when modeling becomes spontaneous, immediate, and integrated, the model becomes a *reflector*, mirroring the learners and their contexts. At this point the trainer as model is interacting fully and equally with the participants.

Modeling that stops short of the integrated ideal proposed by the authors narrows operation to an overuse of one of these four functions. The director refuses to let go of power and control and elevates himself to an elitist position. The encourager turns challenging into competition, and learners are left to their own devices for "winning." The supporter controls feedback in ways that foster dependence, and the reflector becomes involved in personal issues and thinks and reacts without clarity. A combination of these functions is crucial to effective modeling, just as is a blending of the dimensions of modeling discussed previously—conscious/unconscious, verbal/nonverbal, and personal/impersonal. Although movement from one end of these continua to the other must take place to live one's theory, the move must be developmental, evolutionary, and continually balanced against the factors involved in a particular learning situation.

REFERENCES

Bandura, A. *Principles of behavior modification.* New York: Holt, Rinehart and Winston, 1969.

Bandura, A. Vicarious processes: A case of no-trail learning. In L. Berkowitz (Ed.), *Advances in experimental social psychology* (Vol. II). New York: Academic Press, 1965.

Bandura, A., & Walters, R.H. *Social learning and personality development.* New York: Holt, Rinehart and Winston, 1963.

Carlock, C.J., & Byrum-Gaw, B. Group energy, group stage, and leader interventions. In J.W. Pfeiffer & L.D. Goodstein (Eds.), *The 1982 annual for facilitators, trainers, and consultants.* San Diego, CA: University Associates, 1982.

Gaw, B.A. The pendulum swing: A necessary evil in the growth cycle. In J.W. Pfeiffer & J.E. Jones (Eds.), *The 1978 annual handbook for group facilitators.* San Diego, CA: University Associates, 1978.

Pfeiffer, J.W., & Jones, J.E. Introduction to the theory and practice section. In J.W. Pfeiffer & J.E. Jones (Eds.), *The 1974 annual handbook for group facilitators.* San Diego, CA: University Associates, 1974.

Robinson, J.A., & Gaines, D.L. Seven questions to ask yourself before using behavioral modelings. *Training/HRD,* December 1980, pp. 60-74.

Robinson, J.C. *Developing managers through behavior modeling.* San Diego, CA: Learning Concepts, 1982.

Weigel, R.G., Dinges, N., Dyer, R., & Straumfjord, A.A. Perceived self-disclosure, mental health, and who is liked in group treatment. *Journal of Counseling Psychology,* 1972, *19,* 47-52.

Zemke, R. Building behavior models that work—The way you want them to. *Training/HRD,* January 1982, pp. 22-27.

Beverly Byrum-Gaw, Ph.D., *is an associate professor of communication at Wright State University in Dayton, Ohio. She also conducts workshops in listening, interviewing, coaching/counseling, assertiveness, conflict management, team building, and managerial communication skills. Her special areas of expertise are interpersonal, small-group, managerial, and organizational communication. Dr. Gaw has had several articles published in previous* Annuals *and she is editorial consultant for* The 1983 Annual.

C. Jesse Carlock, Ph.D., *is a counseling psychologist in private practice and an adjunct professor of counseling education at Wright State University, Dayton, Ohio. Part of her general practice involves working with recovered alcoholics and persons with eating disorders, Gestalt therapy, and feminist therapy. Dr. Carlock's special interests include women's issues and group work, and she has published articles on both of these topics.*

DANCE/MOVEMENT THERAPY: A PRIMER FOR GROUP FACILITATORS

Susan Frieder Wallock and Daniel G. Eckstein

A common goal of group process involves assisting individuals in identifying and affirming personal values as well as learning to appreciate and respect other life styles. This constant interplay between individual expression and group cohesiveness is mutually beneficial. As James (1897) said:

> The community stagnates without the impulse of the individual. The impulse dies away without the sympathy of the community. (p. 26)

Similarly, Yalom (1975) reported that a supra-individual focus—the cohesiveness and norms of the large group—can facilitate the attainment of each member's individual goals.

A significant tenet of the human-potential movement is that everyone has paradoxical needs to be a unique individual and to be part of the total group or community. O'Connell (1981) expressed the relationship between these needs in the following equation: $NH = SE + SI$. He believes that a natural, "self-actualized" high (NH) consists of an effective integration of self-esteem (SE) and social interest (SI). Thus, "inner" wholeness is dependent on the ability to merge with an "outer" community.

The purpose of this paper is to identify dance/movement therapy (DMT) as an innovative approach for enhancing both self-esteem and social interest. This therapy focuses on physical movement and the creative process as the context for assessment and intervention.

Schmais (1974) noted the following major assumptions concerning the practice of DMT:

- Movement reflects personality;
- The relationship between the therapist and the participant, which is exhibited through movement, precipitates and supports behavioral change; and
- Significant changes occur in movement, and these changes can affect total functioning.

The basic premise is that movement is essential in discharging suppressed emotions and in releasing energy from psychic and somatic blocks. Such an energy release facilitates new levels of perception, which lead toward the integration of body, mind, and spirit. Dance/movement therapy fosters respect for individual differences, aids in the development of a positive body image, and encourages creativity through exploration of inner feelings. Freedom of personal movement, coupled with group interaction, can result in a reaffirmation of one's inner life and greater freedom of spontaneous expression.

In addition, because DMT is primarily nonverbal in approach, it enhances social feeling by counteracting the human tendency to create social distance through verbalization. As Burton (1974) observed:

> ...individuals who have learned such effective verbal defenses from silence to intellectualization need new methods of communication. Movement responses, which involve a lower brain level and are less a part of conscious awareness, are more reliable expressions of feelings than words. (p. 21)

In DMT, the participants are challenged to relate interpersonally in the present. The processes used, such as body-awareness techniques, improvisation, authentic movement, and movement interaction, all aid in developing a common bond and a sense of community support.

A BRIEF HISTORY OF DANCE/MOVEMENT THERAPY

Dance has always been a fundamental part of life as an expression of individual themes and life passages, permitting dramatization of deep feelings and synthesizing experience into structured sequence and rhythms. Group improvisational movement conveys universal, cross-cultural themes, such as those of harvest, fertility, and tribal unity. As evidenced by the activities of medicine men, forms of dance have even been used therapeutically to cure disease and to deal with natural and supernatural forces. It has also been suggested that dance in ritual is a naturally generated form of therapy that helps individuals to deal with crises and events that could otherwise be problems (Wallock, 1977).

The use of dance and movement in formal psychotherapy evolved from the theory and practice of prominent modern dancers. These dancers favored a spontaneous and authentic dance experience, which they accomplished by turning inward to their personal experiences for emotional content and themes. This interpretation resulted in a new definition of dance that laid the foundation for its use in therapy.

Pioneering work was started in the Forties by dancers who recognized that movement had therapeutic value and felt that it could be a powerful tool for working with the emotionally disturbed. Each of these pioneers went through a personal transformation from performing artist to empathetic catalyst in the healing relationship (Wallock, 1977). For example, Marian Chace, a former Densihawn dancer, worked with psychiatric patients at St. Elizabeth's Hospital in Washington, D.C., while Trudi Schoop, a mime, developed a way of working with psychotic populations by helping them to form their fantasies and hallucinations into movement and drama. Mary Whitehouse developed an approach called "Movement in Depth," a combination of dance and Jungian psychology. Others, including Liljan Espenak, Blanche Evans, and Irmgard Bartenieff, also made a strong impact on the emerging profession.

The disciples of these pioneers as well as other dance/movement therapists who have been trained in the eleven graduate-school programs around the country now function as clinicians, as members of treatment teams, or as primary therapists. Largely because of DMT's emphasis on nonverbal communication and expression, many different types of groups have been successfully helped through this approach: the developmentally disabled, the autistic, the physically handicapped, the elderly, the chemically dependent, the visually and hearing impaired, the psychotic, and those with learning disabilities. Adults and children who are free from such encumbrances can also benefit from the use of DMT as a healing, educational, and growth-oriented activity (Wallock, 1977).

The American Dance Therapy Association (ADTA) currently has over 1,100 members and 250 registered dance therapists who have met professional standards of education and clinical practice. The ADTA defines the basic goals of the profession as follows:

> (1) The development of body image, self-concept and a wider movement repertoire, (2) increased awareness of inner physiological states and their psychological counterpart, emotional and physical tension and alternatives for verbal and non-verbal behavior, and (3) expression of body-mind integration, social and ritual interaction, including individual and group statements.[1]

---

[1] From ADTA, "What is Dance Therapy?," 1981. Additional information is available from the American Dance Therapy Association, 2000 Century Plaza, Columbia, Maryland 21044.

PRINCIPLES OF DANCE/MOVEMENT THERAPY AS RELATED TO PSYCHOLOGICAL THEORIES

Body Awareness

Freud maintained that the ego is, first and foremost, a body ego and that all experience comes through the senses as the individual develops. He described various psychosexual stages, which are determined by acts and sensations that are motivated by the libido or sexual energy. As the individual develops, a conflict arises between the libidinal urges and the dictates of society. To cope with the resulting stress, defense mechanisms are formed. Reich (1949), a student of Freud, claimed that such defenses are not only psychological but also manifested in the body as muscular rigidities and tensions, resulting in "the body armour." Reich did extensive work on the function of movement in behavior, the physiological aspects of neuroses, and the relationship between physiological behavior and psychic behavior. He observed and analyzed the muscular patterns and rigidities of his patients and believed such patterns to be an essential part of each patient's mode of dealing with primitive feelings. Consequently, he viewed therapy as a process aimed at allowing the free flow of energy by systematically dissolving these rigidities and the associated psychic resistance.

Many dance/movement therapists have found these theories valid in their work. Assisting an individual in reducing muscular tension can help him or her to regain basic health and functioning by allowing for the expression of repressed feelings. The first step in this process is to develop body awareness. Adler (1930), for instance, maintained that movement acts as a metaphor for life and is a tool for assessing life style. The purpose of a systematic, Adlerian life-style investigation is to help an individual to identify his or her characteristic way of moving and operating in the world. In the same way, DMT reveals the individual's movement repertoire and preferences. After awareness of personal style has been developed, this style can be expanded and behavioral and expressive alternatives can be encouraged.

Free Improvisation

Free improvisation is central to most types of DMT. Burton (1974) described the psychodynamic goals of improvisational activities as conscious regression in the service of the ego, play, getting in touch with the child, spontaneity, and preconscious exploration. She also distinguished improvisation from an individual's nonproductive "acting out" in a group. For example, the group milieu provides an ideal structure in which to observe the Freudian concept of projective transference of past relationships into the "here-and-now" group context. The goal is to bring unconscious transference into conscious awareness so that the participants can learn to use spontaneous, symbolic relationships in an exploratory, conscious fashion.

Empathy and "Interactional Synchrony"

The development of social interest, an essential theme of DMT, is predicated on the ability to empathize. The dance/movement therapist models empathic behavior by being sensitive to the energy level and movement of the individual and of the group as a whole. In turn, the participants learn to be sensitive to one another and to move not only in isolation but also in harmony with others.

In DMT, moving in unison, which is called "interactional synchrony," generates a strong bonding of all group members. By giving open-ended directions and not demonstrating one "correct" way to perform a movement, the dance/movement therapist encourages different interpretations, all of which are acceptable. Adler defines this attitude in one community as the "horizontal plane," in which individual differences are recognized and respected, as opposed to the "vertical plane," an attitude that the qualities or abilities of some are above or beneath those of others (Eckstein, 1981; Driscoll & Eckstein, 1982). In the caring, nonevaluative environment established by a dance/movement therapist, participants become involved and learn to focus on their own and one another's strengths, thereby allowing themselves to develop as individuals and to take advantage of the healing power of the "horizontal-plane" community.

DANCE/MOVEMENT THERAPY IN PRACTICE

Dance/movement therapists do not focus on particular dance skills, the mastery of techniques, or performance; instead, they promote intrapsychic and interpersonal learning by using the developmental, expressive, communicative, and rhythmic aspects of dance as well as the existing movement patterns of the individual.

The dance/movement therapist serves as facilitator, guide, and mediator of the movement process, helping each participant to rediscover the joy of moving, to expand his or her range of movement, and to gain insight through the clarification of movement experiences. The methodology involves both action-oriented processes and the participants' own cognitive insights, which lead to greater self-awareness and behavioral change. The relating of these experiences to personal life experiences aids in the process of integration of feelings with thought and action. The therapist consciously uses his or her own movement as a tool in the process and is aware of personal responses and movement preferences.

In addition, the therapist may focus on verbal cues that can be translated into movement. For example, if a participant says that he or she has feelings of being "pulled in two different directions," the therapist may ask the participant to experiment with the movements associated with those feelings. Thus, the therapist concentrates on listening and watching for themes that may emerge through words or movement. In one case in the authors' experience, a participant was noted to be having difficulty with transition and flow in movement; in fact, this participant later related that she had labeled her problem as a "perch-and-flight" syndrome. After being confronted with this tendency, she learned to feel and acknowledge the natural ending of a pattern in her movement and to respond to the emergence of the new in a less abrupt manner. This learning carried over into her daily life and resulted in more satisfying relationships.

The therapist also frequently notes interferences in the psychodynamic process, such as feelings that are being left unspoken during an interaction. When dealing with such a situation, the therapist might suggest that these feelings be conveyed through movement rather than through words. Kadis (1969) observed that:

> There is evidence to support the conclusion that in our culture, where a heavy burden of defenses are carried by verbalization, it is motor behavior that is most effective in breaking through the verbal defenses. (p. 111)

Body movement can be both map and guide. Movement can be a graphic representation of the intrapsychic dynamics of the personality. In other words, the way in which an individual moves in improvisation can be seen by the dance/movement therapist as symbolic of the entire operational system of that individual. Subsequently, the therapist can suggest structures within which the individual may experiment with alternative ways of moving and being.

For example, family members may be asked to move in ways that express how they feel within the context of the family. Then they may be asked to exchange roles and to move in accordance with their new identities. Through this process the family members develop greater empathic understanding. Freedom to improvise within the designed structure is integral to DMT and can lead to more authentic movement responses and new clues to behavior.

THREE MODELS FOR DANCE/MOVEMENT THERAPY IN GROUPS

The three models for group DMT sessions that follow reflect the approaches of three of the major pioneers in the field: Mary Whitehouse, Trudi Schoop, and Marian Chace. With DMT, as with training, knowing when and how to intervene is as important as the intervention itself. The therapist must be flexible and creative and must feel comfortable with the use of movement in psychotherapy.

Whitehouse

Whitehouse's approach, which she called "Movement in Depth," promoted a shift from left- to right-brain consciousness—from analytical processing to intuitive processing. This shift includes a willingness to suspend judgment, to relate to conditions as they are at the present moment, to grasp metaphoric relationships, to see things in relation to other things, and to perceive how parts might form a whole (Wallock, 1981).

This approach provides the participants with a direct experience of one of the premises of DMT: Physiological and psychological responses are intertwined. The following paragraphs describe how a typical session might progress.

1. The participants are instructed to close their eyes, to concentrate their attention on internal events, and to move in any way they like. This process often results in bringing forth memories and images that were previously inaccessible. The inner impulses that are initiated result in what Whitehouse called "authentic movement," which is frequently manifested as very subtle shifts in body tension and flow of breath. Sometimes instrumental music in the background can induce a relaxed state and evoke movement. Another option open to the therapist is to suggest that the participants themselves decide how they would like to begin—lying, sitting, or standing. Then both the therapist and the participants adopt a "wait-and-see" attitude regarding the movement that occurs.

2. Subsequently, the participants are asked to discuss their experiences and then write about them in journals. The therapist also may request that the participants develop images that are consistent with their physical experiences (Alperson, 1979). In this way the participants learn to stay in touch with the evolving movement-image interaction, thereby developing an understanding of the relationships between current life experiences and unfinished, problematic situations from the past.

3. After the participants have experienced moving on their own, each participant is asked to move in relationship to another. Sometimes physical contact occurs spontaneously, and the participants may be instructed to let this contact happen, to continue moving, and then to make contact with different partners. If each individual can stay in connection with his or her internal movement and, at the same time, relate to the movement of another, a heightened feeling of synchrony can occur and a type of physical "dialog" on a very deep level can take place.

For example, Whitehouse (1969-1970) incorporated into her work a movement structure in which two people face each other; one person moves; and the other acts as a mirror, reflecting the first person's movements. This exercise requires great sensitivity on the part of both the person initiating movements and the person reflecting these movements; the actions must be slow and simple enough that they can be mirrored accurately. Subsequently, the roles of leader and follower are reversed within each dyad. In the final stage, neither partner is a leader, but each picks up cues from the other. Occasionally, without any effort or intellectualization, the initiator of movements and the imitator move as if they were one; each is in tune with the other's subtle movements, and neither knows who is the leader. This unity, which is achieved only when the participants involved have a great deal of experience and body awareness, is the goal toward which Whitehouse worked. She allowed time and space for the development of each experience, knowing that even when only subtle movements are visible, internal movement is occurring.

> ...this sharing can be extended gradually to include three, five, a larger group. Sometimes there comes a wonderful moment in which a spontaneous rhythm or dynamic intensity gradually catches all the members of the group, lifting them into a leaderless whole, uniting them in a common action or common direction, a spontaneous order, a statement growing and expanding, swelling and changing until it comes to its own natural ending. From the outside, it has a quality of unpremeditated choreography. From the inside, it is an experience of participating in a totality made up of more than the sum of its parts but including each part equally. (Whitehouse, 1969-1970, p. 64.)

Schoop

Schoop preferred to work with groups in hospital settings. She borrowed from her performing background as a mime and encouraged patients to form their feelings into short productions rather than to improvise. Her rationale was that the process of forming a fantasy can free a person from emotional bondage.

In order to generate a particular feeling, the therapist using this method applies the movements most commonly associated with that feeling. For example, when a participant engages in actions universally associated with anger—such as stamping, kicking, punching, clawing, pushing, and pulling—the body forces that person into feeling the emotion that he or she is trying to conceal. After the participants have expressed anger fully, the therapist helps them to transform their anger into healthy, functional self-assertion. They are given the right to be angry and are helped to form this feeling by actually dancing the anger with a rhythm.

The goals of this approach to DMT (Schoop, 1974) are the following:

- To identify for each participant the specific parts of his or her body that have been unused or misused, and to direct the person's actions into functional patterns;
- To establish the unifying, interactive relationship between mind and body and between fantasy and reality;
- To transform subjective, emotional conflict into an objective, physical form so that it can be perceived and dealt with constructively; and
- To use any aspect of movement that will increase the individual's ability to adapt adequately to his or her environment and to experience himself or herself as a whole, functioning human being.

A session that employs this approach might involve working with contrasting extremes of an emotion or a physical state (such as tension and relaxation). The process is as follows:

1. The therapist leads exercises that increase the functional capabilities of the body while preparing it for the expression of the contrasting extremes that have been chosen. For example, preparation for the extremes of active and passive can include work with tensing and relaxing muscles. Through observation at this point, the therapist can determine various movement patterns as well as the group's general mood.

2. During the expression phase, the participants connect the extremes to life situations. For example, the group may work with identifying active and passive moments in life, learning to access both extremes and to recognize both as valid.

3. The next step consists of creating a functional balance between the two extremes, which is accomplished by changing the energy level of both extremes until the body approximates physical and emotional balance.

4. The conclusion reinforces the two extremes in a manner that leaves the participants in a state of well-being (Schoop, 1974).

Chace

The third model is based on the work of Marian Chace, another pioneer in DMT. At St. Elizabeth's Hospital in Washington, D.C., Chace established a dance-therapy program that provides services for patients as well as an internship for dance-therapy students.

Chace felt that dance was a means of transcending blocks in communication; that dance therapy was based on aware, nonverbal communication; and that rhythmic action was the tool used by the therapist (H. Chaiklin, 1975). She defined three stages in the DMT process: warm-up, development, and closure (H. Chaiklin, 1975). These stages are described in the following paragraphs.

1. The therapist uses the first step, the *warm-up*, to observe carefully and to pick up cues regarding the communications and needs of individuals and the group as a whole (S. Chaiklin, 1975). For example, when the room is alive with motion, the therapist might form a group circle and initiate a simple step that all participants can perform in unison. Several participants then take turns leading the movement, introducing improvisations that the others can follow and that eventually lead to performances of original dances (Rosen, 1957).

2. In the second phase, *development*, the session builds in intensity. The participants break through patterns of isolation and manifest more complex and spontaneous movement patterns, and interaction is a shared creation. During this process, themes can be developed that parallel psychological concepts (H. Chaiklin, 1975). For example, activities involving space and touch on the physical level can equate to a sense of belonging and trust on the symbolic level. Movements of giving and receiving can be translated literally in the social context. Verbalization increases, and the participants make cognitive connections with what they are doing in the group. Actions are accompanied by words; for example, jabbing movements can be accompanied by comments such as "I'm poking at the people who laugh at me." Through the dynamics of movement, concerns are explored and emotions are differentiated.

3. During the *closure*, intensity diminishes and a level of resolution is reached for parting. A closing ritual clarifies boundaries, solidifies each participant's sense of body integrity, and stimulates a feeling of group continuity. With this approach to DMT, group activity frequently begins and ends in a circle as a definition of a communal space.

APPLICATIONS FOR PRACTICAL GROUP FACILITATING

Dance/movement therapy offers many specific applications for training. For example, workshop participants may be asked to identify the following attributes: a specific physical characteristic; a habit that connotes energy, such as rapid speaking; and a behavior that represents a fantasized self-ideal, such as assertiveness. The participants then take turns sharing these attributes, integrating body movement with descriptive phrases. As each group member shares, the others give spontaneous feedback on the congruity between the movement and the phrases.

Another integrating process is useful as a communication-skills activity. After forming "client"/"helper" dyads, the participants complete the following processes. (After each process, the roles are reversed.)

- The helper confidently assists the "helpless" client in crossing the room.
- The client resists help.
- The client gives a mixed message in which the words spoken and the movements used contradict each other.
- The helper convinces the client to cross the room in any way desired (to react spontaneously and freely).

In addition, *individuation* can be stressed through free movement precipitated by facilitator comments such as the following: "Stretch and yawn. [Pause.] Breathe deeply. [Pause.] Become aware of your feelings and any past associations or memories that come to mind. [Pause.] How do you perceive your relationship with the other group members? [Pause.] Now use the others for support or balance." Similarly, *group cohesion* can be enhanced by asking the participants to move together.

The purpose of this paper has been to provide an introduction to dance/movement theory and practice. Physical movement is an important component that allows people to rediscover their bodies as instruments of expression, to restore awareness of the interactive relationship between their bodies and their minds, to reaffirm themselves as creative beings, and to renew these connections with the whole of life. The authors hope that facilitators will be able to apply these concepts in new and beneficial ways.

REFERENCES

Adler, A. *The science of living.* London: Allen & Unwin, 1930.

Alperson, E. The intrapsychic and the interpersonal in movement psychotherapy. *American Journal of Dance Therapy,* 1979, *3,* 20-31.

Burton, C. Movement as group therapy in the psychiatric hospital. In K. Mason (Ed.), *Focus on dance VII: Dance therapy.* Washington, D.C.: American Alliance for Health, Physical Education and Recreation, 1974.

Chaiklin, H. (Ed.) *Marian Chace: Her papers.* Columbia, MD: American Dance Therapy Association, 1975.

Chaiklin, S. Dance therapy. *American Handbook of Psychiatry.* New York: Basic Books, 1975.

Driscoll, R., & Eckstein, D. An introduction to life-style assessment. In J.W. Pfeiffer & L.D. Goodstein (Eds.), *The 1982 annual for facilitators, trainers, and consultants.* San Diego, CA: University Associates, 1982.

Eckstein, D. An Adlerian primer. In J.E. Jones & J.W. Pfeiffer (Eds.), *The 1981 annual handbook for group facilitators.* San Diego, CA: University Associates, 1981.

James, W. *The will to believe.* New York: Longman's Green, 1897.

Kadis, A.L. Acting out in group therapy. Panel discussion in H. Ruitenbeck (Ed.), *Group therapy today: Styles, methods and theories.* New York: Atherton Press, 1969.

O'Connell, W. *Essential readings in natural high actualization.* Chicago: Alfred Adler Institute, 1981.

Reich, W. *Character analysis.* (J.P. Wolfe, Trans.) New York: Noonday, 1949.

Rosen, E. *Dance in psychotherapy.* New York: Teacher's College Press, Columbia University, 1957.

Schmais, C. Dance therapy in perspective. In K. Mason (Ed.), *Focus on dance VII: Dance therapy.* Washington, D.C.: American Alliance for Health, Physical Education and Recreation, 1974.

Schoop, T. *Won't you join the dance? A dancer's essay into the treatment of psychosis.* Palo Alto, CA: National Press Books, 1974.

Wallock, S. *Dance movement therapy: A survey of philosophy and practice.* Unpublished doctoral dissertation, United States International University, 1977.

Wallock, S. Reflections on Mary Whitehouse. *American Journal of Dance Therapy,* 1981, *4*(2), 45-56.

Whitehouse, M. Reflections on a metamorphosis. *Impulse,* 1969-70, pp. 62-65.

Yalom, I. *Theory and practice of group psychotherapy.* New York: Basic Books, 1975.

Susan Frieder Wallock, Ph.D.*, is the director of the dance/movement therapy master's program at John F. Kennedy University in the San Francisco Bay area. A registered dance therapist and licensed marriage and family therapist, Dr. Wallock is also a lecturer in the Department of Health and Movement Studies at Mills College and maintains a private practice in movement psychotherapy. She also has done cross-cultural research in the areas of ritual, healing, and health care.*

Daniel G. Eckstein, Ph.D.*, is a licensed psychologist and a senior consultant for University Associates, Inc., San Diego, California. He is the co-author of four books on life-style assessment and affective education. His current interests include personal and systems power; sports psychology; organization development; and encouragement laboratories. He also is a professor of psychology for the University of Humanistic Studies, San Diego/Maui.*

VIDEO-ENHANCED HUMAN RELATIONS TRAINING: SELF-MODELING AND BEHAVIOR REHEARSAL IN GROUPS

Jerry L. Fryrear and Stephen A. Schneider

The use of video technology in human relations training involves the learners in passive viewing of programed material, interactive procedures with videotaped programs, and active procedures in which the video serves as an integral part of a structured program. The purpose of this paper is to present a human relations training program that combines elements of modeling, video playback, self-confrontation, behavior rehearsal, and group discussion and interaction. This model is adaptable to virtually any training need.

VIDEOTAPED MODELING

The concept of learning by observing models and imitating their behavior is central to using video in human relations training. Videotaped modeling in human-growth settings, which requires participants to act both as learners and models, is a logical outgrowth of the documented effects of live modeling (Thelen, Fry, Fehrenbach, & Frautschi, 1981). Much social learning is fostered by exposure to models who engage, intentionally or unintentionally, in patterns of behavior that are emulated by others. Performances of modeled behavior provide cues that are clearer and substantially more relevant than those that can be conveyed with a simple verbal description. In fact, the establishment of complex social repertoires is generally achieved through a gradual process in which people pass through an orderly, progressive learning sequence toward the final form of the desired behavior.

Modeling, in general, has been used to effect change in three broad and important areas of psychological functioning (Dawley & Wenrich, 1976):

- To transmit new behavior patterns;
- To eliminate unwarranted behavior patterns; and
- To facilitate the expression of pre-existing response modes.

By observing a model, people learn to overcome the behavioral anxieties and inhibitions that are connected with a specific behavior as well as to perform that behavior themselves. This type of modeling is overt and is governed by four interrelated processes:

- *Attention.* The learner attends to what he or she observes and recognizes and differentiates the model's behavior.
- *Retention.* The learner retains the original observations in some symbolic form, either imaginal or verbal.
- *Motoric Reproduction.* The learner uses symbolic representation to guide his or her own performance.
- *Reinforcement/Motivation.* The learner determines the consequences of the observed behavior.

Bandura (1969) states that a combination of verbal and demonstrational modeling procedures is the most effective means of transmitting new patterns of behavior to those who are found to have behavior deficits. In addition, behavior is more likely to be learned from observing a model when the following conditions are met:

- The learners are given specific instructions on what to look for.
- Conflicting, competing, or irrelevant stimuli are minimized.
- The learners give full, discriminative attention to the modeled behaviors.
- In a succession of scenarios, different models are used, and the behavior they perform is vivid and novel.
- The model is attractive in an interpersonal sense.
- The model is seen as having expertise and as being similar to the observer.
- The model is visibly rewarded for engaging in the depicted behavior.
- The learners are given positive feedback and otherwise rewarded for their own modeling.

For the following reasons, video-enhanced human relations training with a group is well suited to meet these important modeling conditions.

- Through group discussion and guidance from the trainer, the group members are given specific guidelines for evaluating the effectiveness of their behaviors.
- Because the models work from a script, conflicting and irrelevant stimuli are minimized.
- Because the learners watch themselves, they are likely to give full, discriminative attention to the videotape. Furthermore, they actively evaluate their own performances with a view toward improvement.
- The group format, in which each member acts as a protagonist, automatically provides different models, each of whom acts out vivid and novel behavior from a script that is developed by the group.
- Inasmuch as social skills contribute to interpersonal attractiveness, the participant models who act out such skills are seen as having that attribute.
- Because the script is designed to demonstrate maximally effective behavior, the model is perceived as having expertise. During the script-writing process, the group members contribute their own concerns, which tend to be similar to one another; consequently, when these concerns are presented on a screen, the learner perceives the model as similar to himself or herself.
- The script is designed to ensure positive social responses from others.
- The group, the trainers, and the other actors in the scenarios all give positive feedback to the participant model.

An additional variable that has been shown to be crucial to the effective modeling of social behavior is the portrayal of a model who copes rather than one who has mastered the behavior involved. The model who copes performs in a progressively improving manner, while a model as behavioral master consistently performs a desired behavior in an ideal way. In the context of interpersonal problems, most studies have reported more positive effects from using a "coping model" than from using a "mastery model" (Thelen, et al., 1981). Meichenbaum (1971) proposed that these effects might stem from the coping model's presentation of techniques that are an inherent feature of the coping condition, rather than from the perceived similarity between the learner and the model per se. The self-as-model procedure is a coping-model program that involves the repeated practice of a behavior by an initially unskilled protagonist.

SELF-CONFRONTATION: THE SPECIAL CASE OF SELF AS MODEL

Pfeiffer, Heslin, and Jones (1976) have stated the case for self-confrontation succinctly:

> It is our contention that more growth can occur for a group participant if he is provided with a method for specifically focusing on his own behavior. This is in addition to the feedback he receives from fellow group members, which can be growthful on a different and equally important level.
>
> It is not enough that an individual leave a laboratory learning situation feeling exhilarated, more open, charged, and so on. He must have been given the opportunity to understand himself and his behaviors in highly specific ways and be able to make decisions concerning behavior change based on this learning. (p. 7)

The self-as-model procedure is an excellent method for promoting self-understanding and growth; it depends on covert and overt imitation of one's own videotaped behavior. The imitation is followed by changes in self-perception and, subsequently, changes in social behavior outside the training setting.

Two theories of behavioral change following self-observation in training situations tend to support the use of self as model. The first is a cognitive-mediation theory of social learning (Bandura, 1969, 1971, 1973, 1977). Hosford (1980) describes the process as follows:

> In self-modeling, one learns from observing *exemplars of one's own behavior*, that is, a client observes only those instances of his/her own behavior in which he/she is performing in the way desired. Instances of inappropriate behavior (understand verbal/nonverbal response patterns) are deleted from the model. This, of course, differs considerably from self-observation per se in which clients are confronted with instances of their actual behavior which may include more undesired than desired examples of behavior. Self-modeling is also distinguished from standard modeling advocated in social learning theory in that the client, rather than someone else, models the new behavior to be learned. (p. 52)

It is important that the self-as-model procedure provide positive feedback so that the protagonists are not forced to focus only on their perceived mistakes. An exclusive focus on negative behaviors can lead to a failure to strengthen the positive behaviors being modeled; can provide a participant with evidence to support his or her own self-fulfilling, negative hypotheses; and can cause the participant to associate feelings of unpleasantness with the self-observation process itself (Hosford, 1980; Salomon & McDonald, 1970).

A second theoretical rationale for the self-as-model approach is that the self-image evokes strong arousal in the learner, "priming" him or her for positive change. From a psychoanalytic point of view, anxiety aroused by viewing oneself on video may eventually result in replacing immature or narcissistic ego functions with heightened, more adaptive, and more mature ones. Certainly, visual or auditory self-confrontation can result in sensory arousal (Fuller & Manning, 1973; Ho & Hosford, 1979; Holzman, Berger, & Rousey, 1967). It is unlikely, however, that the increased arousal automatically results in positive gain; what is more likely is that this state of arousal makes the learner more open to intervention and suggestion.

The "arousal" rationale for positive behavioral change based on visual self-confrontation is supported by the theory of objective self-awareness developed by Duval and Wicklund (1972). In essence, this theory claims that a state of objective self-awareness occurs whenever one is confronted with oneself as an object, such as when one views one's own televised image. That state of objective self-awareness leads to a comparison of one's objective self with an internalized standard. If the comparison reveals a negative discrepancy between the standard and the objective self, a state of aversive arousal will exist, resulting in the person's attempting to escape the state of objective self-awareness. If escape is not possible, then he or she will eventually attempt to change the objective self by changing either behavior or appearance.

Of course, the trainer would have to keep the client in a state of objective self-awareness for the amount of time necessary for change to occur. This time requirement undoubtedly varies, but Wicklund (1975) has reported behavioral changes in relatively short periods. Furthermore, the group program proposed by the authors is likely to encourage learners to complete the training because of the mutually supportive atmosphere developed as well as the emphasis on action.

BEHAVIOR REHEARSAL

Behavior rehearsal has been shown to be effective in human relations training, largely because the learners are allowed to practice in a safe environment. Lazarus (1966), for example, conducted a study in which the efficacy of four thirty-minute sessions each of behavior rehearsal, direct advice, and nondirective therapy were compared with respect to the subjects' resulting improvement in the management of interpersonal difficulties. Behavior rehearsal led to the greatest change.

In addition, behavior rehearsal to video simulations, called simulation interaction training (SIT), was developed by Doyle (1981) and found to be effective in developing social skills. The technique basically consists of having a person interact with video scenarios and rehearse appropriate behavior responses. Doyle has successfully applied SIT to many human relations problems, including police-cadet training, foreman training, assertiveness training, confrontation management, job interviewing, and management training. Doyle's work is especially germane to the program proposed by the authors because of his extensive use of video technology. He has found that "hardware-supported" training has numerous advantages, the most important being the opportunity for abundant rehearsal.

THE TRAINING PROGRAM

Modeling, self-confrontation, and behavior rehearsal have all been shown to enhance human relations training. In addition, the advantages of group training are well documented. The video-enhanced group-training procedure combines what the authors believe are the best-supported elements of modeling, self-confrontation, and behavior rehearsal. By using a group structure, several positive elements are added: peer support, group problem solving, multiple models, a sense of universality, and group cohesiveness.

The authors' training program is diagramed in Figure 1. It assumes that a small group of people with human relations concerns has been assembled, that some measure of rapport has been established, and that the program has been outlined and explained to the group members during an orientation session. Furthermore, the authors recommend that activities designed to provide a warm-up and to build cohesiveness be conducted prior to implementation.

At the outset of this program, one group member serves as the focal protagonist of a behavioral sequence or scenario and, with the support and assistance of the other members, progresses through a procedure of preparation, execution, and evaluation. The entire procedure consists of nine steps, but Steps 6 through 9 may need to be repeated at least once and perhaps several times. Subsequently, beginning with Step 2, the procedure is completed with a different protagonist and then repeated until each learner has played this role. A session of one and one-half to two hours (minimum) is required to accommodate each protagonist. In addition, a separate session should be conducted at the end of the program for summary purposes. Consequently, with an ideal group size of five to eight members, the program requires seven to ten sessions, including orientation and summary.

The nine-step procedure is as follows:

1. The first step is a general group discussion. The trainer begins this discussion by asking each learner to state a problem situation that he or she is currently faced with or has recently

experienced. This process initiates a discussion of similarities and differences in the reported situations; in fact, it is likely that the learners will automatically begin to offer one another advice, share supportive experiences, or state that they are at a loss and have no suggestions to offer. An important benefit of openly sharing in this manner is the creation of a greater sense of group cohesiveness.

2. The second step involves the selection of a focal protagonist. At this point the trainer can ask for a volunteer, ask the group to vote or reach consensus regarding who should go first, or choose someone on the basis of a perceived interest level as well as a perceived ability to provide a productive first experience.

3. The third step is to help the protagonist to clarify and specify his or her problem situation. This procedure involves the entire group. The protagonist is asked to state the situation as clearly and simply as possible; subsequently, each learner is instructed to ask questions and request additional information as necessary until the situation is clearly understood. In this way the situation is ultimately reduced to a specific, manageable example that can be transformed into an action-oriented script.

4. In the fourth step, the group selects effective behaviors for the protagonist. The trainer starts this process by asking the protagonist to relax for a moment, to think about his or her situation, and to imagine himself or herself acting as effectively as possible. The protagonist then shares this fantasy with the group, and the learners respond with thoughts as to why the protagonist's approach would or would not be the most effective way to handle the situation. The learners also offer their own suggestions, providing new ideas for the protagonist to consider. Step 4 continues until the trainer and the entire group are satisfied that the most suitable alternatives have been explored and the best approach and behaviors have been chosen.

5. Step 5 involves developing and writing an actual script for the protagonist. At the top of the script sheet, the protagonist writes a brief, concise statement of the specific problem. Next he or she lists the names of the characters in the order in which they appear in the situation. Then, with the trainer's help, the protagonist writes the script, creating lines for each actor that are consistent with that actor's character and ensuring that his or her own statements accurately reflect the newly determined effective behaviors. Once the script has been devised, the protagonist reads it aloud to the learners and elicits their comments and ultimate approval.

6. In Step 6 the protagonist selects learners to play the various parts. The chosen actors then learn their lines, determine appropriate nonverbal behaviors for their assigned characters, and participate with the protagonist in one or two rehearsals. When the protagonist and the other actors feel that they are ready, they act out the script as the proceedings are videotaped with full sound.

7. In Step 7 the tape is rewound and played for the entire group. It is important during this step that the trainer help the learners to focus on nonverbal cues as well as verbal content. The tape may be stopped and replayed at any point so that certain behaviors or sequences can be emphasized, or it may be run without interruptions.

8. In the eighth step, the group is asked to respond to the video reproduction of the scripted situation. The protagonist shares his or her feelings about having performed the "most effective" behaviors; the other actors describe how they felt in the roles that they played; and the learners who observed offer critiques and/or share experiences and feelings from their own lives that might be appropriate and useful. In general, the discussion focuses on whether the videotaped playback did, in fact, represent the ideal behaviors called for in the script. If this was not the case, the reasons should be explored, and the behaviors needed for improvement should be identified.

9. A ninth step is used if the discussion in Step 8 uncovers weaknesses in the script or

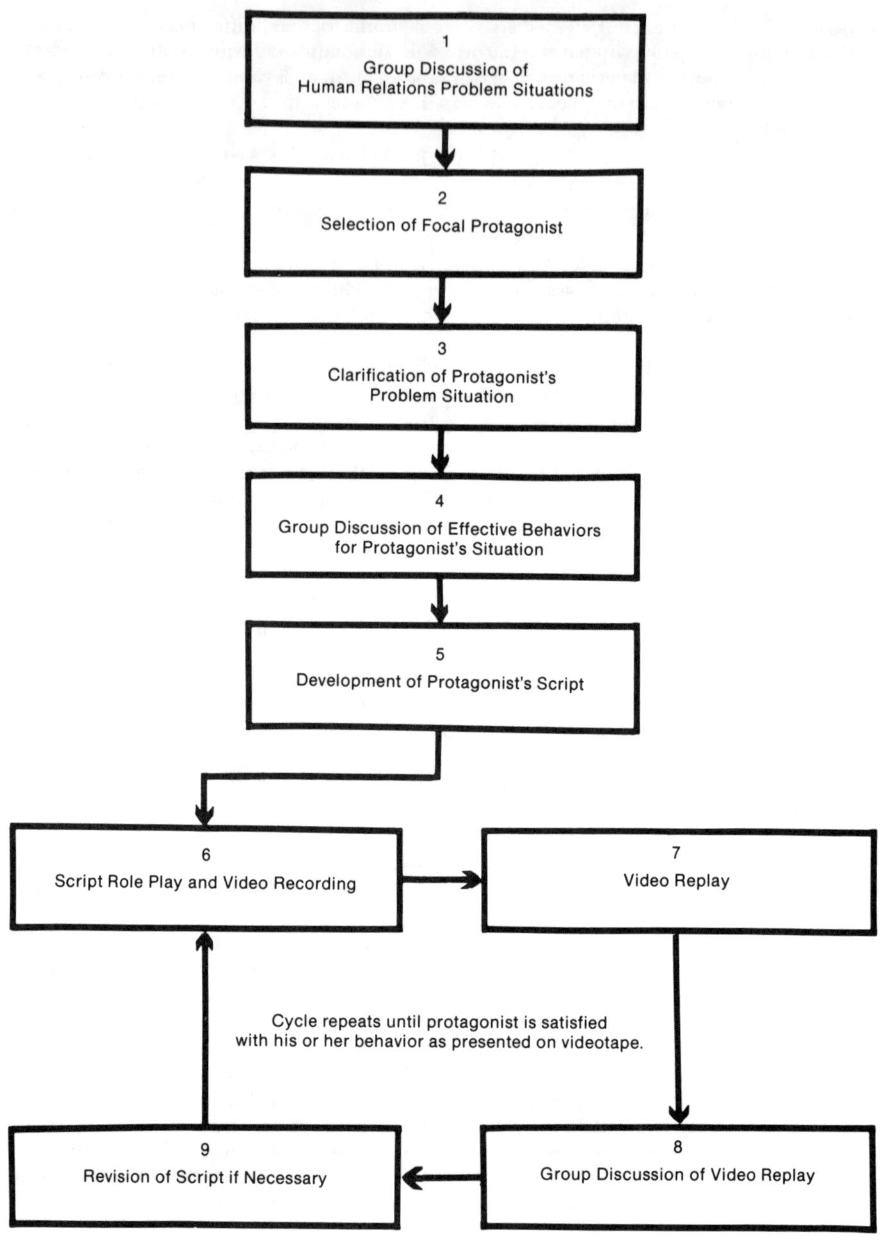

Figure 1. Diagram of Program for Video-Enhanced Human Relations Training

produces new ideas about behaviors that might be more effective than those written into the script. In this event, the script is revised, and Steps 6 through 9 are repeated as many times as necessary to ensure that the new behaviors are learned and the protagonist is satisfied.

When the group is ready to begin the process again with a new protagonist, the first protagonist joins the learners and participates in this capacity. Throughout the program, protagonists who have already enacted their problem situations are encouraged to try out their new behaviors between sessions and to report their experiences to the group.

EXAMPLES OF THE PROGRAM IN PROCESS

The following paragraphs present two examples from an assertiveness-training group that was designed according to the program just described. Eight participants and two trainers were involved.

Example 1

Jim, one of the participants, worked as a foreman in a large manufacturing plant. During Step 1, the group discussion, he identified a problem situation. Subsequently, when it was Jim's turn to serve as the focal protagonist, his problem was clarified; a script was developed; and Jim and Dave, another group member chosen to play the role of his boss, played out the scenario. The group then discussed the performance. The script was deemed adequate; but, because Jim was not satisfied with his performance, he and Dave repeated the scenario three times until he was satisfied with his behavior. The total elapsed time for that session was approximately one and one-half hours.

After input from the learners was incorporated, the statement of Jim's problem situation read as follows: *I refused a request from a subordinate to change to a straight evening shift; after this refusal, the president of the subordinate's union intervened, and my boss was asked to reverse my decision.* The following script was developed from this statement.

> *Dave:* Jim, I have a request from Sam that due to medical difficulties with his older son, he needs to work a straight evening shift. I understand that you turned down his request yesterday, and I'd like to hear why.
>
> *Jim:* Dave, I know that Sam's son's medical problems are extreme, but allowing Sam to work this way could set a bad precedent. There are a number of employees who would love to work straight shifts. Also, I'm against his being on my shift for half of the month because of his inexperience with the machine that he'd be helping to operate. It would certainly affect productivity.
>
> *Dave:* I realize that we may lose production initially, but I feel that I must overrule your decision and show the union that management does have compassion for employees' problems. I'd like you to keep track of production and see if Sam does cause a decrease in productivity.
>
> *Jim:* I don't agree with your decision. I feel that we could be setting ourselves up for a rash of special requests, and the loss of production on my shift could hurt the attitude of the machine's regular operator. Of course, you're the boss; if you want me to grant Sam's request, I'll do it.

It is important to remember that this script is imagined dialog. The actual incident was completely different; Jim simply complied with his boss's request without saying anything and felt anxious and resentful for not having stated his opinion.

After the first video replay of the scenario, Jim and the learners agreed that he had been gritting his teeth and glaring as well as fidgeting and swiveling in his chair. During the second taping, he attempted to change these nonverbal behaviors; this time it was agreed after the replay that Jim had better eye contact with Dave, his voice sounded less angry, his facial expression was softer, and he did not fidget in his chair. In order to practice these new behaviors, Jim requested another taping. Finally, after the third replay, he was satisfied with his performance and felt that he had acted in an appropriately assertive manner.

Example 2

Joyce, another participant in the same group, was a volunteer assistant in a community agency. The final statement of her problem situation was as follows: *I was unable to say no when my supervisor asked me to work with an adolescent in a counseling situation.* Joyce chose Karen, a fellow group member, to play her supervisor, and together they enacted the following script of a phone conversation.

> *Karen:* I really need your help. I've got this serious case, and I feel that you're the only volunteer who is qualified to deal with it. It involves a fourteen-year-old boy who's an alcoholic. Do you think you can find time to assist the case worker?
>
> *Joyce:* Karen, I really would like to help, but, as you know, my schedule at school is very full this semester. I feel that I couldn't devote the time that's necessary for a case like that, at least not right now.
>
> *Karen:* Yes, I understand. Could you hold? I've got another call. . . . Sorry I had to keep you waiting. Now, where were we? By the way, how have you been doing?
>
> *Joyce:* I've been fine, but, as I said, I'm really busy right now. I can't afford the time to assist with the case you mentioned.
>
> *Karen:* This is really a tough case. I certainly wish you had time to work on it—I think you'd learn a lot.
>
> *Joyce:* I'm sure I would learn a lot; I usually do. But at this point I believe I'd be doing a disservice to myself, the client, and the agency.
>
> *Karen:* Well, if you change your mind, let me know.
>
> *Joyce:* I will. Good-bye.
>
> *Karen:* Good-bye.

After the first replay, Joyce had reservations about the verbal content of the script and made some minor revisions with the help of the learners. She also felt that her tone of voice showed too much frustration and that she was not positive enough. Two more tapings were required before she was finally satisfied with the replay results.

APPLICATIONS

As stated previously, the authors' program is adaptable to most training needs. To illustrate its versatility, four applications are described in the following paragraphs.

Training in Business and Industry

The key to the strategy of any training action in business or industry is the selection of the most appropriate method to be used in the instructional design. In order to bring about cost-effective behavioral changes and improved on-the-job performance, the training method selected should meet the following criteria (Bass & Vaughan, 1966):

- Each learner participates actively.
- The learners are given feedback about their attempts to improve.
- A meaningful transfer of learning from the training setting to the job setting is promoted.

- Appropriate behavior is reinforced.
- Practice and repetition are accommodated when needed.
- Motivation is provided for the learners to improve their performance.
- The learners are assisted in their efforts to change.

The training program presented in this paper meets these criteria. It can be used in any business situation in which the development of human relations skills is the goal; for example, such an application might involve the development of cooperation among employees, the development of effective work teams, or leadership training. Furthermore, the authors believe that the program improves on many other training methods used in business by emphasizing participant re-enactment of actual situations rather than lectures or predetermined simulations.

Parenting-Skills Training

In 1981 the authors used their program to teach parenting skills to parents of difficult teenagers (Schneider, 1981). The parents involved contributed actual situations in which they felt that they had not been maximally effective in dealing with their children. With each parent protagonist, the selected incident was stated and clarified, and the group offered suggestions for more productive handling of the event. Subsequently, a script was written; the scenario was enacted; and the protagonist and the other parents discussed and tried to improve on the enactment, as portrayed on the video. The real children were not present; their parts were played by other parents or the authors, who served as the trainers.

The parents found the procedure to be both enlightening and helpful in developing more effective ways of relating to their children, and the authors were impressed with the rapidity with which the parents learned new skills.

Assertiveness Training

The authors' training program is particularly appropriate for assertiveness training for the following reasons:

- Many people who participate in such training know how to be assertive but cannot or will not act in accordance with their knowledge; therefore, it is a small step from discussion to the development of an ideal script.
- It is easy for most participants to pinpoint incidents during which they wish they had acted more assertively.
- Asking the participants to write a script and then to alter it and improvise as necessary meets the needs of most people who are learning to become more assertive.

Training of Trainers and Therapists

Currently the authors are applying their program to the training of students in a therapy practicum. The students identify particular problems that they face with clients; then each protagonist completes the procedure, thereby practicing ideal therapeutic interventions. The clients' roles are played by other students, and the students learn from one another.

An interesting variation is to employ dyads, within each of which the partners take turns being the protagonist as they work on a variety of client-related therapy strategies. If the two students have acted as a team previously during the practicum, they are familiar with each other's clients and can play these roles realistically.

CONCLUSION

The authors have presented a human relations training paradigm in which video recording and playback are an integral part. With many other group training programs, video usage is adjunctive rather than integrated into the procedures. However, because video can play an important role in self-modeling and behavior rehearsal, it becomes central to any theoretical model that incorporates those concepts. Video has enormous potential in human relations training, and adjunctive uses do not allow trainers to take full advantage of this potential.

It is important that trainers incorporate any training tool—video, photography, instruments, and so forth—into a coherent theoretical framework. The authors have tried to provide such a framework, and it is hoped that others can use it productively.

REFERENCES

Bandura, A. *Principles of behavior modification.* New York: Holt, Rinehart and Winston, 1969.

Bandura, A. Psychotherapy based upon modeling principles. In A.E. Bergin & S.L. Garfield (Eds.), *Handbook of psychotherapy and behavior change: An empirical analysis.* New York: John Wiley, 1971.

Bandura, A. *Aggression: A social learning analysis.* Englewood Cliffs, NJ: Prentice-Hall, 1973.

Bandura, A. *Social learning theory.* Englewood Cliffs, NJ: Prentice-Hall, 1977.

Bass, B.M., & Vaughan, J.A. *Training in industry: The management of learning.* Belmont, CA: Wadsworth, 1966.

Dawley, H.H., & Wenrich, W.W. *Achieving assertive behavior: A guide to assertive training.* Monterey, CA: Brooks/Cole, 1976.

Doyle, P. Behavior rehearsal to video simulations: Applications, techniques and outcomes. In J.L. Fryrear & R. Fleshman (Eds.), *Videotherapy in mental health.* Springfield, IL: Charles C Thomas, 1981.

Duval, S., & Wicklund, R.A. *A theory of objective self-awareness.* New York: Academic Press, 1972.

Fuller, F., & Manning, B. Self-confrontation reviewed: A conceptualization for video playback in teacher education. *Review of Educational Research,* 1973, *43,* 469-520.

Ho, P., & Hosford, R. *The effects of anxiety on recall in self vs. other model observations.* Unpublished manuscript, University of California, Santa Barbara, 1979.

Holzman, P., Berger, A., & Rousey, C. Voice confrontation: A bilingual study. *Journal of Personality and Social Psychology,* 1967, *7,* 423-428.

Hosford, R.E. Self-as-a-model: A cognitive social learning technique. *The Counseling Psychologist,* 1980, *9*(1), 45-62.

Lazarus, A. Behavior rehearsal vs. nondirective therapy vs. advice in effecting behavior change. *Behavior Research and Therapy,* 1966, *4,* 209-212.

Meichenbaum, D. Examination of model characteristics in reducing avoidance behavior. *Journal of Personality and Social Psychology,* 1971, *17,* 298-307.

Pfeiffer, J.W., Heslin, R., & Jones, J.E. *Instrumentation in human relations training* (2nd ed.). San Diego, CA: University Associates, 1976.

Salomon, G., & McDonald, F. Pretest and posttest reactions to self-viewing one's teaching performance on videotape. *Journal of Educational Psychology,* 1970, *61,* 280-286.

Schneider, S.A. *Video enhanced self-modeling in the development of assertive behavior.* Unpublished master's thesis, University of Houston, Clear Lake City, 1981.

Thelen, M.H., Fry, R.A., Fehrenbach, P.A., & Frautschi, N.M. Developments in therapeutic videotape and film modeling. In J.L. Fryrear & R. Fleshman (Eds.), *Videotherapy in mental health.* Springfield, IL: Charles C Thomas, 1981.

Wicklund, R.A. Objective self-awareness. In L. Berkowitz (Ed.), *Advances in experimental social psychology* (Vol. 8). New York: Academic Press, 1975.

Jerry L. Fryrear, Ph.D., *is a professor and coordinator of clinical training for the Human Sciences Program at the University of Houston at Clear Lake City and is co-director of the Institute for Psychosocial Applications of Video and Photography at the university. Dr. Fryrear also teaches courses in psychopathology and psychotherapy, conducts research on the use of video and photography in counseling and psychotherapy, and has co-authored several books on the subject. He is managing editor of the journal* Phototherapy.

Stephen A. Schneider is the director of the Ecumenical Sponsoring Committee, Inc., in San Jose, California, and is an organizational consultant in the areas of value-based leadership training, fund raising, listening and communication-skills training, meeting-effectiveness training, and managerial-skills training. Mr. Schneider's special interest is in the development and growth of individuals in organizational settings, leading to more creative and productive output and satisfaction. He also is interested in video-enhanced human relations training.

THE ART OF CREATIVE FIGHTING

H.B. Karp

Whether the particular setting is the family, the small group, the agency, or the business unit, training individuals to deal effectively with conflict requires a great deal of skill and awareness on the part of the facilitator. When training is unsuccessful in other areas of human resource development, such as communication, problem solving, or motivation, the worst that usually happens is that the situation does not improve with time; in other words, communication remains ineffective, problems are not solved, or productivity fails to increase. In dealing with conflict, however, the situation is quite different. A training error or an inappropriate intervention can make the situation immediately more risky and volatile than it was previously. It also becomes less likely that a positive outcome will emerge.

Several elements contribute to making conflict training such a touchy area:

- The topic itself has a strong tendency to initiate deep feelings on the part of most participants and some facilitators. Most people either do not like conflict or are afraid of it even before they deal with it.

- Training in conflict management is not just a matter of cognitive understanding of relevant theory and technique. Facilitators must be comfortable with conflict and their own unique approaches to dealing with it *before* they can assist others in this regard.

- Despite disclaimers to the contrary, there appears to be a highly preferred, "one-best way" to deal with conflict from the viewpoint of human resource development: collaboration. Facilitators work effectively with people in developing collaborative approaches to conflict issues, but they often ignore or avoid other approaches in the process. This tendency has the effect of limiting alternatives and can lead to an impasse. In fact, such a unidirectional approach may increase rather than lessen the fear of conflict. Although collaboration may be the most preferable method for dealing with conflict, on some occasions a collaborative solution simply is not available.

A pragmatic view of training in the area of conflict indicates that the first essential step is to help people to see the simplest and most basic aspects of conflict, thereby stripping it of its mystic and awesome nature. Conflict certainly demands respect, but it need not generate fear and wonder. The second essential step is to legitimize the *process* of conflict. The most valuable skill needed in handling a conflict is not the ability to get along well; it is the ability to fight well. The time to get along well is after the fight is over. Indeed, when people are able to fight fully and creatively, it is probable that they will get along better after the resolution than they did before the conflict arose.

THE NATURE OF CONFLICT

Conflict occurs when two or more people attempt to occupy the same space at the same time. This space can be physical, psychological, intimate, political, or any arena in which there is room for only one view, outcome, or individual. Whether cast in the home or the work setting, conflict is absolutely unavoidable as a normal condition of active life. In addition, it is neither good nor bad in itself; it simply is. Whether the outcome of a conflict situation is positive or negative is almost totally determined by the way in which it is managed. When managed effectively, conflict actually becomes a vital asset in that it is a prime source of energy and creativity in a system.

The four major categories of areas in which conflict arises are described as follows, in descending order of the objectivity involved.

1. *Fact.* Conflict over fact is the most frequent variety, the most objective in nature, the least volatile, and by far the easiest to resolve. This type of conflict centers on *what a thing is or is not.* Resolution is usually achieved by comparing the object of the conflict to a standard or by referring to a mutually acceptable authority. For example, if one person believes that a specific object is a hammer and another believes it to be an axe, resolution is simple to achieve: Obtain a picture of each and hold them next to the object in question.

2. *Method.* Conflict over method is a little more subjective and volatile than conflict over fact. Those involved disagree about a procedure and are in conflict over *what is to be done.* Although personal opinion enters into the process, the conflict can be managed objectively for the most part. For example, a conflict about how to conduct a sales campaign can be resolved most easily by achieving mutual agreement on market conditions, advertising capabilities, budget constraints, and so forth.

3. *Objectives.* Conflict over objectives is more subjective and has a greater potential for volatility than the two types previously discussed. It concerns *what is to be accomplished* and is harder fought due to the fact that it incorporates higher degrees of personal commitment and risk, in terms of both personal and organizational variables. For example, "what is best for the company," such as the next project, is often intertwined with "what is best for me," such as the next promotion. Critical to managing this type of conflict is the recognition that the subjective elements involved are as legitimate as the objective elements.

4. *Values.* Conflict over values is almost totally subjective in nature and is, therefore, the most volatile type. It pertains to *what is right or wrong.* Mismanaged conflicts over values can result in divorces and even wars. The basic strategy in dealing with such a conflict is to avoid it if at all possible. If it is unavoidable, the best tactic is to objectify the issue as much as possible, dealing with behaviors or events that arise from the value rather than dealing with the value itself. For example, a heated argument over the morality of capital punishment has a high probability of ending in nothing but rage, self-righteousness, and moral indignation. However, a discussion of capital punishment in terms of its deterrent effects and legal ramifications has a somewhat better chance of resulting in agreement and resolution.

STRATEGIES FOR MANAGING CONFLICT

The three basic strategies that are used to manage conflict are described in the following paragraphs. These strategies concern the way in which the conflict is resolved rather than the way in which it is conducted.

1. *Competition* is known as the "win/lose" approach to conflict; people compete to see who wins, and the winner takes all. The most obvious example of the competitive approach to conflict is an athletic event.

2. *Compromise* is a "lose/lose" approach. All parties agree to sacrifice equal portions of what they want. Subsequently, another mutual cut may be established and another until everyone settles for very little of what he or she originally wanted. An illustration of the result of conflict that is dealt with through compromise is the comparison between the wording of a bill in the House of Representatives prior to its first committee hearing and the final wording when that bill is enacted into law.

3. *Collaboration* is called the "win/win" approach. When this strategy is employed, people agree ahead of time to work with their conflict until they come up with a unique solution that provides each of them with all or almost all of what he or she wants.

There is little question that the collaborative approach to conflict, although it is the most costly in terms of time and energy, has the highest probability of producing the most creative and highest yielding results. However, as mentioned previously, there are times when a collaborative approach is not available and the issues are too important and vital to the individuals involved even to consider compromise. Some conditions that tend to preclude collaboration are harsh time deadlines, poor interpersonal relationships between or among the conflicting parties, severely limited resources, or differing values. Under these circumstances, competition is the only means available for managing the conflict.

Frequently a conflict is first approached competitively due to disinterest in or unawareness of a collaborative alternative; then, after those involved have competed for a while, they discover a collaborative solution. If the fighting is creative and effective, there is a higher probability that this will occur, given the potential availability of a collaborative solution at the outset.

CREATIVE FIGHTING

It is often the case that people in conflict are unwilling to engage each other powerfully simply because they do not possess the basic skills required for effective fighting. Paradoxically, once an individual has acquired these skills and is comfortable with them, it is much less likely that he or she will have to use them. The newly acquired knowledge and abilities produce a clear confidence that is observable to others, thereby making the individual less subject to unilateral attacks. On the other hand, if a fight becomes unavoidable, he or she can handle it.

Anger is as appropriate and productive a reaction to events as is any other human response. It is as unavoidably reflexive a response to being frustrated as laughter is to being amused. The issue involved is not whether it is appropriate to feel anger when frustrated, but rather how to deal with anger appropriately when it occurs. People must be made aware that there are techniques of fighting that can be learned and used skillfully. Also, they must be given the opportunity to practice these techniques in a neutral, low-risk setting, such as a training workshop. When all parties involved in a fight have acknowledged the legitimacy of conflict, established the norms for fighting, and are confident in their own abilities and strength, they are likely to approach one another with respect. Under such circumstances, there is little threat to ongoing relationships; in fact, there is a great potential for solidifying and enhancing these relationships.

The following paragraphs describe ten guidelines for the process of preparing people to fight creatively.

Establish the Legitimacy of Fighting

Fighting must be seen as a natural and sometimes appropriate thing to do. Occasionally it is even fun, as long as all parties agree to do it. Above all, fighting must not be viewed as an activity to be avoided at all costs. Whenever two or more people are working or living together, conflicts of interest arise. Sometimes these conflicts can be resolved through peaceful negotiation or willing compliance; sometimes they cannot. When the latter condition exists, fighting is the ultimate and appropriate response, unless one or more of the parties disempower themselves and give in because of fear of confrontation.

As stated previously, when fighting is approached creatively, it has several positive aspects that should be recognized: It is energizing; it honors all of its participants; it frequently produces the best solution under the circumstances; it strengthens, rather than weakens, relationships; and the arena in which it occurs becomes a safer, more "human" place in which to live and work. When fighting is not engaged in creatively, personal relationships deteriorate and become characterized by spite, sniping, silent vows of vengeance, sulking, self-pity, and complaints about being misunderstood.

Deal with One Issue at a Time

In an ongoing relationship, unfinished business frequently co-exists with the current source of contention. The temptation when fighting is to bring up unresolved arguments from the past and catch an opponent off guard. When this ploy is successful, the person who initiated it achieves the upper hand and places the opponent on the defensive; the parties involved start a different fight that bears no relevance to the present conflict, and both (or all) of them become vulnerable to attack in this fashion.

Therefore, it is important for those in conflict to maintain a focus on the point of contention. When one person confronts another with an unrelated issue, the individual who is attacked should not respond except to say "That's not what we're dealing with at the moment." Subsequently, the parties may agree to discuss the secondary issue at some time in the future.

Occasionally, during the course of a fight, it becomes obvious that a secondary issue from the past is actually blocking the resolution of the issue at hand. For example, one person might say to another, "The last time you asked me for support and I helped you, you refused to acknowledge my contribution in the final report." When such a situation arises, the current issue should be set aside until closure of the unfinished issue is achieved, at which point the original fight can be continued with greater energy and a higher probability of a successful outcome. The important point is that only one issue should be addressed at a time.

Choose the Arena Carefully

Just because one person is angry with another and wants to fight does not automatically mean that the second party is ready or willing to oblige. Too often, one of the parties is dragged into "the combat zone" when totally unprepared or disinterested, and this situation frequently creates further unnecessary defensiveness, resentment, and personal animosity. To prevent such a development, all parties involved must understand and agree that if one person does not want to fight at a particular moment, no fight takes place at that time. There are three basic responses to consider when a fight is impending.

1. *Engage.* If the timing is right and the point is legitimate, the sooner it is brought into the open and dealt with creatively, the better. The usual outcome of avoiding a fight is that the longer it stays internalized, the higher the probability that it will fester and become more interpersonally volatile.

2. *Accede.* If an issue is important to one party but not to another, the person who feels it to be unimportant may accede to the point. Before engaging in a fight, everyone involved should determine whether the issue is worth his or her time and effort. It makes little sense to pursue a goal that is of no personal consequence. One benefit of this response is that it transforms an opponent into an ally. Another positive aspect is that the individual who consciously chooses to accede to another's wishes experiences no loss of power.

3. *Postpone.* If a person is prematurely engaged in a conflict, he or she may choose to acknowledge the issue and then put it aside. This approach involves listening to what the other person says, acknowledging an understanding of the point being made and its importance, and setting a time for assembling everyone involved and dealing with the issue. This response has a

tendency not only to defuse the issue for the individual who brought it up, but also to prevent its escalation. In addition, postponing a fight allows time to consider the issue fully and to develop appropriate tactics.

The individual who initiates a confrontation and is met with postponing as a response must remember that an opponent should never be forced to fight before he or she is ready. Agreeing to the postponement can be advantageous in that a fully prepared opponent is less likely to overreact or to wage unwarranted counterattacks than is an opponent who is caught off guard.

Avoid Reacting to Unintentional Remarks

Frequently, in the heat of battle, things are said that are regretted an instant later. This is particularly true if the issue at hand is of deep, personal significance to one or both of the parties; if ego involvement is high; or if the relationship is an important one. A related consideration is the fact that often people do not know precisely what they feel or think until they hear themselves verbalizing these feelings or thoughts.

An important aspect of creative fighting is to establish the norm that when unexpected or unintentional comments are made, none of the parties involved will respond by escalating the fight into a more volatile stage that no one wants. Instead, the preferred tactic should be to stop the conversation when a questionable comment is made and determine whether the comment accurately conveys what the speaker meant. If the speaker disavows the comment, everyone— including the speaker—should ignore it; if he or she confirms it, a deeper point of contention may have arisen. In the latter case, those involved in the fight must then decide which issue to focus on.

Avoid Resolutions That Come Too Soon or Too Easily

Newly married couples are often told, "Never let the sun set on an argument." However, this advice may be too simplistic. When a fight is resolved too quickly or a simple but incomplete resolution is agreed to, there are several negative side effects that are usually more painful and damaging in the long run than the original fight itself.

For example, if a fight ends prematurely, its unfinished elements do not go away; they are temporarily repressed and will almost certainly manifest themselves later. Also, the easiest solution is not always the best one in that it tends to treat symptoms and thereby obscure the real problem. Still another negative effect is that if the solution is complete for one party but not for another, the person who feels unsatisfied is not emotionally free to enter into future fights with total enthusiasm. This last effect, although very subtle, can seriously damage the relationship(s) involved.

Each fight has its own, unique level of intensity. Some fights involve simple disagreements and are resolvable "by sundown," whereas those that involve intense feelings, deep-seated values, or complex issues require much more time to be dealt with effectively. With each fight, it is essential that the parties recognize and remain aware of the time element.

There are two ways to approach the handling of time. The first is to recognize clearly and specifically the complexity and importance of the issue and then to agree to devote as much time as required to achieve a resolution. The second approach, known as "bracketing," is also quite useful, particularly when complex, interdependent relationships are involved and the issue at hand is complicated. Many times, reality dictates that even though a fight is taking place, everyday life must go on. When this is the case, it is appropriate to fight for the length of time available; "bracket" the fight by setting it aside completely, but on a temporary basis; devote energies to other concerns as necessary; and resume the fight when possible. In many instances, this approach allows adversaries to work together well and energetically in areas that are not affected by the fight; the harmonious functioning is possible because the point of contention, although "on hold," is still actively being honored by the adversaries.

Avoid Name Calling

The function of creative fighting is to manage conflict in such a way that the following outcomes are ensured.

- An effective resolution is found;
- Everyone involved maintains a clear sense of personal dignity throughout; and
- The relationship(s) is (are) in no way damaged.

Nothing blocks these outcomes more effectively than resorting to name calling.

Creative fighting is unlike many other approaches to conflict in which the participants devote their efforts to injuring their opponents as much as possible; instead, when fighting creatively, each participant strives to achieve a specific objective. In most cases these individual objectives are mutually exclusive so that a clear choice must be made as to which will constitute the final outcome. When accomplishing a specific objective is a person's reason for fighting, it is very much in that individual's best interest not to dehumanize the opponent(s).

Name calling usually occurs when logical arguments fail or when one or more of the parties have become frustrated beyond tolerance. In order to avoid name calling, the safest and most productive stance to maintain throughout the fight is to speak strictly for oneself. When everyone invariably speaks only in terms of what he or she wants, feels, or thinks, there is little risk that anyone will be personally offended; consequently, there is little risk that the fight will escalate to a more volatile and unmanageable level.

Avoid Cornering an Opponent

Occasionally, being "right" and devastating one's opponent may be more personally satisfying than achieving the best resolution possible. However, this approach produces only momentary satisfaction and can be very costly. The practice of cornering and devastating an opponent may preclude a solid resolution. Also, the party who is the object of such an attack may eventually retaliate in kind.

One important aspect of conflict is that, regardless of the point of contention, the longer the fight goes on or the greater the intensity, the higher the ego involvement and the greater the need to save face. Everyone involved should keep this in mind and make it as easy as possible to accommodate one another's wishes. Above all, opponents must be allowed to save face. For example, if it is obvious to everyone that an opponent cannot win a particular argument, it is best to let that opponent retire gracefully. The adversary who allows such a retreat not only achieves what he or she wants, but also accords the opponent the respect that is deserved. Thus, this stance usually results in some degree of appreciation on the part of the vanquished opponent, particularly when all parties realize that pain and humiliation could have been inflicted had the party with the upper hand chosen to do so.

Agree To Disagree

Creative fighting demands the generation of alternatives and a conscious choice of one of these alternatives. Although a mutually acceptable resolution is always the desired outcome, sometimes the reality is that such a resolution is not available. In a fight in which the point of contention is basically impersonal, such as an argument over a fact or a method, a mutually acceptable resolution is almost always available. However, in a fight that is waged over a deeper, more personal issue, such as an objective or a value, mutuality is much more difficult and sometimes impossible to achieve. In the latter case, each viewpoint is so innately a part of the individual who holds it that any attempt to minimize its validity will be taken as an attack on the individual personally. Thus, it is almost impossible for someone involved in such a fight to concede a point without feeling personally diminished in the process.

As mentioned previously, the best and most obvious choice in dealing with arguments of a personal nature is to avoid them completely, if at all possible. Sometimes, however, a discussion about one point reveals a more intense point that is really what is at issue. As soon as it becomes evident that the parties involved are diametrically opposed on a deeply personal issue, there is little or no chance that anything can be said to alter the situation. In fact, the longer the confrontation continues, the higher the probability that each party will become more firmly entrenched in his or her position. Thus, the parties should simply agree to disagree and drop the subject for the moment. Once everyone agrees that it is perfectly acceptable to see things differently and that no attempts at conversion will be made, the subject is much safer to discuss in the future should it arise again. In the meantime, all parties can live or work together productively, because the point of difference can be side-stepped.

It is highly improbable that people involved in a long-term work or personal relationship will share all core values. Not to recognize this fact invites unnecessary squabbling. Although there seems to be constant pressure in interdependent relationships to locate common ground, it may be just as important to isolate irreconcilable differences and acknowledge them as being equally natural and "human."

In some rare instances in which a relationship between two people is extremely interdependent and long term, the parties may hold such polarized values that when one pursues his or her value, the pursuance automatically creates pain or severe problems for the other. Some examples of this type of polarization are the need for autonomy versus the need for participation, the need for isolation versus the need for intimacy, and concern with production versus concern for people. When the situation is so extreme that any concession on the part of either person will result in a loss of self-respect, the following procedure should be considered.

1. *Accept the polarity.* The two parties involved must establish the norm that both have a right to their viewpoints, but that neither is required to like the opposite viewpoint.

2. *Establish the importance of the relationship.* The parties should determine all of the positive, productive aspects of the relationship. It is preferable that they complete this task together rather than separately. They must review the basic values that they hold in common as well as their past successes in the relationship. During this process, enjoyable times and instances of mutual support should be recalled, and the potential for similar occurrences in the future should be accepted. In addition, the interdependent nature of the relationship should be acknowledged and defined.

It is important to note, however, that this step might reveal the possibility that the two parties do not have a solid relationship and that permanent disengagement may be the most realistic, mutually benefical resolution.

3. *Stay with the fight to the end.* If the parties determine that the relationship is important and worth saving, they must agree to endure the fight. However, neither should acquiesce only to please the other person or to reduce the other's pain; both should be appreciative of attempts to please, but they should not accept concessions that are made strictly for this purpose. If they have evaluated their relationship correctly, they will find ways to continue to work together productively, even though they are both experiencing some degree of pain. Both parties must remember that although they seriously disagree on a specific issue, they do not disagree on all others.

Working or living with someone under these conditions represents an incredibly heavy burden for both parties. Sooner or later, only because of exhaustion, it is probable that they will mutually agree to "let go" of the troublesome issue. More to the point, as the exhaustion increases, so does the importance of other issues, and the originally polarized viewpoints tend to become modified. When this happens, it may be possible to achieve a resolution.

Focus on What Is Wanted Rather Than Why It Is Wanted

Almost all fights, creative or otherwise, arise from the fact that the participants want different things. Also, in many cases compliance from the opponent(s) is necessary for the attainment of each person's objective. Thus, it is essential to establish clearly what each party wants and how these objectives differ. On the other hand, spending time and energy exploring *why* each party wants what he or she wants is, at best, a total waste of time and, at worst, an invitation to a psychological melee.

The point to remember is that people have a right to want what they want and to want all of it. This point has tremendous impact on creative fighting. When participants answer opponents' inquiries as to why they want specific objectives, they become "defendants" and the opponents become "judges" who can rule on the worthiness of the reasons supplied. These reasons, once verbalized, are usually anything but convincing. The reality is that very few people know exactly why they want what they want. In fact, most are not too concerned with their own motivation in this regard; for them, it is simply enough that they want.

In addition, the answer to the first "why?" usually leads to another "why?" and still another, and each time the defendant is forced to stray farther from the original objective to provide an answer. Eventually, the issue that generated the fight becomes obscured. The roles may even be reversed; the defendant may become the judge and counter with questions of his or her own. Thus, all parties are compelled to defend themselves, and as a result the fight may escalate.

Therefore, the best strategy is to avoid asking and answering queries about motivation. Instead, each person should concentrate on accomplishing his or her specific goal.

Maintain a Sense of Humor

Fighting is most often viewed as a grim and serious business. In many cases, of course, it is quite serious and certainly deserves to be respected. However, even when the subject of the fight is important and tempers are aroused, it is important that the participants not lose their perspectives. The best way to retain one's perspective during a fight is to exercise a sense of humor. For example, a married couple may be arguing vehemently about finances when suddenly the husband exclaims, "Not only *that*, but you never really liked my mother!" At such moments, it is perfectly legitimate to recognize the humor of the situation and respond accordingly. In fact, the parties involved may be unable to control their laughter and subsequently may find that the fight has disintegrated. Although the tendency when engaged in a fight is to become more "righteous" as the confrontation progresses, the participants would do well to remember that it is the fight that should be taken seriously—not themselves.

SUMMARY

Training people to deal with conflict in an effective manner requires much of a facilitator. Participants must be taught that conflict is a natural part of life and that dealing with it creatively can actually enhance rather than destroy relationships.

Part of the facilitator's responsibility is to help the participants to see that there are four different sources of conflict—fact, method, objectives, and values—and that each source represents a different level of volatility. In addition, the three basic strategies for handling conflict—competition, compromise, and collaboration—should be presented and explained, and the facilitator should take care not to convey an exclusive prejudice in favor of collaboration.

When all participants are aware of the basic aspects of conflict, they should be allowed to practice fighting creatively in a relatively nonthreatening environment, such as a workshop. As they practice, the facilitator should help them to adhere to the ten guidelines that are detailed in this paper.

H. B. Karp, Ph.D., serves as a consultant through his own organization, Personal Growth Systems, in Norfolk, Virginia. He conducts public and in-house workshops in the areas of leadership and supervisory effectiveness and consults to organizations in the areas of team building and conflict management. Dr. Karp's background is in organizational psychology, organization development, human motivation, and Gestalt applications to individual and organizational growth.

A MODEL FOR TRAINING DESIGN: SELECTING APPROPRIATE METHODS

Donald T. Simpson

Many trainers and consultants who are skilled at facilitating learning groups hesitate to attempt the design of a major training program. Instead, they adapt designs from their experience and rely heavily on instinct. In doing so, they restrict themselves to using methods with which they are comfortable—with the potential that the trainer's comfort may come at the learners' expense. What is needed, therefore, is a systematic, rational approach to designing a learning program that is based on current, sound research rather than on personal intuition. In this paper, the author presents such an approach in model form, concentrating on guidelines for selecting needs-analysis methods, a design strategy, and training methods.

THE NEED FOR A DESIGN MODEL

One effective way to bridge the gap between research and application is through the use of models. A model describes the reality of research, just as a set of blueprints describes a house. Of necessity, the individual who conceives a model of a particular process makes some assumptions and/or eliminates some variables. The resulting abstract thus allows its users to clarify their understanding of the process and to describe it with a common language.

The purpose of a training-design model is to describe the complex phenomena of adult learning in terms that can be used to design the training process. Ideally, the originator of such a model starts with research findings and philosophies about how adults learn and then works toward educational strategies described as methods and media. If a model is to be useful, it also should be applicable over a wide range of learning situations.

THE ROLE OF RESEARCH

Trainers base their actions with learning groups on their assumptions about the way in which people learn. These assumptions may be the result of an understanding of current research, personal values, and/or personal experience as learners. Whatever the source, it is helpful and necessary to examine these assumptions periodically and to determine their validity.

As designers of training programs, trainers become consumers of research. The designer begins with the philosophy and research of education, sociology, and psychology; combines the resulting data with the practical applications and constraints of "the real world"; and then develops a useful learning vehicle.

The model described in this paper is based on the philosophy of Pine and Horne (1969), who described the conditions that facilitate adult learning. It also draws on the ideas of Krathwohl, Bloom, and Masia (1964), who classified different types of learning as follows:

- The cognitive domain, which allows an individual to learn and recall facts, concepts, and principles. In the author's model, this element is called the *knowledge component*.
- The psychomotor domain, which involves the motor or neuromuscular skills and allows

an individual not only to move as desired, but also to solve problems and to communicate interpersonally. The author refers to this element as the *skill component.*

● The affective domain, which allows an individual to form and exercise values, attitudes, and feelings. This element is termed the *attitudinal component* in the author's model.

In addition, the model relies on Knowles' (1970) description of the way in which adults learn and the methods that are most effective in helping them to learn. The connection between the model and Knowles' work is explained later in this paper.

THE DEVELOPMENTAL SEQUENCE OF THE MODEL

Figure 1 depicts a sequence for designing a training program. Each of the steps involved is dealt with separately in the following paragraphs.

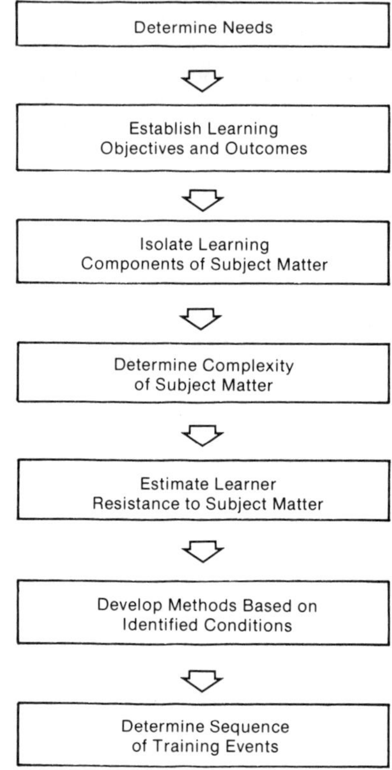

Figure 1. A Model for Designing a Training Program

Determine Needs

If a trainer designs and trains in accordance with incorrectly defined needs, that work is in vain. Before considering design strategies or delivery, the trainer must be confident that the right issues are being addressed. Often, management identifies as a training problem an issue that cannot be addressed properly through training. Thus, it is the trainer's responsibility, whenever possible, to provide the objectivity demanded by a needs determination. It would be desirable, of course, always to conduct the most accurate and complete analysis possible. Most organizations, however, do not have unlimited resources, especially during difficult economic times; in addition, the training effort under consideration may not warrant a costly, time-consuming needs assessment. Therefore, it is often necessary to compromise for the sake of practicality.

Newstrom and Lilyquest (1979) describe five criteria that affect the selection of needs-analysis methods. For simplicity in application, these five are combined into three as follows:

1. *Cost.* When planning a needs assessment, the cost must be considered in terms of money and time. In general, the more accurate and the more complete the assessment, the more it will cost and the longer it will take. Also, as more people are involved in the effort, both types of expenditure tend to increase. Some anticipated learner populations are so large that the cost of surveying or interviewing all participants becomes prohibitive; in these cases the trainer must employ sampling techniques.

2. *Accuracy.* The degree of accuracy required varies with the type of program being contemplated. Some training programs are so critical to the organization that the needs must be determined with absolute accuracy; interventions involving the way in which people control a major manufacturing process or the way in which a hospital staff carries out key medical procedures are examples of such critical efforts. Other types of training, however, may not demand a high degree of accuracy; examples are orientation programs for new employees or introductions of new administrative procedures within which there will be reviews and checks. Obviously, when extreme accuracy is a necessity, the cost of the assessment is increased.

3. *Commitment.* A commitment to the training effort, especially on the part of the prospective learners, is an important factor. Conducting a timely, accurate assessment of training needs is a wasted effort if the would-be learners resist the program. Thus, it is important that the trainer build commitment into the design. One way to accomplish this—although it usually involves time, effort, and money—is to involve the learners in the assessment of their own needs. Similarly, management commitment to a training effort can be enhanced by involving the decision makers early and often.

Thus, it becomes apparent that the degrees of accuracy and commitment required in a given situation affect the cost of needs assessment. Figure 2 is a categorization of assessment methods that are appropriate under various circumstances. Different methods often can be combined to achieve a balance among the factors of cost, accuracy, and commitment. For example, a general survey may be used to indicate trends as well as to identify specific individuals for in-depth interviews. Examination of data, such as records of customer complaints or funding sources, may be combined with task analysis of selected positions and interviewing. Combining methods is also a way of effecting a reality check on the determination of training needs.

Establish Learning Objectives and Outcomes

It is essential that the trainer design the program in accordance with appropriate learning objectives and the corresponding knowledge, behaviors, and/or skills to be gained. If people are trained to know or do something for which they have no use in "real life," the training program becomes a waste of trainer time, learner time, and money. In addition, learners who are unable to apply their learnings because of organizational regulations or other factors often experience a deep sense of frustration. Under these circumstances, training becomes dysfunctional. Thus, it is important to ensure that all of those whose functioning might be affected by a training program—management as well as participants, for example—understand fully and commit themselves to the learning objectives and content. One way to enhance such commitment, as noted earlier, is to involve everyone throughout the process of program development.

Involvement need not mean one-on-one interviews with every person who might be affected. It often takes the form of negotiating training time and objectives with management, feeding back survey results to learners, and educating both management and learners regarding the rationale behind the training design. Removing the element of mystery from the design fosters commitment and trust.

Another important reason for involving others in establishing objectives and outcomes is that this approach provides another reality check. Those who are closest to the environment in which the training will be applied can easily identify anything impractical or unworkable.

Isolate Learning Components of Subject Matter

In designing a training experience, the trainer should start by re-examining the program objectives in terms of the knowledge, skills, and/or attitudes to be gained. For example, it is a good idea to look for the verbs in the objectives: Verbs such as *know, list, describe,* and *discuss* indicate a strong knowledge component, whereas verbs like *conduct, operate, construct,* and *perform* indicate a strong skill component. Although all learning involves all three components, isolating the three allows the trainer to consider specific methods best suited to the subject matter.

Knowledge Components

In general, these components are most effectively addressed through some method that allows self-paced learning. Such methods include assigned reading; written or computer-assisted, programed instruction; and individual, analytical work, such as with case studies. Many professionals in the field of adult education have published research strongly indicating that

	Low Demands for Accuracy	High Demands for Accuracy
Moderate Commitment Required	General survey Trend data Opinions/instinct	Task analysis Mission analysis Assessment center with limited feedback Detailed data analysis
High Commitment Required	One-on-one interviews Group interviews Critical incidents followed by interviews	A combination of methods: mission/task analysis, survey, interviews, and feedback/clarification meetings

Figure 2. Needs-Assessment Methods That Accommodate Requirements for Accuracy and Commitment

everyone gains knowledge in an individualized, self-paced way (Knowles, 1970); yet training in knowledge components often continues routinely to be done in groups. In addition, bringing people together unnecessarily for this purpose increases the cost of training in terms of effort, time, and money. Thus, it would seem to be more desirable to develop materials that can be sent to individual learners rather than to send the learners to the materials.

Skill Components

Components dealing with skills suggest a strategy of interaction with the materials, machines, or people involved. The need to learn interpersonal skills, for example, implies that the participants must work with other people during the training experience, whereas the need to learn how to operate a machine implies that the participants must actually use that equipment during training. In other words, learning skills means learning by doing. Often the trainer must turn to simulation for practical reasons; learners need to practice new skills in the relatively safe environment provided by a training setting before they feel confident enough to risk using them in "the real world." However, the greater the similarity between the training environment and the "real-life" environment, the more effective the training.

Attitudinal Components

These components, which deal with the affective domain, suggest an experiential approach designed to evoke specific behaviors and to provide continued positive reinforcement of a particular attitude. Training seldom effects total and instant conversions because attitudes form over time, usually as the long-term result of specific behaviors and the experienced consequences of those behaviors. Thus, in most training programs, attitudinal components become variables associated with the more immediate objectives related to knowledge and skill. If the trainer provides a design that enables learners to acquire the knowledge and skill needed to accomplish a particular task and if he or she follows up with positive reinforcement, then it is likely that the learners will develop a positive attitude toward that task.

Determine Complexity of Subject Matter

As the complexity of the subject matter increases, so must the learner interaction with that subject matter. Too much interaction with a simple topic either bores or insults learners, and too little interaction with complex material results in a failure to learn. The facilitator can gauge whether the chosen methods are appropriate in this regard by evaluating learnings at intervals during a field test.

Learner readiness for a given subject matter is a related concern. If readiness is overestimated or if some learners do not meet prerequisites, the trainer may need to spend more time on the topic than planned.

Estimate Learner Resistance to Subject Matter

The learners' resistance to the subject matter, as anticipated by the trainer, is an important consideration. The ability to estimate resistance depends on one's knowledge of the topic, the organization involved, the sociology of the learners as a group, and the events that led to training. Dealing with resistance is similar to dealing with complexity of subject matter: The higher the level of anticipated resistance, the greater the need for planned interaction between and among the learners. For some topics and with some learners, learning can occur with no learner interaction whatsoever. When the anticipated resistance is particularly high, confrontation is in order, leading not only to increased learner/learner interaction, but also to greater learner/trainer interaction.

Develop Methods Based on Identified Conditions

In order to develop appropriate training methods, it is necessary to combine the determinations regarding the isolation of learning components, the complexity of the subject matter, and the anticipated resistance to the subject matter. The key principle involved is that methods are chosen according to their ability to address the identified conditions. Adhering to this principle keeps the trainer from inappropriately designing personal biases into the program. For example, many trainers favor experiential methods because of their particular applicability in fostering the learning of interpersonal skills. But to apply such methods to a simple knowledge component might be inappropriate; a precourse or intersession reading assignment might not only suffice for this purpose, but also save group time for a more suitable use, such as skill practice. Figure 3 presents methods that are appropriate under specific circumstances.

The use of many training methods or tools can be varied in accordance with specific conditions. For example, a case study can be used in several ways, as illustrated in Figure 4.

Appropriate Methods

Emphasis on Knowledge Components

	Low Complexity	*High Complexity*
Low Resistance	Reading Lecture/panel discussion Film/slide/tape	Programed instruction Case study/analysis Experiential/lecture
High Resistance	Group discussion	Interactive case study Interactive instruments Simulation/game

Emphasis on Skill Components

	Low Complexity	*High Complexity*
Low Resistance	Demonstration (e.g., film) + practice	Modeling On-the-job training + feedback Instruments
High Resistance	Structured experience Group role play Modeling	Role play Psychodrama Simulation/game

Figure 3. Training Methods That Are Appropriate Under Specific Circumstances

Identified Conditions	Suggested Learner Activities
Emphasis on Knowledge Components	
Low complexity, low resistance	Read the case as an example of some concept described earlier.
High complexity, low resistance	Read and analyze the case, perhaps by responding to summary questions or by writing essays.
Low complexity, high resistance	Read and discuss the case.
High complexity, high resistance	Read, analyze, and discuss the case, perhaps developing a group analysis or recommendation.
Emphasis on Skill Components	
Low complexity, low resistance	Read the case as an example of a skill such as problem identification
High complexity, low resistance	Read and analyze the case, perhaps working out a problem-analysis sequence.
Low complexity, high resistance } High complexity, high resistance }	Read the case, analyze it, and develop a role play or simulation from it that includes interaction with others.

Figure 4. Example of Ways To Use a Case Study To Accommodate Different Conditions

Determine Sequence of Training Events

When establishing the sequence of events in a training program, the trainer should consider the following issues:

1. *Prerequisite Learning.* Some types of knowledge and skill are dependent on other types as prerequisites. For instance, one must know how to add and subtract before attempting to learn multiplication and division. Similarly, basic communication skills are prerequisite to counseling. The trainer must keep prerequisites in mind when establishing a sequence of training activities.

2. *Affective Set.* It is a good idea to begin a training program by building learner rapport, confidence, and receptivity. Getting acquainted activities and ice breakers pave the way for later learning, including the development of deeper trust and teamwork.

3. *Participation.* Generally, participation by learners increases over time as they become more comfortable with the trainer, one another, and the learning environment. Depending on other factors, the more participative elements of the program usually should be scheduled to take place after a degree of comfort has been established.

4. *Complexity/Risk.* The learners' willingness to offer opinions, deal openly with feelings, and tackle complex material also increases with time spent in the learning environment. Thus, progressing from the familiar to the unfamiliar is a useful guide.

5. *Theory/Practice.* An emphasis on knowledge components often dictates that theory be presented before practice. When the emphasis is on skill or attitude components, the trainer may present theory and rationale before practice or, as in the experiential or laboratory approach, draw conclusions from experience.

SUMMARY

The author's model for designing a training program is based on current research regarding the way in which people learn. The developmental sequence of the model begins with an assessment of the specific needs involved. Then objectives for the learning program are determined, along with expected outcomes. Subsequently, the learning components of the subject matter are categorized as consisting of knowledge, skill, and/or attitudes so that they can be addressed properly. At this point, it is important that the trainer involve all those who might be affected by the training; allowing them to have input not only increases their commitment and trust, but also provides valuable information as to what may or may not be possible to achieve in the actual work environment. The next step is to determine the complexity of the subject matter so that the trainer can select appropriate methods and time frames. The degree of learner readiness is also assessed at this point; resistance to subject matter as well as prerequisite knowledge or abilities are issues that must be analyzed and incorporated into the design.

After all existing conditions have been identified, the trainer is ready to develop a program that allows for the treatment of these conditions. Once methods have been selected, the trainer can establish a sequence of training events to follow.

Thus, with this model, the learning objectives dictate content as well as methods so that the trainer can overcome any predisposition for using only a few favorite techniques. In this way, program participants can be provided with effective learning experiences.

REFERENCES

Knowles, M.S. *The modern practice of adult education*. New York: Association Press, 1970.

Krathwohl, D.R., Bloom, S., & Masia, B.B. *Taxonomy of educational objectives: Book 2—Affective domain*. New York: Longman, 1964.

Newstrom, J.W., & Lilyquest, J.M. Selecting needs analysis methods. *Training and Development Journal*, October 1979, pp. 53-57.

Pine, G., & Horne, P. Principles and conditions for learning in adult education. *Adult Leadership*, October 1969, pp. 108-110; 126, 133-134.

Donald T. Simpson *is a personnel and organization development consultant to business and the community in the Rochester, New York, area. His current efforts are in the design of management development programs in the private and public sectors. Mr. Simpson's background is in military logistics management, industrial engineering, adult education, management education, and educational design.*

MANAGING SUPERVISORY TRANSITION

Raymond J. Zugel

Turnover in managerial or supervisory positions is a fact of life in our society. This type of transition, when unmanaged, produces effects that are well known to those who have experienced the situation: a short-range orientation, role ambiguity, reduction in openness of communication, jockeying for position, and a general lack of knowledge about the future of the organization and relationships. These common problems as well as others lead to reduced performance.

Organizations deal with managerial transition in a variety of ways. Many simply let it happen and accept the cost as a natural part of doing business; others manage it in order to reduce the cost to the organization and to maintain stability. This paper addresses a consultant-facilitated method of managing supervisory transition that has been in use for over four years and has become an effective, routine practice in a department of the Federal government.[1]

THE SITUATION

Once a change in managers is announced, organizational processes are affected. The outgoing manager focuses his or her attention more on what has to be done before the departure and less on future activities, more on task-related behaviors and less on relationship behaviors. Communication is reduced, and decisions tend either to be made very quickly with limited consultation or to be delayed until the new manager assumes authority. As the date of departure approaches, the outgoing manager becomes more and more preoccupied with his or her new position and personal concerns; however, when that day arrives, he or she becomes concerned about the future of the organization and the subordinates. In fact, the outgoing manager may be beset with contradictory feelings about how well he or she wants the new manager to perform.

Throughout this period, the subordinates develop anxiety about what will happen to them and the organization. They sense changes in their relationships and involvement with the outgoing manager as well as the creation of a vacuum because of the manager's withdrawal. Frustration builds regarding decision making, and concerns about the future are heightened. As the change of managers approaches, they tend to become increasingly cautious, anxious about the shift of power, and concerned with their own positions and prerogatives. If the new manager is unknown to them or if he or she is known to be different from the outgoing manager, their anxiety is even greater.

After the new manager has taken control, the processes of the organization adjust slowly. The new manager may be insufficiently informed about substantive matters and, therefore, unable to make decisions. Also, he or she may not know the subordinates well enough to rely on them for information and advice. As a result, decisions are often made slowly and painfully. The manager's focus is short ranged; efforts are geared toward learning what must be done to supervise the most immediate and pressing operations. Consequently, task-related behaviors

---

[1]The basic idea for this approach is not the author's. It is, rather, the product of learnings derived from a number of consultants and academicians. Michael D. Mitchell of Chico State College and Gerald D. Pike of Signetics Corporation provided the major content.

assume primary importance, and relationship behaviors are limited. In the meantime, the subordinates look for clues as to what the new manager's wants and idiosyncrasies might be, what he or she thinks is important, and how he or she wants to operate. The results of these developments are a reduction in communication and a continuance of the already-reduced organizational performance.

Figure 1 was designed to illustrate data derived from interviews with government personnel involved in unmanaged transitions. As interpreted in this figure, a small dip in performance was usually evident at approximately two and one-half months before the managerial change; it was at this point that those interviewed were informed of the upcoming transition. Subsequently, a surge in performance generally occurred as the outgoing manager sought to accomplish as much as possible before leaving. Then, with increasing proximity to the date of leaving, performance dropped. The interview data indicate that the total period of reduced performance is four to six months. In some organizations this may be acceptable; in most it probably is not.

In the department of the Federal government from which the interview data were derived and in which managers habitually changed every eighteen to twenty-four months, the loss of continuity and waste of resources were determined to be unacceptable. To counter these problems and attempt to lessen the impact of managerial change, the department adapted and employed a meeting design that was originally developed and published by Mitchell (1976, 1977). The consultant-facilitated "transition meeting," as it is known, has been found to be highly effective in this department and in private enterprise as well. It may be used in almost any transitional situation, although it is most profitable when the level of anxiety experienced by the incoming manager and/or the subordinates is high.

IMPLEMENTATION

The basic design is essentially the same as that of the team-building meeting proposed by Reilly and Jones (1974). One major addition is the inclusion of an evaluative measure for the meeting itself and one for the organization in which the meeting is conducted. Implementation of the design is accomplished in three phases: prework, the actual meeting, and follow-up.

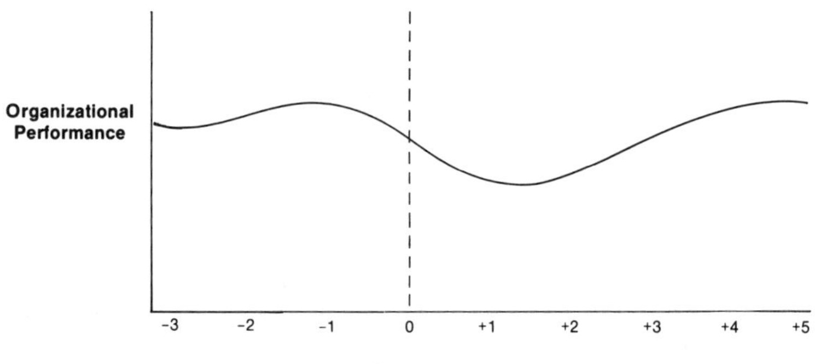

Figure 1. Example of the Impact of Managerial Change on Organizational Performance

Prework

Generally, the consultant's first step is to contact the outgoing manager when the departure is announced. The concept for the procedure is discussed, and the outgoing manager is asked whether the meeting would be appropriate. If the manager supports the proposal and is willing to be involved in the meeting, he or she is questioned concerning hopes and fears for the transition and the organization. If the manager is unwilling or unable to attend, he or she is asked to introduce the idea to the incoming manager and to make suggestions regarding who should attend.

Subsequently, the incoming manager is introduced to the concept, invited to express views toward it, and then asked to decide whether he or she supports the idea. It should be made clear that this decision should not be considered final until all subordinates have been interviewed and the needs of the organization have been identified. However, the incoming manager's support is critical; without it, the project cannot succeed.

The next step is to interview the subordinates for the purpose of introducing them to the meeting agenda, advising them about what they will be asked to do, and eliciting their hopes and fears for the transition and the organization. These interviews can be conducted individually or as group sensing sessions. In either case, at the conclusion of the process, the consultant should administer assessment instruments (Figures 2 and 3) to evaluate the status of essential organizational processes and each individual's understanding of the transition meeting. Outcomes of the interviews should be a reduction of anxiety about the meeting, a positive attitude toward the meeting, and an identification of the major issues that should be addressed during the meeting.

The consultant reviews the information contributed by the outgoing manager and the subordinates, revises the basic agenda as necessary to meet the organization's needs, and presents the revised agenda to the incoming manager. At this point, the major issues that are likely to be brought up should be discussed. If some of these issues are determined to be inappropriate to the meeting, the incoming manager must be advised and means of dealing with the issues developed. As a final step, the consultant should coach the incoming manager and the outgoing manager, if he or she plans to attend, regarding their involvement in the meeting and the types of behavior that will make the meeting most productive. For the incoming manager, beneficial behaviors include active listening, encouraging openness, and resisting the urges to pontificate or to make decisions under pressure; for the outgoing manager, they normally include active listening, encouraging openness, and guarding against defensiveness.

The Meeting

Objectives selected for the meeting must be appropriate for the group involved. The following ones are standard and are applicable to most transition meetings:

- Get acquainted;
- Clarify concerns and expectations;
- Reach a clear and shared understanding of the major priorities and goals of the organization for the next six to nine months;
- Determine what needs to be done to manage the transition; and
- Plan how to do it.

The paragraphs that follow present an agenda that addresses these objectives.

Introduction and Get-Acquainted Period

Opening remarks are made either by the outgoing manager, if he or she is present, or by the

For each of the statements below, circle the number that indicates the degree to which that statement is true for you.

<table>
<tr><td></td><td>Not at all</td><td>Very little</td><td>Undecided</td><td>Somewhat</td><td>A great deal</td></tr>
<tr><td>1. The information that I receive through formal channels is generally accurate.</td><td>1</td><td>2</td><td>3</td><td>4</td><td>5</td></tr>
<tr><td>2. I obtain all of the information that I need about what is happening in other sections of the organization.</td><td>1</td><td>2</td><td>3</td><td>4</td><td>5</td></tr>
<tr><td>3. I feel that decisions are made in this organization at the level at which the most adequate information is available.</td><td>1</td><td>2</td><td>3</td><td>4</td><td>5</td></tr>
<tr><td>4. I feel that decisions are made in this organization after obtaining information from those who actually do the jobs involved.</td><td>1</td><td>2</td><td>3</td><td>4</td><td>5</td></tr>
<tr><td>5. I have a clear understanding of the major priorities and goals of this organization.</td><td>1</td><td>2</td><td>3</td><td>4</td><td>5</td></tr>
<tr><td>6. My co-workers understand the major priorities and goals of this organization.</td><td>1</td><td>2</td><td>3</td><td>4</td><td>5</td></tr>
<tr><td>7. I believe that this organization has a plan for the achievement of its stated goals.</td><td>1</td><td>2</td><td>3</td><td>4</td><td>5</td></tr>
<tr><td>8. I believe that work priorities are established in accordance with the organization's objectives.</td><td>1</td><td>2</td><td>3</td><td>4</td><td>5</td></tr>
<tr><td>9. I recognize and understand the concerns and expectations of my co-workers.</td><td>1</td><td>2</td><td>3</td><td>4</td><td>5</td></tr>
<tr><td>10. I recognize and understand the concerns and expectations of my supervisor.</td><td>1</td><td>2</td><td>3</td><td>4</td><td>5</td></tr>
<tr><td>11. My supervisor and co-workers are aware of my concerns and expectations.</td><td>1</td><td>2</td><td>3</td><td>4</td><td>5</td></tr>
</table>

Figure 2. Organizational-Status Assessment

The items in this instrument were adapted with permission from the following sources: Dyer, TEAM BUILDING: ISSUES AND ALTERNATIVES, © 1977, Addison-Wesley, Reading, MA, p. 54; U.S. Army Organizational Effectiveness Training Center, *General Organizational Questionnaire Manual*, 1976, U.S. Army, Fort Ord, CA.

For each of the statements below, circle the number that indicates the degree to which that statement is true for you.

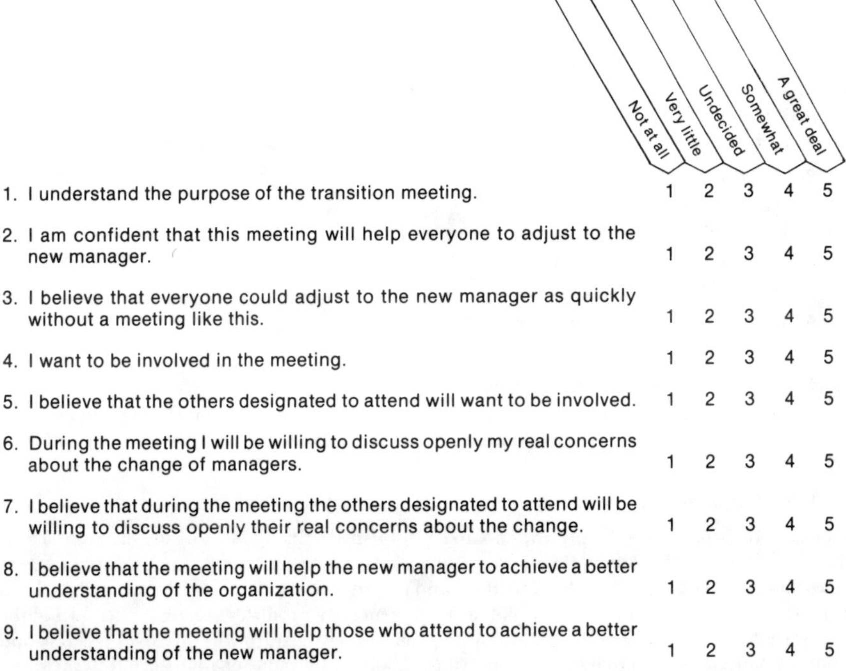

1. I understand the purpose of the transition meeting.
    1 2 3 4 5

2. I am confident that this meeting will help everyone to adjust to the new manager.
    1 2 3 4 5

3. I believe that everyone could adjust to the new manager as quickly without a meeting like this.
    1 2 3 4 5

4. I want to be involved in the meeting.
    1 2 3 4 5

5. I believe that the others designated to attend will want to be involved.
    1 2 3 4 5

6. During the meeting I will be willing to discuss openly my real concerns about the change of managers.
    1 2 3 4 5

7. I believe that during the meeting the others designated to attend will be willing to discuss openly their real concerns about the change.
    1 2 3 4 5

8. I believe that the meeting will help the new manager to achieve a better understanding of the organization.
    1 2 3 4 5

9. I believe that the meeting will help those who attend to achieve a better understanding of the new manager.
    1 2 3 4 5

Figure 3. Premeeting Assessment

The items in this instrument were adapted with permission from the following sources: Dyer, TEAM BUILDING: ISSUES AND ALTERNATIVES, © 1977, Addison-Wesley, Reading, MA, p. 54; U.S. Army Organizational Effectiveness Training Center, *General Organizational Questionnaire Manual*, 1976, U.S. Army, Fort Ord, CA.

incoming manager. The remarks are brief and address the manager's hopes for the meeting as well as the norms to be followed. If the outgoing manager makes these remarks, the incoming manager should follow with comments indicating support of the desired outcomes and norms. Subsequently, the consultant reviews the meeting objectives and the agenda and then asks the group members to voice their expectations so that any disparity between goals can be dealt with before proceeding.

The next step, a get-acquainted activity, can take any of several forms depending on the participants, how well they know one another, and their willingness to take risks. The consultant should use procedures that are acceptable to the participants but that lead to the establishment of openness and risk taking as acceptable norms. A common procedure is to ask each person to introduce himself or herself by completing the following statements:

- I am...
- My chief responsibility is...
- The word that best describes me as a person is...
- The word that best describes me on the job is...
- My chief strengths as a person are...
- My chief weakness as a person is...
- My morale on the job is...
- The way I feel about this meeting is...

Normally, the outgoing manager introduces himself or herself first; then the key subordinates and, finally, the incoming manager do the same.

Identification of Issues and Concerns

If the data obtained from the prework are to be published, this segment of the meeting begins with publication of those data. If not, the group members are asked to develop lists of important issues and concerns regarding the transition and the organization. This task can be completed individually or in small groups. Individual work generally produces greater ownership of the data, greater risk taking, and larger amounts of data; small-group work involves less risk and produces data in more manageable proportions. Each participant (or small-group representative) spends one or two minutes presenting his or her list (or the small group's list) to the entire group. After each sharing, the participants are allowed to ask questions for clarification only.

After all data have been published, posted, and clarified, the members are encouraged to speak about the issues that are important to them. During the discussion, the consultant should facilitate carefully to ensure that the crucial issues are covered sufficiently, that the discussion is not dominated by anyone, that it focuses on problem definition, and that the desired norms are followed. After the major issues have emerged, the consultant helps the participants to establish the priority of these issues.

Goal Setting

For this activity, the consultant asks each member to develop a list of goals for the total organization, for his or her department or immediate area, and for himself or herself. Subsequently, each list is presented to the total group and posted; the outgoing manager makes the first presentation and is followed by each subordinate and then the incoming manager. Again, only questions and requests for clarification are permitted.

After all goals have been presented and clarified, an open discussion is focused on organizational goals and continues until the major ones have been identified adequately. Then the priority of these goals is established, primarily for the benefit of the incoming manager. If the organization has an established management-by-objectives (MBO) program, the objectives of that program should be considered and may even serve as the basis for this discussion.

At the completion of the discussion, the outgoing manager should depart from the meeting. It is at this point that the incoming manager begins to take a more active and directive role in the meeting.

Transition Issues

The participants are asked to review the data posted thus far and individually determine which issues and concerns relate specifically to the transition. In an open session or in small groups, the members then publish, clarify, and discuss these issues and determine their priority. Finally, the new manager selects those items for which he or she would like actions to be planned.

Action Planning

Action planning is usually accomplished in small groups, with each group working on a different issue or set of issues. This process is most effective when the groups are allowed to choose their own assignments. During planning, the new manager moves from group to group, providing guidance and information as appropriate. The desired outcome of this activity is a list of actions in which everyone, including the incoming manager, takes part in order to facilitate the transition. These actions should be specific and should include timetables or milestones as well as clearly defined responsibilities.

Closure

The final segment of the meeting focuses on the new manager, who is given an opportunity to respond to what has happened during the meeting, to state his or her expectations regarding the functions of the subordinates, and to explain his or her personal way of doing business. Also, this is an excellent time for the new manager to address the ways in which his or her behavior and expectations differ from those of the outgoing manager. This portion of the agenda is most useful when the manager allows the subordinates to ask questions and make comments.

To conclude the session, the manager and the consultant should review the objectives and the agenda to determine whether the meeting has been successful; then the meeting is adjourned by the manager.

Follow-Up

Within a day or two, the consultant should meet with the new manager to review the meeting and its outcomes. Both process and content should be discussed to ensure that the manager receives maximum benefit from the meeting. The discussion should include a review of action plans, commitments made by the manager, and any coaching on future managerial behavior that seems appropriate.

Approximately two weeks later, the assessment instruments that appear as Figures 2 and 4 should be administered to all of the subordinates; subsequently, six to eight weeks after the meeting, the subordinates are again asked to complete the instrument that constitutes Figure 2. After all resulting data have been compiled, the consultant and the manager discuss the implications of these data. Variations in responses to the Organizational-Status Assessment (Figure 2) can indicate the effect of the meeting on key processes. When considered in total, the instrument results provide not only a tool for measuring the utility of the meeting but also a basis for future actions to be taken by the manager. They also provide a beneficial side effect by focusing people's attention on key processes during the transition period.

For each of the following statements, circle the number that indicates the degree to which that statement is true for you.

Scale: Not at all / Very little / Undecided / Somewhat / A great deal

1. I feel that the transition meeting accomplished its stated objectives.   1   2   3   4   5

2. The meeting helped me to adjust to the new manager.   1   2   3   4   5

3. I believe that I could have adjusted to the new manager as quickly without the meeting.   1   2   3   4   5

4. The time I spent in the meeting was well spent.   1   2   3   4   5

5. I believe that the others who attended the meeting wanted to be involved.   1   2   3   4   5

6. During the meeting I discussed my real concerns about the change of managers.   1   2   3   4   5

7. I believe that the others who attended the meeting discussed their real concerns.   1   2   3   4   5

8. I believe that the new manager gained a better understanding of the organization as a result of the meeting.   1   2   3   4   5

9. I believe that those who attended gained a better understanding of the new manager as a result of the meeting.   1   2   3   4   5

10. I believe that a meeting of this type should be conducted for every change of managers.   1   2   3   4   5

Complete each item below:

11. The most obvious result of the meeting was:

12. The most valuable part of the meeting for me was:

13. The least valuable part of the meeting for me was:

14. If the meeting were to be conducted in this organization again, something that I think should be changed is:

Figure 4. Postmeeting Assessment

The items in this instrument were adapted with permission from the following sources: Dyer, TEAM BUILDING: ISSUES AND ALTERNATIVES, © 1977, Addison-Wesley, Reading, MA, p. 54; U.S. Army Organizational Effectiveness Training Center, *General Organizational Questionnaire Manual*, 1976, U.S. Army, Fort Ord, CA.

CONSULTANT CONSIDERATIONS

The following issues merit the consultant's special consideration:

1. *The Timing of the Meeting.* Experience shows that the meeting is most effective when conducted on or near the actual date of the managerial change. At this point the new manager does not own any of the specific problems involved and has maximum flexibility. The subordinates recognize these factors and feel relatively free to discuss issues in the hope of having an early impact on the manager. If the meeting cannot be conducted until later, the new manager may be more a part of the problem and may have established his or her own method of operation that people feel unwilling to address. If the session is conducted more than thirty days after the change, it becomes something other than a transition meeting.

2. *The Length and Design Components of the Meeting.* These components are extremely flexible. The minimum time for a productive meeting seems to be about four hours, which allows for introductory activities, identification of issues and concerns, and the new manager's closing remarks. However, the optimal length for most organizations is one to one and one-half days, which accommodates each of the suggested design components and has proven to be most productive for organizations that are unaccustomed to organization development (OD) activities. For organizations with previous OD experience, the meeting can be extended and more emphasis placed on action planning, role clarification, or team-building activities.

3. *The Outgoing Manager's Level of Involvement.* This matter must be carefully considered when designing and conducting the meeting. If the outgoing manager chooses to attend, he or she may find the meeting threatening and may be defensive when criticism of current operations arises. If the relationship between the subordinates and their outgoing manager is even marginally good or better, the subordinates may edit their comments so that the manager will leave feeling good. The end result may be a limiting of subordinates' openness and domination of the group by the outgoing manager. However, if the group has had previous experience with OD activities and the consultant is an effective facilitator, this potential problem can be lessened. If the outgoing manager does attend, the situation can be handled in such a way that he or she provides unique insights and helps to ensure that key issues are discussed.

In addition, if the outgoing manager participates, the transference of power to the new manager must be considered in all activities. Each manager's role should change during the course of the meeting. Initially, the outgoing manager should be active while the new manager listens, asks questions, and observes. As the meeting progresses, the roles should be gradually reversed; by the end of the meeting, the former manager should be "out" and the new manager fully "in."

4. *Pressure on the New Manager.* The new manager may feel significant pressure to make decisions about substantive issues. It is best to address this subject before the meeting and to advise him or her to defer any decisions except those that directly pertain to the transition. All of the participants should be similarly advised. During the meeting, the consultant may have to intervene to clarify the norms governing decision making.

OUTCOMES

The most common outcomes of a transition meeting are increased information flow, clearer understanding of major issues and goals, and a reduction of the amount of ambiguity experienced by the new manager and his or her subordinates. During the meeting the new manager generally identifies key subordinates and becomes familiar with their personalities and methods of operation. A common reaction on the part of the manager is that the meeting was well worth the effort because of the time saved in becoming established in the job. Also, as a result of the discussions conducted, the subordinates gain a better understanding of one another's views and tend to operate more as a team after the meeting.

In addition, experience indicates that the meeting can strongly affect intervening variables. The resulting effect on end-result variables was evaluated in a study conducted within the United States Army between December, 1976, and March, 1979 (Stewart, 1980). The study concluded that the transition meeting had significant positive effects on statistical indicators of organizational performance.

USE TO THE CONSULTANT

Experience indicates that the transition meeting is useful to the consultant as well as to the client. The meeting is seen as a relatively low-risk venture by people who would normally be unwilling to try an OD approach to organizational change. As such, it gives them a chance to experiment with OD and to gain confidence in the technology and the consultant. The structure of the meeting and the evaluation procedure tie the consultant and the client together over a two- to three-month period; as a result, many consultants who have employed the procedure have established a significant number of ongoing OD operations in organizations that probably would not have asked for help otherwise. The author's experience is that more than 50 percent of the organizations that have used the transition meeting have requested further OD involvement within six months of the meeting.

SUMMARY

The transition meeting is a simple and direct approach that clearly meets the needs of client organizations that are contemplating managerial change. It has positive effects on both organizational climate and performance indicators. In addition to its usefulness to the consultant as a marketing tool, it is easy to conduct, requires little time, and presents only limited risk to the client or the consultant. For all of these reasons, the transition meeting is an OD intervention that can be useful to virtually any organization that seeks to control the potentially volatile circumstances arising from this type of change.

REFERENCES

Dyer, W.G. *Team building: Issues and alternatives.* Reading, MA: Addison-Wesley, 1977.

Mitchell, M.D. The transition meeting: A technique when changing managers. *Harvard Business Review*, May-June 1976, pp. 9-11.

Mitchell, M.D. Dealing with personnel changes in a working team. In J. Adams, J. Hayes, & B. Hopson (Eds.), *Transition.* Montclair, NJ: Allanheld, Osmun, 1977.

Reilly, A.J., & Jones, J.E. Team building. In J.W. Pfeiffer & J.E. Jones (Eds.), *The 1974 annual handbook for group facilitators.* San Diego, CA: University Associates, 1974.

Stewart, W.L. Fort Carson evaluation of organizational effectiveness operations. In P.J. Rock (Ed.), *OE Communique*, Winter 1980, pp. 95-116.

U.S. Army Organizational Effectiveness Training Center. *General organizational questionnaire manual.* Ford Ord, CA: U.S. Army, 1976.

Raymond J. Zugel is an organizational effectiveness consultant for the Headquarters, U.S. Army, Office of the Chief of Staff, Washington, D.C. He consults with senior civilian and military leaders in the areas of transition management, performance management, crisis management, strategic planning, survey-guided development, and human resource development. Major Zugel's background is in line management and training. He also has served as organizational effectiveness consultant to the U.S. Army Combat Developments Experimentation Command.

ORGANIZATIONAL ANALYSIS, DESIGN, AND IMPLEMENTATION: AN APPROACH FOR IMPROVING EFFECTIVENESS

David A. Nadler

In the last twenty years, there has been an explosive development of new tools for improving the effectiveness of organizations. Both research and practice have answered many questions about how organizations function and how different patterns of organizational behavior contribute to or detract from organizational performance. However, the insights gained from research, theoretical development, and practice have presented another, more formidable question: How can these insights be applied?

Over time, it has become apparent that different approaches for improving organizational effectiveness have certain characteristics in common. As a result of attempts to apply some of these technologies, consultants have learned that the following elements are important, if not essential, to any approach.

1. *Diagnosis.* The effective solution of organizational problems is dependent on a thorough diagnosis (Lawrence & Lorsch, 1969; Levinson, 1972). In the absence of diagnosis, the consultant may begin to apply solutions in search of problems, and this approach can lead to the prescription of treatments for ailments that do not exist.

2. *Systematic Processes.* Organizations are complex systems. The data that are essential to diagnostic and problem-solving endeavors must be collected in such a way that validity is ensured and that the collection itself does not endanger the organization or its members (Nadler, 1977). This requires the development of a systematic approach to identifying problems, generating solutions, and implementing those solutions.

3. *Research-Based Models.* The complexity of organizational phenomena requires that diagnosis and problem solving be conducted according to some kind of "road map." It has become more and more obvious that organizations are dynamic systems and that the simple application of common sense is not enough to understand problems and develop solutions. Aids are required in the form of theories, concepts, and models validated by both research and practice.

4. *Employee Participation.* It has been shown that when an organization's employees participate in solving problems and implementing solutions, the effectiveness of these procedures can be greatly enhanced (Coch & French, 1948; Vroom, 1964; Vroom & Yetton, 1973). This speaks for involvement whenever appropriate.

5. *Timeliness.* Diagnoses and action sequences that are timely produce great benefits. Frequently, systematic problem analysis is erroneously equated with lengthy problem analysis. For example, when diagnostic studies continue six or eight months, managers find themselves either having to solve problems on their own or learning to live with those problems. Thus, interventions that address important problems must be conducted in a timely manner.

6. *Senior-Management Involvement.* Numerous studies and projects have reaffirmed the conviction that senior management should be involved in, or at least supportive of, the problem-

solving activity. More specifically, research indicates that senior managers approach problem solving with their own "road maps" or models (Argyris & Schon, 1974); when these models differ from those used by the people who are doing the actual problem-solving work, conflict is inevitable and implementation of solutions becomes problematic.

As mentioned previously, the importance of these elements is well supported by theory, research, and the experiences of managers and consultants; however, some of the elements seem inherently contradictory. For example, how can problem solving include employee participation and still be timely? How can it depend on research-based models and still allow for participation? How can both management and nonmanagement personnel be involved?

In fact, the literature on organizational improvement is full of reports of efforts in which one element (for example, employee participation) was present and a seemingly contradictory element (for example, senior-management involvement) was not, resulting in failure. The conclusion seems to be that there has been a need to develop a technology that makes effective tradeoffs among these criteria.

This paper describes one such technology that is applicable to many different situations. It has two major components. The first of these is a *model of organizational effectiveness* (Nadler & Tushman, 1977, 1981) that aids in diagnosing problems, developing solutions, and implementing those solutions. The second is a structured *process for problem solving* or a sequenced set of phases, each with its own goals, structures, and activities.

THE CONGRUENCE MODEL OF ORGANIZATIONAL BEHAVIOR

There are many different ways of viewing organizations and the patterns of behavior that occur within them. During the past two decades, however, there has been an emerging view of an organization as a complex and open social system (Katz & Kahn, 1966) that receives input from the larger environment and subjects the input to various transformation processes that result in output.

As a system, an organization is composed of interdependent parts. Change in one part of the system results in changes in other parts. However, an organization also has the property of equilibrium; the system generates energy to move toward a state of balance among its parts. In addition, it needs to maintain favorable transactions of input and output with the environment in order to survive over time.

Although this system perspective is useful, by itself it may be too abstract to be a usable tool for managers. Thus, a number of organizational theorists have attempted to develop more pragmatic theories or models based on the system paradigm. The author's particular approach, called the Congruence Model of Organizational Behavior (Nadler & Tushman, 1977, 1979, 1981), represents such an attempt. This model depends on the relationships among input, transformation process, and output. In this framework, the principal inputs to the system of organizational behavior are the following:

- The *environment*, which provides constraints, demands, and opportunities;
- The *resources* available to the organization;
- The *history* of the organization; and
- The organization's *strategy*, perhaps the most crucial input because it consists of key decisions regarding the match of the organization's resources with the constraints, demands, and opportunities in the environment and within the context of history.

In general, the output of the system is the effectiveness of the organization in performing in a manner consistent with the goals of its strategy. Specifically, the output includes not only *organizational performance* as a whole, but also its major contributors, *group performance* and *individual behavior and affect*. Thus, as shown in Figure 1, the organization is viewed as a

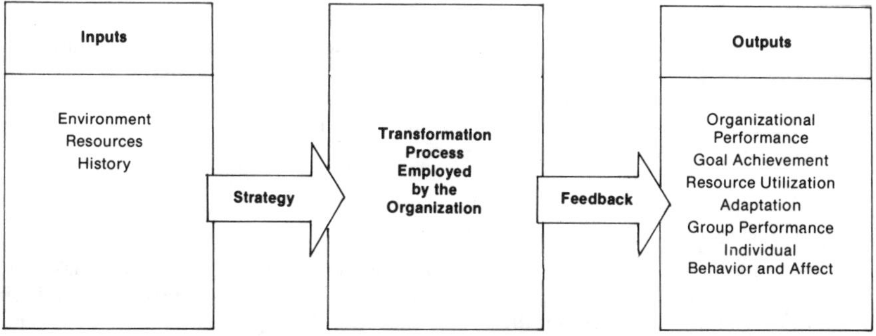

Figure 1. The System Model Applied to Organizational Behavior

mechanism that takes inputs (strategy and resources in the context of history and environment) and transforms them into outputs (patterns of individual, group, and organizational behavior).

The major focus of organizational analysis, therefore, is this transformation process. The Congruence Model conceives of the organization as being composed of four major components as follows:

- The *tasks* of the organization, or the work to be done and its critical characteristics;
- The *individuals* who are to perform organizational tasks;
- The *formal organizational arrangements*, which include various structures, processes, and systems that are designed to motivate individuals and to facilitate task completion; and
- The *informal organizational arrangements*, which include patterns of communication, power, and influence as well as values and norms that are neither planned nor written, but tend to emerge over time and ultimately characterize actual functioning.

The basic hypothesis of the model is that *an organization is most effective when its major components are congruent with one another.* The relationships among these components are illustrated in Figure 2. When an organization faces problems of ineffectiveness, these problems stem from poor fit, or lack of congruence, among organizational components. For example, the skills and abilities of the individuals available to do the necessary tasks must be congruent with the demands of those tasks; at the same time, the rewards that the work provides must be congruent with the needs and desires of the individuals.

Thus, this approach to organizations is a contingency approach. There is not one best organizational design or style of management or method of working; rather, different patterns of organization and management are most appropriate in different situations. The model recognizes the fact that individuals, tasks, strategies, and environments may differ greatly from organization to organization.

A PROCESS FOR PARTICIPATIVE DIAGNOSIS, DESIGN, AND IMPLEMENTATION

Any substantive model of organizational behavior, such as the Congruence Model, assists the manager or consultant by suggesting which elements should be analyzed and by aiding in identifying both the causes of problems and possible solutions. However, most models do not indicate how to accomplish diagnosis and problem solving. What is needed, therefore, is a process model or a set of sequenced phases of activity that serves as a guide for using a substantive model. One such process is described in the following paragraphs. It is designed for use by a consultant in implementing a participative approach to addressing organizational problems—an approach in which employees are involved in diagnosing problems, developing solutions, and implementing those solutions.

Process Overview

As shown in Figure 3, the process consists of five phases of activity. In the first phase, *needs identification*, the consultant collects data in a limited fashion for the purpose of developing diagnostic hypotheses and determining whether the problems and their causes are organizational in nature. In the second phase, *diagnosis*, the consultant and a team of people from the organization participate in an in-depth data-collection and -analysis activity aimed at identifying problems, their costs, and their causes. The third phase is *design*, during which the consultant and another team of organizational members develop and design solutions for the problems identified in diagnosis. In the fourth phase, *implementation*, a transition team consisting of organizational members coordinates the movement of the organization from its current state toward the full implementation of the design-phase recommendations. Finally, in the *evaluation* phase, the diagnostic activities are repeated to determine whether the projected benefits of the design were realized.

Throughout this process the bulk of the work and analysis is done by teams of employees (including managers) who are aided by the consultant. While these activities are being

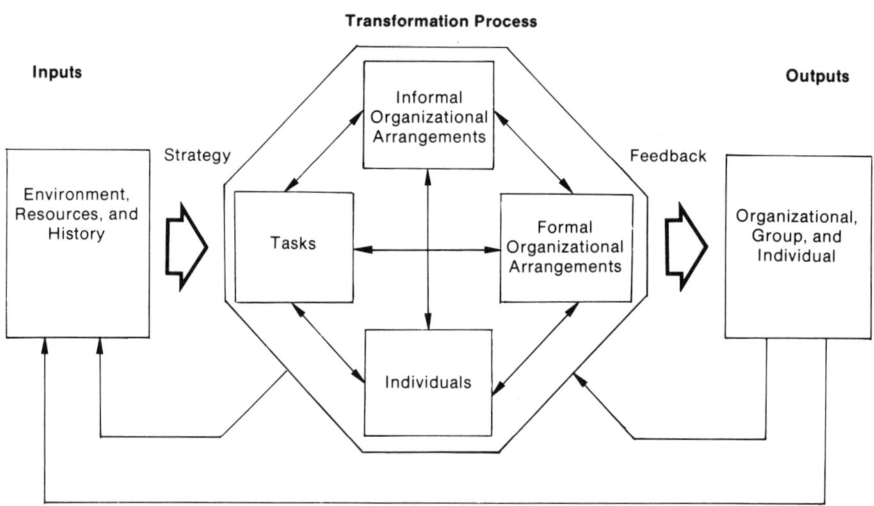

Figure 2. The Congruence Model of Organizational Behavior

Figure adapted from D.A. Nadler and M.L. Tushman, "A Congruence Model for Diagnosing Organizational Behavior," in D. Kolb, I. Rubin, and J. McIntire. *Organizational Psychology: A Book of Readings* (3rd ed.), Prentice-Hall, 1979.

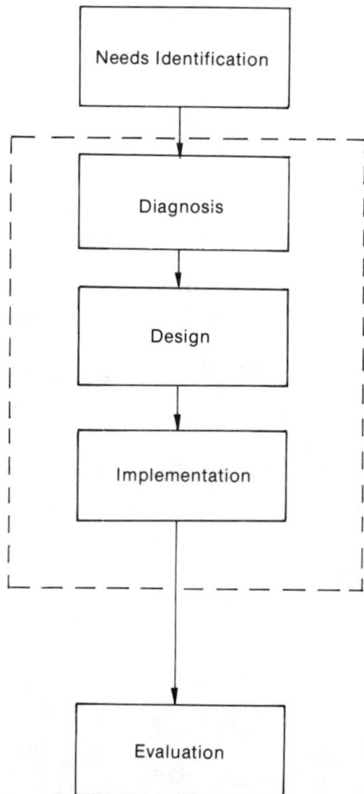

Figure 3. An Overview of the Organizational Diagnosis, Design, and Implementation Process

completed, the senior management of the client unit is also involved in a series of workshop activities that parallel the employee-team phases. In each case, the client participants use specific tools to accomplish data collection, analysis, design, and implementation, and most of these tools are provided within the context of the Congruence Model.

The Structure and Activities of Each Phase

The total process is designed to be applicable in a number of settings with limited input and support from an "expert" or consultant. As illustrated in Table 1 and described in the following paragraphs, in each phase specific individuals or groups are designated to complete specific activities.

1. *Needs Identification.* In this phase, the consultant and the chief operating officer of the particular client unit, department, or group work jointly to identify major problems, to determine whether the subsequent phases of diagnosis and design are needed, and to ensure that these activities will be responsive to the identified problems and needs. Typically, this phase starts when the client, usually a senior manager, approaches the consultant; during an ensuing discussion, the client talks about his or her perception of problems and needs in the

organizational unit, and the consultant describes the analysis, design, and implementation process. This discussion may be repeated in a separate session for other members of the senior management of the unit.

These initial discussions are usually followed by a limited data-collection activity. The consultant conducts interviews with employees in the unit who represent different levels and different functional groupings. The interview is structured but open ended, with questions derived from the Congruence Model. These data, as well as observational data and pertinent information from sources such as performance results and annual reports, are analyzed using the Congruence Model. Subsequently, a series of diagnostic hypotheses is developed; these hypotheses are recorded as testable-but-tentative statements of problems and their causes. The entire analysis is then presented to the senior management of the unit along with a proposal (if appropriate) outlining the scope and nature of a recommended diagnostic effort. Management then makes a decision whether to stop the process at this point or to proceed to diagnosis.

2. *Diagnosis.* The goal of the diagnostic phase is to identify problems (discrepancies between expected and actual outputs), to estimate the costs associated with those problems, to

Table 1. Major Phases of the Organizational Analysis, Design, and Implementation Process

Phase	Designated Individual or Group	Activities
Needs Identification	Consultant	Initial discussion with management Employee interviews Analysis and hypothesis formation Feedback of analysis Diagnosis proposal Decision about proceeding
Diagnosis	Consultant Diagnostic team composed of organizational members; assigned full-time	Data collection: work flows, interviews, instruments, observations, archival sources Data analysis: problems, costs Diagnostic report and presentation Decision about proceeding
Design	Consultant Design-team leader Design team composed of organizational members; assigned full-time	Design or redesign of work flows, the organization (grouping of functions), jobs, and/or support systems and mechanisms Design report and presentation Decision about proceeding
Implementation	Consultant Transition manager Transition team composed of organizational members; assigned part-time	Analysis of transition issues Development of transition plan (activity network, benchmarks, evaluation points) Development of "marketing" strategy Execution and monitoring of transition plan
Evaluation	Consultant Evaluation team composed of organizational members	Repetition of diagnostic phases Review of findings compared with design-report predictions

identify factors causing the problems, and to identify opportunities or arenas for action aimed toward solutions. Again, the Congruence Model serves as the basic diagnostic device, although other, more specific models are employed as well. Among the models frequently used are those of performance (Lawler, 1973), organization design (Galbraith, 1973, 1977), job design (Hackman & Oldham, 1980), and organizational climate (Litwin & Stringer, 1968).

During this phase, a team is formed and assigned to work full-time on diagnosis. Its members come from the organization and are chosen on the basis of their specific subject-matter expertise (as related to the work and technology of different parts of the unit), their roles in the informal organization (opinion leaders), their credibility, and their oral and written communication skills. Usually, eight to twelve people are selected from different levels of the organization.

The consultant trains the team in the conceptual models and the specific diagnostic tools to be used. The team then collects information that includes descriptions of work flows as well as data derived from individual and group interviews, instruments, observations, and archival sources. These data are analyzed to identify problems and to estimate costs (usually in dollar terms, accounting for additional expense, lost revenue, and so forth). Then the team writes a diagnostic report that details the methodology and identifies problems, causes, and penalties (costs).

The diagnostic activities are designed to take no more than twenty to twenty-five working days. The team formally presents its report to the management of the unit, whose members then make a decision regarding whether to proceed to the design phase.

3. *Design.* The design phase also depends on a team of organizational members who are assigned to work on their task full-time and who are chosen according to approximately the same criteria that governed selection of the diagnostic team. However, there are a few differences in team composition, partially because of the scope of the design activities and the segments of the organization that will be the focus of the design. Also, the average hierarchical level of employee is generally higher for the whole team because a somewhat broader perspective is frequently needed for the design of solutions than for the diagnosis of problems. In addition, this team requires a designated leader to manage its work; usually, the individual chosen is someone who reports directly to the chief operating officer of the unit. Thus, in this phase the consultant functions more as a teacher and a facilitator than as a manager, as is the case during diagnosis.

The basic goal of the design team is to design or develop solutions for the problems identified in the diagnostic phase. The main conceptual tool used in addition to the Congruence Model is a specific theory of organizational design based on information-processing concepts (Galbraith, 1977; Tushman & Nadler, 1978) of job design (Hackman & Oldham, 1980). However, the solutions developed may not be restricted to job design; depending on the nature of the problems identified in the diagnostic phase, solutions may also encompass training, team building, changes in management practices, and so forth. When these types of solutions are called for, still other conceptual tools are required.

The design team delves into and may provide alternative approaches to the actual work flow, the organization itself (including the grouping of functions and the relationships among various functions), specific jobs, and support systems and mechanisms (rewards, measurements, methods and procedures, supervisory relationships, and so forth). Recommendations are summarized in a report that is formally presented to management. Then management is faced with a decision about whether to accept the design as is or to alter it and whether to continue to implementation.

The training of the design team is accomplished in a somewhat different way from the training of the diagnostic team. Members are not trained completely at the beginning of the process; instead, they are trained in modules corresponding to the different types of design tasks to be completed (for example, work-flow redesign or function regrouping). Each module is conducted immediately before the team is required to do that particular work.

As is the case with the diagnostic phase, the design phase, including training, is structured to be completed within twenty to twenty-five working days.

4. *Implementation.* Experience has indicated the vital role of a specific implementation program in bringing about organizational improvements (Nadler, 1981). However, this phase is frequently given insufficient attention. Consequently, the process described in this paper places a good deal of emphasis on managing the implementation of the design recommendations.

A transition team is assembled to manage the implementation. This team has an officially designated leader, usually someone who reports directly to the chief operating officer of the unit. The consultant trains the members by conducting an "implementation-strategies workshop" and then guides the team through a process of identifying the issues (both technical and political) involved in the implementation. Subsequently, the team members collectively develop a transition plan that includes an activity network, such as a Program Evaluation and Review Technique (PERT) chart (Miller, 1974); benchmarks; evaluation points; and so forth. In addition, a strategy for "marketing" the implementation is developed.

When the transition plan is approved by management, the team is responsible for monitoring the implementation process until the new structure has been instituted completely. This period varies from a few weeks to a number of months, depending on the scope, size, and intensity of the changes being implemented.

5. *Evaluation.* During this final phase, the diagnostic activities are repeated to determine whether the problems originally identified were solved, whether the design was implemented and produced the results predicted, and whether any new problems arose or were created as a result of the new design. These determinations may lead to the repetition of the cycle with a different scope or with new problems to address.

The Management Workshop "Parallel Path"

Early experiences with the five-phase model presented in this paper indicated that it was relatively successful through the end of the design phase. Clients tended to agree to conduct diagnosis, accept the diagnostic report, authorize the establishment of a design, and accept the design recommendations. Frequently, however, severe problems were encountered during implementation because the senior management of the unit did not fully understand, support, or feel involved in the new structure and the implementation process. This situation led to the development of another set of activities aimed at helping senior management to understand, influence, and thus "own" the design, all with the goal of increased success in the implementation phase. What was developed was a series of workshop sessions involving the chief operating officer of the unit and his or her two immediately subordinate levels. These workshops run concurrently with the diagnostic, design, and implementation phases and are thus referred to as the "parallel-path" activities (see Figure 4). The general goals of the parallel path are as follows:

- To introduce the managers to the concepts, models, and tools that the diagnostic, design, and implementation teams are using;
- To provide an opportunity for the managers to look at their own operations and develop their own informed views about problems, solutions, and implementation processes;
- To transform the managers into informed, critical consumers of diagnostic and design reports; and
- To enable the managers to provide active support during the implementation of new designs and solutions.

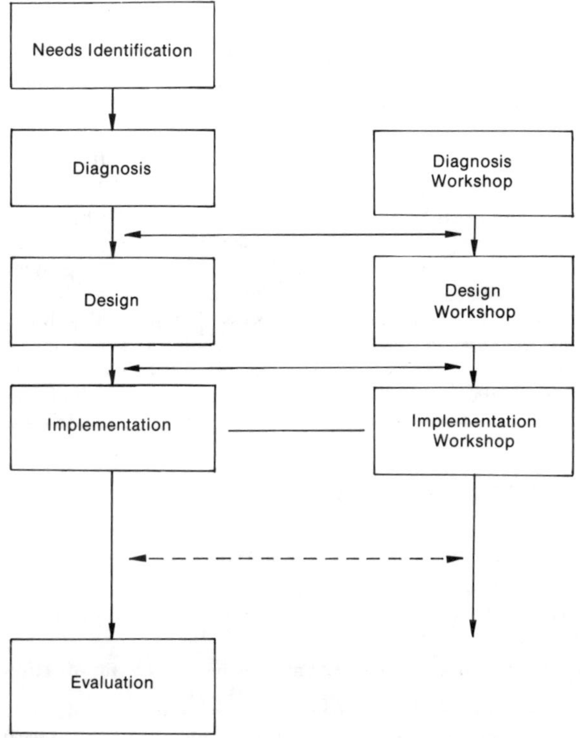

Figure 4. The Employee-Led Process and the Parallel Path of Senior Management

There are three workshops, each associated with a particular phase of the employee-led process:

1. *Diagnosis Workshop.* This workshop is a series of sessions conducted on four separate half-days. The participants are introduced to the concept of models for diagnosis and design and are taught the general diagnostic model (Nadler & Tushman, 1977) as well as some of the basic concepts of motivation, job design, and organization design. They gain experience with the concepts through analysis of case studies and case discussions, and finally they apply these concepts to the unit of which they are all part. In a fifth session, the parallel-path group meets with the diagnostic team to hear and react to its report.

2. *Design Workshop.* The next workshop is aimed at familiarizing the managers with tools for design and allowing them to make some basic, fundamental design decisions about the configurations of the organization as a macrocosm. The managers are taught both the concepts and the techniques of the information-processing model of design (Galbraith, 1973, 1977; Tushman & Nadler, 1978), and then they apply that model to case studies and their own organization. The final session usually transpires immediately before the design team presents its report, although throughout the process there is contact between the two groups (via the consultant and through overlapping membership) so that all activities coincide.

3. *Implementation Workshop.* The implementation workshop actually precedes the activities of the implementation team. The goal of this workshop is to develop the managers' sensitivity to the critical importance of effectively managing the transition between a current state and the desired future state. The managers work on a complex case in which an appropriate new design was implemented but the transition was managed poorly, leading to major problems. Then the members are presented with concepts of transition management and the implementation of change (Beckhard & Harris, 1977; Nadler, 1981), after which they establish a set of issues and recommendations for the transition team to consider.

At the conclusion of the workshops, the management group continues to function during the period of implementation and transition. It meets at fairly regular intervals (for example, once a month) to hear reports from the transition team and to monitor progress.

Thus, the mainstream activities (from needs identification through evaluation) and the parallel-path workshops form an integrated process that not only allows for employee participation in the diagnosis, design, and implementation activities, but also maintains the involvement and builds the support of senior management. In the mainstream phases, the employee teams complete the work of the transition; meanwhile, the senior managers are trained to understand and appreciate this work so that they can support the end products.

CHARACTERISTICS OF THE PROCESS

The entire process provides one way of incorporating and making tradeoffs among the desirable characteristics of an effort to improve organizational effectiveness.

- The approach is *diagnostic*; it provides for two phases of diagnosis to ensure that the particular methods, tools, and processes selected are appropriate for the client organization.

- It is also *systematic*; it is comprehensive and can be outlined ahead of time and managed.

- The process is built on the use of *research-based models* for diagnosis, design, and implementation. It enables the use of scientific tools in an applied setting.

- The team structure provides a method for *employee participation* in the actual work of diagnosis, design, and implementation.

- The structure of the process and the use of intensively managed teams and task forces allows for *timeliness* in completion.

- Finally, through the parallel-path activities, *senior-management involvement* is ensured.

RESULTS

The process has been used in various forms in a number of organizations. An overview of the results obtained with one client organization illustrates the effectiveness achieved.

In a large corporation in the communications industry, the process was used for approximately thirty different projects in different settings, including the departments of sales, manufacturing, operations, and staff. An analysis of the team reports from these projects revealed that the diagnostic and design teams were able to develop solutions that resulted in an average net reduction in expenses of 16 percent per year for all of the projects. At the same time, productivity—from the standpoint of both quality and quantity—was maintained.

In the same organization, an examination of the projects using the parallel path versus those without the parallel path revealed an implementation success rate of approximately 30 percent without the parallel path and approximately 75 percent with this component.

These sample analyses are only preliminary; more detailed examinations of the process are currently being conducted. It appears, however, that the process provides one viable method for doing systematic work to improve organizational effectiveness through participative processes.

OTHER APPLICATIONS

Over time it has become evident that the technology represented in this paper could be used in ways other than the full five-stage process dictates. Specifically, it appears that the process can be entered at any of a number of points (see Figure 5). The diagnosis, for example, could be initiated with the design phase. This alternative approach might be possible in situations in which other diagnostic approaches have been used, and it would be particularly applicable when a new organization is being formed or when existing ones are merging. Some abbreviated diagnostic work could be done to determine the key strategic and work-flow issues, and the design phase could be the first full-scale activity.

Finally, the implementation phase could be used by itself. For example, other processes might be used to develop the design (such as a "top-down" design, a senior-management design, or an outside "expert" design); then the implementation phase would be used as a way of implementing the design in a participative fashion. Similarly, the implementation process could be used to implement other types of major organizational changes (such as the reduction of the work force, implementation of new technology, changes in physical location, and so forth).

These applications are primarily illustrative; others undoubtedly exist. Much work needs to be done to explore the full range of possibilities.

SUMMARY

This paper has presented a systematic approach for improving organizational effectiveness through participative processes. The approach is dependent on a general diagnostic model of organizational behavior and a structured process for the participative application of that model

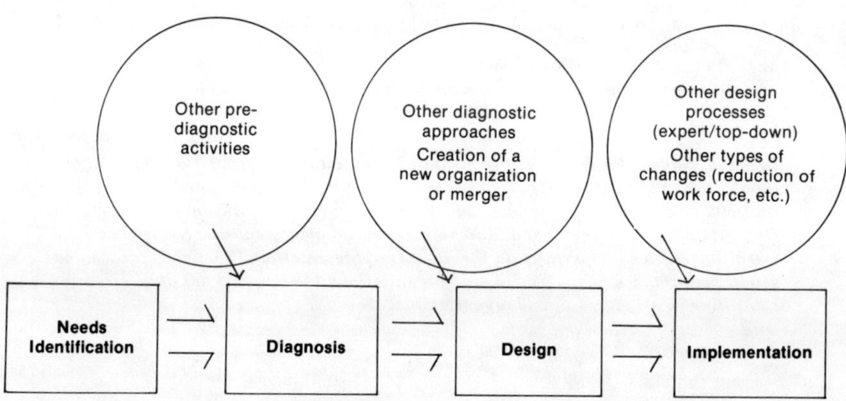

Figure 5. Alternative Applications of the Process

in an organizational setting. At the core of this process is a structured method of completing diagnosis, organizational and solution design, and the implementation of changes.

Initial experiences with the process are promising. It appears to be a cost-effective way of involving organizational members in the improvement of organizational effectiveness. Clearly, this is not the only way of addressing the improvement of organizational effectiveness, nor is it necessarily the best approach for all situations. Further experimentation and research are needed to determine what types of problems, settings, or work technologies are most amenable to this approach. At this stage, however, it provides some direction and one set of options for the manager who wishes to enhance the effectiveness of his or her organization.

REFERENCES

Argyris, C., & Schon, D.A. *Theory in practice.* San Francisco: Jossey-Bass, 1974.

Beckhard, R., & Harris, R. *Organizational transitions.* Reading, MA: Addison-Wesley, 1977.

Coch, L., & French, J.R.P., Jr. Overcoming resistance to change. *Human Relations,* 1948, *11,* 512-532.

Galbraith, J.R. *Designing complex organizations.* Reading, MA: Addison-Wesley, 1973.

Galbraith, J.R. *Organization design.* Reading, MA: Addison-Wesley, 1977.

Hackman, J.R., & Oldham, G.A. *Work redesign.* Reading, MA: Addison-Wesley, 1980.

Katz, D., & Kahn, R.L. *The social psychology of organizations.* New York: John Wiley, 1966.

Lawler, E.E. *Motivation in work organizations.* Belmont, CA: Wadsworth, 1973.

Lawrence, P.R., & Lorsch, J.W. *Developing organizations: Diagnosis and action.* Reading, MA: Addison-Wesley, 1969.

Levinson, H. *Organizational diagnosis.* Cambridge, MA: Harvard University Press, 1972.

Litwin, G.H., & Stringer, R.A. *Motivation and organizational climate.* Boston: Harvard University Graduate School of Business Administration, 1968.

Miller, L.R. *A peek at PERT—A brief introduction to Program Evaluation and Review Technique.* Escondido, CA: The Center for Leadership Studies, 1974.

Nadler, D.A. *Feedback and organization development: Using data based methods.* Reading, MA: Addison-Wesley, 1977.

Nadler, D.A. An integration theory of organizational change. *Journal of Applied Behavioral Science,* 1981, *17*(2), 191-211.

Nadler, D.A., & Tushman, M.L. A diagnostic model for organizational behavior. In J.R. Hackman, E.E. Lawler, & L.W. Porter (Eds.), *Perspectives on behavior in organizations.* New York: McGraw-Hill, 1977.

Nadler, D.A., & Tushman, M.L. A congruence model for diagnosing organizational behavior. In D. Kolb, I. Rubin, & J. McIntyre (Eds.), *Organizational psychology: A book of readings* (3rd ed.). Englewood Cliffs, NJ: Prentice-Hall, 1979.

Nadler, D.A., & Tushman, M.L. A congruence model for diagnosing organizational behavior. In D.A. Nadler, M.L. Tushman, & N.G. Hatvany (Eds.), *Approaches to managing organizational behavior: Models, readings, and cases.* Boston: Little, Brown, 1981.

Tushman, M.L., & Nadler, D.A. Information processing as an integrating concept in organizational design. *Academy of Management Review,* 1978, *3,* 613-624.

Vroom, V.H. *Work and motivation.* New York: John Wiley, 1964.

Vroom, V.H., & Yetton, P.W. *Leadership and decision making.* Pittsburgh, PA: University of Pittsburgh Press, 1973.

David A. Nadler, Ph.D., *is the president of Organizational Research & Consultation, Inc., in New York City and is an adjunct associate professor in the Graduate School of Business at Columbia University, where he also directs the Advanced Program in Organization Development and Human Resource Management. Dr. Nadler has done extensive research and writing on the subjects of organizational change, feedback and group performance, management, and organizational design, and has done extensive consulting in management and organizational areas.*

INTRODUCTION TO THE RESOURCES SECTION

A resource published in the *Annual* series is an informational tool to aid in the dissemination and utilization of knowledge important to the further understanding of human behavior.

Many types of resources are found in the *Annuals*. Some are listings of either conceptual, content material such as books and other printed references, services, and educational programs (software), or technical, equipment-related material such as training or media packages (hardware). Networks are another area of resources—these are organizations and people who are connected because of common professional interests or special individual and organizational purposes.

This section is of particular use to the practitioner in staying abreast of trends in the field, in updating knowledge in particular content or technical areas, and in developing further sources of information. Furthermore, the network and linkage resources are helpful in putting the practitioner in touch with like-minded people and organizations who can be stimulating to career and professional growth.

This year's *Annual* has four varied resources. They reflect some themes from other sections of this *Annual*: self-awareness, understanding work-group behavior, career pathing. The first article is a network resource: "Applied Behavioral Science Consulting Organizations: An Updated Directory" is a revision of a list last published in the 1980 *Annual*. Then Diedrich's "Team Building/Team Development: A Reference List" is a bibliography of books, case studies, and articles organized around content topics of team development: purposes, design, leader and consultant behavior. Pikoff's "Biofeedback: An Outline of the Literature and Resource Directory" provides information on both software and hardware as well as biofeedback networks. The directory covers a wide range of literature, including overviews, special topics, and professional concerns; biofeedback equipment and media presentations; and a list of professional organizations involved in biofeedback research, training, and treatment. Finally, Whitaker's "Executive Recruiters: A Directory" provides a potential source of linkage for interested professionals and organizations. Sixty executive recruiting organizations are listed with their organizational specialties, executive salary ranges, representative client lists, and client fees. Whitaker also includes a realistic discussion of the recruiting process as well as issues involved in using small versus large recruiting organizations. All of these resources provide up-to-date information that offers consultants additional access to the important tools of their trade.

APPLIED BEHAVIORAL SCIENCE CONSULTING ORGANIZATIONS: AN UPDATED DIRECTORY

In the 1975 *Annual* we published a directory of applied behavioral science consulting organizations as a resource for both consultants and those seeking consulting services. We updated the listing for the 1980 *Annual*; for this revision, we contacted the organizations listed in the 1980 directory as well as those that had asked to be included since that time and requested that they bring their listings up to date.

Many organizations in the original listings have moved, and many requests for an update were not forwardable. Because the listings were obviously incorrect, we deleted them if neither the principals nor the organization was listed in other available directories. Clearly, many eligible organizations have not been included—simply because we did not have information about them. Users of the *Annual* are invited to send corrections, alterations, additions, or suggestions for updated versions of the directory to be published in later issues of the *Annual*.

CANADA

C.I.M., Inc.
(Centre Interdisciplinaire de Montreal, Inc.)
5055 Gatineau Avenue
Montreal, Quebec H3V 1E4
(514) 735-6595
Principals: J. M. Aubry, President; L. Auger, Secretary-Treasurer.
Founded: 1969
Full-time Consultants: 3
Part-time Consultants: 10
Major Services: Human relations training; management/leadership development; organization development; community development; psychotherapy.
Area of Emphasis: Interdisciplinary approach.
Typical Clients: Education; government; hospitals; organizations.

International Communications Institute
Box 8268, Station F
Edmonton, Alberta T6H 4P1
(403) 432-1319
Principals: A.C. Lynn Zelmer, Partner; Amy Elliott Zelmer, Partner.
Founded: 1969
Full-time Consultants: 2

Major Services: Human relations training (in-house); management/leadership development; design and production of educational materials (films, television, simulations, training programs, etc.).
Areas of Emphasis: Community use of and access to media services (especially low-budget production); international development education; appropriate or intermediate technology; simulations and games; cross-cultural education.
Typical Clients: Colleges and universities; adult education agencies; government and industry training departments; community groups (voluntary agencies).

Management Renewal Limited
P.O. Box 6071, Station J
Ottawa, Ontario K2A 1T1
(613) 829-9319
Principals: Frank T. Laverty, President; Michael R. Laverty, Vice President; Joy J. Laverty, Business Manager.
Founded: 1970
Full-time Consultants: 3
Part-time Consultants: 12
Major Services: Human relations training; management/leadership development; organization development.

Areas of Emphasis: Management by objectives; transactional analysis; consulting skills; support staff development; positive action for women.
Typical Clients: Government; industry; education; health care; service industries.

Quetico Centre
Box 1000
Atikokan, Ontario P0T 1C0
(807) 929-3511
Principals: C.M. McIntosh, President; V. Prokopchuk, Chairman of the Board; B. Badana, Vice Chairman; L. E.Wiens, Secretary.
Nonprofit Organization
Founded: 1958
Full-time Consultants: 3
Part-time Consultants: 2
Major Services: Constructive organizational change; developing organizational philosophy, goals, and objectives; management/leadership development; community development; human relations training; creative arts development; youth leadership; health and wellness learning.
Areas of Emphasis: Training materials on system changes; in-house and public activities.
Typical Clients: Business and industry; municipal and provincial government agencies; community agencies; schools and colleges; individuals.

EASTERN and SOUTHERN UNITED STATES

The Atlanta Consulting Group, Inc.
2028 Powers Ferry Road, Suite 190
Atlanta, Georgia 30339
(404) 952-0898
Principals: Hyler J. Bracey, President; Aubrey C. Stanford, Vice President; Roy W. Trueblood, Vice President.
Founded: 1972
Full-time Consultants: 3
Part-time Consultants: 8
Major Services: High-quality, custom-designed, in-house skill-building events for middle-and upper-level managers.
Areas of Emphasis: People skills; organization development; team work; rational decision making; problem solving and planning.
Typical Clients: Fortune 500; banks over $2 billion; Fortune Top 50 (nonindustrial).

Block Petrella Weisbord/ Designed Learning, Inc.
1009 Park Avenue
Plainfield, New Jersey 07060
(201) 754-5100
Principals: Anthony Petrella, President; Peter Block, Senior Vice President; Marvin R. Weisbord, Senior Vice President; C. James Maselko, Senior Vice President.
Founded: 1968
Full-time Consultants: 9
Part-time Consultants: 10
Major Services: Human relations training; management/leadership development; organization development; community development; training of in-house trainers and organization development specialists.
Areas of Emphasis: Team-building and consultation skills; management training for first-line supervisors; career planning; conflict management; organizational diagnosis.
Typical Clients: Industry; government; hospitals and medical centers; school systems; volunteer organizations.

The Gemini Group
RD #2, Box 117
Bedford, New York 10506
(914) 764-4938
Principal: Kenneth Finn
Founded: 1977
Full-time Consultants: 2
Part-time Consultants: 5
Major Services: Large personnel systems; management development; organization development; cost effectiveness; survey feedback; consultation-skills development; growth-dynamics management.
Areas of Emphasis: Total systems approach; measurement technology; strategy planning; business growth; marketing.
Typical Clients: Small growing companies; high technology companies; large personnel groups; Fortune 500.

Human Resources Institute (HRI)
(Scientific Resources, Inc.)
Tempe Wick Road
Morristown, New Jersey 07960
(201) 267-1496
Principals: Robert F. Allen, President; Barry Certner, Vice President; Elaine J. Allen, Secretary-Treasurer.
Founded: 1965
Full-time Consultants: 10
Part-time Consultants: 20
Major Services: Human relations training; management/leadership development; organization development; community development; health promotion programs.
Area of Emphasis: Working with normative systems, which assist organizations in understanding and modifying the organizational cultures of which they are a part.
Typical Clients: Corporations; prisons; government; school systems; hospitals; communities; colleges and universities.

Human Systems Development
1310 W. Colonial Drive, Suite 30
Orlando, Florida 32804
(305) 841-0343
Principal: Larry E. Webb, Senior Consultant.
Founded: 1978
Full-time Consultants: 1
Part-time Consultants: 6
Major Services: Human relations training; management/leadership development; organization development; conflict and stress management; communication skills training; creative problem-solving training; team building.
Areas of Emphasis: Helping individuals and organizations to achieve their goals through effective human systems.
Typical Clients: Business; government agencies; school systems; church organizations; community organizations; health-care delivery systems.

The Institute for Organization Development
3384 Peachtree Road, N.E.
Atlanta, Georgia 30345
(404) 237-8962
Principals: Arthur M. Cohen, President & Treasurer; Lois P. Cohen, Vice President & Secretary.
Founded: 1972
Full-time Consultants: 2
Part-time Consultants: 2
Major Services: Human relations training; management/leadership development; organization development; community development.
Areas of Emphasis: Individual adjustment problems; performance analysis and career development; conflict management.
Typical Clients: Business and industry; religious systems; professional organizations.

Interact Associates
2566 Elmwood Avenue
Rochester, New York 14618
(716) 271-2421
Principals: Kenneth Rabinowitz, President; John N. Brennan, Secretary; Anthony S. Caiazza, Treasurer.
Founded: 1978
Full-time Consultants: 2
Part-time Consultants: 1
Major Services: Organizational diagnosis; organizational development; human relations training; management/leadership development.
Areas of Emphasis: Interpersonal skill training for managers; team building and leadership training; organizational assessment of business, government, and social-service agencies.
Typical Clients: Business and industry; school systems; government agencies; social-service agencies.

Lopez Assessment Services, Inc.
14 Vanderventer Avenue
Port Washington, New York 11050
(516) 883-4041
Principals: Felix M. Lopez, Chairman; Felix E. Lopez, President.
Founded: 1970
Full-time Consultants: 6
Part-time Consultants: 4
Major Services: Human relations training; management/leadership development; organization development; management by objectives; performance evaluation.
Areas of Emphasis: Restructuring selection systems of EEOC conformation; individual and corporate accountability programs.
Typical Clients: Business; government agencies; school systems; religious organizations.

McBer and Company
137 Newbury Street
Boston, Massachusetts 02116
(617) 437-7080
Principals: David C. McClelland, Chairman, Board of Directors; Richard E. Boyatzis, President/Chief Executive Officer; Lyle M. Spencer, Jr., Vice President; W.J. Burns, Vice President; James A. Burruss, Vice President; George O. Klemp, Jr., Vice President; Tomas Perez, Vice President; Murray K. Dalziel, Vice President.
Founded: 1963
Full-time Consultants: 35
Part-time Consultants: 27
Major Services: Management/leadership development; organization development; competency testing and assessment and competancy-based training; alcohol treatment; career and life planning; consultant and trainer training; sales training.
Areas of Emphasis: Preparing client personnel to provide internal consulting, training, and development services; empirical research.
Typical Clients: Corporations; government agencies; schools and colleges; nonprofit and volunteer agencies; foreign countries.

Mid-Atlantic Association for Training and Consulting, Inc.
1500 Massachusetts Avenue, N.W. (Suite 325)
Washington, D.C. 20005
(202) 223-0582
Principals: Al Rollins, President; Anna Barton-Thomas, Coordinator of Public Events; Ann Paulen, Coordinator of Contract Services; Frank Johnson, Chairman; Benjamin F. Bray, Vice Chairman; Jack Andersen, Treasurer; David Caldwell, Secretary.
Nonprofit organization
Founded: 1965
Full-time Consultants: 2
Part-time Consultants: 160

Major Services: Human relations training; management/leadership development; organization development; personal planning; training of trainers; personal growth; training of lay ministers.

Areas of Emphasis: Training and consulting for religious and voluntary systems (general consulting skills, etc.); conflict and power utilization; educational design skills; training and consulting for business and professions.

Typical Clients: Church jurisdictions and organizations; prisons; school systems; voluntary organizations such as drug education centers and charities; business; government.

NTL Institute

1501 Wilson Boulevard, Suite 1000
P.O. Box 9155, Rosslyn Station
Arlington, Virginia 22209
(703) 527-1500
Principals: Harold L. Hodgkinson, President; Stanley Schwartz, Controller; Virginia L. Sprecher, Executive Director of Marketing and Admissions; Marilyn D. Swenson, Executive Director of Programs and Management.
Nonprofit organization
Founded: 1947
Full-time Consultants: 2
Part-time Consultants: 350 professional members
Major Services: Human relations training; management/leadership development; organization development; community development; training of trainers; AU/NTL Master's Program in human resource development.
Area of Emphasis: Programs for executives, managers, trainers, and consultants.
Typical Clients: Education; hospital and health care agencies; national and international business and industry; social service agencies; police; service academies; Federal and local government agencies.

O.D.C., Inc.

4905 Radford Avenue (Suite 206)
Richmond, Virginia 23230
(804) 358-9184
Principal: Kenneth I. Newman, Executive Director.
Founded: 1967
Full-time Consultants: 3
Part-time Consultants: 7
Major Services: Management/leadership development; organization development; community development; management by objectives; career planning and development.
Areas of Emphasis: Utilization and development of human resources; consultation on problem solving, decision making, conflict management, etc.
Typical Clients: Government; educational institutions; prisons; industry; hospitals.

ORC, Inc.

(Organization Resources Counselors)
Rockefeller Center
1211 Avenue of the Americas
New York, New York 10036
(212) 719-3400
Principal: Charles A. Tasso
Founded: 1926
Full-time Consultants: 60
Major Services: Organization planning and development; attitude research; management/leadership development; productivity assessment; compensation surveys and consulting (national and international); EEO and OSHA; labor relations; selection practices.
Areas of Emphasis: Executive consulting; organization diagnosis; strategic planning; training design and delivery; attitude surveys; salary surveys; international compensation; EEO program and policy consulting; safety and health consulting; quality circles.
Typical Clients: Business and industry; educational systems; government agencies; foreign government agencies and industry.

Paster Associates

15 Floral Drive
Hastings-on-Hudson, New York 10706
(914) 478-1168
Principals: Nic Paster, President & Executive Secretary; Vera Paster, Vice President.
Founded: 1971
Full-time Consultants: 2
Major Services: Human relations training; management/leadership development; organization development; community development; group therapy.
Areas of Emphasis: Personal growth; life planning; team building; couples laboratories; conflict management; humanizing education and administration.
Typical Clients: School systems; colleges and universities; public health agencies; professional groups and associations; personnel departments of business and industry; consulting firms; couples and families.

Personnel Development Corporation

717 Light Street
Baltimore, Maryland 21230
(301) 547-0909
Principals: Robert B. Sprague, President; Richard R. Cappe, Vice President; Jeanette F. Cozzolino, Secretary; Michael Hinkle, Treasurer.
Founded: 1972
Full-time Consultants: 3
Part-time Consultants: 1
Major Services: Human relations training; management; career guidance; personal assessment; public seminars; sales and sales management training.
Areas of Emphasis: Effective selection techniques.
Typical Clients: Business and industry.

Robert Saunders Associates
Candlewood Isle
New Fairfield, Connecticut 06810
(203) 746-2473
Principal: Robert C. Saunders, President.
Founded: 1970
Full-time Consultants: 1
Part-time Consultants: 1
Major Services: Management/leadership development; human relations training; organization development.
Areas of Emphasis: Career and self-development; supervision and consulting skills; sales and sales management; in-house and public training programs.
Typical Clients: Business and industry; government agencies; executives and professionals.

Robert H. Schaffer & Associates
401 Rockrimmon Road
Stamford, Connecticut 06903
(203) 322-1604
Principals: Robert H. Schaffer, President; Richard A. Bobbe, Vice President; Robert A. Neiman, Vice President.
Founded: 1959
Full-time Consultants: 9
Major Services: Management/leadership development; organization development; consulting development; planning development.
Areas of Emphasis: Increasing an organization's achievement as well as its basic capacity to sustain higher levels of accomplishment; consultation with key people; programs for executives, staff groups, or technical groups; programmed materials for use by an organization's internal consulting staff.
Typical Clients: Manufacturing, processing and service industry; public service agencies; R&D groups; internal consulting groups; training and development departments.

S. M. Scherzer & Associates, P.C.
11 Poplar Plain Road
Westport, Connecticut 06880
(203) 226-3100
Principals: Saul M. Sherzer, President; Jack Butler, Associate; Ray Forbes, Associate.
Founded: 1972
Full-time Consultants: 3
Part-time Consultants: 3
Major Services: Management and organization development; coaching and counseling; opinion surveys; white collar productivity; outplacement counseling; behavior modification.
Areas of Emphasis: Organization development top-down model; management consultation; outplacement counseling.
Typical Clients: Conglomerates; home building industry; service industries; consumer business.

Synectics, Inc.
17 Dunster Street
Cambridge, Massachusetts 02138
(617) 868-6530
Principals: George M. Prince, Chairman; Richard A. Harriman, President; John C. Philipp, Vice President; Marvin L. Smith, Vice President.
Founded: 1960
Full-time Consultants: 15
Major Services: Training courses for groups and individuals; Innovation Sessions™; human resource development consulting.
Areas of Emphasis: Teaching skills for cooperative accomplishment; innovation; meeting structure; creative problem solving with groups.
Typical Clients: All levels of business, industry, service organizations, and the private sector.

CENCOAD, Inc.
2118 South Summit Avenue
Sioux Falls, South Dakota 57105
(605) 336-5236
Principals: Victor V. Pavlenko, Director; Irma E. Herrboldt, Administrative Assistant.
Founded: 1969
Full-time Consultants: 2
Part-time Consultants: 1
Major Services: Human relations training; management/leadership development; organization development; community development; clinical pastoral education; environmental conflict resolution.
Areas of Emphasis: Participative management systems; decision making; problem solving; planning processes.
Typical Clients: Rural communities; community agencies; business; religious organizations; local governments.

The Center for Applied Behavioral Sciences
P.O. Box 829
Topeka, Kansas 66601
(913) 273-7500
Principals: Roy W. Menninger, President; Glenn Swogger, Center Director; Jerry W. Johnson, Director of Administration; Jack Fitzpatrick, Director of Consultations.
Nonprofit organization
Founded: 1973
Full-time Consultants: 10
Part-time Consultants: 15
Major Services: Human relations training; management/leadership development; community development.
Areas of Emphasis: Seminars for executives; personal and organizational consultations.
Typical Clients: Private executives; government.

Communication Consultants, Inc.
8 York Drive
Athens, Ohio 45701
(614) 594-7539
Principals: Sue DeWine, President; Jacqueline Rumley, East Coast Associate; Marie Shafe, Florida Associate; Craig Brubaker, Indiana Associate; Anita James and Lynda Swenson, Midwest Associates.
Founded: 1973
Full-time Consultants: 6
Part-time Consultants: 6
Major Services: Human relations training; management/leadership development; organization development; operations research; future planning; career development; communications, multimedia programs.
Areas of Emphasis: Optimizing human potential in organizations; management science; interpersonal communication; group dynamics.
Typical Clients: School systems; college faculties; business and industry; hospitals; prisons; voluntary organizations; state agencies; Federal programs.

Community Psychology Institute
University of Cincinnati
336 Dyer
Cincinnati, Ohio 45221
(513) 475-5981
Principals: W. Brendan Reddy, Director; Dan Langmeyer, Coordinator of Research.
Nonprofit organization
Founded: 1966
Full-time Consultants: 2
Part-time Consultants: 6
Major Services: Human relations training; management/leadership development; organization development; community development; program evaluation; surveys.
Area of Emphasis: Local human and public service organizations.
Typical Clients: Schools; agencies; institutions.

David L. Ward and Associates, Inc.
360 West Wellington Street
Chicago, Illinois 60657
(312) 929-3993
Principals: David L. Ward, President; Terry Bartlett, Vice President.
Founded: 1968
Full-time Consultants: 4
Part-time Consultants: 3
Major Services: Seminars/workshops; ombudsman programs; needs analysis; counseling; consulting.
Areas of Emphasis: Art of managing people; motivational techniques for managers; time management; problem solving/decision making.
Typical Clients: Business and industry; government.

Educational Administration Development Associates (E/A/D/A)
P.O. Box 1206
Manhattan, Kansas 66502
(913) 539-4528
Principals: Eddy J. Van Meter, President; Susan J. Scollay, Vice President.
Founded: 1973
Full-time Consultants: 3
Part-time Consultants: 4
Major Services: In-service and staff development; proposal preparation and review; project management and evaluation.
Area of Emphasis: Publication of the Educational Organization Development Handbook.
Typical Clients: Public and private school systems; community and junior colleges; four-year and graduate educational institutions.

Growth Associates, a division of Prairie View, Inc.
Box 467
Newton, Kansas 67114
(316) 283-2400
Principals: Merrill F. Raber, Division Director; Gordon Funk, Director, Organization Consultation; George Lehman, Organization Consultant; Jane Hershberger, Special Services.
Nonprofit organization
Founded: 1968
Full-time Consultants: 3
Part-time Consultants: 2
Major Services: Management/leadership development; organization development; community development; continuing education.
Areas of Emphasis: Management training and consultation; continuing education for health care professionals.
Typical Clients: Colleges; government agencies; business; industry; social service and mental health agencies; churches.

Hobert-Martin Consulting Psychologists, Inc.
4428 IDS Center
Minneapolis, Minnesota 55402
(612) 338-8461
Principals: Robert D. Hobert, President; James F. Martin, Secretary-Treasurer;
Founded: 1972
Full-time Consultants: 6
Part-time Consultants: 1
Major Services: Personnel assessment; career planning; management/leadership development; organization development; management consulting.
Areas of Emphasis: Appraisal and development of human resources; career development; management/leadership development seminars; consultation with managers; organization audits/surveys; personnel

research and planning; organization development and planning.

Typical Clients: Corporations; government; law-enforcement agencies; professional organizations; education; hospitals.

Human Resource Associates, Inc.

755 Westview Drive
P.O. Box 303
Hastings, Minnesota 55033
Principals: David W. Helmstetter, President; Donald G. May, Vice President.
Founded: 1969
Full-time Consultants: 13
Part-time Consultants: 30
Major Services: Employee-assistance programs; clinical demonstration programs; dissemination of educational alternatives; in-service training in affective education; management/leadership consulting.
Areas of Emphasis: Leadership and group dynamics; problem solving; human relations skills; designing and implementing nontraditional human service delivery systems.
Typical Clients: Schools; mental health centers; government agencies; private business and industry.

Human Resource Development Associates of Ann Arbor

1820 Green Road
Ann Arbor, Michigan 48105
(313) 994-4732
Principals: Kendall W. Cowing, President; Della K. Cowing, Vice President; George E. Sproule, Principal.
Founded: 1973
Full-time Consultants: 4
Part-time Consultants: 10
Major Services: Executive planning and consultation; employee development programs; supervisory training; strategic long-range planning; quality circles implementation; performance appraisal systems; employee attitude/opinion surveys, orientation programs, and assistance; career counseling.
Areas of Emphasis: Executive consultation; management training; staff/team development; communication; conflict management; change; quality circles.
Typical Clients: Business/industry; health and medical care; government; communities.

Human Synergistics, Inc.

39819 Plymouth Road
Plymouth, Michigan 48170
(313) 459-1030
Principals: J. Clayton Lafferty, Chief Executive Officer; D. Joseph Fisher, President; Justs Grinvalds, Executive Vice President.
Founded: April 1970
Full-time Consultants: 3

Part-time Consultants: 7
Major Services: Management counsulting; training material and program development; selection system development; leadership, communication, and organization development; safety awareness and training programs.
Areas of Emphasis: Diagnostic evaluation; achievement motivation; group processes; human resource utilization.
Typical Clients: Public utilities; manufacturers; retailers; food industry; educational and government institutions; finance and banking data processors; health care; consultants.

Industrial Administration Department

GMI Engineering & Management Institute
1700 West Third Avenue
Flint, Michigan 48502
(313) 762-7959
Principals: Tony Hain, Dept. Head; J.P. Zima, Prof., Org. Comm.; R. Widgery, Prof. Org. Psych.; S.L. Tubbs, Prof., Org. Comm.; Georgia Chao, Asst. Prof., Org. Psych.; Barbara T. Ward, Org. Comm.
Nonprofit organization
Founded: 1982
Full-time Consultants: 6
Part-time Consultants: 20
Major Services: Management/leadership development; organization development; community development; quality circles; management education.
Areas of Emphasis: Management of change; human resources accounting; communication audits; management information systems; lead indicators of social change; Japanese management methods.
Typical Clients: Business; industry; education.

Organizational Consultants, Inc.

16 West Erie, 3S
Chicago, Illinois 60610
(312) 642-5124
Principals: William J. Fillmore, President; Joseph E. Engel, Vice President; Robert T. deFilippis, Vice President.
Founded: 1972
Full-time Consultants: 3
Part-time Consultants: 6
Major Services: Consultation on the integration of business strategy and corporate culture; consultation to key executives and to senior management teams on the management of major organizational change; team building at senior, middle, and line-management levels; consultation on the impact of management style on the attainment of corporate objectives.
Areas of Emphasis: System-wide organizational change; integration of strategy and culture; individual and group style; the management of organizational behavior; individual, group, and organization development; cross-cultural issues.

Personnel Decisions, Inc.
Foshay Tower, Suite 2300
821 Marquette Avenue
Minneapolis, Minnesota 55402
(612) 339-0927
Principals: Wayne K. Kirchner, Chairman; Lowell W. Hellervik, President; James L. Sheard, Vice President; John C. Buchanan, Vice President; Marlys M. Gimble, Secretary-Treasurer.
Founded: 1966
Full-time Consultants: 8
Part-time Consultants: 3
Major Services: Appraisal and evaluations; assessment centers; management training; organizational development; personnel research; human resource system development.
Area of Emphasis: Psychological consultation in all areas of human resource management and development.
Typical Clients: Business and industry; government and municipalities.

Roland S. Larson & Associates, Inc.
2442 Gettysburg Avenue South
Minneapolis, Minnesota 55426
(612) 545-6077
Principals: Roland S. Larson, President; Doris E. Larson, Secretary-Treasurer.
Founded: 1967
Full-time Consultants: 2
Part-time Consultants: 8
Major Services: Career development; outplacement counseling; staff development; customized training events and workshops.
Areas of Emphasis: Life work planning; stress management; team effectiveness; marriage enrichment; value clarification; communication skills; peer counseling; positive learning programs.
Typical Clients: Schools; colleges; religious institutions; government; community agencies; business and industry.

V. Harvey & Associates
1315 Greenwood Avenue
Kent, Ohio 44240
(216) 673-6208
Principal: Virginia P. Harvey
Founded: 1976
Major Services: General management consulting; quality improvement; organizational climate surveys; in-company seminars; organization development.
Areas of Emphasis: Group dynamics for quality circles; conflict management; task-group development; interpersonal skill development; T-group training.

Center for Human Resources and Organizational Development
7124 Highway 17
Santa Cruz, California 95066
(408) 354-4041
Principals: Patrick M. Williams, Director; Gay Williams, Partner.
Founded: 1969
Full-time Consultants: 2
Part-time Consultants: 3-5
Major Services: Organization and management change and development; human relations training; leadership development; quality of working life.
Areas of Emphasis: Team building; training internal organization development consultants; leadership skill building; good management practices.
Typical Clients: Business organizations; school systems; city governments.

Counseling and Educational Development Service, Inc.
P.O. Box 7158
Missoula, Montana 59807
(406) 543-3550
Principals: John Harris, Associate Director for Consulting and Training; Rowan W. Conrad, Associate Director for Research.
Nonprofit organization
Founded: 1976
Full-time Consultants: 3
Part-time Consultants: 8
Major Services: Management skills training; organization development; personnel systems design and staff development; counselor-skills-training evaluation; employee-assistance program development; stress and conflict-management programming and training.
Areas of Emphasis: Human relations training for management and supervisory staffs; workshop and conference planning; systems designing; team building; primary to advanced skills training for counselors in high-risk populations.
Typical Clients: Government agencies; Native American organizations and tribes; business; industry; schools; substance-abuse programs; private individuals and families.

Edward Glaser & Associates
10889 Wilshire Boulevard (Suite 1120)
Los Angeles, California 90024
(213) 879-1280
Principal: Edward M. Glaser, Managing Associate.

Founded: 1952
Full-time Consultants: 2
Part-time Consultants: 14
Major Services: Executive development; individual appraisal; organization planning and development; quality of work life and productivity improvement; communications analysis; leadership training; innovation facilitation.
Areas of Emphasis: Psychological consultation to management; organization development; personnel assessment and development; managerial and supervisory training.
Typical Clients: Private organizations; government or public agencies.

Harris International, Ltd.
2702 Costebelle Drive
La Jolla, California 92037
(619) 453-2271
Principals: Philip R. Harris, President; Dorothy L. Harris, Chairperson. Affiliated with Mark Silber & Associates, Ltd.
Founded: 1971
Full-time Consultants: 2
Part-time Consultants: 45
Major Services: Management and executive development; organization development; behavioral science/human-factor research; learning systems development.
Areas of Emphasis: Cross-cultural training; management of change; organizational culture and communications; high-performing personnel and companies; foreign deployment; performance management. Centered around publications of principals.
Typical Clients: Multinational corporations; government agencies at all levels; national/international associations; educational and health systems.

Herman Associates, Inc.
25532 Jesmond Dene Road
Escondido, California 92026
(619) 747-0264
Principal: Stanley M. Herman, President.
Founded: 1973
Full-time Consultants: 2
Part-time Consultants: 6
Major Services: Programs for organizational excellence; management coaching and development; organization development; training of consultants.
Areas of Emphasis: Authentic management; development of individualized approaches for improving personal and organizational performance.
Typical Clients: Business and industry; government.

Human Interaction Research Institute
10889 Wilshire Boulevard
Los Angeles, California 90024
(213) 879-1373
Principals: Edward M. Glaser, President; Bernice T. Eiduson, Vice President; Robert J. Swenson, Financial Officer; Kathalee N. Garrison, Secretary.
Nonprofit organization
Founded: 1961
Full-time Consultants: 3
Part-time Consultants: 21
Major Services: Management/leadership development; organization development; community development; program evaluation; human-services research; consultation.
Areas of Emphasis: Knowledge utilization and management of change; problem solving; quality of work life improvement.
Typical Clients: Federal, state, and local government agencies; school systems; hospitals; industrial organizations.

Humetrics
7761 Starlight Drive
La Jolla, California 92037
(619) 453-2239
Principals: Lawrence N. Solomon; Evelyn K. Solomon.
Founded: 1972
Full-time Consultants. 2
Major Services: Human relations training; management/leadership development; organization development.
Areas of Emphasis: Personal growth; male-female roles in work world; team building; conflict management; communication.
Typical Clients: School systems; hospitals; municipal government; industry; civil service; military.

International Training Consultants, Inc.
1135 E. Verdugo
Burbank, CA 91501
Principals: Edmund John Phillips, III, President; Rowena von Dornum, Director, Creative Services; Farhad Fred Ebrahimi, Computer Sciences.
Founded: 1967
Full-time Consultants: 15
Part-time Consultants: 8
Major Services: Human relations training; management/leadership development; organization development; community development; educational and vocational training; multimedia development.
Areas of Emphasis: Analytical, educational, evaluative, social research; managerial; related technical services.
Typical Clients: Government agencies and private organizations in the U.S. and abroad.

John A. Hawley Associates/Team Climate Associates
517 First Street
Manhattan Beach, California 90266
(213) 376-5448
Principal: Jack Hawley, President
Founded: 1970
Full-time Consultants: 2
Part-time Consultants: 6
Major Services: Vertical linking; quality of work life; human relations training; management/leadership development; organization development.
Areas of Emphasis: Large organization development programs; organization development resources development; multidisciplinary approaches to organizational improvement; creation of positive work environments using vertical linking; "total" team-building methods.
Typical Clients: Private industry; Federal, state, and local government.

Leadership Institute of Spokane (LIOS)
P.O. Box 8444
Spokane, Washington 99203
(509) 534-4324
Principals: Bob Crosby, President; John Scherer, Director, Organization Development Services.
Nonprofit organization
Founded: 1968
Full-time Consultants: 3
Major Services: Human relations training; management/leadership development; organization development; community development; life direction and personal skill assessment.
Areas of Emphasis: Training designed for specific needs; an M.A. program in Applied Behavioral Science.
Typical Clients: Community mental health; government; religious organizations.

Mark Silber Associates, Ltd.
16776 Bernardo Center Drive
Professional Suite 110-B
San Diego, California 92128
(619) 451-1133
Principals: Mark B. Silber, President; David Brewer, Vice President; Philip Harris, Senior Vice President.
Founded: 1971
Full-time Consultants: 8
Part-time Consultants: 3
Major Services: Executive effectiveness retreats; manager-development workshops; supervisory training; inter-departmental team building; and employee climate analyses.
Areas of Emphasis: Training-needs analyses; design and implementation of O.D. and managerial education for extension of performance competence.

Typical Clients: Health-care systems; bank and financial institutions; heavy and light multinational corporations; trade associations—both domestic and international.

National Indian Training and Research Center
2121 South Mill Avenue (Suite 218)
Tempe, Arizona 85282
(602) 967-9484
Principals: Lawrence Hart, President; Cecil Corbett, Vice President; Lucy Covington, Secretary; Alfreda Bergan, Treasurer.
Nonprofit organization
Founded: 1969
Full-time Consultants: 3
Part-time Consultants: 10
Major Services: Human relations training; management/leadership development; organization development; community development; consultation; workshops.
Area of Emphasis: Minorities, especially American Indians.
Typical Clients: Education; health; government; Indian tribes.

Organization Resources Counselors, Inc.
4966 El Camino Real, Suite 216B
Los Altos, California 94022
(415) 962-8590

11645 Wilshire Boulevard
Los Angeles, California 90025
(213) 820-3800

1800 East Garry, Suite 213
Santa Ana, California 90025
(714) 540-6616
Principals: Anthony Tasca; Robert Formento; Raymond Busch
Founded: 1926
Full-time Consultants: 15
Major Services: Organization planning and development; attitude research; management/ leadership development; productivity assessment; compensation surveys and consulting (national and international); EEO and OSHA; labor relations; selection practices.
Areas of Emphasis: Executive consulting; organization diagnosis; strategic planning; training design and delivery; attitude surveys; salary surveys; international compensation; EEO program and policy consulting; safety and health consulting; quality circles.
Typical Clients: Business and industry; educational systems; government agencies; foreign government agencies and industry.

The Results Company
P.O. Box 81171
San Diego, California 92138
(619) 444-1901
Principals: Edward T. Pidgeon, Jr., President; Joan E. Hoemann, Secretary/Research Coordinator.
Founded: 1979
Full-time Consultants: 2
Major Services: Organizational climate surveys; management/leadership development; organizational development.
Areas of Emphasis: Data gathering; identification of issues impacting on productivity; custom-designed workshops and training sessions.
Typical Clients: Hospitals; financial institutions; government agencies; industry; professional associations.

Thoren Consulting Group, Inc.
5410 S. Lakeshore Drive
Tempe, Arizona 85283
(602) 838-7406
Principals; Donald A. Thoren, President; Charles A. Bivenour, Senior Vice President.
Founded: 1969
Full-time Consultants: 7
Part-time Consultants: 1
Major Services; Human relations training; management/leadership development; organization development; personal growth; motivation seminars; sales training; interpersonal effectiveness; quality control circles.
Areas of Emphasis: Training of supervisors; personnel practices; sales training.
Typical Clients: Small to medium-sized business; government.

University Associates Publishers and Consultants
8517 Production Avenue (P.O. Box 26240)
San Diego, California 92126
(619) 578-5900
Principals: J. William Pfeiffer, President; Leonard D. Goodstein, Chairman.
Founded: 1968
Full-time Consultants: 6
Part-time Consultants: 2
Major Services: Training of human resource development practitioners; management/ leadership development; organization development; publishing of current practical and theoretical materials for human resource development; Master's Degree in human resource development; laboratory education intern program.

Areas of Emphasis: Custom-designed training programs; use of structured experiences; practical applications; widespread distribution of information; public workshops; customized consultation; large system interventions; personal and professional growth.
Typical Clients: Business and industry; religious groups; human-service organizations; health-care services; educational systems; government.

Western Center Associates
11326 Magnolia Boulevard, Suite 2
North Hollywood, CA 91601
(213) 980-7878
Principals: Harold T. Marckwardt, President; Noble F. McKay, Vice President.
Founded: 1966
Full-time Consultants: 3
Part-time Consultants: 16
Major Services: Human relations training; management/leadership development; organization development; community development; training of trainers; career-development training; publishing materials for self-directed job seeking.
Areas of Emphasis: Custom-designed interracial and interdisciplinary involvement efforts at organizational improvement; large-scale usages of small-group methodology; implementing affirmative action; applied adult learning; designers and publishers of total training packages in the areas of productivity and career development.
Typical Clients: School systems; Federal government; county trainers; business and industry; national service organizations; universities.

ENGLAND

Dale Loveluck Associates Ltd.
"Little Oaks"
6 Mitchell Walk
Amersham, Bucks, HP6 6NN
England
Amersham 5224 STD Code 024-03
Principals: Alan Dale, Chairman; Anne Dale, Secretary.
Founded: 1968
Part-time Consultants: 30
Major Services: Human relations training; management/leadership development; organization development; community development; consultant development; personal development; publications.
Areas of Emphasis: Eclectic frameworks and methods: behavior, structure, tasks, technology, culture.
Typical Clients: Industry; health; education; training boards; new enterprises.

**International Institute for Organizational
and Social Development (I.O.D.)**
Predikherenberg 55
B-3200 Leuven (Kessel-lo)
Belgium
(016) 251-671 (& 672)
Principals: Leopold Vansina, Director; Ludo Janssens;
Willem de Jong; Luc Hoebeke; Herm Eikenbroek.
Founded: 1970
Full-time Consultants: 4
Part-time Consultants: 1
Major Services: Development of organizations; training
and management development; professional develop-
ment for organization consultants; career guidance and
counseling; action research.
Areas of Emphasis: Systemic and interdisciplinary
approach to organizational problems in a consultative
relationship with the client; non-ideological approach
to education and organizational issues; and a continuous search for validation of opinions and practice by
using empirical data and scientific findings.
Typical Clients: Industrial organizations and hospitals.

TEAM BUILDING/TEAM DEVELOPMENT:
A REFERENCE LIST

Richard C. Diedrich

The following reference list was developed for a Region I ASTD conference session on team building and team development held in Hartford, Connecticut, in September of 1981. The numbers in the outline refer the reader to the references that follow.

PURPOSES AND ISSUES

1, 3, 4, 6, 7, 9, 11, 13, 16, 19, 23, 24, 28, 29, 31, 39, 40, 45, 47, 51, 54, 59, 65, 68, 69, 73, 75, 76, 87, 89, 90, 91, 93, 95, 99, 100, 101, 103, 104, 107, 108, 111, 113, 118, 120.

DESIGN FORMAT

General

1, 7, 9, 20, 24, 28, 45, 46, 47, 67, 73, 91, 96, 99, 105, 107, 108, 111, 113.

Specific/Detailed

5, 11, 12, 13, 18, 21, 25, 27, 29, 31, 32, 34, 37, 39, 40, 52, 55, 56, 58, 60, 61, 62, 63, 64, 70, 71, 72, 74, 77, 78, 82, 83, 86, 88, 92, 93, 94, 98, 100, 106, 109, 110, 114, 115, 117, 120.

LEADER BEHAVIOR

5, 7, 17, 24, 31, 36, 45, 54, 65, 72, 75, 91, 93, 103.

CONSULTANT BEHAVIOR

4, 5, 7, 11, 20, 24, 29, 31, 36, 45, 52, 54, 71, 72, 91, 93, 100.

CASE STUDIES

5, 6, 7, 8, 10, 11, 13, 14, 18, 19, 20, 21, 22, 26, 27, 28, 30, 31, 32, 36, 42, 44, 46, 55, 56, 61, 63, 64, 70, 71, 72, 74, 78, 79, 80, 83, 84, 88, 89, 92, 94, 98, 99, 100, 102, 105, 110, 115, 116.

RESEARCH STUDIES

2, 8, 15, 17, 22, 32, 41, 43, 47, 48, 49, 53, 55, 57, 60, 61, 80, 84, 85, 106, 109, 112, 114, 116, 119.

BOOKS

33, 35, 38, 50, 81, 97.

SHORT COURSE

Articles

1, 6, 7, 9, 13, 24, 31, 51, 52, 73, 75, 76, 89, 100, 108, 120.

Books

33, 38, 81.

REFERENCES

1. Alban, B.T., & Pollitt, L.I. Team building. In T.H. Patten, Jr. (Ed.), *OD—Emerging dimensions and concepts.* Madison, WI: American Society for Training and Development, 1973.

2. Aram, J.D., & Morgan, C.P. The role of team collaboration in R&D performance. *Management Science,* 1976, *22,* 1127-1137.

3. Atkins, S. Getting your team in tune. *Nation's Business,* March 1975, pp. 91.93.

4. Baker, H.K. The hows and whys of team building. *Personnel Journal,* 1979, *58,* 367-370.

5. Beckhard, R. The confrontation meeting. *Harvard Business Review,* 1967, *45,* 149-155.

6. Beckhard, R. *Organization development: Strategies and models.* Reading, MA: Addison-Wesley, 1969. (See Chapter 3: "Strategies, Tactics, and Activities in Organization Development," pp. 26-42; and two case studies, pp. 57-66, 67-73.)

7. Beckhard, R. Optimizing team-building efforts. *Journal of Contemporary Business,* 1972, *1,* 23-32.

8. Beckhard, R., & Lake, D.G. Short- and long-range effects of a team development effort. In H.A. Hornstein *et al., Social intervention: A behavioral science approach.* New York: The Free Press, 1971.

9. Beer, M. The technology of organization development. In M.D. Dunnette (Ed.), *Handbook of industrial and organizational psychology.* Chicago: Rand McNally, 1976.

10. Belleveau, N. Team management: Putting the reins on the performance horserace. *Institutional Investor,* 1976, *10,* 74-75.

11. Bidwell, A.C., Farrell, J.J., & Blake, R.R. Team job training—A new strategy for industry. *Training Directors,* 1961, *15,* 3-23.

12. Blake, R.R., & Mouton, J.S. Headquarters-field team training for organizational improvement. *Journal of American Society of Training Directors,* 1962, *16,* 3-11.

13. Blake, R.R., & Mouton, J.S. Group and organizational team building: A theoretical model for intervening. In C.L. Cooper (Ed.), *Theories of group processes.* London: John Wiley & Sons, Ltd., 1975.

14. Blake, R.R., & Mouton, J.S. *The new managerial grid®.* Houston: Gulf, 1978. (See Chapter 10: "9, 9 Teamwork," pp. 140-156.)

15. Blake, R.R., Mouton, J.S., Barnes, L.B., & Greiner, L.E. Breakthrough in organizational development. *Harvard Business Review,* 1964, *42,* 133-138.

16. Blake, R.R., Mouton, J.S., & Blansfield, M.G. The logic of team training. In I.R. Weschler & E.H. Schein (Eds.), *Issues in human relations training.* Washington, DC: NTL Learning Resources Corporation, 1962.

17. Boss, R.W. The effects of leader absence on a confrontation teambuilding design. *Journal of Applied Behavioral Science,* 1978, *14,* 469-478.

18. Boss, R.W. It doesn't matter if you win or lose, unless you're losing: Organizational change in a law enforcement agency. *Journal of Applied Behavioral Science,* 1979, *15,* 198-220.

19. Boyer, R.K. Development for the new organizational team. *Business Quarterly*, 1969, *34*, 64-71.

20. Bradford, L.P. Using a consultant. *Making Meetings Work*. San Diego, CA: University Associates, 1976.

21. Bragg, J.E., & Andrews, J.R. Participative decision making: An experimental study in a hospital. *Journal of Applied Behavioral Science*, 1973, *9*, 727-735.

22. Brown, L.D., Aram, J.D., & Bachner, D.J. Interorganizational information sharing: A successful intervention that failed. *Journal of Applied Behavioral Science*, 1974, 533-554.

23. Browning, L.D. Diagnosing teams in organizational settings. *Group & Organization Studies*, 1977, *2*, 187-197.

24. Burke, R.J., & Weir, T. Team building for more effective work groups. *Canadian Banker and ICB Review*, 1976, *83*, 40-45.

25. Corbin, A. Using a team approach to market-oriented planning. *Management Review*, 1977, *66*, 9-15.

26. Crockett, W.J. Team-building—One approach to organization development. In W.W. Burke & H.A. Hornstein (Eds.), *The social technology of organization development*. San Diego, CA: University Associates, 1972.

27. Curtis, H.B. Employee participation in solving production problems. *Personnel Administrator*, 1977, *22*, 33-36, 49.

28. Davis, S.A. An organic problem-solving method of organizational change. *Journal of Applied Behavioral Science*, 1967, *3*, 3-19.

29. Davis, S.A. Building more effective teams. *Innovation*, 1970, *15*, 32-41.

30. Day, T.L. *Team-building: Bargaining for performance—the Sawmill saga*. Madison, WI: American Society for Training and Development, 1978.

31. Dayal, I., & Thomas, J.M. Operation KPE: Developing a new organization. *Journal of Applied Behavioral Science*, 1968, *4*, 473-506.

32. Dirks, M.J., Rottinghaus, M.K., & Lansky, L.M. Argyris' intervention theory: A small-group application. *Group & Organization Studies*, 1978, *3*, 317-329.

33. Dyer, W.G. *Team building: Issues and alternatives*. Reading, MA: Addison-Wesley, 1977.

34. Ely, D.D. Team building for creativity. *Personnel Journal*, 1975, *54*, 226-227, 243.

35. Ends, E.J., & Page, C.W. *Organizational team building*. Cambridge, MA: Winthrop, 1977.

36. Farrell, J. Organization development in a federal government setting. In J.J. Partin (Ed.), *Current perspectives in OD*. Reading, MA: Addison-Wesley, 1973.

37. Francis, D., & Woodcock, M. *Unblocking your organization*. San Diego, CA: University Associates, 1979. (See Part Three: "Common Blockages—Poor Teamwork," pp. 69-73.)

38. Francis, D., & Young, D. *Improving work groups: A practical manual for team building*. San Diego, CA: University Associates, 1979.

39. French, W.L., & Hollman, R.W. Management by objectives: The team approach. *California Management Review*, 1975, *17*, 13-22.

40. French, W.L., & Bell, C.H., Jr. *Organization development*. Englewood Cliffs, NJ: Prentice-Hall, 1973. (See Chapter 10: "Team Interventions," pp. 112-120; and Chapter 11: "Intergroup Interventions," pp. 121-126.)

41. Friedlander, F. The impact of organizational training laboratories upon the effectiveness and interaction of ongoing work groups. In W.W. Burke & H.A. Hornstein (Eds.), *The Social technology of organization development*. San Diego, CA: University Associates, 1972.

42. Galbraith, J. *Designing complex organizations*. Reading, MA: Addison-Wesley, 1973. (See Chapter 6: "A Case Study/Teams," pp. 67-88.)

43. Gavin, J.E., & McPhail, S.M. Intervention and evaluation: A proactive team approach to OD. *Journal of Applied Behavioral Science*, 1978, *14*, 175-194.

44. George, W.W. Task teams for rapid growth. *Harvard Business Review*, 1977, *55*, 71-80.

45. Gibb, J.R. TORI theory: Consultantless team-building. *Journal of Contemporary Business*, 1972, *1*, 33-41.

46. GM's test of participation. *Business Week*, February 23, 1976, pp. 88, 90.

47. Golembiewski, R.T., & Blumberg, A. The laboratory approach to organization change: The "confrontation design." *Journal of the Academy of Management*, 1968, *11*, 199-210.

48. Golembiewski, R.T., Carrigan, S.B., Mead, W.R., Munzenrider, R., & Blumberg, A. Toward building new work relationships: An action design for a critical intervention. *Journal of Applied Behavioral Science*, 1972, *8*, 135-148.

49. Golembiewski, R.T., Hilles, R., & Kagno, M.S. A longitudinal study of flex-time effects: Some consequences of an OD structural intervention. *Journal of Applied Behavioral Science*, 1974, *10*, 503-532.

50. Gorden, W.I., & Howe, R.J. *Team dynamics in developing organizations.* Dubuque, IA: Kendall/Hunt, 1977.

51. Harley, K. Team development. *Personnel Journal*, 1971, *50*, 437-443.

52. Harrison, R. Role negotiation: A tough minded approach to team development. In W.W. Burke & H.A. Hornstein (Eds.), *The social technology of organization development.* San Diego, CA: University Associates, 1972.

53. Harvey, J.B., & Boettger, C.R. Improving communication within a managerial workgroup. *Journal of Applied Behavioral Science*, 1971, *7*, 164-179.

54. Hausser, D.L., Pecorella, P.A., & Wissler, A.L. *Survey-guided development II: A manual for consultants.* San Diego, CA: University Associates, 1977. (See: "Module 5, Work-Group Feedback Meeting," pp. 66-82.)

55. Hautaluoma, J.E., & Gavin, J.F. Effects of organizational diagnosis and intervention on blue-collar "blues." *Journal of Applied Behavioral Science*, 1975, *11*, 475-496.

56. Hill, M. Organization development in an aerospace setting. In J.J. Partin (Ed.), *Current perspectives in OD.* Reading, MA: Addison-Wesley, 1973.

57. Hill, R.E. Managing interpersonal conflict in project teams. *Sloan Management Review*, 1977, *18*, 45-61.

58. Hines, W.W. Increasing team effectiveness. *Training and Development Journal*, 1980, *34*, 78-82.

59. Karp, H.B. Team building from a Gestalt perspective. In J.W. Pfeiffer & J.E. Jones (Eds.), *The 1980 annual handbook for group facilitators.* San Diego, CA: University Associates, 1980.

60. Kegan, D.L., & Rubenstein, A.H. Trust, effectiveness and organizational development: A field study in R & D. *Journal of Applied Behavioral Science*, 1973, *9*, 498-513.

61. Kimberly, J.R., & Nielsen, W.R. Organization development and change in organizational performance. *Administrative Science Quarterly*, 1975, *20*, 191-206.

62. Koehler, W.R., Lehner, G., & Fisher, F.E. Team effectiveness training. *Training and Development Journal*, 1974, *28*, 3-6.

63. Koppes, D.L. OD in an aluminum and chemical setting. In J.J. Partin (Ed.), *Current perspectives in OD.* Reading, MA: Addison-Wesley, 1973.

64. Kuriloff, A.H., & Atkins, S. T-group for a work team. *Journal of Applied Behavioral Science*, 1966, *2*, 63-94.

65. Lewis, J.W. Management team development: Will it work for you? *Personnel*, 1975, *52*, 11-25.

66. Likert, R. Improving cost performance with cross functional teams. *Management Review*, 1976, *65*, 36-42.

67. Likert, R., & Fisher, M.S. MBGO: Putting some team spirit into MBO. *Personnel*, 1977, *54*, 40-47.

68. Lippitt, G.L. *Team building for matrix organizations* (PAI Reprint RP1). Washington, DC: Project Associates, 1969.

69. Locander, W.B., & Scamell, R.W. Team approach to managing the market research process. *MSU Business Topics*, 1977, *25*, 15-26.

70. Louis, A.M. They're striking some strange bargains at Diamond Shamrock. *Fortune*, January 1976, pp. 142-146; 148-152; 156.

71. Luke, R.A., Jr., Block, P., Davey, J.M., & Averch, V.R. A structural approach to organizational change. *Journal of Applied Behavioral Science*, 1973, *9*, 611-635.

72. Mangham, I. Building an effective work team. In M.L. Berger & P.J. Berger (Eds.), *Group training techniques*. Epping, Essex, England: Gower Press Limited, 1972.

73. Mangham, I. Team development in industry. In C. L. Cooper (Ed.), *Developing social skills in managers*. New York: John Wiley, 1976.

74. Margulies, N., & Raia, A.P. People in organizations—A case for team training. *Training and Development Journal*, 1968, *22*, 2-11.

75. Margulies, N., & Wallace, J. *Organizational change*. Glenview, IL: Scott, Foresman, 1972. (See Chapter 7: "Changing Team Relationships," pp. 99-121.)

76. Marksbury, H. Casting light on what makes us tick. *Management Review*, 1979, *68*, 8-14. (See Part 1: Managerial Team Building.)

77. Marksbury, H. A manager's trip through the hall of mirrors of the psyche. *Management Review*, 1979, *68*, 53-57. (See Part 2: "Managerial Team Building.")

78. Mather, A.F., & Schuttenberg, E.M. A team development project. *Training and Development Journal*, 1971, *25*, 15-24.

79. McGill, M. *Organization development for operating managers*. New York: AMACOM, 1977.

80. McMillan, C.B. Organizational change in schools: Bedford-Stuyvesant. *Journal of Applied Behavioral Science*, 1975, *11*, 437-456.

81. Merry, U., & Allerhand, M.E. *Developing teams and organizations*. Reading, MA: Addison-Wesley, 1977.

82. Miller, N. The accountability chart—A tool for team building. *Personnel*, 1977, *54*, 51-56.

83. Mitchell, M.D. Dealing with personnel changes in a working team. In J. Adams, J. Hayes, & B. Hopson (Eds.), *Transition: Understanding and managing personal change*. Montclair, NJ: Allanheld, Osmun & Co., 1976.

84. Moore, M.L. Assessing organizational planning and teamwork: An action research methodology. *Journal of Applied Behavioral Science*, 1978, *14*, 479-491.

85. Nadler, D.A., & Pecorella, P.A. Differential effects of multiple interventions in an organization. *Journal of Applied Behavioral Science*, 1975, *11*, 348-366.

86. Owens, J. Organizational conflict and team building. *Training and Development Journal*, 1973, *27*, 32-39.

87. Parlour, R.R. Executive team training. *Journal of the Academy of Management*, 1971, *14*, 341-344.

88. Patten, T.H., Jr., & Dorey, L.E. Long-range results of a team-building OD effort. *Public Personnel Management*, 1977, *6*, 31-50.

89. Petrella, T. *Managing with teams*. Wynnewood, PA: Block Petrella Associates, 1974.

90. Pickering, W.D., & Rogers, G.W. *The anatomy of teamwork* (Management Psychologist, Series 3, No. 1). Chicago: Rohrer, Hibler & Replogle, Inc., 1965.

91. Plovnick, M., Fry, R., & Rubin, I. New developments in OD technology: Programmed team development. *Training and Development Journal*, 1975, *29*, 19-25.

92. Pneuman, R.W. A team development intervention (Aerospace Electrical Division, Westinghouse). Paper presented at the meeting of the O.D. Institute, Hartland, MI, April 1979.

93. Reilly, A.J., & Jones, J.E. Team-building. In J.W. Pfeiffer & J.E. Jones (Eds.), *The 1974 annual handbook for group facilitators*. San Diego, CA: University Associates, 1974.

94. Rush, H.M.F. *Behavioral science* (SPP No. 216). New York: The Conference Board, Inc., 1969. (See the case study on American Airlines, pp. 72-86.)

95. Scherer, J.J. Can team building increase productivity or how can something that feels so good not be worthwhile? *Group & Organization Studies*, 1979, *4*(3), 335-351.

96. Schrello, D.M. How interdisciplinary training pays off. *Training and Development Journal*, 1975, *29*, 16-20.

97. Scientific Methods, Inc. *Grid team building* (2nd ed.). Austin, TX: Scientific Methods, Inc., 1975. (See "Organizational Team Building," pp. 3-24.)

98. Scott, T. Organization development in a bank setting. In J.J. Partin (Ed.), *Current perspectives in OD*. Reading, MA: Addison-Wesley, 1973.

99. Slaughter, J.M., & Schmid, R.O. Effective team action improves plant operations. *Personnel Journal*, 1975, *52*, 435-437.

100. Solomon, L.N. Team development: A training approach. In J.E. Jones & J.W. Pfeiffer (Eds.), *The 1977 annual handbook for group facilitators*. San Diego, CA: University Associates, 1977.

101. Stone, A.R. The interdisciplinary research team. *Journal of Applied Behavioral Science*, 1969, *5*, 351-365.

102. Sweedar, P. Team approach to community relations and how it's working. *Telephony*, 1976, *191*, 25-28.

103. Team management: Are two (or more) heads better than one? *Savings and Loan News*, 1977, *98*, 548-553.

104. Team working together is the key to success. *Purchasing*, 1977, *82*, 74-75.

105. Teamwork through conflict. *Business Week*, March 20, 1971, pp. 44-50.

106. Van Zelst, R.H. Sociometrically selected work teams increase production. *Personnel Psychology*, 1952, *5*, 175-186.

107. Varney, G.H. Building an effective management team. *The Business Quarterly*, 1976, *41*, 38-45.

108. Varney, G.H. *Organization development for managers*. Reading, MA: Addison-Wesley, 1977. (See Chapter 9: "Building an Effective Management Team," pp. 151-165.)

109. Varney, G.H., & Hunady, R.J. Energizing commitment to change in a team-building intervention: A FIRO-B approach. *Group & Organization Studies*, 1978, *3*, 435-466.

110. Wampler, K.F. Organization development in an airline setting. In J.J. Partin (Ed.), *Current perspectives in OD*. Reading, MA: Addison-Wesley, 1973.

111. Weihrich, H. TAMBO: Team approach to MBO. *University of Michigan Business Review*, 1979, *31*, 12-17.

112. Wilson, J.E., Mullen, D.P., & Morton, R.B. Sensitivity training for individual growth—Team training for organizational development. *Training and Development Journal*, 1968, *22*, 47-53.

113. Winning, E.A. Integrating management theory into action programs. *Personnel*, 1976, *53*, 21-29.

114. Woodman, R.W. *Effects of team development intervention: A field experiment*. Unpublished doctoral dissertation, Krannert Graduate School of Management, Purdue University, 1978.

115. Zand, D.E. Collateral organization: A new change strategy. *Journal of Applied Behavioral Science*, 1974, *10*, 63-89.

116. Zand, D.E., Steele, F., & Zalkind, S.S. The impact of an organizational development program on perceptions of interpersonal, group and organization functioning. *Journal of Applied Behavioral Science*, 1969, *5*, 393-410.

117. Zeira, Y. Training the top-management team for planned change. *Training and Development Journal*, 1974, *28*, 30-36.

118. Zemke, R. Team building: Helping people learn to work together. *Training*, 1978, *15*, 23-26; 32-34.

119. Zenger, J.H. *The effect of a team human relations training laboratory on the productivity and perceptions of a selling group*. Unpublished doctoral dissertation, University of Southern California, 1968.

120. Zenger, J.H., & Miller, D.E. Building effective teams. *Personnel*, 1974, *51*, 20-29.

Richard C. Diedrich, Ph.D., *is the manager for Boston and corporate psychologist for Rohrer, Hibler & Replogle, Inc. He has over twenty years of experience as a consultant, teacher, and trainer in business, industry, and educational institutions. Before joining Rohrer, Hibler, & Replogle, he was an assistant professor at Purdue University. Dr. Diedrich is a member of the American Psychological Association, American Society for Training and Development, and OD Network.*

BIOFEEDBACK: AN OUTLINE OF THE LITERATURE AND RESOURCE DIRECTORY (1983 UPDATE)

Howard Pikoff

Interest in biofeedback has mushroomed in the last five years. A computer search of *Psychological Abstracts* from 1967 to early 1982 shows a year-by-year increase in publishing activity, with some 1,400 references appearing under the term "biofeedback" during this period. Almost 1,000 of these have been published since 1976.[1] Along with increased publishing, expansion of the field has been marked by the founding of a number of professional societies and journals; the establishment of graduate training programs (Feuerstein & Schwartz, 1977); the appearance of new manufacturers, advanced equipment, and multimedia training aids on the market (Rugh & Schwitzgebel, 1975); a concern over legislation, ethics, and certification (Fuller, 1978); and dozens of imaginative applications, a call or two for restraint, and a host of unanswered questions (Miller, 1976, 1978). All of these attest to the growing importance of biofeedback as a technology.

The present article is a working guide to these areas presented in two sections: (a) an outline of the literature covering frequently cited papers, research reviews, bibliographies, introductions, overviews, questions, problems, and professional issues and (b) a resource directory of training, instrumentation, multimedia aids, and professional organizations. It is intended as a road map for the new traveler on a growing frontier.

OUTLINE OF THE LITERATURE

Frequently Cited Papers

The *Social Sciences Citation Index* was used to identify reports that helped to shape the research literature in the formative decade of the 1970s. A group of sixty-five authors who were well known in the field or who had published two or more articles on biofeedback between 1970 and 1979 was selected. These authors were then checked in the *Social Sciences Citation Index* for the period 1977 through 1979 to determine how many times each of their papers on biofeedback had been cited.

Listed below are the five most frequently cited reports, with the number of citations for each shown in parentheses. (Due to variations and occasional errors in the citing of references, the number of citations indicated should be seen as approximate.) The list presents no surprises. Blanchard has been the premier critic of biofeedback methodology from its infancy; Budzynski's seminal headache papers spawned an entirely new clinical field. Neal Miller has for more than

[1] It should be noted that the focus here is biofeedback per se. During this period, numerous additional references have appeared dealing with the operant conditioning of autonomic and somatic responses in humans and animals, which could be considered variants of biofeedback but which were not so labeled by their authors.

thirty years been at the forefront of American psychology with his work on instrumental conditioning in animals and humans.

Blanchard, E.B., & Young, L.D. Self-control of cardiac functioning: A promise as yet unfulfilled. *Psychological Bulletin*, 1973, *79*, 145-163. (39)

Blanchard, E.B., Young, L.D., & Jackson, M.S. Clinical applications of biofeedback training: A review of evidence. *Archives of General Psychiatry*, 1974, *30*, 573-589. (67)

Budzynski, T., Stoyva, J., & Adler, C. Feedback-induced muscle relaxation: Application to tension headache. *Journal of Behavior Therapy and Experimental Psychiatry*, 1970, *1*, 205-211. (55)

Budzynski, T.H., Stoyva, J.M., Adler, C.S., & Mullaney, D.J. EMG biofeedback and tension headache: A controlled outcome study. *Psychosomatic Medicine*, 1973, *35*, 484-496. (64)

Miller, N.E. Learning of visceral and glandular responses. *Science*, 1969, *163*, 434-445. (77)

Research Reviews and Bibliographies

The literature of biofeedback is being abundantly reviewed and documented. Of particular interest are Blanchard et al. (1974) for their systematic, critical analysis of the methodology in the early studies; Shapiro and Schwartz for the variety of clinical issues discussed (psychosomatic etiology, patient motivation, symptom substitution, placebo effects); and a book-length review of the literature by Yates. In addition to the references listed below, three important sources are *Biofeedback and Self-Control*, an annual review series published by Aldine; *The Biofeedback Syllabus* (Brown, 1975), a compilation of abstracted references to biofeedback and related psychophysiology; and the massive bibliography, *Biofeedback: A Survey of the Literature* (Butler, 1978).

General Literature

Birbaumer, N. Biofeedback training: A critical review of its clinical applications and some possible future directions. *European Journal of Behavioural Analysis and Modification*, 1977, *4*, 235-241.

Blanchard, E.B., Young, L.D., & Jackson, M.S. Clinical applications of biofeedback training: A review of evidence. *Archives of General Psychiatry*, 1974, *30*, 573-589.

Center for Behavior Modification. *Clinical applications of biofeedback: Review of the literature.* Minneapolis: Author, 1976.

Epstein, L.H., & Blanchard, E.B. Biofeedback, self-control and self-management: An integration and reappraisal. *Biofeedback and Self-Regulation*, 1977, *2*, 201-212.

Schaefer, S., & Engel, R.R. Operant control of autonomic functions: Biofeedback bibliography. *Perceptual and Motor Skills*, 1973, *36*, 863-875.

Shapiro, D., & Schwartz, G.E. Biofeedback and visceral learning: Clinical applications. *Seminars in Psychiatry*, 1972, *4*, 171-184.

Steiner, S.S., & Dince, W.M. Biofeedback efficacy studies: A critique of critiques. *Biofeedback and Self-Regulation*, 1981, *6*, 275-288.

Wenrich, W.W., & LeTendre, D. Operant control of autonomic behavior: An annotated bibliography (1954-1974). JSAS *Catalog of Selected Documents in Psychology*, 1975, *5*, 231. (Ms. No. 924)

Yates, A. *Biofeedback and the modification of behavior.* New York: Plenum Press, 1980.

Special Topics

Blanchard, E., Andrasik, F., Ahles, T., & Teders, S. Migraine and tension headache: A meta-analytic review. *Behavior Therapy*, 1980, *11*, 613-631.

Blanchard, E.B., & Young, L.D. Self-control of cardiac functioning: A promise as yet unfulfilled. *Psychological Bulletin*, 1973, *79*, 145-163.

Budzynski, T. Biofeedback in the treatment of muscle-contraction (tension) headache. *Biofeedback and Self-Regulation*, 1978, *3*, 409-434.

Diamond, S., Diamond-Falk, J., & DeVeno, T. Biofeedback in the treatment of vascular headache. *Biofeedback and Self-Regulation*, 1978, *3*, 385-408.

Fernando, C.K., & Basmajian, J.V. Biofeedback in physical medicine and rehabilitation. *Biofeedback and Self-Regulation*, 1978, *3*, 435-455.

Fotopoulos, S.S., & Sunderland, W.P. Biofeedback in the treatment of psychophysiologic disorders. *Biofeedback and Self-Regulation*, 1978, *3*, 331-361.

Frumkin, K., Nathan, R.J., Prout, M.F., & Cohen, M.C. Nonpharmacologic control of essential hypertension in man: A critical review of the experimental literature. *Psychosomatic Medicine*, 1978, *40*, 294-320.

Hatch, J.P., & Gatchel, R.J. The role of biofeedback in the operant modification of human heart rate. *Biofeedback and Self-Regulation*, 1981, *6*, 139-167.

Jessup, B.A., Neufeld, R.W.J., & Merskey, H. Biofeedback therapy for headache and other pain— Evaluative review. *Pain*, 1979, *7*, 225-270.

Kostes, H., & Glaus, K.D. Applications of biofeedback to the treatment of asthma: A critical review. *Biofeedback and Self-Regulation*, 1981, *6*, 573-593.

Masterson, J.P., & Turley, W.B. Biofeedback training with children. *American Journal of Clinical Biofeedback*, 1980, *3*, 137-143.

Morley, S. Partial reinforcement in human biofeedback learning. *Biofeedback and Self-Regulation*, 1979, *4*, 221-227.

Plotkin, W.B. The alpha experience revisited: Biofeedback in the transformation of psychological state. *Psychological Bulletin*, 1979, *86*, 1132-1148.

Prima, A., Agnoli, A., & Tamburello, A. A review of the application of biofeedback to migraine and tension headaches. *Acta Neurologica*, 1979, *34*, 510-521.

Qualls, P.J., & Sheehan, P.W. Electromyograph biofeedback as a relaxation technique: A critical appraisal and reassessment. *Psychological Bulletin*, 1981, *90*, 21-42.

Reeves, J.L., & Shapiro, D. Biofeedback and relaxation in essential hypertension. *International Review of Applied Psychology*, 1978, *27*, 121-135.

Rotberg, M.H., & Surwit, R.S. Biofeedback techniques in the treatment of visual and ophthalmologic disorders: A review of the literature. *Biofeedback and Self-Regulation*, 1981, *6*, 375-388.

Sappington, J.T., Fiorito, E.M., & Brehony, K.A. Biofeedback as therapy in Raynaud's disease. *Biofeedback and Self-Regulation*, 1979, *4*, 155-169.

Seer, P. Psychological control of essential hypertension: Review of the literature and methodological critique. *Psychological Bulletin*, 1979, *86*, 1015-1043.

Tarler-Benlolo, L. The role of relaxation in biofeedback training: A critical review of the literature. *Psychological Bulletin*, 1978, *85*, 727-755.

Taub, E., & Stroebel, C.F. Biofeedback in the treatment of vasoconstrictive syndromes. *Biofeedback and Self-Regulation*, 1978, *3*, 363-373.

Travis, T.A., Kondo, C.Y., & Knott, J.R. Alpha enhancement research: A review. *Biological Psychiatry*, 1975, *10*, 69-89.

Turk, D.C., Meichenbaum, D.H., & Berman, W.H. Application of biofeedback for the regulation of pain: A critical review. *Psychological Bulletin*, 1979, *86*, 1322-1338.

Whitehead, W.E. Biofeedback in the treatment of gastrointestinal disorders. *Biofeedback and Self-Regulation*, 1978, *3*, 375-384.

Williamson, D.A., & Blanchard, E.B. Heart rate and blood pressure biofeedback: I. A review of recent experimental literature. *Biofeedback and Self-Regulation*, 1979, *4*, 1-34.

Williamson, D.A., & Blanchard, E.B. Heart rate and blood pressure biofeedback: II. A review and integration of recent theoretical models. *Biofeedback and Self-Regulation*, 1979, *4*, 35-50.

Zimet, G.D. Locus of control and biofeedback—Review of the literature. *Perceptual and Motor Skills*, 1979, *49*, 871-877.

Introductions and Overviews

The following present perspectives both broad and narrow, theoretical and applied. Blanchard and Epstein are worth noting for their clear and concise presentation of clinical research; Budzynski's article and Fuller's book for practical how-to-do-it guidance; and Brown, author of several books on biofeedback, for her vision.

Astor, M. An introduction to biofeedback. *American Journal of Orthopsychiatry*, 1977, *47*, 615-625.

Basmajian, J.V. (Ed.). *Biofeedback principles and practice for clinicians*. Baltimore: Williams & Wilkins, 1979.

Blanchard, E., & Epstein, L. *Biofeedback primer*. Reading, MA: Addison-Wesley, 1978.

Brown, B. *Stress and the art of biofeedback*. New York: Harper & Row, 1977.

Budzynski, T.H. Biofeedback procedures in the clinic. *Seminars in Psychiatry*, 1973, 5, 535-547.

Fuller, G. *Biofeedback: Methods and procedures in clinical practice*. San Francisco: Biofeedback Press, 1977.

Gaarder, K.R. *Clinical biofeedback: A clinical manual in behavioral medicine* (2nd ed.). Baltimore: Williams & Wilkins, 1981.

Gatchel, R.J., & Price, K.P. (Eds.). *Clinical applications of biofeedback: Appraisal and status*. Oxford, England: Pergamon Press, 1979.

Peper, E. *From the inside out: A self-teaching and laboratory manual for biofeedback*. New York: Plenum Press, 1981.

Rosenboom, D. (Ed.). *Biofeedback and the arts: Results of early experiments*. Vancouver, British Columbia: Aesthetic Research Centre of Canada, 1976.

Schwartz, G.E., & Beatty, J. (Eds.). *Biofeedback: Theory and research*. New York: Academic Press, 1977.

Questions, Problems, Professional Issues

Of particular interest in this final group of papers are Fuller's broad overview of such diverse topics as instrumentation, insurance, professional groups, ethics, training, legislation; Stroebel and Glueck's analysis of the therapeutic value of properly managed placebo effects; and a lecture on research problems by Miller, whose closing caveat—"In opening up this new era, we should be bold in what we try but cautious in what we claim" (p. 24 of manuscript cited below)—serves as a fitting conclusion to the present outline of the biofeedback literature.

Amar, P.B. Role of the therapist in biofeedback training. *Psychotherapy and Psychosomatics*, 1978, *30*, 179-186.

Basmajian, J.V. Fact vs. myth in EMG biofeedback. *Biofeedback and Self-Regulation*, 1976, *1*, 369-371.

Borgeat, F., Hade, B., Larouche, L.M., & Bedwani, C.N. Effect of therapist's active presence on EMG biofeedback training of headache patients. *Biofeedback and Self-Regulation*, 1980, *5*, 275-282.

Butterfield, W. & Schwitzgebel, R. Implications of the medical device amendments of 1976. *Behavioral Engineering*, 1976, *3*, 103-104.

Farr, S.P., Smith, R.P., & Meyer, R.G. Promise and problems in biofeedback research. *Psychologia*, 1975, *18*, 212-220.

Ferguson, D.C. Biofeedback and behavioral medicine: Prospects for the 1980's. *American Journal of Clinical Biofeedback*, 1981, *4*, 8-15.

Fuller, G. Current status of biofeedback in clinical practice. *American Psychologist*, 1978, *33*, 39-48.

Holroyd, J.C., Nuechterlein, K.H., Shapiro, D., & Ward, F. Individual differences in hypnotizability and effectiveness of hypnosis on biofeedback. *International Journal of Clinical and Experimental Hypnosis*, 1982, *30*, 45-65.

Kimmel, H.D. The relevance of experimental studies to clinical applications of biofeedback. *Biofeedback and Self-Regulation*, 1981, *6*, 263-271.

Kleinman, K.M. The role of reinforcement and motivation in biofeedback performance. *Physiology & Behavior*, 1981, *26*, 921-925.

Lazarus, R.S. A cognitively oriented psychologist looks at biofeedback. *American Psychologist*, 1975, *30*, 553-561.

Miller, N. Fact and fancy about biofeedback and its clinical implications. JSAS *Catalog of Selected Documents in Psychology*, 1976, *6*, 92-93. (Ms. No. 1329)

Onoda, L. Ethical and professional issues for psychologists and counselors employing biofeedback in counseling settings. *Personnel and Guidance Journal*, 1978, *57*, 214-217.

Plotkin, W.B. The role of attributions of responsibility in the facilitation of unusual experiential states during alpha training: An analysis of the biofeedback placebo effect. *Journal of Abnormal Psychology*, 1980, *89*, 67-78.

Plotkin, W.B. A rapprochement of the operant-conditioning and awareness views of biofeedback training: The role of discrimination in voluntary control. *Journal of Experimental Psychology: General*, 1981, *110*, 415-428.

Sanders, S.H., & Collins, F. The effect of electrode placement on frontalis EMG measurement in headache patients. *Biofeedback and Self-Regulation*, 1981, *6*, 473-481.

Schwartz, G. Biofeedback as therapy: Some theoretical and practical issues. *American Psychologist*, 1973, *28*, 666-673.

Schwartz, M.S. Biofeedback Certification Institute of America—Blueprint knowledge statements. *Biofeedback and Self-Regulation*, 1981, *6*, 253-262.

Shapiro, D. Recommendations of ethics committee regarding biofeedback techniques and instrumentation: Issues of public and professional concern. *Psychophysiology*, 1973, *10*, 533-535.

Shapiro, D. Biofeedback and behavioral medicine in perspective. *Biofeedback and Self-Regulation*, 1979, *4*, 371-381.

Silver, B.V., & Blanchard, E.B. Biofeedback and relaxation training in the treatment of psychophysiological disorders: Or are those machines really necessary. *Journal of Behavioral Medicine*, 1978, *1*, 217-239.

Stenger, C.A. The emergence of biofeedback technology and pain management programs in the Veterans Administration: An overview. *American Journal of Clinical Biofeedback*, 1980, *3*, 3-4.

Stroebel, C.F., & Glueck, B.C. Biofeedback treatment in medicine and psychiatry: An ultimate placebo? *Seminars in Psychiatry*, 1973, *5*, 379-393.

Willis, S.L. Biofeedback treatment failures and motivational problems. *American Journal of Clinical Biofeedback*, 1980, *3*, 79-85.

Wineburg, E.N. Should you incorporate biofeedback into your practice? *Behavioral Medicine*, 1981, *8*, 30-34.

Resource Directory

A directory in a field as fluid as biofeedback is probably outdated from the moment of conception and certainly incomplete by the time of publication. The associations shown under "Professional Organizations" are excellent sources for updating the following listings.

Training

The following psychology programs offer graduate training, including clinical practica and laboratory apprenticeships, in biofeedback and clinical psychophysiology: Bowling Green State University, University of Colorado, University of Denver, University of Georgia, University of Manitoba, University of Michigan, University of Mississippi, Ohio University, University of Oregon, Pennsylvania State University, Purdue University, University of Rochester, University of South Dakota, State University of New York at Stony Brook, Washington State University, and Yale University.

Additional data on biofeedback training and a listing of anticipated programs, many of which may now be operational (e.g., State University of New York at Buffalo), will be found in

Feuerstein and Schwartz (1977). Information about graduate programs in the related areas of behavioral medicine and health psychology may be obtained from the Society of Behavioral Medicine (P.O. Box 8530, Knoxville, Tennessee 37916) and the Division of Health Psychology of the American Psychological Association (1200 17th Street N.W. Washington, D.C. 20036). For a description of biofeedback treatment and internship facilities, see Warrenburg and Cram (1978) and Cram and Warrenburg (1977).

Instrumentation

In addition to supplying equipment, some of the larger companies (e.g., Cyborg of Massachusetts) offer training and seminars as well as information about applications and general developments in the field. More complete listings of manufacturers and suppliers are available in Rugh and Schwitzgebel (1975) and from the Biofeedback Society of America. Several discussions of equipment selection and evaluation have also been published (e.g., Girdano, 1976; Paskewitz, 1975; Schwitzgebel & Rugh, 1975).

United States

Alabama
  Cybersystems
  8300 Viceburg Drive
  Huntsville 35805

Arizona
  Semantodontics
  3714 Indian School
  Phoenix 85060

California
  Autogenic Systems
  809 Allston Way
  Berkeley 94710

  Biofeedback Research Institute
  6399 Wilshire Boulevard
  Los Angeles 90048

  Electro Labs
  366 South Lemon Avenue
  Walnut 91766

Colorado
  Biofeedback Systems
  2736 47th Street
  Boulder 80301

  Staodynamics
  1225 Florida Avenue
  Longmont 80501

Illinois
  Neuronics
  105 West Madison
  Chicago 60611

Indiana
  Medical Device Corporation
  1555 North Bellefontaine Street
  Indianapolis 46208

Bio-Temp Products
1950 West 86th Street
Indianapolis 46208

Kansas
  Systec
  1546 East 23rd Street
  Lawrence 66044

Maryland
  BRS/LVE
  5301 Holland Drive
  Beltsville 20705

Massachusetts
  Cyborg Corporation
  55 Chapel Avenue
  Newton 02158

  G & W Applied Science Laboratories
  335 Bear Hill Road
  Waltham 02154

Michigan
  Bio-Medical Instruments
  2387 Eight Mile
  Warren 48090

Minnesota
  Medical Devices
  833 3rd Street S.W.
  St. Paul 55112

Nebraska
  Farrell Instruments
  P.O. Box 1037
  Grand Island 68801

New Jersey
  Edmund Scientific Company
  101 East Gloucester Pike
  Barrington 08007

New Mexico
Ouroboros Instruments
215 Sierra Drive
Albuquerque 87106

New York
Biofeedback Instrument Company
255 West 98th Street
New York 10025

BMA Audio Cassette Programs/
Biomonitoring Applications
200 Park Avenue South
New York 10003

Ohio
Marietta Apparatus Company
P.O. Box 671
Marietta 45750

Pennsylvania
Coulborn Instruments
RD #2
Wescoesville 18001

Tennessee
Ortec
Life Sciences Products
Oak Ridge 37830

Texas
Narco Bio-Systems
7651 Airport Boulevard
P.O. Box 12511
Houston 77017

Utah
Motion Control
1005 South 300 West
Salt Lake City 84101

Vermont
Med Associates
P.O. Box 47
East Fairfield 05448

Wisconsin
Nicolet Instrument Company
5225 Vernona Road
Madison 53711

Foreign

England
Biofeedback Systems
6 Lower Ormond Street
Manchester 1

Canada
EKEG Electronics Company
P.O. Box 46199
Station G
Vancouver 8, British Columbia

Thought Technology
2193 Clifton Avenue
Montreal, Quebec H4A 2N5

The Netherlands
Enting Instruments
VIJFTIG Bunderweg 1
Dorst

Multimedia Aids

The following is a sample of aids available for instruction (films and video cassettes in particular), keeping abreast of the field (the BMA catalog reads like a "Who's Who" of biofeedback), and direct use by clients (e.g., tapes on relaxation in conjunction with at-home exercises).

Audio

Available from BMA Audio Cassettes, 200 Park Avenue South, New York, New York 10003.

Adler, C., & Adler, S. *Biofeedback in psychotherapy.*

Basmajian, J. *Biofeedback and rehabilitation medicine.*

Blanchard, E. *Biofeedback in modification of cardiovascular disorders.*

Brown, B. *EEG biofeedback: Clinical applications and research frontiers.*

Budzynski, T. *Biofeedback in systematic desensitization.*

Danskin, D., & Lowenstein, T. *Biofeedback applications in counseling and education.*

Diamond, S. *Effective headache management through biofeedback training.*

Fuller, G. *Developing a biofeedback practice and clinic.*

Gaarder, K. *Selecting patients for biofeedback therapy.*

Gregg, R., & Frazier, L. *Biofeedback applications in pregnancy and labor.*

Miller, N. *Clinical applications of biofeedback: Appraisal and status.*

Rugh, J. *Evaluating and selecting of instrumentation.*

Stoyva, J. *Stress disorders: Why use biofeedback.*

Available from the Cyborg Corporation, 55 Chapel Avenue, Newton, Massachusetts 02158.

Diamond, S. *Proper selection of headache patients for biofeedback.*

Engel, B. *Biofeedback in control of cardiac function.*

Peper, E. *Current status of biofeedback technology: Clinical and research perspectives.*

Rickles, W. *Psychodynamics of biofeedback therapy.*

Sargent, J. *Thermal biofeedback in migraine headache treatment: The Menninger Foundation studies.*

Available from the Biofeedback Institute, 3428 Sacramento Street, San Francisco, California 94118:

Development of a biofeedback practice or clinic.

How to relax some more.

How to teach relaxation techniques and how to relax.

Progressive relaxation techniques.

Visual

Biofeedback (transparencies). Lansford Publishing, P.O. Box 8711, 1088 Lincoln Avenue, San Jose, California 95155.

Biofeedback; Part 2 of *The behavioral revolution* (video cassette). Pennsylvania State University, Audio-Visual Services, University Park, Pennsylvania 16802.

Biofeedback: Conscious control of the unconscious (filmstrip or slides). Informative Image, 115 W. McDowell Road, Phoenix, Arizona 85003.

Biofeedback—Listening to your head (17-mm film). Documents Associates, 43 Britain Street, Toronto 285, Ontario, Canada.

Biofeedback—The yoga of the west (16-mm film). Hartley Publications, Cat Rock Road, Cos Cob, Connecticut 06807.

Clinical uses of biofeedback (video cassette). Growth Associates, Division of Prairie View, P.O. Box 467, Newton, Kansas 67114.

Dialogue on biofeedback (film). U.S. Department of Agriculture, Office of Communications, Motion Picture Services, 14th and Independence Avenue, Washington, D.C. 20251.

EMG biofeedback: A new tool for physical and occupational therapy (slide/tape). Cyborg Corporation, 55 Chapel Avenue, Newton, Massachusetts 02158.

Mind over body (16-mm film). Time-Life Films, 42 W. 16th Street, New York, New York 10011.

Video cassettes available from the Biofeedback Institute, 3428 Sacramento Street, San Francisco, California 94118:

Biofeedback samples, excerpts.

Case studies in biofeedback.

Instrumentation in biofeedback.

Introduction to biofeedback.

Procedures in biofeedback.

Troubleshooting problems in biofeedback.

Professional Organizations

A number of groups have formed to deal with issues of public and professional concern (Fuller, 1978). Many can also supply information on local certification requirements, treatment facilities, educational opportunities, workshops, and the like.

National

Founded as the Biofeedback Research Society in 1968, this organization adopted its present name in 1976 to reflect a growing interest in applied as well as experimental biofeedback. The society has a membership in excess of 2,000, holds an annual conference, sponsors workshops, and publishes the journal *Biofeedback and Self-Regulation*.

Biofeedback Society of America
4301 Owens Street
Wheat Ridge, Colorado 80033

The American Association of Biofeedback Clinicians publishes the *American Journal of Clinical Biofeedback*.

American Association of Biofeedback Clinicians
2424 Dempster Street
Des Plaines, Illinois 60016

State

Addresses of statewide organizations may be obtained from the Biofeedback Society of America.

REFERENCES

Biofeedback and self-control: An Aldine annual on the regulation of bodily processes and consciousness. Chicago: Aldine, 1971-1978.

Brown, B. *The biofeedback syllabus: A handbook for the psychophysiologic study of biofeedback.* Springfield, IL.: Charles C. Thomas, 1975.

Butler, F. *Biofeedback: A survey of the literature.* New York: Plenum Press, 1978.

Cram, J., & Warrenburg, S. *A survey of biofeedback training opportunities at clinical internship facilities.* Denver, CO: Biofeedback Society of America, 1977.

Feuerstein, M., & Schwartz, G.E. Training in clinical psychophysiology: Present trends and future goals. *American Psychologist,* 1977, *32,* 560-567.

Fuller, G. Current status of biofeedback in clinical practice. *American Psychologist,* 1978, *33,* 39-48.

Girdano, D.A. Buying biofeedback. *Health Education,* 1976, *7,* 14-16.

Miller, N. Fact and fancy about biofeedback and its clinical implications. JSAS *Catalog of Selected Documents in Psychology,* 1976, *6,* 92-93 (Ms. No. 1329)

Miller, N.E. Biofeedback and visceral learning. *Annual Review of Psychology,* 1978, *29,* 373-404.

Paskewitz, D. Biofeedback instrumentation: Soldering closed the loop. *American Psychologist,* 1975, *30,* 371-378.

Rugh, J.D., & Schwitzgebel, R.L. Biofeedback apparatus: List of suppliers. *Behavior Therapy,* 1975, *6,* 238-240.

Schwitzgebel, R., & Rugh, J. Of bread, circuses, and alpha machines. *American Psychologist,* 1975, *30,* 363-370.

Warrenburg, S., & Cram, J.R. Biofeedback training opportunities in clinical internship facilities: An extension of the Feuerstein and Schwartz survey. *American Psychologist,* 1978, *33,* 190-191.

Howard Pikoff *has been an adjunct lecturer in the Department of Psychology at the State University of New York at Buffalo for the past five years. Mr. Pikoff's treatment and research interests currently are in headache and pain management. He also has published several reviews of the literature on biofeedback and behavior modification.*

EXECUTIVE RECRUITERS: A DIRECTORY

Leslie Whitaker

You run a company and you have a position to fill. It is a newly created, top-level job with particular technical requirements. There is no one within your company who would be just right for the job. You are not quite sure how much salary and other benefits you must offer to get the executive you need. You are even less sure where to find candidates for the job. You certainly cannot call up your competition and ask them who you might lure away to your company. What will you do?

Well, until twenty years ago, your only option would have been to conduct the search process yourself. Even though you might have been able to ask for significant help from executives in your personnel division, they would have been rather inexperienced at recruiting top-level people, and therefore, your search, though it may have taken much of your valuable time, could have turned out to be fruitless in the end.

Now, however, one option is to get assistance from one of the many professional recruiting firms which operate in most cities throughout the country. Headhunters, as they are sometimes called, specialize in recruiting top executives for corporations.

Most important in the executive recruiting process is choosing the "right" recruiting firm for you. All professional recruiters interviewed by *Wharton* stressed the importance of getting along well not only with the firm, but with the particular recruiter who will actually be conducting your search. You and the recruiter should be in frequent communication during the course of the search. He or she must be able to understand from the beginning what the "chemistry" of your organization is, so that the intangible aspects of filling the job are well understood. Therefore, you must trust your recruiter, so that you can willingly reveal highly confidential information.

You must trust your recruiter's expertise, also, so that if he or she recommends offering a higher salary or a change in job description, you will be sure that the recommendation is based on an intelligent, reliable assessment of the market. As Anne Hyde, president of Boyden/ Management Woman, says, "Anybody can find people. What you're buying is our judgment and evaluation."

Most likely your initial working relationship—the length of the search—will last from eight to sixteen weeks. However, if you are well pleased with the placement, your relationship with the recruiting firm may be ongoing for many years.

What follows is a rough outline of the recruiting process as it is generally practiced.

The first step an executive recruiter will take is to determine what are the qualifications you (as client) require to fill the vacancy—skills, past experience, education. Equally important for the recruiter to determine is the management style of your corporation. The recruiter will want guidance as to the intangible aspects of the job—office dynamics, dress, do's and don't's—things you take so completely for granted that you may even have trouble articulating them.

The recruiting firm, which has a data base made up of the hundreds (or thousands) of resumes it has on file—computerized or not—begins to search for a list of candidates who might qualify for your open position. The recruiting firm also uses its data base as a source of people who can recommend executives to fill the position.

The initial list of possible candidates the recruiter gathers (perhaps twenty) is checked rather informally, although complete confidentiality must be maintained. The candidates' reputations in their field, with their past employers, and if possible with their present employers, are all investigated. (Collecting preliminary data is easiest for senior-level searches where candidates have more visibility.) All of this is done before the executives are even contacted about the position.

Those candidates who seem the best qualified are then approached for preliminary interviews. Over the telephone only enough information is exchanged to determine if there is a shared interest in meeting. It is not until the recruiter interviews the candidate personally that the name of your firm and the details of the position should be revealed.

Those candidates whom the recruiter judges to be the best able to work successfully in your organization are then interviewed again. Their references are checked thoroughly, but still with complete confidentiality to protect both the candidates and the client. Because those references initially supplied by the candidate are likely to be purely positive, the recruiter asks these references for other contacts—contacts who might reveal negative information. These "second generation references" may be former roommates, social contacts, business associates, or professors.

Once the recruiter has narrowed the list to the top few candidates and has met with you to discuss them, it is your turn to do the interviewing. You should meet the candidates promptly and should remember that they are not in the market for a new job but, rather, that you are looking for an executive. When you interview the candidates, you should discuss the specifics of the job, including salary and other compensation issues. It is important that you be as candid as possible with each applicant. Try to discuss both the pressures and the rewards of the job, the character of the organization, and what you will expect of the person who comes to hold the position.

After each interview you should let the search firm know exactly how the meeting went. The firm will also be receiving the candidates' impressions of their interviews. This part of the process supplies very helpful data for the search firm, both for the conclusion of the search and in the event of future searches for your company. If all goes well, you will be able to choose from among the candidates and make a decision promptly. If not, the search firm will use its increased knowledge of your requirements to look for more recruits.

There are, of course, risks associated with the executive recruiting process. Perhaps the most significant is that the new executive may not work out, despite all the care taken by you, the search firm, and him or her. There have recently been a number of highly publicized departures of new arrivals, and though most of these may have had less to do with shortcomings of the search process than with ongoing problems of the company doing the hiring, it is well to remember that neither recruiters nor recruitees are magicians. A new arrival, whatever his or her talents, needs time to learn the company and may therefore, in the short run at least, be less effective than someone promoted from the inside.

Ethical recruiting firms do recognize that they may have some responsibility if the new hire doesn't work out. If the executive leaves within a year, and the problem can be traced to an oversight which is the fault of the recruiter—such as a failure to detect a gap in the client's technical training—many firms guarantee that they will find a replacement without charge, except for additional expenses.

Another problem is breach of confidentiality. In the course of the search, the recruiter learns quite a lot of potentially damaging information about you and the candidates, not the least of which is that they are available and that your organization is short of top-level talent. There is a professional association in the field, the Association of Executive Recruiting Consultants (AERC). It has sixty members, all of whom subscribe to the organization's published code of ethics, which includes high standards for confidentiality. The AERC's code of ethics also includes the following guidelines:

- Reference investigation and reporting should be conducted with the candidate's prior knowledge and within the spirit and intent of applicable Federal and state laws and regulations.

- Under no circumstances will a member firm accept payment for counseling or assisting an individual to find employment.

- Whenever a "non-candidacy" opinion is made by a client, the prospect should be informed as quickly as possible.

Certainly there are numerous reputable firms that do not belong to this association, but you should be sure that whatever firm you engage complies with ethics similar to those of the AERC.

There are some people who simply consider the whole executive recruiting process to be unethical. Many large firms make a point of growing their own talent internally. They pride themselves in their strength on the bench and are naturally upset when an executive who represents a substantial long-term investment by the company decides to leave. Lingering doubts on this level may go a long way toward explaining the relatively poor performance of executive recruiters in a recent opinion poll. The *Wall Street Journal* and the Gallup organization surveyed 782 chief executives about their attitudes toward such providers of services as lawyers, investment bankers, accountants, public relations advisors, and executive recruiters. The chief executives were least satisfied with the headhunters, with only 11 percent saying they were "very satisfied." Another 42 percent, however, said they were "fairly satisfied."

Clients are not the only people who can be dissatisfied with the behavior of some executive recruiting firms. McGraw-Hill, the parent firm of *Business Week* magazine, recently settled a suit out of court against Bacci Bennett Owen Webb, a San Francisco-based executive recruiting firm. McGraw-Hill charged that an employee of the firm was calling companies, informing them that she was "Kathy Morrison of *Business Week*," and soliciting and receiving sensitive and restricted company information from the firms on that basis.

In the light of some of the problems that can arise, probably the best way to choose a recruiting firm is to get recommendations from executives you can trust in other firms that have had satisfactory client relationships with an executive recruiter.

The Issue of Size

Before you make a final decision, though, there are several more issues that you have to decide for yourself. One is size: There are two opposing schools of thought as to whether a larger or smaller firm is better. Carl Menk, president of Boyden Associates, one of the largest executive recruiting firms in the country, puts it this way: "Smaller firms provide more personal attention, but a large firm has more research clout. You will get quicker attention from a larger firm with rapid computer access to a huge data bank. Thirty percent of our searches are filled from our data bank. Larger firms also generally have more prior experience."

On the other hand, W. Glenn Luckett, principal of Stumbaugh Associates, a small firm located in Georgia, lists three advantages of working with a small recruiting firm.

First, "they are more inclined to turn down search assignments which they do not feel can be completed successfully and promptly. They do not have the expenses required for supporting a multitude of offices and a large staff."

Second, "they are more responsive and sensitive to the needs of a client. The loss of a few clients to a large firm is seldom felt."

Third, "from a candidate's point of view, a smaller firm provides a higher level of confidentiality because their data may not be computerized and their personal information is not circulated among so many researchers."

You should keep in mind the fact that once a firm has established a client relationship with a corporation, it is against accepted ethical standards to recruit from within that corporation for at least two years following. If your field is a small one, you may not want to deal with a large firm that has client relationships with all of your possible sources of candidates. Richard Conarroe, in his book *Executive Search*, recommends that you draw up a list of possible sources of candidates and ask the recruiting firm how many of those it may not be able to use.

Another issue which will be of major concern to you when hiring an executive recruiter is whether you want a "generalist" or a "specialist." A specialist conducts searches in only a few related areas, such as finance and accounting. A specialist has the advantage of knowing the field intimately—the jobs, the executives, and the salaries. However, with a specialist you may run into the same problem as with a large firm: lack of sources from which to recruit because of previously established client relationships with those sources. Gregory J. Wallang, vice-president of Ability Search, Inc., a firm which works mainly in high-technology fields, is a strong believer in going only to a "cross-industry specialist" because of the limited sources of candidates. He believes that in going to a specialist restricted by industry, you're "giving up more than you're gaining."

Gary Stevens, president of Stonehill Management Consultants, Inc., argues in favor of specialization, depending on the area involved in the search. His firm specializes in economics, econometrics, corporate planning, and operations research. "There is no lack of candidates because Washington is a constant source" of economists, he says. "Specialists have a point of reference to know what is average, above average, and what is exceptional."

A specialty handled by some headhunters is the recruitment of women and minorities. If you need help complying with affirmative action regulations, you may consider going to a firm such as Boyden/Management Woman for assistance. Anne Hyde, president, explains, "We recruit professionals who happen to be women. Clients come to us for finding people to penetrate a level where women or minorities haven't been."

There are two ways in which executive recruiting firms are paid. Some firms wish to be hired on a contingency basis, not to be paid unless the position is filled. Most firms, however, are paid on a retainer—that is, they are paid whether or not the position is filled. Most recruiters agree that your search will get superior treatment if the firm is hired on a retainer basis. The firm can then be involved in fewer searches at once, because its income is guaranteed, and it therefore will devote more time and attention to each search. There will be no incentive to present you with inferior candidates merely to speed up the search, get the job filled, and get paid.

The contingency basis, however, is attractive if you do not have the funds to hire a search firm on a retainer basis. Stevens of Stonehill Management Consultants often works on a contingency basis, though he prefers the retainer arrangement. "Though it is more risky for my firm, I don't want to ignore those searches that cannot afford a retainer fee. Frequently the manager searching to fill a position in economics does not have the power or budget to handle a retainer fee."

Once a good relationship has been established, you may keep the recruiting company on a retainer basis, to keep its eyes open for any good candidates, or you may return to it later when you have a specific position to fill. In any case the recruiter will already have an intimate knowledge of your corporation and will be even more likely to conduct a successful search for you.

One final note. If you are looking for a job yourself, most of these firms will accept resumes. However, you will probably not receive any response from them until you happen to match a current search.

What follows is a list of sixty executive recruiters located throughout the country, both specialists and generalists. This list is not intended to be comprehensive, but rather is a selection designed to give the reader an idea of the great variety of services now available in executive recruiting. The information on the chart was supplied by the firms listed.

Suggested Reading

Richard R. Conarroe (Ed.), Executive Search, A Guide for Recruiting Outstanding Executives, *Van Nostrand Reinhold, 1976. An in-depth guide to the executive search process.*

Consultants News and Executive Recruiter News, *James Kennedy (Ed.) (published monthly), Kennedy & Kennedy, Inc., Templeton Rd., Fitzwilliam, N.H. Confidential newsletters for the consulting and recruiting professions.*

Directory of Executive Recruiters, *Consultants News, 1981. A comprehensive list of executive recruiters nationwide. Updated yearly.*

Roger K. Williams, How to Evaluate, Select and Work with Executive Recruiters, *Cahners, 1974. A concise handbook for the client.*

NAME / ADDRESS	SPECIALTY	SALARY RANGE	REPRESENTATIVE CLIENT LIST	FEE TO CLIENT
Ability Search, Inc. 1629 K Street, N.W. Washington, DC 20006	Data processing; operations research; management science; strategic planning.	$25,000 + Avg. $30,000-40,000	Pfizer; AT&T; Chase Manhattan; Citibank.	30%.
Accounting Resources International 500 C Newport Ctr. Drive Newport Beach, CA 92660	Accounting; finance.	$25,000-100,000	Big Eight accounting firms; major consulting firms.	25% + expenses.
Ahrens, Davis & Associates, Inc. 20 Tower Lane Avon, CT 06001	Insurance; energy; general business.	$30,000 + Avg. $55,000	Manufacturers; banks.	30% first year's income.
Peter W.A. Ambler Associates 1215 Country Club Lane Fort Worth, TX 76112	Energy; general manufacturing.	$30,000-40,000 +	ITT; Emerson Electric; Cabot Corporation; Texas Instruments.	30% + expenses.
Antell, Nagel, Moorhead & Assoc. 230 Park Avenue New York, NY 10169	General management across the board.	$40,000 +	Confidential.	30% of first year's total compensation.
Bowden & Company, Inc. 5000 Rockside Road Cleveland, OH 44131	Generalist.	$40,000 +	TRW; American General; AmeriTrust; SOHIO.	30% first year's salary.
Boyden Associates, Inc. 260 Madison Avenue New York, NY 10016	Generalist.	$40,000 +	Confidential.	One-third first year's compensation (salary + bonus).
Boyden/Management Woman 151 Railroad Avenue Greenwich, CT 06830	Generalist.	$35,000-300,000	Confidential; one-half of Fortune 500.	30% first year's compensation package.
Bradbeer & Company 349 Lancaster Avenue Haverford, PA 19041	Marketing; advertising.	$25,000 +	Advertising agencies; consumer industries.	20% estimated middle salary range.
Breitmayer Associates 72 Park Street New Canaan, CT 06840	Generalist.	$40,000 +	Petroleum; metals fabrication; communications.	30% first year's income.

NAME ADDRESS	SPECIALTY	SALARY RANGE	REPRESENTATIVE CLIENT LIST	FEE TO CLIENT
Thomas A. Buffum Associates 2 Center Plaza Boston, MA 02108	Generalist.	$40,000 +	Northeast primarily; Exxon; Norton; Itek.	30% first year's compensation.
E.A. Butler Associates, Inc. 1270 Avenue of the Americas New York, NY 10020	Generalist.	$45,000 +	Automotive; oil; heavy industry.	30% first year's salary.
William H. Clark Associates, Inc. 330 Madison Avenue New York, NY 10017	Generalist.	$60,000-100,000	Confidential.	Retainer; 30%.
Coker, Tyler & Company 1835 Savoy Drive Atlanta, GA 30341	Finance; accounting; health care specialists.	$20,000 +	Hospitals; administrative and executive levels.	Retainer; 30% first year.
Conley Associates, Inc. 810 Cardinal Lane Hartland, WI 53029	Generalist.	$40,000-500,000	Banking; heavy manufacturing; family health.	Depends on assignment.
Corry, Howe Associates, Inc. Time & Life Building New York, NY 10020	Generalist; general management; planning; human resources.	$75,000-100,000's Avg. $100,000	Confidential.	30%.
Crosby & Company P.O. Box 171 Chadds Ford, PA 19317	Generalist; upper level management; engineering; aerospace.	$50,000 +	Confidential.	30% base salary first year.
Deane, Howard & Simon, Inc. 630 Oakwood Avenue West Hartford, CT 06110	Generalist.	$30,000 + Avg. $50,000	Loctite.	30% + expenses.
Thorndike Deland Associates 1440 Broadway New York, NY 10018	Consumer package goods; retailing; textile; apparel.	$50,000-75,000	R.J. Reynolds; General Foods; AMF.	30% of first year's salary.
Devine, Baldwin & Peters, Inc. 250 Park Avenue New York, NY 10177	Generalist.	$40,000 +	Salomon Brothers; Avon Products; Morton-Norwich; Kennecott.	30%.
R.M. Donaldson Associates 25 Commerce Drive Cranford, NJ 07016	Hospitality; restaurant; hotel; food service.	$18,000-250,000	ARA Services; Steak & Ale Restaurants of America; Stouffer.	15%.
Eastman & Beaudine, Inc. 111 W. Monroe Street Chicago, IL 60603	Generalist.	$40,000 + Avg. $90,000-100,000	Ford; American Express; Singer.	30% first year's income.
Einstein Associates 122 East 42nd Street New York, NY 10017	Generalist.	$35,000 +	Manufacturing; consumer products.	30% first year's income.
Ernst & Whinney/Executive Search 1300 Union Commerce Building Cleveland, OH 44115	Executive positions; generalist.	$50,000 +	Confidential.	Hourly charge.
Executive Women, Inc. 65 LaSalle Road West Hartford, CT 06107	Generalist (women).	$20,000 +	Connecticut General; Stanley Works; United Technologies; Hartford Insurance.	25% first year's salary.
Foster & Associates, Inc. 1 Market Plaza San Francisco, CA 94105	Generalist (upper and middle management).	$50,000 base salary	Confidential.	30% of first year's salary.

NAME ADDRESS	SPECIALTY	SALARY RANGE	REPRESENTATIVE CLIENT LIST	FEE TO CLIENT
Genovese & Company 1880 Century Park E. Los Angeles, CA 90067	Technical companies; data processing; general managers.	Avg. $64,500	Citicorp (L.A. division).	30% first year's income + expenses.
Gilbert Tweed Associates, Inc. 630 Third Avenue New York, NY 10017	Generalist; heavy industrial.	Avg. $50,000-55,000	Mobil; FMC; ITT; CBS; National Steel.	30%.
Halbrecht Associates Inc. 1200 Summer Street, Box 3540 Stamford, CT 06905	High management; decision science; economics.	$40,000 + Avg. $45,000-55,000	Consulting firms; Big Eight accounting firms.	30% total compensation.
Heidrick & Struggles, Inc. 125 S. Wacker Drive Chicago, IL 60606	Generalist.	$50,000 +	All industries.	One-third first year's compensation.
Huxtable Associates, Inc. P.O. Box 621 Bridgeton, MO 63044	Generalist.	Avg. $40,000-100,000	Deere & Company; Burroughs Corporation.	30% annual beginning compensation.
Impact Associates 14407 12th Place, N.E. Bellevue, WA 98007	Senior management.	$30,000 + Avg. $45,000-50,000	Plastics; steel; energy; financial; general manufacturing.	30% retainer.
Industry Search Inc. 3100 Monroe Avenue Rochester, NY 14618	Generalist.	$25,000-75,000 Avg. $35,000	General Signal; General Electric; University of Rochester; Eastman Kodak; American Airlines.	20% up to $25,000; 25% over $25,000.
The Interface Group, Ltd. 1212 Potomac Street, N.W. Washington, DC 20007	Generalist; government; EEOC.	$40,000-six figures	Philip Morris; Amtrak; Bristol-Myers.	30% first year's total guaranteed salary.
Kensington Executive Search 25 Third Street Stamford, CT 06905	Generalist.	$40,000 +	Confidential.	Varies.
Korn/Ferry International 277 Park Avenue New York, NY 10172	Generalists; specialty divisions include: government, energy.	$50,000 +	Union Carbide; Chase Manhattan; Citicorp; Mattel; General Mills.	33.3% base salary + bonus.
Oliver & Rozner Associates, Inc. 598 Madison Street New York, NY 10022	Generalist.	$40,000 +	All industries.	One-third first year's compensation.
Parker, Eldridge Sholl & Gordon, Inc. 440 Tottin Pond Road Waltham, MA 02154	Generalist.	$35,000 + Avg. $50,000-60,000	Computer and energy systems manufacturers.	30% base salary.
Pinsker & Shattuck, Inc. 14375 Saratoga Avenue Saratoga, CA 95070	Middle and top management.	$40,000-200,000	Manufacturing (high technology).	30% estimated first year's cash compensation.
Placement Associates, Inc. 645 Madison Avenue New York, NY 10022	Public affairs and communications.	$18,000-150,000	Confidential.	1% per 1000 up to 30%.
Poirier, Hoevel & Company 606 Wilshire Blvd. Santa Monica, CA 90401	Generalist.	$35,000 + $70,000-75,000	ITT; 20th Century Fox; Bank of America.	Retainer; 30% of first year's base salary.

NAME ADDRESS	SPECIALTY	SALARY RANGE	REPRESENTATIVE CLIENT LIST	FEE TO CLIENT
Eugene C. Pressler Box 132 Blue Bell, PA 19422	Generalist.	$25,000 +	International and domestic industrial and commerical.	Varies.
Harry J. Prior Associates, Inc. 700 112th Avenue, N.E. Bellvue, WA 98004	Top management.	$40,000 + Avg. $60,000-70,000	Banks; retail; transportation; manufacturing; health care.	No flat fee; based on time and effort.
Pro Source 1001 Steadwick Road Gaithersburg, MD 20878	Hospitals; administrative.	$30,000 +	Confidential.	Unfixed percentage of first year's salary + expenses.
Paul R. Ray & Company, Inc. 1208 Ridglea Bank Bldg. Fort Worth, TX 76116	Top management across the board.	$40,000 + Avg. $60,000-65,000	General Mills; General Dynamics; Chase Manhattan; American Express.	30% first year's guaranteed compensation.
R.E.A. Associates 11906 Manchester Road St. Louis, MO 63131	Engineering; accounting; finance; industrial sales.	$20,000-60,000 (middle management)	Confidential.	25% + adjustments for time and feasibility study.
Pamela Reeve Agency 409 N. Camden Drive Beverly Hills, CA 90210	Advertising; marketing; creative (art); accounting.	$18,000 +	Young & Rubicam; D'arcy McManus & Masius.	30%.
Russell Reynolds Associates, Inc. 245 Park Avenue New York, NY 10167	Senior management.	$50,000 + Avg. $85,000	Confidential.	Retainer; one-third first year's salary + expenses.
Raymond H. Riley Associates 717 17th Street Denver, CO 80202	Technical and senior management.	$50,000-100,000	Oil & gas companies.	30%.
Search America/Personnel Consultants 12700 Hillcrest Road Dallas, TX 75230	Senior management.	Avg. $40,000-45,000	Food; lodging; energy; data processing.	Retainer; fee $8,000-$15,000.
Stuart Associates, Inc. 270 Amity Road Woodbridge, CT 06525	Technical; manufacturing; finance sales; data processing.	$24,000-28,000 + (junior and senior management)	United Technologies Corporation.	Avg. $6,000; $1,500-15,000.
Stumbaugh Associates 4319 Covington Hgwy. Decatur, GA 30035	Generalist.	Avg. $36,900 $35,000-45,000	RCA; National Data; Allegheny Ludlum.	Retainer basis; 30-35% + expenses.
Sturm, Burrows & Company 1420 Walnut Street Philadelphia, PA 19102	Generalist.	$25,000 + Avg. $40,000	Metals & minerals; electrical connector field.	Sliding scale; 20% of $20,000; 25% of $25,000.
Tasa, Inc. 2199 Ponce de Leon Blvd. Coral Gables, FL 33134	Generalist.	$40,000 +	Confidential.	30% gross annual; 35% transnational.
Technical Recruiting Systems, Inc. 836 S. Northwest Highway Barrington, IL 60010	Engineering; banking.	$20,000-75,000	American Hospital Supply; C.R. Bard; Johnson & Johnson.	30%.

NAME ADDRESS	SPECIALTY	SALARY RANGE	REPRESENTATIVE CLIENT LIST	FEE TO CLIENT
Vine Associates, Inc. 10911 Riverside Drive North Hollywood, CA 91602	Executives; line and staff positions; petroleum; coal mining.	$35,000-150,000	Leading petroleum and coal mining companies; Fortune 1000.	30-35% first year's salary.
Walters & Company 4418 Davidson Avenue Atlanta, GA 30319	Generalist.	$30,000 +	Confidential; conglomerates; banks; textiles.	25%.
Warren Management Consultants 306 East 50th Street New York, NY 10022	Senior management.	$40,000-200,000 + Avg. $50,000-100,000	All areas of banking.	30% first year's compensation.
Webster Positions, Inc. 76 N. Broadway Hicksville, NY 11801	Electronic industry; engineering; scientific programming.	$18,000 +	Grumman Data Systems; Raytheon; ITT-Electronic.	—
Windsor-Greene Associates 545 Boylston Street Boston, MA 02116	Accounting; finance.	$20,000-75,000	Polaroid; ComputerVision; Commercial Union Insurance.	Percentage of first year's salary.

Leslie Whitaker is assistant editor of *The Wharton Magazine.*

CONTRIBUTORS

Ralph R. Bates
Vice President for OD
Trans Century Corporation
1789 Columbia Road, N.W.
Washington, D.C. 20009
  (202) 328-4440

Robert P. Belforti
Distribution Services Manager
IBM Corporation
1049 Asylum Avenue
Hartford, Connecticut 06105
  (203) 727-6461

C. Jesse Carlock, Ph.D.
Adjunct Assistant Professor
Counseling Education
Wright State University
Dayton, Ohio 45435
  (513) 223-5213

Tom Carney, Ph.D.
Professor
Department of Communication Studies
University of Windsor
401 Sunset Avenue
Windsor, Ontario N9B 3P4, Canada
  (519) 253-4232

Phyliss Cooke, Ph.D.
Director of Professional Services
University Associates, Inc.
8517 Production Avenue
P.O. Box 26240
San Diego, California 92126
  (619) 578-5900

Paul David
Consultant-Trainer
Human Development Trust, Inc.
1716 East Highland Drive
Seattle, Washington 98112
  (206) 324-1644

Richard C. Diedrich, Ph.D.
Manager, Boston
Rohrer, Hibler & Replogle, Inc.
470 Totten Pond Road
Waltham, Massachusetts 02154
  (617) 890-7791

Daniel G. Eckstein, Ph.D.
Senior Consultant
University Associates, Inc.
8517 Production Avenue
P.O. Box 26240
San Diego, California 92126
  (619) 578-5900

Dean Elias
Regional Director
Antioch University Seattle
1165 Eastlake Avenue East
Seattle, Washington 98109
  (206) 323-2270

Jerry L. Fryrear, Ph.D.
Professor of Psychology
Program in Human Sciences
University of Houston
  at Clear Lake City
2700 Bay Area Boulevard
Houston, Texas 77058
  (713) 488-9480

Susan Frieder Wallock, Ph.D.
Director
Dance/Movement Therapy Master's Program
Graduate School of Professional Psychology
John F. Kennedy University
12 Altarinda Road
Orinda, California 94563
  (415) 254-0200

Beverly Byrum-Gaw, Ph.D.
Associate Professor
Department of Communication
Wright State University
Dayton, Ohio 45435
  (513) 873-2710

Christine Glaser
Vice President
Organization Design and Development, Inc.
101 Bryn Mawr Avenue
Bryn Mawr, Pennsylvania 19010
  (215) 525-9505

Rollin Glaser
President
Organization Design and Development, Inc.
101 Bryn Mawr Avenue
Bryn Mawr, Pennsylvania 19010
  (215) 525-9505

Robert N. Glenn, Ph.D.
Coordinator of Clinical Supervision
  and Training
Henrico Area Mental Health and
  Retardation Services
10299 Woodman Road
Glen Allen, Virginia 23060
  (804) 266-4991

Joel Goodman, Ed.D.
Director, The HUMOR Project and
  Consultation Services
Sagamore Institute
110 Spring Street
Saratoga Springs, New York 12866
  (518) 587-8770

Jeanette Goodstein
Freelance Consultant
  and Trainer
16134 Ladera Piedra
Poway, California 92064
  (619) 485-9857

Leonard D. Goodstein, Ph.D.
Chairman of the Board
University Associates, Inc.
8517 Production Avenue
P.O. Box 26240
San Diego, California 92126
  (619) 578-5900

Dwight L. Gradin
Internship and Language Coordinator
Missionary Internship
36200 Freedom Road, P.O. Box 457
Farmington, Michigan 48024
  (313) 474-9110

Laura M. Graves, Ph.D.
Assistant Professor of Management
  and Organization
School of Business Administration
University of Connecticut
Storrs, Connecticut 06268
  (203) 486-3638

Lauren A. Hagan
Life Insurance Agent
Fidelity Union Life
19 Pond Point Road
Milford, Connecticut 06460
  (203) 878-5737

H.B. Karp, Ph.D.
Principal
Personal Growth Systems
1441 Magnolia Avenue
Norfolk, Virginia 23508
  (804) 489-2586

William W. Kibler
Director, Organization and
  Management Development
R.J. Reynolds Tobacco Company
401 North Main Street
Winston-Salem, North Carolina 27102
  (919) 777-6910

Charles A. Lowe, Ph.D.
Professor of Psychology and
  Head, Division of Social Psychology
University of Connecticut
Storrs, Connecticut 06268
  (203) 486-4910

Tony McNulty
Senior Training Adviser
Lucas CAV Limited
P.O. Box 36
Warple Way, Acton
London W3 7SS, England
  (01) 743-3111

Ben Markens
Operations Manager
Laurino Packaging Corporation
360 Cold Spring Avenue
West Springfield, Massachusetts 01089
  (413) 737-1121

William T. Milburn
Training and Development Manager
R.J. Reynolds Tobacco Company
401 North Main Street
Winston-Salem, North Carolina 27102
  (919) 777-6250

Mike M. Milstein, Ph.D.
Professor of Educational Administration
State University of New York
  at Buffalo
470 Baldy Hall
Amherst Campus
Buffalo, New York 14260
  (716) 636-2471

Cheryl A. Monyak
Assistant Underwriter
Special Accounts Marketing
Travelers Insurance Company
One Tower Square
Hartford, Connecticut 06115
  (203) 277-0320

Dan Muller
Curriculum and Training Coordinator
Value Management Resource Office
City of Phoenix
324 West Washington Street
Phoenix, Arizona 85003
  (602) 262-4673

David A. Nadler, Ph.D.
President
Organizational Research and Consultation, Inc.
9 East 41st Street, Eighth Floor
New York, New York 10017
  (212) 370-1111

Stella Lybrand Norman
Supervision, South Clinic
Crossroads Drug Abuse Program
6301 Richmond Highway
Alexandria, Virginia 22306
  (703) 765-7945

Udai Pareek, Ph.D.
Larsen and Toubro Professor
  of Organizational Behavior
Indian Institute of Management
Vastrapur, Ahmedabad,
Gujarat, India 380 015
  (307) 450041

George J. Petrello, Ph.D.
Dean, School of Business and
  Administration
St. Mary's University
One Camino Santa Maria
San Antonio, Texas 78284
  (512) 436-3705

Howard Pikoff
Adjunct Lecturer
Department of Psychology
State University of New York
  at Buffalo
Buffalo, New York 14226
  (716) 831-3067

Gary N. Powell, Ph.D.
Associate Professor of
  Management and Organization
University of Connecticut
Box U-41
Storrs, Connecticut 06268
  (203) 486-3862

Brent D. Ruben, Ph.D.
Professor and Chairperson
Department of Communication
Rutgers University
4 Huntington Street
New Brunswick, New Jersey 08903
  (201) 932-7911

Stephen A. Schneider
Director
Ecumenical Sponsoring Committee, Inc.
389 East Santa Clara Street
San Jose, California 95113
  (408) 932-5134

Mark P. Sharfman
Instructor
Department of Management
University of Arizona
Tucson, Arizona 85721
  (602) 626-1474

John M. Shearer
Program Manager
Community Services Division
Montana Department
  of Social and Rehabilitation Services
P.O. Box 216
Kalispell, Montana 59901
  (406) 755-5950

Annette N. Shelby, Ph.D.
Associate Professor of Management
School of Business
Georgetown University
Washington, D.C. 20057
  (202) 625-4044

Karen Sykas Sighinolfi
Sales Representative
Thomas J. Lipton, Inc.
800 Sylvan Street
Englewood Cliffs, New Jersey 07662
  (201) 567-8000

Donald T. Simpson
Educational Design Consultant
104 Tarrytown Road
Rochester, New York 14618
  (716) 244-8556

Karen J. Troy
Career Development Specialist
Minnesota Gas Company
201 South 7th Street
Minneapolis, Minnesota 55402
  (612) 372-5136

Timothy R. Walters
Partner
Avant Video
513 West 5th Street
Tempe, Arizona 85282
  (602) 966-8544

Leslie Whitaker
Assistant Editor
The Wharton Magazine
The Wharton School
Centenary Hall C C
University of Pennsylvania
Philadelphia, Pennsylvania 19104
  (215) 243-8999

Raymond J. Zugel
Organizational Effectiveness Consultant
Headquarters, U.S. Army
Office of the Chief of Staff
Washington, D.C. 20310
  (202) 695-6491

Please add the following name to your mailing list.

____

____

____

____ Zip _____________

Primary Organizational Affiliation: ☐ fill in with one number from below

1. Education
2. Business & Industry
3. Religious Organization
4. Government Agency
5. Counseling

6. Mental Health
7. Community, Voluntary, and/or Service Organization
8. Health Care
9. Library
0. Consulting

Please add the following name to your mailing list.

____

____

____

____ Zip _____________

Primary Organizational Affiliation: ☐ fill in with one number from below

1. Education
2. Business & Industry
3. Religious Organization
4. Government Agency
5. Counseling

6. Mental Health
7. Community, Voluntary, and/or Service Organization
8. Health Care
9. Library
0. Consulting

BUSINESS REPLY CARD

FIRST CLASS   PERMIT NO. 11201   SAN DIEGO, CA

POSTAGE WILL BE PAID BY ADDRESSEE

UNIVERSITY ASSOCIATES
Publishers and Consultants
8517 Production Avenue
P.O. Box 26240
San Diego, California 92126

BUSINESS REPLY CARD

FIRST CLASS   PERMIT NO. 11201   SAN DIEGO, CA

POSTAGE WILL BE PAID BY ADDRESSEE

UNIVERSITY ASSOCIATES
Publishers and Consultants
8517 Production Avenue
P.O. Box 26240
San Diego, California 92126